PEARSON

ALWAYS LEARNING

Len Karakowsky
York University

Exploring the Canadian Business Environment

Excerpts taken from:
Business Essentials, Sixth Canadian Edition
by Ronald J. Ebert, Ricky W. Griffin, Frederick A. Starke, and
George Dracopoulos

Canadian Industrial Relations, Third Edition
by Jon Peirce and Karen Joy Bentham

Economics for Life: Smart Choices for All?
by Avi J. Cohen and Ian Howe

Cover images courtesy of Debbie Karakowsky and Yuri Arcurs/iStockphoto.

Excerpts taken from:

Business Essentials, Sixth Canadian Edition
by Ronald J. Ebert, Ricky W. Griffin, Frederick A. Starke, and George Dracopoulos
Copyright © 2012, 2009, 2006, 2003, 2000, 1997 by Pearson Canada, Inc.
Published by Prentice Hall
Toronto, Ontario

Canadian Industrial Relations, Third Edition
by Jon Peirce and Karen Joy Bentham
Copyright © 2007, 2003, 2000 by Pearson Canada, Inc.
Published by Prentice Hall

Economics for Life: Smart Choices for All?
by Avi J. Cohen and Ian Howe
Copyright © 2011 by Pearson Canada, Inc.
Published by Addison Wesley
Toronto, Ontario

Pearson Learning Solutions, 501 Boylston Street, Suite 900, Boston, MA 02116
A Pearson Education Company
www.pearsoned.com

Printed in Canada

7 8 9 10 XXXX 16 15 14 13 12

000200010270764963

MHB/JG

ISBN 10: 1-256-34775-2
ISBN 13: 978-1-256-34775-0

COPYRIGHT ACKNOWLEDGMENTS

Grateful acknowledgment is made to the following sources for permission to reprint material copyrighted or controlled by them:

"Canada Earns a C Grade in Global Economic Rankings," by Eric Beauchesne, reprinted by permission from *iPolitics*, May 17, 2011.

"Canadian Consumers Changing Habits: Study," by Derek Abma, reprinted from the *Financial Post*, January 27, 2011, by permission of National Post Inc.

"Gross Domestic Product by Industry, 2001 to 2009" and "Unemployment Rate, Canada, 1976–2009," courtesy of Statistics Canada and Public Works and Government Services Canada.

"Whose Auto Bailout Is Most Expensive? Go Canada!" by Erik Heinrich, reprinted by permission from *Time*, May 6, 2009.

"Employment by Industry, 2006–2010," courtesy of Statistics Canada.

"Employment Rate, by Gender, 1976–2009," courtesy of Statistics Canada and Public Works and Government Services Canada.

"Imports, Exports and Trade Balance of Goods" (2011), courtesy of Statistics Canada.

"Canadian Firms Reduce Reliance on U.S. Trade," by Gordon Isfeld, reprinted from the *Times Colonist*, April 8, 2011, by permission of National Post Inc.

"Innovation Out of Our Hands in a Branch–Plant Economy," by David Olive, reprinted by permission from the *Toronto Star*, March 23, 2010.

"What Facebook Learned from Apple and What We Can Learn from Facebook," by Andy Ramirez, reprinted from *Executive Street*, May 28, 2010, by permission of Vistage International.

Chapters 1 and 2 reprinted from *Business Essentials*, Sixth Canadian Edition, by Ronald J. Ebert, Ricky W. Griffin, Frederick A. Starke, and George Dracopoulos (2012), Pearson Canada, Inc.

"Canadian Economy Lures International Retail Interests," reprinted from *The Retail Report* (2011), Colliers International.

"Borders Bankruptcy and Our Changing World," by Walter Riker, reprinted by permission from *The Curious Voyager*, March 3, 2011.

"Block Chocolate – Breaking the Impasse," by Jane Simms, reprinted from *Marketing*, June 9, 2004.

"Is the Newspaper Industry at Death's Door?" by Shameem Mahmud, reprinted from the *Daily Star*, May 7, 2009.

"Groupon Is Hastening the Demise of the Newspaper Industry," by Kris Ashton, reprinted by permission from *Daily Deal Media*, April 3, 2011.

"Print Me a Stradivarius," reprinted by permission from the *Economist*, February 10, 2011.

"The Hidden Dangers of Outsourcing," by Freek Vermeulen, October 28, 2010, reprinted by permission of the author.

"Nothing to Fear from Teleworking," by Danny Bradbury, reprinted from the *Financial Post*, March 16, 2010, by permission of National Post Inc.

"Outsourcing Deal Gives P&G Clout with HP," by Patrick Thibodeau, reprinted by permission from *Computerworld*, March 22, 2010.

"Corporate 'Welfare' More than $200 Billion over 13 Years," by John Morrissy, reprinted from the *Vancouver Sun*, November 28, 2009, by permission of National Post Inc.

"The Scope of Federal Regulation in Canada," originally titled "Appendix A: Scope of Federal Regulatory Activity," reprinted from the Red Tape Reduction Commission, courtesy of Public Works and Government Services Canada.

"Used Car Buyers Are Protected," by Monique Savin, reprinted from the *Globe and Mail*, March 16, 2010, by permission of the author.

"What Is the Competition Bureau?" (2011), reprinted from the Competition Bureau, Public Works and Government Services Canada.

"Auto Bailouts: Good or Bad Idea?," reprinted from *Business in the News*, July 7, 2009, by permission of Pearson Canada.

"Ottawa Loans Pratt & Whitney $300 Million to Help 'Create and Maintain' Jobs," reprinted by permission from the *Canadian Press*, December 13, 2010.

"Canada Post Is a Prime Candidate for Privatization," reprinted from the *Montreal Gazette*, February 13, 2007.

"Good Time to Sell Government Assets? Depends on the Asset," by Bryne Purchase, reprinted from the *Globe and Mail*, January 22, 2010, by permission of the author.

"Should Government Support Pratt & Whitney?" by Adrian MacNair, reprinted from the *National Post*, December 14, 2010.

Excerpts from Chapter 9 reprinted from *Economics for Life: Smart Choices for All?*, by Avi J. Cohen and Ian Howe (2011), Pearson Canada, Inc.

"No Graceful Exit," by Byron Christopher, reprinted from *Our Times*, November 5, 2002.

"The Rise of Walmart's Small Box," by Joe Castaldo, reprinted from *Canadian Business*, March 14, 2011.

"Brazil at Heart of Google's Latin America Strategy," by Alejandro Lifschitz and Helen Popper, March 7, 2011, by permission of Helen Popper.

"Forces Driving Competition within an Industry," by Michael E. Porter, reprinted from *Competitive Strategy* (1980), by permission of The Free Press, a division of Simon & Schuster, Inc. Copyright © 1980, 1998 by The Free Press.

"The Profits and Perils of Supplying to Wal–Mart," by Emily Schmitt, reprinted by permission from *Businessweek*, July 14, 2009.

"Lazy Worker or Flawed Work Culture?" by Chris Atchison, reprinted from the *Globe and Mail*, May 12, 2011, by permission of the author.

"BCE–CTV Deal Remakes Media Landscape," by Iain Marlow, reprinted by permission from the *Globe and Mail*, September 10, 2010.

"Starbucks Targets Quebec's 'Café Culture,'" by S. John Tilak, reprinted by permission from *Reuters*, April 13, 2011.

"Tim Hortons Tiptoes into Starbucks Territory," reprinted from the *National Post*, January 6, 2006, by permission of National Post Inc.

"This Revolution Is Changing Companies," by Michael Slaby, reprinted from the *Globe and Mail*, February 23, 2011.

"More Women in the Workplace Is Good for Business," by Deborah Gillis, reprinted from the *Globe and Mail*, October 12, 2010, by permission of Catalyst.

BRIEF CONTENTS

CONTENTS

PREFACE

The Canadian business landscape has changed dramatically in recent years. Bankruptcies, mergers and foreign takeovers are just a few of the common business events that we continue to witness.

Clearly, we live in a rapidly changing environment. Business is influenced by a host of factors that exist outside the walls of the company. What exactly are these challenges? The aim of this text is to introduce the student to many of these critical concerns facing today's organizations. However, I hope that you find this book goes beyond a mere presentation of current issues affecting organizations.

A fundamental aim of any university education is to encourage critical thinking skills. I have tried to develop this book with that objective in mind. That is, this book is not so much a description of the business environment; rather, it is intended as a springboard for critically examining the central challenges that organizations face. It presents the reader with questions, concepts, theories and ideas. And it is aimed at encouraging students to think about these concepts and assess how they might add value to an understanding of the nature of the business environment.

As with the completion of any book, much thanks must be given to the many individuals who contributed directly or indirectly to the writing process. First, I wish to thank all the staff at Pearson, including Nick Durie, Susan Erickson, Marika Brenes, Liz Faerm and the rest of their team. Thank you to my colleagues at York University. Thanks to You-Ta Chuang for authoring Chapter 9, Eytan Lasry for co-authoring Chapters 3 and 4 and to Igor Kotlyar for co-authoring Chapter 10. Finally, I must express my gratitude to my dear wife, Debbie, whose support and encouragement made all this possible.

Len Karakowsky
Toronto, Canada

INTRODUCTION

The central aim of this book is:

- To examine current issues affecting the management of organizations.
- To offer insight into the unique nature of the Canadian business context.
- To help generate conceptual frameworks for identifying and analyzing key business issues.
- To encourage critical thinking regarding the challenges facing business.

This book presents conceptual frameworks, ideas and theories drawn from the work of management scholars and organizational research. In order to enhance critical thinking skills, each chapter emphasizes concept application through the infusion of extensive "real-life" business illustrations, largely drawn from the Canadian popular press. Each chapter begins with **The Business World**, which reports current real-life business issues and themes explored within the chapter. The chapters are also filled with real-life business illustrations. Each chapter also contains end-of-chapter **Concept Applications** with questions. These cases are also largely drawn from the Canadian popular press, and are intended to give you an opportunity to apply chapter concepts to real business contexts.

In addition to encouraging critical thinking skills, this book is equally concerned with relating ideas and issues voiced by practitioners and communicated through such popular press sources as *Business Week, Canadian Business, Fortune, Report on Business, The Globe and Mail, The National Post,* and the *Ottawa Citizen.*

Structure of the Book

The Environment of Business: A Framework For Study

Chapter 1 presents our framework for study of the broader context within which business operates. The environment of organizations. This chapter helps us appreciate the challenges of developing managerial strategies to cope with the environment. The framework employed is one that underscores external forces directed at the organization. The ability to adequately address these forces will, ultimately, determine the organization's fate.

Chapter 2 explores the economic context of business. We identify the factors of production and consider different types of global economic systems. This chapter also examines how demand and supply affect resource distribution in Canada. Indicators of economic stability and growth are also presented.

Chapter 3 describes the competitive environment and identifies key issues in understanding prospects and challenges for any business. Chapter 4 considers the role that technology can play in business success. Chapter 5 presents issues pertinent to the labour pool in Canada. We will consider the implications of demographic diversity for the workplace. An examination of the nature and role of unions in Canada is also included in this chapter. Chapter 6 discusses organizations in the global or international context. This chapter explores the notion of globalization, and outlines a number of central considerations in any organizational efforts to expand internationally. Chapter 7 considers the roles that government can play with regard to business, and how these roles have been changing. Issues such as privatization and deregulation are discussed.

Chapter 8 raises the issue of social responsibility in its discussion of the societal context of business. We will consider why businesses may need to go beyond addressing purely financial objectives. Consideration is also given to corporate responsibilities arising in the global context. Chapter 9 explores the connection of business strategy with the environment. The nature and challenges of strategic management are discussed.

Chapter 10 explores the issue of change. What is change, and how do organizations experience change? We will consider factors that either create or reduce resistance to change in organizations. This chapter also discusses the notion of the learning organization, and addresses the question of whether organizations are capable of facilitating learning and development among their members. Current issues such as mergers, tipping-point change are examined.

The Context of Business:
A Framework For Study

What are the key factors that determine business success or failure? How does one make sense of the current state of business? Assessing the prospects of organizations requires a careful examination of the contexts within which organizations operate. Much of this chapter and, indeed, this book is intended to address those factors that critically impact the functioning and fate of business. These factors compose the environment of business. To develop an effective business strategy, every organization must understand its environment.

LEARNING OBJECTIVES

After studying this chapter, you should be able to:

1. Understand the notion of organizations as open systems.
2. Identify the forces that comprise the specific and general environments of organizations.
3. Discuss six forces confronting organizations.
4. Explain the importance of each of the external forces within the Canadian business context.
5. Describe the framework that this text will use to examine the environment of business.

THE BUSINESS WORLD

Canada earns a C grade in global economic rankings

Eric Beauchesne

Canada is a middling global economic performer, and its lagging productivity and relatively weak outward foreign investment are to blame, according to the Conference Board of Canada's annual global ranking of Canada's relative economic performance.

"Canada gained ground on its international peers during the recession, but is again slipping back to the middle of the pack compared to the leading economies in the world," the think-tank said in Thursday's report.

Canada is expected to rank ninth this year—a C grade—up a notch from tenth in 2010, but down from sixth—a B grade—in both 2008 and 2009, it said.

(Continued)

The U.S., despite being hit much harder by the financial crisis than Canada and having a jobless recovery, is expected to earn the same grades as Canada, slipping to eleventh spot, or a C, this year from eighth, or a B, last year.

"Canada seems to be slipping back into old patterns as it comes out of the recession," said Glen Hodgson, the conference board's chief economist. "Our ranking improved during the recession years—even when our performance did not—because we suffered much less economic damage than other countries."

In fact, during the recession Canada's performance slipped markedly on key economic indicators, such as income per capita, growth in gross domestic product, and on employment and unemployment, it said.

While Canada's performance on most indicators has improved during the recovery, it has slipped in the ranking because other countries are improving even more, it explained.

"Of particular concern, Canada's labour productivity growth is expected to rank in thirteenth place—a D grade—in 2011," it said. "Canada also continues to perform poorly on outward foreign direct investment, dropping from seventh place—a C grade—in 2009 to eleventh—a D grade—in 2011."

"Canada had it too good for too long," Hodgson said in an interview with iPolitics.ca, explaining that the formerly weak loonie allowed businesses here to compete internationally without boosting their productivity while easy access to the rich U.S. market allowed them to ignore other foreign markets.

With the mature U.S. market stagnating and the loonie above parity, that may be changing, he said, noting there's been an increase in foreign capital investment in recent quarters, but adding that Canada has a lot of catching up to do.

"On a more positive note," the conference board said Canada gets an A on employment growth in 2010, and is expected to do so again this year.

That may be due to the positive hiring response of employers to the federal government's stimulus program, and possibly an attempt by employers to identify and grab talented workers in advance of the expected tightening of the labour market as baby boomers start retiring, it said.

The problem, however, is that Canadian firms have increased production by hiring more workers rather than boosting their productivity, it said, noting that low productivity growth is the flip side of the strong rebound in employment.

What Canadian businesses should be doing is creating jobs by boosting their productivity, Hodgson said.

"Ultimately, we want to maximize wealth creation through productivity growth," he said. "But we also want that wealth to be widely shared through more jobs."

The weakness in outward-bound foreign investment, meanwhile, suggests Canadian firms have been slow to adapt to increasing globalization and tap into international supply chains and are failing to take advantage of the strong Canadian dollar to invest in new or existing foreign businesses, it said.

In the annual benchmarking exercise, Australia and Sweden are expected to earn "A" grades in both 2010 and 2011, the only two countries to do so in Canada's peer group of major industrial countries.

Australia was the only major industrial country to avoid the 2008–09 recession, thanks to its deep trade and investment relationship with China and other Southeast Asian economies, it noted. Sweden, meanwhile, was hit hard by the recession, but has been experiencing an equally sharp recovery.

MAKING SENSE OF ORGANIZATIONS AND MANAGEMENT

What constitutes the business context or environment, and what factors play the strongest role in determining whether a business will prosper or fail? This question requires a closer examination of the environment of business and of the contexts within which all business operates. To understand the forces that act on business, we can examine issues that are part of the organization's external environment. This chapter sets the stage for that examination.

THE ORGANIZATION AS AN OPEN SYSTEM

It is an obvious fact that we are a society of organizations. From our hospitals, to our schools to our multi-national organizations, it is hard to imagine life without organizations. And, for better or worse, those very institutions and organizations that we have grown up with are continuing to undergo dramatic change. But what exactly are organizations?

What Is an Organization?

What do you think of when you think of an "organization"? We can identify three broad categories of organizations:

1. public/governmental organizations that provide goods and services without necessarily generating a profit;
2. private/non-governmental organizations, including voluntary organizations, that offer goods or services without necessarily generating a profit; and
3. private organizations that produce goods or services with the intent of making a profit for the benefit of their owners or shareholders.

Though we can observe such diverse organizations that operate in these very different sectors, we can also identify underlying characteristics that are common to all organizations. In fact, it is useful to consider a very fundamental question as a starting part in our examination of the nature of organizations. What is an organization? How do we define it? GM, Microsoft, your high school, St. John Ambulance—what do all these entities have in common? Organizations may be large corporations or small non-profit organizations; they might be housed within a large skyscraper; or they could simply be composed of members who are spread across a wide location. What makes all these things organizations?

1. **Organizations are social entities.** Clearly, all the examples cited above have at least one common element—they are made up of people! They are entities that have been generated and are maintained by people. They involve some level of human interaction.
2. **Organizations are created to achieve goals.** That is, they are goal directed. Whether it is a profit-making organization or a non-profit organization, all organizations have some kind of goal or objective they were designed to achieve.
3. **Organizations interact with the environment.** Can you think of any organization that is not somehow linked to its external environment? Think about it. An organization obtains inputs from its environment, whether in the form of people, raw materials, technology or financial capital. All these inputs are transformed by the organization and become outputs: the goods, services or knowledge that the organization generates.

Using Metaphors to Describe Organizations

One helpful method of understanding the nature of organizations is through the use of metaphors. According to Gareth Morgan, a management scholar and author of *Images of Organization*, we can consider the notion of an organization as, essentially, a social construction. That is, we are giving a tangible name to something that we take for granted. Words, names, concepts, ideas, facts, observations, etc., do not so much denote external "things" as conceptions of things activated in the mind. They are not to be seen as a representation of a reality "out there," but as tools for capturing and dealing with what is *perceived* to be "out there."[1] Hence, we understand the usefulness of metaphors. A metaphor is often regarded as no more than a literary and descriptive device for embellishment, but more fundamentally it is a creative form that produces its effect through a crossing of images. A metaphor proceeds through assertions that "subject A is like B and . . ." Through the processes of comparison, between the images of A and B, we generate new meaning. The use of metaphors serves to generate an image for studying a subject. Different images of a subject guide and, ultimately, shape what is seen.

- Organization as machine
- Organization as living organism
- Organization as political system
- Organization as theatre
- Organization as sports team
- Organization as family

EXHIBIT 1.1   What does *organization* mean to you?

In more practical terms—what are the common features of these things that we call *organizations*? Why does this label fit a variety of entities, from non-profit to for-profit contexts? Metaphors are useful to help us describe and, ultimately, understand these social constructions. Consider dictionary definitions of the term *organization*. The Oxford English Dictionary has defined it as a term used primarily to describe the action of organizing or the state of being organized, particularly in a biological sense. Also, the term has been considered as referring to an organized body, system or society. The state of being organized in a biological sense was the basis of the metaphor of arranging or coordinating.

The term *organization* as a depiction of a social institution is relatively new, and creates a new meaning through metaphorical extension of older meanings. Ultimately, the importance of the metaphors we use to describe our hospitals, businesses, places of worship, etc., are important because they lead our thinking about the nature of these places, how they should be designed and how they should function. Let's consider an example of how metaphors guide our thinking in the area of management philosophy.

For example, the "organism metaphor" encompasses a conception of organizations as systems of mutually connected and dependent parts constituted to share a common life. This metaphor suggests that we can conceive organizations as living organisms that contain a combination of elements differentiated yet integrated, attempting to survive within the context of a wider environment. The open-systems approach of organizations, discussed next, is based on this metaphor.

Certainly, we can apply myriad metaphors to try to advance our understanding of what organizations really represent. Among some of the more popular conceptions of organizations in terms of metaphors are organizations as political systems;[2] organizations as loosely coupled systems;[3] organizations as theatres;[4] organizations as a collection of cultures.[5] (See Exhibit 1.1.) No one metaphor can capture the total nature of organizational life. New metaphors can be created for viewing and understanding organizations. Indeed, the very nature of the study of organizations and the field of organizational theory is metaphorical—that is, it is subjective in many ways. The notion of "organizations as systems" is one such metaphor whose implications we will explore in more detail below. This metaphor has guided organizational theories regarding structure and design.

ORGANIZATIONS AS OPEN SYSTEMS

Scholars who have studied organizations have generated countless perspectives on the nature of these entities. One useful perspective involves the view of organizations as systems. How might the metaphor of an organization as a "system" guide our understanding with regard to how organizations operate and sustain themselves?

A system can be defined as interdependent elements working together to achieve a goal or goals. The interdependence of the elements creates an entity that is more than just the sum of its parts—something is achieved beyond the mere putting together of these separate components. The notion of organizations as systems is intended to guide our understanding of what organizations are all about and how they function and survive.[6] Specifically, the notion of an **open system** asserts that organizations are entities that are embedded in, and dependent on exchanges with the environment they operate within. In addition, organizations can be viewed as social systems, with people constituting the basic elements.

Interestingly, there have been times when organizations have been viewed as closed systems, with the belief that how organizations function and survive depends on their ability to remain divorced from their environment. Closed systems have been defined as fully self-sufficient entities requiring no interaction with the environment, and this clearly makes this metaphor difficult to find in practice. This guiding metaphor led much organizational thinking to focus on the organization's internal environment with regard to dealing with organizational functioning and survival. At the same time, this approach failed to recognize the role that the external environment can have in the organization's operations.

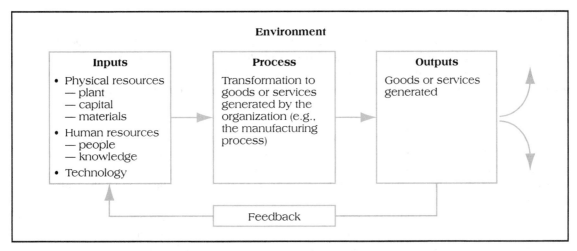

EXHIBIT 1.2 Organizations as open systems.

It was only when the environment became sufficiently volatile and complex that theorists recognized the futility of viewing organizations as closed systems. It became necessary to embrace the open systems metaphor and further acknowledge the critical importance of the notion that organizations are embedded in their environment, requiring resources from and generating outputs to their environment. This also underscored the importance of further understanding the nature of the organization's external environment. (See Exhibit 1.2.)

An organization's environment represents all elements that exist outside the organization and that, potentially, influence or affect the organization in some way. As mentioned elsewhere, the open-systems perspective of organizations emphasizes the importance of the environment and interaction with the environment. Clearly, organizations are dependent on the environment for their survival and success. Without obtaining the necessary environmental inputs, whether they are suitable employees or the raw materials for production, organizations cannot function effectively. Similarly, if organizations fail to generate the types of products or services sought by the environment, then, too, these organizations will cease to exist. As suggested earlier, organizations are created in response to societal or environmental needs; and ultimately, it is the environment that will determine the organization's fate. How an organization chooses to respond to its environment encompasses the notion of business strategy.

The External Context of Business

We can refer to the external context of organizations as their environment. Management scholars have typically defined the environment of an organization along two dimensions: the organization's *specific or task environment*, and the organization's *general environment*. Each factor in an organization's external environment can be considered as existing in two spheres: a specific sphere or environment within which the organization directly operates and a general sphere or environment that would encompass the external environments of all organizations in a society. The specific sphere has been referred to as the environmental domain of the organization. For example, changes in the international environment may be a common factor for all organizations with, say, trade agreements affecting Canadian industry in general. However, some industries may have been differentially affected by changes in the international environment via trade agreements. Not all organizations within an industry or within different industries are equally affected by changes in the environment. There are changes that affect all or some industries, and there are changes or factors that influence the direct sphere or environment of the organizations.

Specific or Task Environment

Any organization is surrounded by external stakeholders. These are parties or groups that have direct influence on the organization's ability to obtain resources and generate outputs. Stakeholders have some kind of stake or interest in the organization, and could include such parties as the organization's customers, suppliers, the labour pool from within which the organization obtains employees, competitors, unions, distributors, creditors, the local public and the government. (See Exhibit 1.3.) While not all of these stakeholders may exist or exert influence on every organization, they are the types of factors that potentially constitute the specific environment of an organization.

General Environment

The sphere surrounding the organization's specific environment is typically referred to as the **general environment**. The forces that make up the general environment ultimately shape the specific environment of the organization. Consequently, the general environment will also influence the organization's ability to obtain resources. General environmental factors typically include: economic, competitive, technological, societal, global and political forces. (See Exhibit 1.3.)

Economic Forces   Whether it is a recession or strong economic health in Canada, the economic environment acts as a strong influence on the present and future prospects of any organization. Moreover, given the strong global ties in Canada, we can also consider the international economic environment as exerting an influence on Canadian organizations. Certainly, we understand the strong influence that the United States and its economy exert on Canadian business.

Any organization, in considering how it will obtain resources from the environment, must ask the question, Is the economy healthy or weak? Organizations are continuously forced to adapt to changing economic conditions. Downsizings are more likely to occur in lean times than in rich. For example, the development of a temporary workforce was partly an outcome of the recession that occurred in the 1990s and the consequent introduction of massive downsizings and layoffs of permanent members of the workforce. Economic changes have also facilitated changes to the nature of the employer–employee relationship. Lifetime employment appears to be a thing of the past. Consider the 1950s or the 1970s—those were times when employment actually meant security. In fact, the dominant model was long-term employment stability. However, a change to these implicit employment promises occurred sometime in the 1980s, when the age of downsizing began, with large, secure

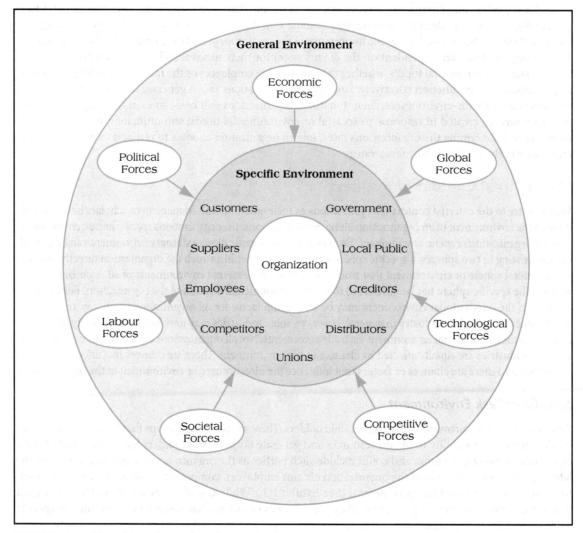

EXHIBIT 1.3   The external context of organizations.

organizations beginning to lay off employees. Today, part-time and temporary work arrangements have become much more common than in the past. The economic context of business will be explained in Chapter 2.

Competitive Forces   Competitive forces operate at two levels for any organization. As mentioned, an organization will have its own set of competitors, yet the force of competition can be viewed from a more general level. For example, globalization, as discussed elsewhere in this book, opens the floodgates for competitors in many industries. Clearly, the number of competitors and the nature of competition will dictate changes in organization strategy (see Talking Business 1.1). Competition, both domestic and foreign, certainly has demanded an acceleration in innovation among firms in many industries. Organizations, to compete effectively, must continually create new and better methods of serving customers. While globalization has opened up larger markets for businesses, it has also facilitated much higher levels of competition. Chapter 3 examines the nature of competitive forces and includes a consideration of the different stages of the industry lifecycle model. That chapter also identifies the key drivers of industry evolution and how competitive forces change during the lifecycle. What are the key success factors for firms at each stage of the lifecycle?

Talking Business 1.1

Pop Strategy

With the sales of cola and other pop falling, cash-rich PepsiCo has put itself on a wellness workout as it tries to tilt its offerings toward fast-growing health-conscious snacks and drinks . . . PepsiCo, more so than archrival Coca-Cola of Atlanta, has strategically diversified outside the soft-drink business in recent years as it looks for faster-growing markets, including health-conscious beverages and snacks and international markets. Having a greater assortment of offerings also gives PepsiCo more clout with grocers, who control prized store shelf space . . . The non-pop strategy appears to be working . . . That diversification has put PepsiCo in a stronger market position than Coca-Cola, whose sales and profit are much more dependent on soft-drink sales.

Source: Excerpted from Barrie Mckenna, "Is Pepsi a natural mix with Evian and yogurt?" *The Globe and Mail* (July 20, 2005), B1.

Technological Forces   Chapter 4's discussion of innovation acknowledges the importance of technological forces that surround organizations. Technology plays a central role in how an organization functions, how it obtains resources and, ultimately, how effectively it competes. We will consequently examine different types of innovations and explore the relationship between technological evolution and industry evolution. Furthermore, we will discuss the impact of technology on competitive business practices and technology lifecycle models. The technological environment exerts influence across industries. For example, in the case of Bell Canada, the increase in the number of competitors in the telecommunications industry was partly a consequence of the ability of smaller businesses to enter the industry with the increasingly sophisticated technology that formerly was the domain of big business, given its costly nature. However, with technological advances came reductions in operating costs which led to the ability to attract more competitors who could now afford to enter the industry.

Change in technology is a constant and is a force that permits and demands organizational change. (See Talking Business 1.2.) One benefit of technology is increased flexibility in work arrangements. Telework, or telecommuting, essentially means that, given today's technology, an employee can work from home. Technology has also facilitated business process re-design or "re-engineering," an issue examined in Chapter 4.

Labour Forces   Canadian business operates within a diverse society. The Canadian population reflects a multitude of cultures and demographic backgrounds. For example, recent census figures provided by Statistics Canada show that over 5 million Canadian citizens were foreign-born, comprising nearly 20 percent of the total population. This diversity is increasingly reflected in the Canadian labour pool. Immigrants who came to Canada in the 1990s have accounted for approximately 70 percent of the total growth of the labour force in recent years. Women also comprise a significant component of the Canadian labour force and account for about half of both the employed work force and all union members. Visible minorities and people with disabilities, together with women, make up over 60 percent of Canada's labour force. Diversity in our work

Talking Business 1.2

Harnessing the Force of Technology

Downloading music illegally has been a problem for some time now. Napster pioneered the peer-to-peer technology that enabled file-sharers around the globe to instantly and illegally have access to thousands of songs. Mired in lawsuits, Napster was eventually prohibited from engaging in this activity (but it paved the way for other like-minded services such as Kazaa and Grokster). The music industry had no choice but to provide something that the consumer clearly wanted. Apple Computer, Inc. has led the way with its iPod and iTunes service. Clearly the music industry needs to stay innovative in order to combat sliding sales. The film industry is similarly attempting to harness the power of technology. Film studios are desperately trying to fight a decrease in ticket sales as well as an insurgence of technology that allows pirating to be conducted at a click of the mouse.

Technology has had a similarly powerful impact on the television industry. The life of a TV show has long been determined by the ratings. Recorded by Nielsen Media Research, each new show has to instantly prove itself, otherwise it will be cancelled, often with episodes yet to air never to be seen again. However, with the advent of TV shows on DVD, this perform-or-die ethos has been slowly changing. TV-DVD revenue has been steady, and the network heads are being forced to modify their strategy.

Sources: "Music—Digital Downloading: Finally getting in on the act." *[London] Marketing Week* (September 1, 2005), p. 20.; Robert Poe, "BlingTones' Ringtones Crunk Out the Revenue." (June 1, 2005) <http://onlinenews.itu.int/americas2005onlinenews/article/articleDetail.jsp?id=172176>; "Movie same-time DVD releases" (2005) <http://p2pnet.net/story/6796>

force is also reflected in the growing presence of older workers. All these factors demand that organizations understand the demographic context within which they operate.

In addition, business must also recognize the nature of the industrial relations context within which many operate. Across many industries, unions are the organizations responsible for representing the interests of Canada's working population. It is critical to understand the role of unions and how they can impact the environment of business. Given the range of activities within which unions can operate, they can have an equally broad range of effects on their member's wages and working conditions, as well as on the productivity and overall performance of the firms within which their members work. In addition, unions can have an impact on the Canadian economy and Canadian society as a whole. Chapter 5 will examine these issues within an exploration of the industrial relations context.

Global Forces   **Global forces**, in many ways, are forces that could be embedded in general economic, political, technological or societal forces—but are international in nature.

The tragic and devastating events of September 11, 2001, resulted in a chain reaction of international consequences, including changes in economic and political forces acting on organizations. Global events have an increasingly important impact on local organizations. While there is no universally agreed-upon definition of *globalization*, it is useful to consider this concept as a process: that is, a process involving the integration of world economies. The presence of trade blocs reflects the accelerating pace with which nations are integrating their economies. Globalization also includes the globalization of markets—the notion that consumer preferences are converging around the world. Whether it is for products made by McDonald's, Sony, Gap or Nike, organizations are increasingly marketing their goods and services worldwide. On the other side, production is increasingly becoming a global affair. Businesses will set up operations wherever it is least costly to do so.

Certainly, international trade agreements are global agreements among governments that are changing the nature and functions of many businesses. A Canadian organization may not simply consider consumers within the domestic borders, but may have a significant consumer market overseas; this demands a knowledge of global societies, global competitors and other forces that exist on an international level.

The global forces of the general environment underscore the increasingly tangled web of players in the global business context—domestic and foreign competitors, domestic and foreign workers, domestic and foreign industry, government, national cultures and economies. How business is conducted in light of trade agreements and global arrangements is a key issue for our entire society. And this is a theme we will explore more fully in Chapter 6.

Political Forces   Political forces can exert influence at both the specific and general levels. The government's push toward deregulating many industries was not solely aimed at the telecommunications industry, but rather was designed to welcome more competitors into the Canadian business sector and facilitate freer trade between Canada and the United States. The reduction in trade barriers worldwide has also opened the doors for increasing presence of foreign competition in many industries. Deregulation and privatization, discussed in another chapter, are clear examples of the importance of considering the effect of governmental changes on business strategy. Are government regulations facilitating, or restricting, certain business strategies? The political environment of business can dictate changes in how business competes, or what services it offers and how they can be offered. As we will discuss in a later chapter, the deregulation of protected industries in the 1980s and 1990s created competition for companies where no real competition had previously existed. Industries such as telecommunications, banking, energy and aerospace were dramatically affected by these governmental/regulatory changes. As the dominant companies in these industries were forced to compete in an open market, some responded by downsizing their workforce.

In a general sense, the traditional relationship of government with business is clearly undergoing change. The trend toward increased government involvement after World War II seems to have reversed by about 1980. In fact, some observers have suggested that this massive disposal of government-owned assets and the reduction of government controls in the business sector indicate a minor revolution of sorts. We will examine this issue in more detail in Chapter 7.

Societal Forces   Societal forces have an important impact on organizations. The nature of a society certainly is an entrenched part of any organization's general environment. For example, we have witnessed an increasing concern for individual welfare in the workplace as societies become more cognizant of human rights and how people should be treated. Consequently, the workplace increasingly emphasizes organizational justice—how employees are treated. This has translated into greater laws governing fairness in the workplace. One such area that has been dramatically affected is compensation. Pay equity has been among numerous issues examined in redressing inconsistencies in pay treatment among men and women, for example. We have also witnessed an increasing emphasis on merit-based pay and pay-for-performance—which all attempt to more closely link actual effort to performance instead of seniority-based pay, which bases pay on the number of years an employee has been with the organization.

Business must respond to society. Consumer tastes change, for example, and business must adapt to such changes (see Talking Business 1.3). Similarly, the types of organizations that serve societal demands can change. The aging population suggests that greater emphasis needs to be placed on such industries as the health care sector. In addition, society has a certain set of ethics or values, and these can influence the type of behaviour that organizations will manifest in that society. From a societal standpoint, it is not difficult to understand the importance of adequately addressing the issue of the ethical behaviour of business organizations and their constituents. All sectors of society, including organizations themselves, are drastically affected by a variety of forms of unethical behaviour. There is a growing belief that organizations are social actors responsible for the ethical and unethical behaviour of their employees. Critics of business argue that organizational leaders must examine more closely the "moral sense-making" within organizations and responsibilities to external constituencies. The tolerance of unethical behaviour in a society would seem to be a precursor to the acceptance of corporate unethical behaviour. This is an issue that we will more fully explore in Chapter 8, which also emphasizes the requirement for organizations to address stakeholders in the global context.

Generating a Winning Business Strategy

After fully examining these external forces, deciding what strategies the organization should pursue is a key task of managers. Managers are continually faced with making decisions, both minor and major, on a daily basis. Our aim will be to describe the nature and purpose of strategic management and its connection to the environment. Chapter 9 examines issues that are of critical importance to strategic management. What are the key forces in determining an industry's structure, and what are the strategic implications? We will consider the roles of organizational resources and capabilities in firm performance. Our exploration will also include a discussion of corporate strategy and an identification of three generic strategies, and how organizations go about implementing strategy.

Exhibit 1.4 illustrates the framework we adopt in this book, and also identifies the environment of business. While Chapter 9 identifies strategic responses to the environment, Chapter 10 highlights the challenges of adapting to changes in the external environment.

Talking Business 1.3
Canadian Consumers Changing Habits: Study

Derek Abma

OTTAWA—Canadian consumers are "radically reassessing how they spend their money," according to a study released Thursday by American Express.

The credit card company said Canadians are becoming more particular about getting value for their money, and there is more awareness of the ethical implications of their purchasing decisions.

That's based on a study of 1,000 Canadians, carried out in August by international research group, The Future Laboratory.

"Consumers are moving from the excessive, impulsive spending of the pre-recession era to more careful, considered spending, in which value for money and quality take precedence over branding," the report said.

"They are more thoughtful in what they buy, and looking for more meaning in their purchases, so they increasingly seek products that are ethical and environmentally friendly."

Among the general shopping trends the study says will take hold in 2011 and beyond is a preference for buying goods that are locally produced.

The study said 36% of Canadians in the study support local businesses because they want to have a positive impact on their communities. Almost half said the involvement of local firms in the production of a goods affects their purchasing decisions, and about as many said they have become more aware over the last year of the environmental impact of their buying activities.

No margin of error was provided for the data.

Toronto retail consultant Anthony Stokan, a partner at Anthony Russell and Associates who helped with the research, said there's an increasing awareness among the masses about how their purchasing decisions affect the immediate community around them and bigger world in general. A few years ago, he said, buying decisions were almost solely based on personal reasons.

"I think the interesting thing about moving into this decade is people are making an assessment on every aspect of their behaviour, whether it's driving distance in terms of purchasing, what the impact of that is in terms of the environmental footprint, what the impact is of importing goods or importing fresh food or fresh vegetables during the summer when they can be bought locally," he said.

Mr. Stokan said the baby-boomer generation is driving much of the new consumption trends, given their ample financial resources and the freedom that comes from partial or full retirement.

The shopping habits of people in their 20s and 30s are also changing, but much of this end comes from a lack of financial resources, given the unstable job market they are dealing with, Mr. Stokan added.

Canadians between the ages of 18 to 34 "are choosing to downsize and simplify their possessions," American Express said. Among this group, 57% said they shop for things they "need," versus 37% who said they shop for things they "want."

On the other hand, baby boomers between 55 and 64 are looking to live it up. The survey found 87% of Canadians in this age group make luxury purchases, and 54% said being able to access to the Internet from almost anywhere affects their buying habits.

"These seniors are experiencing a renewed lease of life and enjoying longer, more active and more engaged lifestyles, but they are also very environmentally conscious," the report said.

Consumer trends toward more responsible purchasing and greater demand for quality were also found in parallel studies done by American Express in the United States, United Kingdom, Australia, Japan and Mexico.

However, Mr. Stokan said Canada is leading such changes. He said this is largely the result of Canadians being tech savvy and using the Internet in gaining more awareness of the products they buy and how their consumption relates to global issues.

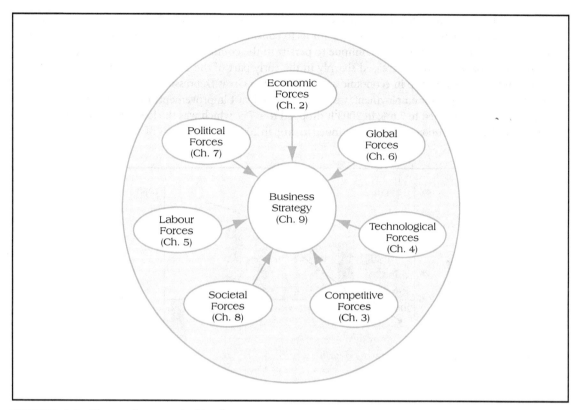

EXHIBIT 1.4   The environment of business.

From the above description of the environment, it can be observed that there is an overlap of factors between the general environment and the specific environment. An organization may have a specific market niche or set of consumers; but demographic changes in the general environment, such as an aging society, will certainly translate into changes to consumer tastes at the specific environment level. Similarly, as noted above, the government's aim to reduce trade barriers at a national level can translate into regulation within an organization's specific environment, or can result in increased competition within the organization's specific environment. This underlines the importance of understanding the impact of the general external environment or the specific environment of the organization.

THE CANADIAN CONTEXT

Let's revisit each of the external environmental forces with regard to the Canadian context.

Economic Forces in Canada

What are some of the indicators of the current state of health of the Canadian economic scene? One indicator of the health of the economy is GDP—**gross domestic product**: the total value of a country's output of goods and services in a given year. The money that is earned from producing goods and services goes to the employees who produce them, to the people who own businesses and to the governments in the form of taxes. The general trend of governments worldwide is to reduce their share of GDP. Obviously, it is good for GDP to grow: from 1979–1989 Canada's GDP grew about 3.2% annually. The compound annual growth of GDP between 2001 and 2009 was 1.6%. Currently, Canada's economy is expected to see compounded annual growth of 2.5% until 2025.[7] (See Exhibit 1.5 for GDP growth between 2001 and 2009.) Canada experienced solid economic growth between 1993 and 2007. However, it went into a severe recession in 2008/2009. Fortunately, it emerged strong after this global financial crisis ended.

The future health of the Canadian economy, as in most economies, is continually the subject of speculation. It appears that economists are not necessarily more accurate in their predictions of economic well-being than are those looking into the proverbial crystal ball. It would seem crucial to understand what underlying forces are ultimately shaping the state of our business system in Canada. This amounts to distinguishing between short-term changes in the domestic economy and ongoing trends in the nature of the business enterprise system. It may be more manageable for us to consider what has been going on around us in recent years and assess what conditions will continue to persist in the coming years.

The unemployment rate increased sharply in the early part of the 1990s due to the severe 1991–1992 recession and the steepest drop in economic activity since the Great Depression of the 1930s. While much of the 1990s were not bright for employment, we have witnessed vast improvements in recent years. By 1999, the unemployment rate dropped to 7.6%; in 2005 it dropped to 6.7%, which was the lowest level achieved in three decades. This decrease in unemployment continued to drop in 2007, reaching a low of about 6%. (See Exhibit 1.6.)

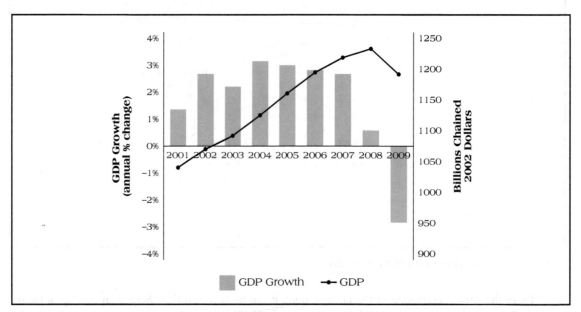

EXHIBIT 1.5   GDP growth in 2001 and 2002 was much slower, with annual growth rates below the 9 year compound annual rate. However, in 2003, annual GDP growth slipped to 2.1, corresponding with a down-turn in the United States economy. GDP growth rates went on to rebound and remained steady around 3% until 2008, when a global recession trimmed annual GDP growth to 0.6%. In 2009, the GDP continued to decline to a low of 2.8%.

Source: Statistics Canada, Gross Domestic Product by Industry, 2001 to 2009.

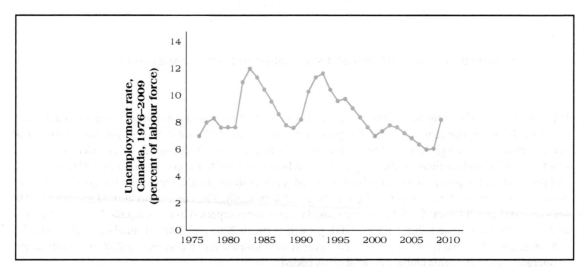

EXHIBIT 1.6   In 2009, the unemployment rate was 8.3%. Between 1976 and 2009, the unemployment rate reached its highest levels in 1983 (12.0%) and 1993 (11.4%), following two major recessions in Canada. In 2007, Canada recorded its lowest unemployment rate (6.0%) since the mid-1970s.

Source: Statistics Canada. *Labour Force Historical Review 2009* (Table 086). Ottawa: Statistics Canada, 2010 (Cat. No. 71F0004XVB).

Competitive Forces in Canada

When you think "Canadian business," what picture do you conjure in your mind? Looking back over Canada's past, it has been argued that we established a certain pattern for ourselves in terms of the type of business activity we emphasized here. During most of our existence, we have developed as a largely open economy, trading internationally, primarily, in resources. Specifically, Canada, for most of our existence, has focused on the extraction and processing of our natural resources. It has been suggested that our emphasis on the export of our natural resources, typically in a relatively unprocessed state, made us more akin to a simple supplier of raw materials, whether it has been logs and lumber, pulp and newsprint, unrefined minerals, agricultural crops, etc. In fact, it has been argued that our corporations are much more involved in the extraction and processing of natural resources than most other countries at comparable stages of economic development. This pattern has led critics to suggest that we have not developed the entrepreneurial and technological expertise of other nations, who used our "raw materials" and added value through their own technological resources. However, it would be unfair to suggest that this is the whole picture. The fact is, we have witnessed major changes in the nature of our economic sector, and we continue to see a major transformation in our economy and in the types of business competitors we have created. As with any capitalist-based system, Canada views competition as an important part of the business enterprise system!

Imagine a situation where there is only one provider of an important good. If society requires this good, then they must be willing to accept whatever price the provider demands. There is also no assurance regarding the quality of the good. There is little incentive for the provider of this good to be efficient in operations—any high costs can be passed on to the consumer in the form of high prices. Similarly, there is little need to innovate or produce higher quality products for the consumer, given that there is no risk of losing this captive market. Consequently, competition is considered to be an important element: this entails firms competing with each other to provide better products at lower prices in order to increase sales and profits.

Pure competition, sometimes referred to as **perfect competition**, exists when there are many small firms producing an identical product, and consequently no single producer has the power to affect the price of the product. Traditionally, the agricultural industry is an example of this type of competition, given the identical nature of the products and the fact that no single producer can influence prices. In fact, these companies are forced to respond obediently to prices set in the market. **Monopolistic competition** involves a large number of small firms whose product or service is perceived as slightly different. As a result, each firm has some influence on the prices, such as may be the case with retail operations. An **oligopoly** exists where there are a small number of producers with a different product. For example, car manufacturers have significant control over prices, and yet competition does play a role in the prices set. Finally, a monopoly exists where there is only one seller or producer.

Our economic system is based on the assumption that sufficient competition exists among business enterprises to ensure that business provides the goods and services required by society at a fair cost. Competition is the "invisible hand" that ensures the market works in this manner. However, if an industry is relatively concentrated, then businesses can act as price setters, not price takers. Of course, with extreme concentration, as is the case with a monopoly, then business can set the price itself or collude with other businesses. Observers suggest that Canada has not taken as strict a stance on industry concentration as the United States, where legislation has been aimed at preventing industry concentration. In Canada, government-legislated competition policy does attempt to discourage industry concentration, but also seeks to control the potential inequities created when a small number of firms dominate a particular market. (See Talking Business 1.4)

Talking Business 1.4
Competition

How does the Canadian corporate landscape shape up in terms of the relative numbers of business competitors? Well, looking across industries, what we tend to see is domination by a relatively small number of firms. That is, we have a relatively small number of corporations in any particular industry. This has been referred to as "industrial concentration in the economy." Statistics Canada recently estimated that the largest 25 firms in Canada are responsible for about 25% of total profits generated in the business sector and own about 41% of the total assets. Of course, some industries are more concentrated than others. For example, we have relatively few large players in the brewery industry, in banking and among department stores.

Technological Forces in Canada

Traditionally, Canada's economy has been resource based. This refers to our emphasis on industries like agriculture, mining, forestry, fisheries, minerals and energy. Natural resources have constituted the bulk of Canada's exports. Given the nature of our primary industries, one important implication is that prices for the output of these industries are very much influenced by the world market. That is, these natural resource industries are highly affected by any fluctuations in the global supply and demand for these commodities, suggesting that many of our industries are highly sensitive to changes in the global or world market. A general criticism that has been levelled at the Canadian business environment is that we need to catch up in the area of technology and innovation rather than relying on our natural resources in largely unprocessed forms.

However, the Canadian economy has been transforming. We have already seen significant changes in the sectoral composition of Canada's economy over the 20th century. At the beginning of the 20th century, there was a balance between employment in the primary sectors of the economy and the industrial and service sectors. What we mean by the primary sector is agriculture, mining, logging, fishing, hunting and trapping. The industrial sector is akin to the manufacturing or goods-producing sectors, while the service sector can include things like the hotel or restaurant industry. At the beginning of the 20th century, we had an abundance of employment in the primary sector, with most of this coming from the agricultural sector. However, even early in the century Canada witnessed a steady decline in agricultural employment right up until World War II—after which time this decline continued even more rapidly.

Canada's employment has clearly shifted away from the agricultural sector. Why? A number of reasons have been offered. Perhaps one of the most obvious reasons for the decline in agricultural employment is a reduced need for human capital: that is, part of the reason is simply due to technological advances that have made human labour obsolete. Many areas have become increasingly mechanized and, consequently, require far fewer workers to achieve the same level of output. Concurrent to this decline has been the increasing urbanization of the Canadian population: increasing numbers of Canadians continue to flock to cities from rural areas in search of employment, and it is the cities that attract the largest share of new immigrants.

If there has been a significant shift in employment away from the agriculture sector, the question is, Where has it shifted to? What we have seen happening in conjunction with that decline in Canada is great increases in the number of Canadians employed in goods-producing and service industries. The manufacturing sector produces tangible goods, such as clothes, oil, food, machines and automobiles. The service sector includes things like banking, insurance, information, marketing, accounting, hospitality and food services, recreation and so on.

The shift to the manufacturing and service sectors was particularly striking in the first 15 years following World War II, after which growth in these areas slowed, although it certainly continued throughout the sixties, seventies and eighties. However, what is particularly striking in the later post-war period is the simultaneous rise in service sector employment, and, at least since the 1950s, the rapid decline in goods-producing industries. We continue to witness this trend, albeit at a reduced rate. Consider this: in 1950, only 42% of Canadians were employed in service-producing industries; by 1993, the figure had risen to over 72%. Whereas at the turn of the century we shifted from an agricultural to an industrial economy, the second shift has been the transition from a goods-producing to a service-oriented economy. This shift is summed up in the observations in Talking Business 1.5.

Talking Business 1.5

Information Technology

Canada's information technology sector will replace rocks and trees as the dominant force in the economy over the coming decade, according to a study from the Toronto Dominion Bank. Despite the recent weaknesses in the New Economy industries, their growth will continue....Canada's economy is expected to be even less resource-based, more heavily wired and more service-driven than ever before. . . . The bank defined the New Economy as eight industries in the area of information technology—four in manufacturing and four in services. Those in manufacturing include communications and electrical equipment; office and business machines; communications, energy, wire and cable; and scientific equipment. Services include telecommunications—both broadcasting and carriers—computers and software sectors. Meanwhile the resource sector, which includes oil and gas, agriculture, forestry, fishing and logging, and resource-based manufacturing, continues to decline.

Source: Excerpted from Marian Stinson, "New economy still seen as future" *The Globe and Mail* (May 31, 2001).

Why are we moving away from the natural resources and the manufacturing sector to the service sector? What is driving this shift? Well, there is not really one accepted reason for this transformation to a service economy. But probably the most often cited reason is technology: just as mechanization of agricultural production decreased the need for human capital, more generally the increasing mechanization of manufacturing facilities has similarly reduced the need for human labour in this sector. We can produce comparable levels of output with far less labour than we did in the past. This is referred to as a productivity improvement. And as far as productivity is concerned, what we have seen is labour productivity growth in manufacturing outpacing productivity growth in services. (See Exhibit 1.7.) Why?

Consider the nature of many service-oriented jobs: social workers who counsel youths, waiters who serve customers, and medical caregivers who treat patients are not easily replaced by machinery. Productivity growth in this sector is thus much slower than in the manufacturing sector. The result of this difference in productivity growth rates is that more Canadians need to be employed in services in order to maintain the relative levels of service and manufacturing output.

Whatever the source, there is little question that services are playing a much greater role in our economy than they have in the past. However, one final question that we can ask related to all this is, Is this shift a good thing? Let's consider several implications of this transition.

On an individual level, anyone planning on entering the job market or remaining employable must consider his or her skill set. Obviously, our workforce must be better educated and capable of attaining the relatively higher skill levels required in the highly paying service sector jobs (in comparison to the manufacturing sector). The notion of the **knowledge worker,** a relatively recent buzzword, underscores the increasing importance of higher education and the value of transferable skills.

EXHIBIT 1.7   Employment by industry (in thousands).

	2006	2007	2008	2009	2010
All industries	**16,410.2**	**16,805.6**	**17,087.4**	**16,813.1**	**17,041.0**
Goods-producing sector	3,975.9	3,975.7	4,013.4	3,724.3	3,740.0
Agriculture	346.9	335.0	323.6	316.1	300.7
Forestry, fishing, mining, quarrying, oil and gas	334.1	341.7	344.6	317.9	329.4
Utilities	121.3	137.7	151.5	147.6	148.3
Construction	1,066.4	1,130.5	1,231.0	1,160.8	1,217.2
Manufacturing	2,107.2	2,030.9	1,962.7	1,781.8	1,744.3
Services-producing sector	12,434.3	12,829.9	13,074.0	13,088.8	13,301.0
Trade	2,616.4	2,673.3	2,684.9	2,652.2	2,677.8
Transportation and warehousing	794.8	819.7	848.9	816.2	805.7
Finance, insurance, real estate and leasing	1,032.9	1,055.8	1,073.6	1,092.1	1,095.7
Professional, scientific and technical services	1,082.1	1,129.9	1,189.3	1,191.9	1,266.7
Business, building and other support services[1]	683.3	699.0	685.0	654.9	672.2
Educational services	1,154.7	1,179.8	1,186.3	1,188.8	1,217.8
Health care and social assistance	1,779.0	1,835.4	1,893.0	1,949.2	2,030.7
Information, culture and recreation	742.3	776.3	758.4	769.6	766.0
Accommodation and food services	1,013.9	1,073.8	1,080.6	1,056.6	1,058.4
Other services	701.1	721.8	748.3	787.0	753.5
Public administration	834.0	865.1	925.7	930.3	956.4

1. Formerly Management of companies, administrative and other support services.

Source: Statistics Canada, CANSIM, table (for fee) 282–0008 and Catalogue no. 71F0004XCB. www40.statcan.gc.ca/l01/cst01/econ40-eng.htm.

But in broader terms, is the service sector better for our economy? Or is manufacturing still very much a critical element? A number of observers suggest that we should say "good riddance" to the old, outdated manufacturing sector and welcome the growing service sector with open arms. For example, economist Nuala Beck, in her popular book *Shifting Gears: Thriving in the New Economy,* referred to a "new knowledge economy" that is quickly replacing the old mass-manufacturing economy. Beck observed that these "knowledge workers" now make up 30% of North America's workforce, while only 10% are actually involved in production. Further, it is the more knowledge-intensive new industries (like the high-tech industries) that are creating most of the jobs and driving the economy.

Labour Forces in Canada

Demographics comprises the characteristics of a population (e.g., age, sex, income, employment status, etc.). What are some defining characteristics of our population? First, there are not many of us—relatively speaking. Canada's total population of approximately 31 million is among the smallest of the industrialized nations. It has been observed that our relatively small market has made it extremely difficult to develop more than a handful of domestic manufacturers of a stature capable of competing on the world markets. Moreover, it has been asserted that Canada has generated too many small operations that have been protected for too long by government. What are the implications of this? Many businesses see an urgent need to expand their markets beyond Canadian borders.

Demographic (population) trends have a significant effect on business planning and activities. In the 20 years following World War II (1946–1966), Canada witnessed an unusual phenomenon. Large numbers of war veterans, aided by government grants, got married and acquired housing for their families. In addition, the hundreds of thousands of immigrants who were entering Canada annually also needed housing. Four children per family was the norm. These were *baby boomers.* This explosive growth in population and family formation led to a 20-year boom in many industries (e.g., housing, furnishings, children's clothing, etc.).

Today, other important demographic trends have emerged that will have a great impact on the next few decades. For example, consider the *aging population.* (See Talking Business 1.6.) The demographics of the workforce have changed gradually over the years, and among these changes we have witnessed a graying or aging of the workforce. In 1921 the median age of the Canadian population was under 24 years; by 1993 it had risen to over 33 years. The median age continues to rise, and could be as high as 50 by the year 2036. In 1981, the largest age bracket was the group between 15 and 24. Population projections show that by 2031 the largest group will be the 70–74 age bracket. By 2011, the portion of the population over 65 and 75 was about double what it was in 1981 (9.7%). At the same time, the portion of the population that is very young continues to decrease because of declining birth rates since the mid-1960s (e.g., in 1971 about 30% of the Canadian population was between 6 and 19; by 2011, it had dropped to about 20%). So businesses will cater to an older population: health care, recreation, travel are among the industries that are predicted to benefit from an older population.

One other major change in the makeup of the workforce is *women in the workforce.* The growing number of women in the workforce is another trend that will have a significant impact on business. In 1921

Talking Business 1.6
An Aging Workforce

The challenges of dealing with a changing workplace demographic were also noted in a recent report by economist Bill Robson for the C.D. Howe Institute, entitled, *Aging Populations and the Workforce: Challenges for Employees.* The report suggested that over the next 20 years, both business and government will need to adapt numerous employment practices and social policies to meet the changing demands of an aging workforce, and a workforce that is more highly educated and largely female. Currently, the federal government has been initiating training and labour policy changes that recognize the aging of the workforce. Recently, the Minister of Human Resources and Development suggested, for example, that Canada accept more immigrants to replace retiring workers. According to the report, private-sector employers will also require new recruitment and training strategies to manage an older workforce and a greater immigrant population.

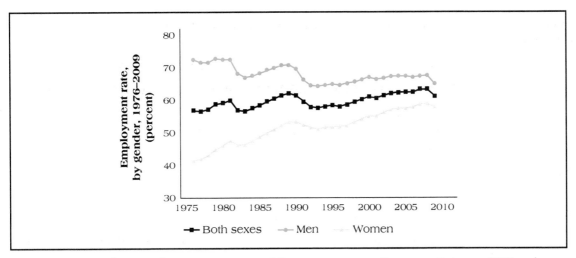

EXHIBIT 1.8 Employment has grown more rapidly among women than men. Between 1976 and 2009, the employment rate for women rose from 41.9% to 58.3%, a 16.4 percentage point increase. On the other hand, the employment rate for men declined by 7.5 percentage points from 72.7% in 1976 to 65.2% in 2009.

Source: Statistics Canada. *Labour Force Historical Review 2009* (Table 002). Ottawa: Statistics Canada, 2010 (Cat. No. 71F0004XVB).

only 20% of the female population worked outside the home. By the 1990s the figure had risen to about 60%. Exhibit 1.8 shows trends in labour participation rates by gender. There are also some interesting patterns to observe within the workforce. Now into the 21st century, we see the continued increase in the number of women in the workforce. We are also observing an increase in the cultural diversity of organizations—a greater heterogeneity of races and nationalities. The changing cultural mix of organizations demands that we place greater attention on efforts to effectively integrate the variety of cultures, along with men and women in the workplace.

Global Forces in Canada

The United States

Clearly, our proximity to the United States is an element that influences the nature of our business environment. Keep in mind that the United States has a population that is approximately 10 times that of Canada. And though we possess one of the largest countries in terms of land mass, the bulk of our population lives within 200 km of the Canada–U.S. border. In fact, the U.S. presence in the Canadian business sector is a defining characteristic of our environment. Moreover, the trade agreements we have entered into with the United States have critical implications for our business sector (an issue we will deal with later in this book).

Importance of International Trade

Currently, Canada exports over 40% of its total annual production (GDP), compared to 25% a decade ago. This underscores the fact that Canada is considered to be a major trading nation. A key concern regarding our international business activity is whether we are selling more to other countries (exporting) than we are importing (buying from other countries). Other than the United States (our major trading partner, consuming more than 85% of our total exports), we have traditionally run a trade deficit with most other countries (i.e., our imports have outweighed our exports), as illustrated in Exhibit 1.9.

A number of issues regarding our trade status have received much attention in the last decade or so: the Free Trade Agreement and the North American Free Trade Agreement (NAFTA) and the consequent increase in the degree of openness to international trade. As mentioned earlier, Canada's traditional reliance on trade in unprocessed natural resources has received much criticism, and its traditional reliance on U.S. trade has been scrutinized, as reflected in Talking Business 1.7.

EXHIBIT 1.9   Imports, exports and trade balance of goods on a balance-of-payments basis, by country or country grouping (in $ millions).

	2005	2006	2007	2008	2009	2010
Exports	**450,210.0**	**453,951.9**	**463,120.4**	**488,754.1**	**369,343.2**	**404,834.2**
United States[1]	368,278.9	361,442.1	355,731.5	370,005.3	271,108.7	296,672.0
Japan	10,172.8	10,278.1	10,026.8	11,784.3	8,861.8	9,716.6
United Kingdom	9,360.5	11,282.2	14,152.3	14,029.3	13,046.0	16,985.8
Other European Union[2]	18,643.8	20,903.7	24,392.7	25,173.5	19,010.3	19,475.8
Other OECD[3]	14,545.6	16,808.1	19,743.6	20,748.6	16,690.6	17,908.3
All other countries	29,208.5	33,237.6	39,073.5	47,013.1	40,625.8	44,075.7
Imports	**387,837.8**	**404,345.4**	**415,683.1**	**443,777.2**	**374,080.9**	**413,832.8**
United States[1]	259,332.9	265,088.3	270,066.9	281,535.0	236,289.6	259,952.7
Japan	11,213.1	11,849.9	11,967.1	11,671.8	9,329.2	10,067.2
United Kingdom	9,066.5	9,547.1	9,962.9	11,232.9	8,529.6	9,560.6
Other European Union[2]	29,487.3	32,547.5	32,403.7	35,461.4	30,240.5	30,788.3
Other OECD[3]	24,282.1	23,680.1	25,159.8	27,380.4	25,961.7	29,012.9
All other countries	54,455.9	61,632.4	66,122.7	76,495.7	63,730.4	74,451.1
Balance	**62,372.2**	**49,606.5**	**47,437.3**	**44,976.9**	**−4,737.7**	**−8,998.6**
United States[1]	108,946.0	96,353.8	85,664.6	88,470.3	34,819.1	36,719.3
Japan	−1,040.3	−1,571.8	−1,940.3	112.5	−467.4	-350.6
United Kingdom	294.0	1,735.1	4,189.4	2,796.4	4,516.4	7,425.2
Other European Union[2]	−10,843.5	−11,643.8	−8,011.0	−10,287.9	−11,230.2	−11,312.5
Other OECD[3]	−9,736.5	−6,872.0	−5,416.2	−6,631.8	−9,271.1	−11,104.6
All other countries	−25,247.4	−28,394.8	−27,049.2	−29,482.6	−23,104.6	−30,375.4

1. Also includes Puerto Rico and Virgin Islands.
2. Other European Union includes Austria, Belgium, Bulgaria, Cyprus, Czech Republic, Denmark, Estonia, Finland, France, Germany, Greece, Hungary, Ireland, Italy, Latvia, Lithuania, Luxembourg, Malta, Netherlands, Poland, Portugal, Romania, Slovakia, Slovenia, Spain and Sweden.
3. Other countries in the Organisation for Economic Co-operation and Development (OECD) include Australia, Canada, Iceland, Mexico, New Zealand, Norway, South Korea, Switzerland and Turkey.

Source: Statistics Canada, CANSIM, table (for fee) 228–0003. Last modified: 2011–06–09.

Foreign Ownership

How "Canadian" is Canadian business? In other words, what proportion of the corporations doing business in Canada are not actually controlled by Canadian sources?

While the level of foreign ownership varies among different industries (e.g., about 67% in chemical product and textile manufacturers, and only about 9% in communications), the average level of foreign ownership is relatively high by world standards. Annual foreign investment in Canadian companies means ownership of assets like factories, land, buildings, machinery, equipment and companies themselves. So, we have a pretty high level of foreign ownership, largely U.S.-based, in Canadian corporations—but what difference does that make to the nature of business in Canada?

What are the implications of foreign investment? There is much debate about this topic. In fact, Canadians have traditionally been ambivalent when it comes to the issue of foreign investment. For some, interest in the Canadian economy is a good thing. On the one hand, we want to attract investors to our country in order to help generate more business and more jobs. The source of ownership shouldn't make a difference when the results are the same—more jobs for Canadians and more money invested in the Canadian economy.

What impact does foreign ownership have on the personality of our corporate sector? Keep in mind that these foreign-owned corporations are largely subsidiaries of U.S.-based "parent" companies. One important

Talking Business 1.7

Canadian Firms Reduce Reliance on U.S. Trade

Gordon Isfeld

Canada's cozy trade relationship with the United States is continuing to chill as companies increasingly turn to other partners overseas.

The country's reliance on its traditional cross-border trade has waned over the past decade, and 2010 was no exception, with ties to other countries—in particular, China and the U.K.—growing stronger.

Trade with the U.S. accounted for 62.5 per cent of all Canadian activity last year, down from 76.3 per cent in 2001, Statistics Canada said in an annual trade review released Thursday.

While the U.S. is still Canada's biggest market, trade with China more than tripled, rising to 3.3 per cent from 1.1 per cent over the same period, while trade with the U.K.—Canada's second biggest trading partner—totalled 4.1 per cent, up from 1.3 per cent.

The shift away from the U.S. reflects the weaker demand for Canadian products south of the border, where the economy has been struggling to rebound from the financial crisis and recession.

The strong appreciation of Canadian dollar against its U.S. counterpart—making Canadian products more expensive—has been a factor in shrinking exports to the U.S., said Douglas Porter, deputy chief economist at BMO Capital Markets. The loonie's advance against other currencies has not been as dramatic as it has with the U.S. dollar.

As well, the growth of emerging markets has continued to open up new avenues for Canadian exports—particularly commodities, which have soared in value since the global economy began turning around.

Copyright © *The Victoria Times Colonist*

---

consideration is the activity that the corporation carries on in order to conduct its business—i.e., strategic planning, research and development, marketing, etc. Many foreign-owned firms, like the car manufacturers or the multinational oil companies, operate Canadian subsidiaries largely to produce or simply market the product. These products are typically designed outside Canada, usually using imported components. These Canadian subsidiaries, then, do not perform the complete range of functions in order to offer a product in the marketplace. These are the traditional so-called **branch plants**.

Some observers believe that we will continue to see the rapid spread of branch plants in Canada, with progressively less important activities being allocated to the Canadian subsidiary. This has led many critics to suggest that these subsidiaries are nothing more than "sales offices" for the U.S. parent company. Mel Hurtig made the following critical observation regarding the significance of foreign ownership in Canada:

> In . . . just over 20 years, there were 11,380 companies in Canada taken over by non-resident-controlled corporations. The total value of the takeovers was just over $548.494 billion. During the same years, new foreign investment for new businesses in this country was just over $18.040 billion. So, it was just over 96.8% foreign investment for takeovers, and a pathetic less than 3.2% for new business investment. Breaking down the numbers further: 11,380 companies over 20 years is 569 companies a year average. Or you can think of it as 3 companies every two days, and an average of 47 a month, EVERY month for the last 20 years![8]

Some critics argue that we have built up a dependence on foreign capital to supply us with the funds for business development. While this financial assistance was welcome, it brought a major cost with it—the establishment of these branch plants, and an economy that is approximately 30% foreign-owned. It has been suggested that the presence of this branch plant economy has impeded the development of an innovative or entrepreneurial spirit in Canadian business (see Talking Business 1.8). In other words, there is a sense that, historically, Canadian managers have not been challenged to do the strategic planning, to engage in the research and development and to develop the technological expertise to add value to the present supply of products or services. However, we are witnessing the increasing presence of Canadian-owned and global competitors, and it is expected that Canada will continue to move beyond its history and carve a bigger niche in the global environment.

Talking Business 1.8

Olive: Innovation Out of Our Hands in a Branch-Plant Economy

David Olive

Nortel Networks Corp. on Friday quietly shed the last of its remaining major businesses, selling its optical and ethernet networking operations to U.S.-based Ciena Corp. for $774 million (U.S.).

There is a bounty of ironies here, of course. A mere decade ago Nortel had a $360 billion stock-market value, making it the 12th most-valuable corporate enterprise in the world. Nortel supplied world markets with its pioneering fibre optical gear that is now the backbone of the global Internet. For a time it nervily supplanted LM Ericsson as a telecom-equipment supplier to the Swedish government. The phones at the White House ran on Nortel's networking gear.

Ciena, meanwhile, was a start-up too small to appear on Nortel's radar when it went on its multi-billion-dollar takeover binge in the late 1990s, which almost saw Nortel merging—and as the dominant partner—with the legendary Corning Inc. of New York State, maker of Thomas Edison's first light bulb.

We coulda been a contendah…

Instead, the steep decline and ultimate dismantling of the 125-year-old Nortel roughly coincided with the loss to foreign owners of such other "national champions" as Alcan, Inco, Falconbridge, Stelco, Ipsco and Dofasco, the latter among the world's best-run and most consistently profitable steelmakers during close to a century of Canadian ownership.

"Canada for sale" was Ottawa's guiding principle, if one wants to dignify with a label the feds' lack of interest, under both the Paul Martin Grits and Stephen Harper Tories. Yes, commitments of continued employment were extracted from or offered by some of the foreign buyers. These were promptly reneged on come the recession by the new Swiss, Brazilian and U.S. owners of Falconbridge, Inco and Stelco, respectively.

It's in that context that we're warned again that Canada lags the world in industrial innovation, this time in the Conference Board of Canada's latest report card, which ranks Canada 14th among 17 peer nations.

"Canada is well-supplied with educational institutions and carries out scientific research that is well-respected around the world," said Giles Rhéaume, vice-president for public policy at the think-tank.

"But, with a few exceptions, Canada does not successfully commercialize its scientific and technological discoveries into world-leading products and services. Canadian companies are rarely at the leading edge of new technology and find themselves a step behind the leaders."

That's an understatement. We're not a step behind, we're nowhere to be found in most industrial sectors. There are no Canadian-owned automakers (South Korea has several).

We have no major players in heavy equipment; chemicals; industrial wiring and electrical controls; motors; prescription and over-the-counter drugs; hygiene, make-up, fragrance and other personal-care products; breakfast cereals, snack foods; liquor; diapers; greeting cards; laundry and other cleaning products; hotel and resort chains; industrial and household tools; pet food; tires; office and home furnishings; or heart stents, Stryker beds and other products of the medical-industrial complex.

The decisions about shape, size, variety, colour, pricing and regional availability of all those things are made beyond our borders. Canada has always been a branch plant, since its first brush with European fur traders. How can we complain that we suffer the backward attributes of a branch-plant economy when we are, in fact, a branch plant?

Innovation is a key to productivity gains, the principal means by which we raise our standard of living. But innovation is largely out of our hands. Industrial R&D for companies that sell their goods in Canada is largely conducted elsewhere. So is the critical decision-making about new-product development and investment in more efficient capital equipment.

With notable exceptions like the auto sector, branch plants rarely have a mandate to export. The entire point of most branch plants is to focus on serving a national or regional market.

We know from the examples of Bombardier Inc., now building China's inter-city rail system; engineering giant SNC-Lavalin, also of Montreal; Magna International with its hundreds of plants in North America and Europe; and BlackBerry developer Research In Motion that Canadian firms are capable of developing world-class products and conquering global markets.

But in contrast with many of our industrialized peers, we have not devised a national industrial strategy that incubates cash-strapped yet promising start-ups that might someday have the required heft of a Bombardier, Magna or RIM; strengthening the bond between universities and teaching hospitals with commercial enterprises; and confronting the dilemma of Canadian owners of world-class firms selling out to foreign interests.

If it feels at times that we're living in someone else's country, in some degree we are. With one of the least domestically owned economies among our industrial peers, it's long past time we confronted the implications of foreign ownership on our lack of control over productivity, on which our prosperity very much depends.

Political Forces in Canada

The Canadian economic system has been described as a mixed system. This refers to the notion that while we possess a capitalist economy, government nonetheless plays an important role. In fact, historically, government has played a critical role in the Canadian economy. In Canada, we have a long history of government involvement in business in the sense of promoting and protecting our industries. Tariffs on imported goods were designed to protect our domestic business by making the cost of foreign goods more expensive relative to those of Canadian goods. It can be argued that a large portion of Canada's industrial development is due to protectionism through tariffs first imposed in 1879 by Sir John A. Macdonald's National Policy. Eventually, the government also offered direct incentives for industrial and resource development. "Incentive programs" were established to encourage managers to conduct business in a manner desired by the government.

Managers may decide to, say, invest in a new product development, or engage in greater export activities, or to locate in an underdeveloped region. Consequently, government incentives will be offered to engage in such activities. Receiving government financial support or reward for such activities would influence decisions to engage in these activities.

In Canada, on-going issues concern the degree to which government can or should help businesses compete—whether in the form of direct subsidies, tax incentives or some other forms of protectionism. For example, one recurring controversy in recent years is the level of government subsidies to businesses operating in the global marketplace and government support for research and development programs. For example, one controversy involved a dispute regarding government subsidies to Canada's aerospace giant Bombardier and its main competitor in the jet market, Embraer SA (Empresa Brasileira de Aeronáutica S.A.) of Brazil. The lumber dispute highlighted in Talking Business 7.5 in Chapter 7 is another example of the difficulty in establishing the degree to which government should aid business. (See Talking Business 1.9.)

Talking Business 1.9

Whose Auto Bailout Is Most Expensive? Go Canada!

Erik Heinrich

Is the Canadian government's bailout of Chrysler Canada the worst deal it has ever made? Quite possibly, some critics say, and more of the same is waiting just around the corner as General Motors prepares to ask that country's taxpayers to fork over a similar amount of money in a few weeks' time.

Ottawa and the Ontario government are contributing at total of $3.2 billion in loans to keep Chrysler Canada alive including $850 million extended to the ailing automaker at the beginning of the year. Prime Minister Stephen Harper and Ontario Premier Dalton McGuinty have characterized the Canadian contribution as proportional to the $12 billion in emergency loans that the Obama Administration has made available to Chrysler LLC, now under Chapter 11 bankruptcy protection.

Not quite. In fact, Canada is paying a significant premium over the U.S. to save Chrysler jobs at home, with no guarantees that the billions it is laying at the automaker's door will ever be repaid or do anything to help maintain the country's 20% production share of the North American auto industry.

The Canadian rescue package works out to more than $340,420 for every employee at Chrysler Canada, which has 9,400 hourly and salaried workers on payroll. That's 15% more than the $295,000

(Continued)

per employee that Washington is shelling out to save about 40,000 Chrysler jobs in the U.S. "This money will never be paid back to the Canadian government," says Toronto analyst Dennis DesRosiers, with DesRosiers Automotive Consultants. "The deal has been spun in a positive way, but if taxpayers understood what's really going on, they would revolt."

What's really going on behind the scenes of the Canadian bailout of Chrysler has more to do with politics than economics. Car dealers and parts suppliers have engaged in a ferocious campaign to save the automaker, both in Ottawa and at the Ontario legislature in Toronto. At the same time, Harper and McGuinty are fearful of the repercussions of having Chrysler Canada fail on their watch, possibly triggering a collapse of Ontario's auto sector.

Harper's minority Conservative government in particular needs votes in Canada's industrial heartland if it is to survive a general election, which might come as early as next month.

Also, the Obama Administration has made it clear that Canada needs to step up with a serious rescue package for Chrysler and General Motors if it wants a voice in how the North American auto industry is restructured. But it's already a silent partner, receiving just 2% of Chrysler and one director on the new board in exchange for $3.2 billion in support. That's poor payback, says Jack Layton, head of the New Democratic Party, Canada's fourth largest federal party, which enjoys strong union ties. "The government did not fight hard enough for job and production-share guarantees," he says.

Societal Forces in Canada

There is much to be proud of with regard to our Canadian business environment. A report produced by the Economist Intelligence Unit (EIU) indicated that Canada is expected to be the best country in the world in which to conduct business in the coming years. According to the EIU's global business rankings for 2009–2013, Canada ranks first in the G7 as "the best place to invest and do business."

Much of Canada's economic strength lies in the diversity of its natural-resource industries that supply ore, oil and gas, lumber, and other commodities internationally. In addition, our rapidly growing high-tech sectors are earning high marks for leading edge research and development. This includes such areas as information and communications technology (ICT), biotechnology, nanotechnology, advanced manufacturing, electronics, aeronautics, pharmaceuticals, and agri-food. Among other achievements, Canada invests more money in education, as a percentage of GDP, than almost every other country in the world. In fact, we have been ranked first by the Organization for Economic Cooperation and Development (OECD) for higher education achievement given that more than half of Canadians (between the ages of 25 and 35) have a post-secondary education.

Canada is indeed poised to earn a distinguished reputation on the world scene. At the same time, it is important to consider how we can maintain and strengthen such a reputation. Perhaps central among the factors to consider is the manner in which we conduct business in this country—the integrity of our business environment. Unfortunately, we have witnessed that Canada, like any other country, is not immune to scandal and corruption. In recent years, both the private and public sectors have been forced to confront a host of misdeeds that speak to the issue of corporate governance, social responsibility, and business ethics. The challenge for Canadian business leaders is to ensure that, along with our industrial development, comes an equally well-developed sense of corporate ethics and social responsibility.

In a recent article for the Ottawa Citizen, journalist Derek Abma,[9] observed that Canadian business is at risk of losing its "clean cut" image if scandals continue to accumulate. Abma cites a number of recent scandals, including a Vancouver-based mining company. Bear Creek Mining Corp. sought to open a silver mine in Peru and this sparked a violent protest by local citizens who were concerned that the company's activities would pollute water while giving few economic benefits. About five people died and a dozen were wounded in clashes, in 2011.

Sadly, Canadian companies have increasingly been appearing in the news in a less than-flattering light globally. Calgary-based Niko Resources Ltd. Was found guilty in 2011 of bribing a government official in Bangladesh. The RCMP had been investigating the case against Niko for six years, along with at least 22 other ongoing investigations involving Canadian companies suspected of bribery. Elsewhere, an engineering firm based in Montreal (SNC Lavalin Group Inc.), was recently exposed in the media as playing a role in building prisons for the Libyan regime of Moammar Gadhafi. (SNC was named as the buyer of the CANDU nuclear-reactor division from federally owned Atomic Energy of Canada Ltd.). In 2009, Toronto-based Barrick Gold Corp. (among the world's largest gold miners) faced public embarrassment after Norway's government pension fund sold off about $230 million worth of stock it held in Barrick because of what it saw as irresponsible environmental practices of the mining company in Papua New Guinea.

Other socially irresponsible practices have been occurring in a host of industries and for many years in Canada. The Canadian oil sands industry in general has been criticized globally for its production of "dirty oil." In terms of criticism, Canada has also been pointed out by the anti-corruption group *Transparency International* for being the only G7 country that continually provides "little or no enforcement" of the Organization for Economic Co-operation and Development's Anti-Bribery Convention.

All those scandals may be "exceptions to the rule" in that business here normally operates with integrity and with a social conscience. These scandals do not detract from the fact that we do have a lot to be proud of in terms of our Canadian business practices. However, it would be foolish to ignore these events and to assume that they will never reappear. We need to better recognize that the societal context within business operates must be fully addressed in order to ensure continued prosperity and success in our business sector.

CHAPTER SUMMARY

Understanding the environment of business is the only way to get a sense of where we are headed in terms of future economic prospects. Whether you are currently a full-time student or in the workplace, an understanding of the context of organizations is a critical part of any intelligent person's portfolio. The aim of the upcoming chapters is to shed more light on the environment of organizations, and to consider the implications for the future of organizations. What are the prospects for business, and what are the challenges we must confront? No organization operates in a vacuum, and so the real world surrounding the organization must be addressed.

CONCEPT APPLICATION

FACEBOOK AND THE BUSINESS CONTEXT

*Facebook, which is just turning six, has achieved a level of maturity most wags thought would never come. Somewhere along the road to becoming the platform of choice for 400 million users in every country on earth, the company grew up. Baby photos now dot the worktables at its Palo Alto headquarters. Chefs provide free gourmet fare in the company cafeteria. And the founder, who once coded the site while dashing between makeshift offices in a beat-up car that didn't need a key, now mingles with his 1,200 employees, recruited and supported by a real HR person, in a new 135,000-square-foot office space. "We used to stand outside of Stanford looking for engineers to help us," laughs Chris Cox, vice president of product, and creator of the original news-feed feature.

Today, Facebook feels the way Google, Intel, and Microsoft likely did at similar stages in their own life cycles—still agile enough to invent the future, but sufficiently stable to handle some real turbulence. In fact, Zuckerberg has been studying those companies, and their histories, closely. "There are advantages to being both bigger and smaller," he tells me. "But the cool thing is, we're in our sweet spot now."

———————————
*Source: Fast Company

WHAT FACEBOOK LEARNED FROM APPLE AND WHAT WE CAN LEARN FROM FACEBOOK

Andy Ramirez

**Lets stop bashing Facebook for five minutes. It's easy to talk about the mistakes of the company, and everyone is. I want to take a look at what the company has done right since making those mistakes. I also want to draw a comparison between these mistakes and those made by the now biggest tech company in the world, Apple. Through this I will show you two simple lessons in what has transpired for both companies, stay close to your roots and be nimble.

In a blog post today Mark Zuckerberg, the creator of Facebook, announced that Facebook was releasing new, simpler privacy controls as a result of "lots of feedback" the company received.

The fact is that there has been a wave of negative backlash against Facebook recently for sharing too much information with the outside world. People have been threatening to drop

(Continued)

the network and send it the way of MySpace. Have people gone mad? Have they forgotten that the information they were posting is on the internet? The answer is no. People reacted the way they did because Facebook broke the cardinal rule, sticking to their own ideals. Facebook forgot where they came from, and what got them to where they are.

Technology, especially web technology, seems to be a great place to see this concept in action. One major example some people may remember is Apple, the poster child for why sticking to your roots matters. Apple changed the world when it introduced the first Macintosh, it also rose quickly to be one of the hottest tech companies around. The reason for the rise is that Apple introduced something unique, different and high end, a successful formula for the company. This success did not last forever, in the late 80's Apple lost its way. It began releasing vague product lines with little differentiation. The company tried to compete in the low cost computer market. The formula was broken and the founders that had brought the company to success were no longer there to help find the way.

However, Facebook and other businesses can learn from what happened next...Apple once again found its way. In 1996 they brought back Steve Jobs, the leader that knew what made Apple different. In 1998 they released the iMac, in 2001 the iPod, in 2001 they also introduced OS X. On and on the hits have kept rolling, all because Apple has decided to not stray from what it does right. There is no denying that this company has rediscovered what made it successful.

So what does this have to do with Facebook? Facebook must go back to the roots that made it successful. The reason people liked the network to start with was the exclusivity it offered. Originally when the social network was only available to college students, a certain kind of privacy was built in. Only your peers could see anything about you. Now the network is mired with privacy backlash. Newspaper stories of people being fired for Facebook pictures, parents spying on children, corporations using it as a background checking tool, all have pushed the Facebook users closer and closer to the edge. When Facebook lent a helping hand to the privacy problems by opening up more information without user interaction the members of the community saw it as an affirmation that Facebook had no interest in keeping things the way it originally intended, between peers.

What has Facebook done right? Simple, they're quick on their feet. In just a few days they went from huge mistake to public solution. Mark Zuckerberg posted his blog about the fix, did interviews around the fix, did everything in his power to show that Facebook is a company that listens and reacts. This will be met with applause by the community so close to giving up. Time could end up showing that it all turned out to be a positive for Facebook because of how quickly they reacted. I know I'm happy to see that they took these steps.

In the business world of technology there are two lessons here, focus and speed. Find what works, focus on that, and do that better than anyone else. Once you have that one thing down like there is nothing else, then think about expanding your offerings. When you do find yourself down the wrong path get back on the right one as quick as you can. Do this by listening to your consumers, listening to your peers, and most of all, listening to your company's soul. Some kind of peer board of advisors you could turn to might be helpful in times like these. I wonder if there is some company around that can help you when you need unbiased advice and guidance.

**Source: "What Facebook Learned From Apple and What We Can Learn from Facebook," Andy Ramirez, *Executive Street*.

Questions:

1. What elements of the external environment do you think contributed to Facebook's success?
2. Which elements are beginning to create challenges for Facebook?
3. Which context must Facebook work hardest to address in order to continue to prosper?

The Economic Context

Are you familiar with the Canadian economic environment? This chapter examines the nature of economic systems. Such issues as demand and supply, and the nature of private enterprises are discussed. We will also identify fundamental indicators of economic stability and growth.

LEARNING OBJECTIVES

By the end of this chapter, you should be able to:

1. Identify the factors of production.
2. Describe different types of global *economic systems* according to the means by which they control the factors of production through *input* and *output markets*.
3. Show how *demand* and *supply* affect resource distribution in Canada.
4. Identify the elements of *private enterprise* and explain the various degrees of *competition* in the Canadian economic system.
5. Define key indicators of economic stability and economic growth.

THE BUSINESS WORLD

Opportunities and challenges in the mobile phone market

During the last decade, a Canadian company called Research In Motion (RIM) has emerged as a high-tech star in the mobile phone industry. The company was started in 1984 by two engineering students—Mike Lazaridis at the University of Waterloo and Douglas Fregin at the University of Windsor. Its first wireless handheld device—called the Inter@ctive Pager—was introduced in 1996. The now-famous BlackBerry hit the market in 1998. In 2009, *Fortune* magazine named RIM as the fastest-growing company in the world. There are over 40 million corporate and consumer BlackBerry users, and RIM's goal is to have 100 million customers.

RIM is a remarkable Canadian success story, but industry analysts see potential challenges on the horizon for companies in the smart phone market. The market potential is huge, but competition is intense and new product introductions are occurring at a dizzying pace.

(Continued)

Unless otherwise credited, content in this chapter is taken from *Business Essentials*, Sixth Canadian Edition, by Ronald J. Ebert, Ricky W. Griffin, Frederick A. Starke, and George Dracopoulos.

There are also two industry trends that make it difficult to predict the future for any of the competitors in the smart phone industry. The first is the so-called "bring your own device" trend, which means that companies are shifting the responsibility for having a phone onto employees. The second trend is "sandboxing," which means separating work functions from the rest of the smart phone for security reasons, and allowing employees to use the phone at work without losing access to other applications like games or social networking. Both these trends may hurt RIM in the corporate market because employees may decide to buy something other than a BlackBerry. Some analysts are now fairly pessimistic about RIM's future; they think the company may continue to grow, but that shareholder returns will decline.

Another major area of concern is patent infringement lawsuits. During the past decade, RIM and other firms have sued and been sued for patent infringement. In 2006, RIM agreed to pay Virginia-based NTP $612.5 million for infringing on NTP's patent. RIM also sued Samsung after Samsung introduced a smart phone called the BlackJack. In 2009, Klausner Technologies filed suit against RIM for infringing one of its visual voicemail patents. These lawsuits have created great uncertainty in the smart phone industry.

Yet another problem is the negative publicity RIM received regarding stock options. In 2007, the company announced a $250 million restatement of earnings after it was learned that hundreds of stock options had been backdated (timed to a low share price to make them more lucrative for managers who received them). In 2009, Canadian regulators were seeking $80 million in penalties from co-CEOs Mike Lazaridis and Jim Balsillie, and several other executives agreed to pay penalties for backdating stock options.

All of these things have had a negative effect on RIM's stock price.

RIM has taken several strategic actions in an attempt to improve its future prospects. Historically, RIM's international footprint has not been large (about 80 percent of RIM's revenue comes from the U.S., Canada, and the U.K.). But in 2009, RIM signed a deal with Digital China to distribute BlackBerrys in China. The potential market in China is obviously large, but consumers in China may not be willing to pay the high price of a BlackBerry. As well, the production of unauthorized copycat phones (knock-offs) is a problem in China. For example, the "BlockBerry" is one of the competing phones sold in China.

RIM is also responding to competitive threats by positioning the BlackBerry as a general purpose smart phone for the average consumer, not just business users. More stylish models are being produced and are aimed at students, "soccer moms," and consumers in general. RIM also developed a new advertising campaign, sponsored a high-profile tour of Irish rock group U2, and provided better web browsers and applications for internet shopping. RIM's security standards mean it is safe for customers to do things like shop online from their smart phone.

According to the research firm IDC, there were 450 million mobile internet users in 2009, but that number should increase to 1 billion by 2013. Over 80 percent of RIM's new subscribers are individuals, not businesses. One positive trend for RIM is increasing consumer interest in smart phones. About 40 percent of the mobile phones purchased in 2010 were smart phones, and that proportion will increase over the next few years.

THE IDEA OF BUSINESS AND PROFIT

The opening case illustrates the dynamic and rapidly changing nature of modern business activity, and the opportunities and challenges that are evident. It also shows how business managers must pay attention to many different things, including the actions of competitors, rapid technological change, new product development, corporate strategy, risk management, stock prices, and a host of other variables that you will read about in this book.

Let's begin by asking what you think of when you hear the word *business*. Do you think of large corporations like Shoppers Drug Mart and Walmart, or smaller companies like your local supermarket or favourite restaurant? Do you think about successful companies like CN and Research In Motion, or less successful companies like GM Canada? Actually, each of these firms is a **business**—an organization that produces or sells goods or services in an effort to make a profit. **Profit** is what remains after a business's expenses have been subtracted from its revenues. Profits reward the owners of businesses for taking the risks involved in investing their time and money. In 2008, the most profitable Canadian companies were Encana Corp. ($6.3 billion), the Canadian Wheat Board ($5.7 billion), and Canadian Natural Resources Ltd. ($4.9 billion).[1]

The prospect of earning profits is what encourages people to start and expand businesses. Today, businesses produce most of the goods and services that we consume, and they employ many of the working people in Canada. Profits from these businesses are paid to thousands upon thousands of owners and shareholders, and business taxes help support governments at all levels. In addition, businesses help support charitable causes and provide community leadership. A 2010 study by KPMG of the G7 industrialized countries revealed that Canada ranked as the most cost-effective place to do business.[2]

In addition to for-profit business firms, there are also many not-for-profit organizations in Canada. **Not-for-profit organizations** do not try to make a profit; rather, they use the funds they generate (from government grants or the sale of goods or services) to provide services to the public. Charities, educational institutions, hospitals, labour unions, and government agencies are examples of not-for-profit organizations. Business principles are helpful to these not-for-profit organizations as they try to achieve their service goals.

ECONOMIC SYSTEMS AROUND THE WORLD

A Canadian business is different in many ways from one in China, and both are different from businesses in Japan, France, or Peru. A major determinant of how organizations operate is the kind of economic system that characterizes the country in which they do business. An **economic system** allocates a nation's resources among its citizens. Economic systems differ in terms of who owns and controls these resources, known as the "factors of production" (see Exhibit 2.1).

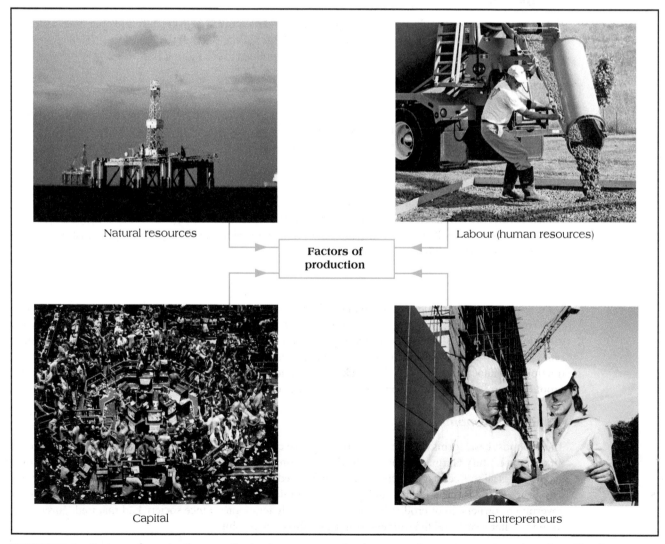

EXHIBIT 2.1   Factors of production are the basic resources a business uses to create goods and services. The four factors are natural resources, labour, capital, and entrepreneurs.

Factors of Production

The key difference between economic systems is the way in which they manage the **factors of production**—the basic resources that a country's businesses use to produce goods and services. Traditionally, economists have focused on four factors of production: *labour, capital, entrepreneurs,* and *natural resources.* Newer perspectives tend to broaden the idea of "natural resources" to include all *physical resources.* In addition, *information resources* are often included now.[3]

Labour

The people who work for a company represent the first factor of production—**labour**. Sometimes called *human resources,* labour is the mental and physical capabilities of people. Carrying out the business of a huge company such as Imperial Oil requires a labour force with a wide variety of skills ranging from managers to geologists to truck drivers.

Capital

Capital refers to the funds that are needed to start a business and to keep it operating and growing. For example, Imperial Oil needs capital to pay for its annual drilling costs, which run into the millions of dollars each year. Major sources of capital for businesses are personal investment by owners, the sale of stock to investors, profits from the sale of products and services, and funds borrowed from banks and other lending institutions.

Entrepreneurs

Entrepreneurs are people who accept the opportunities and risks involved in creating and operating businesses. Mike Lazaridis (Research In Motion), Sergie Brin and Larry Page (Google), Michael Dell (Dell Computer), and Mark Zuckerberg (Facebook) are well-known entrepreneurs (see Talking Business 2.1).

Natural Resources

Natural resources include all physical resources such as land, water, mineral deposits, and trees. Imperial Oil makes use of a wide variety of natural resources. It obviously has vast quantities of crude oil to process each year. But Imperial Oil also needs the land where the oil is located, as well as land for its refineries and pipelines.

Information Resources

Information resources include the specialized knowledge and expertise of people who work in businesses, as well as information that is found in market forecasts and various other forms of economic data. Much of what businesses do results in either the creation of new information or the repackaging of existing information for new users and different audiences.

Types of Economic Systems

Different types of economic systems manage the factors of production in different ways. In some systems, ownership is private; in others, the factors of production are owned by the government. Economic systems also differ in the ways decisions are made about production and allocation. A **command economy**, for example, relies on a centralized government to control all or most factors of production and to make all or most production and allocation decisions. In **market economies**, individuals—producers and consumers—control production and allocation decisions through supply and demand.

Command Economies

The two most basic forms of command economies are communism and socialism. As originally proposed by nineteenth-century German economist Karl Marx, **communism** is a system in which the government owns and operates all sources of production. Marx envisioned a society in which individuals would ultimately contribute according to their abilities and receive economic benefits according to their needs. He also expected government ownership of production factors to be only temporary. Once society had matured, government would "wither away" and the workers would gain direct ownership.

Talking Business 2.1

Entrepreneurship and New Ventures

A Shrine to Wine

Wine connoisseurs, also known as oenophiles, have a love of and devotion to wine, and they take just as much care in the procurement and storage of their vino as they do in the tasting. Robb Denomme and Lance Kingma own Winnipeg-based Genuwine Cellars, which sells custom-designed wine cellars, some of which have six-figure price tags. The company was started somewhat by accident in 1995 when someone asked Kingma if he thought he could build a wine cellar. He took on the challenge, and the first order led to another, and he eventually partnered with Denomme, who was just 17 at the time. As the saying goes, the rest is history. Today, the business is a multimillion-dollar operation selling to clients around the world, with the majority of sales being to the U.S.

Genuwine's international success probably wouldn't have happened, or at least not as easily, without the help of the Department of Foreign Affairs and International Trade (DFAIT). According to Robb, "Working with the TCS [Trade Commissioner Service] you get results, you get where you want to go. Trade commissioners are there to help and always get back to you with the answers you need." The TCS is a division of Foreign Affairs and its goal is to help companies succeed globally. Not only did TCS help Genuwine Cellars get connected with a business consultant, it also helped with financing. Other governmental agencies, including the Prairie Centre for Business Intelligence and the National Research Council, have also provided business support.

In addition to market development strategies, Genuwine Cellars is credited with some other good moves. "Genuwine is doing all the right things a growing company should do—lean manufacturing, continual investments in technology, importing contract manufactured goods from Asia, setting up a design office in Latin America to take advantage of a lower cost structure and access to skilled professionals, the list goes on," says Joanne MacKean, senior manager, Business Development Canada. Further, Genuwine Cellars is one of the largest wine cellar manufacturers in North America and the only company with a manufacturing facility in Canada. Very little competition, niche market, upscale consumer—so just what's "in store" for this business?

According to Denomme, the recent recession had some effect, but the company is still experiencing growth. Denomme's enthusiasm and drive are not quashed, however. He says, "You've got to keep a positive attitude." Sounds like this entrepreneur looks upon his wine glass as being half full rather than half empty.

But Marx's predictions were faulty. During the last 20 years, most countries have abandoned communism in favour of a more market-based economy. Even countries that still claim to be communist (for example, China, Vietnam, and Cuba) now contain elements of a market-based economy. Whether communism can be maintained alongside a market-based economy remains to be seen.

In a less extensive command economic system called **socialism**, the government owns and operates only selected major industries. Smaller businesses such as clothing stores and restaurants may be privately owned. Although workers in socialist countries are usually allowed to choose their occupations or professions, a large proportion generally work for the government. Many government-operated enterprises are inefficient, since management positions are frequently filled based on political considerations rather than ability. Extensive public welfare systems have also resulted in very high taxes. Because of these factors, socialism is generally declining in popularity.[4]

Market Economies

A **market** is a mechanism for exchange between the buyers and sellers of a particular good or service. For example, the internet is a technologically sophisticated market that brings buyers and sellers together through e-commerce. People usually think of e-commerce as being business-to-consumer (B2C) transactions, such as buying books over the internet for personal use. But business-to-business (B2B) transactions are also a very important market. B2B involves businesses joining together to create e-commerce companies that make them more efficient when they purchase the goods and services they need. B2B transactions actually far exceed B2C transactions in dollar value.

In a market economy, B2C and B2B exchanges take place without much government involvement. To understand how a *market economy* works, consider what happens when a customer goes to a fruit stand to buy apples. Assume that one vendor is selling apples for $1 per kilogram, and another is charging $1.50. Both vendors are free to charge what they want, and customers are free to buy what they choose. If both vendors' apples are of the same quality, the customer will likely buy the cheaper ones. But if the $1.50 apples are fresher, the customer may buy them instead. Both buyers and sellers enjoy freedom of choice (but they also are subject to risk, as the financial meltdown of 2008 demonstrated).

A GlobeScan poll of over 20,000 people in 20 countries asked people whether they agreed with the following statement: "The free market economy is the best system." Where do you think the highest support for the free market economy was found? Not in Canada, the United States, Germany, or Japan, but in *China,* where 74 percent of people polled agreed with the statement.[5] This is a surprising finding, given the Chinese government's strong support of the communist economic ideology. It seems hard to believe now, but before 1979, people who sold watches on street corners in China were sentenced to years of hard labour. After China's constitution was amended to legitimate private enterprise, the private sector has become incredibly productive. It is estimated that China produces 60 percent of all the toys in the world.[6] China's reputation for being a low-cost producer of goods is legendary. It is also a vast and rapidly growing market for many of the products that Canadian firms produce—chemicals, ores, cereals, and wood products.

Input and Output Markets A useful model for understanding how the factors of production work in a pure market economy is shown in Exhibit 2.2.[7] In the **input market**, firms buy resources from households, which then supply those resources. In the **output market**, firms supply goods and services in response to demand on the part of the households. The activities of these two markets create a circular flow. Ford Motor Co., for example, buys labour directly from households, which may also supply capital from accumulated savings in the form of stock purchases. Consumer buying patterns provide information that helps Ford decide

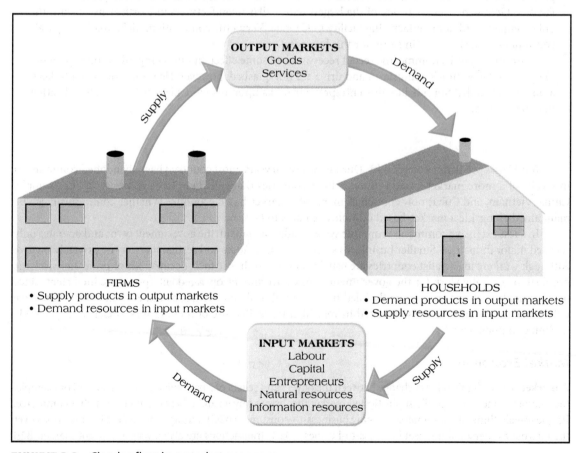

EXHIBIT 2.2 Circular flow in a market economy.

which models to produce and which to discontinue. In turn, Ford uses these inputs in various ways and becomes a supplier to households when it designs and produces various kinds of automobiles, trucks, and sport-utility vehicles and offers them for sale to consumers.

Individuals are free to work for Ford or an alternative employer and to invest in Ford stock or alternative forms of saving or consumption. Similarly, Ford can create whatever vehicles it chooses and price them at whatever value it chooses. Consumers are free to buy their next car from Ford, Toyota, BMW, or any other manufacturer. The political basis for the free market economy is called **capitalism**, which allows private ownership of the factors of production and encourages entrepreneurship by offering profits as an incentive. This process contrasts markedly with that of a command economy, in which individuals may be told where they can and cannot work, companies may be told what they can and cannot manufacture, and consumers may have little or no choice as to what they purchase or how much they pay for items (see Exhibit 2.3).

Mixed Market Economies

Command and market economies are two extremes, or opposites. In reality, most countries rely on some form of **mixed market economy** that features characteristics of both command and market economies. One trend in mixed market economies that began in the 1990s is **privatization**—converting government enterprises into privately owned companies. In Canada, for example, the air traffic control system was privatized, and the federal government sold several other corporations, including Canadian National Railway and Air Canada. The Netherlands privatized its TNT Post Group N.V., and India privatized 18 industries, including iron, steel, machinery, and telecommunications.[8] In 2010, the Organisation for Economic Co-operation and Development (OECD) said that Canada Post's monopoly should be ended and it should be privatized.[9] However, when a worldwide recession began in 2008, the trend slowed. Government bailouts of Chrysler and GM in both Canada and the U.S. meant that government was once again a part-owner of some business firms. A few countries are even pursuing a policy of **nationalization**—converting private firms into government-owned firms. Venezuela, for example, nationalized its telecommunications industry.

As a result of the recession of 2008, mixed market economies are now characterized by more government involvement than was evident just a few years ago. Governments in mixed market economies have

EXHIBIT 2.3   Despite becoming a territory of the communist People's Republic of China in 1997, Hong Kong remains one of the world's freest economies. In Hong Kong's Lan Kwai Fong district, for example, traditional Chinese businesses operate next door to well-known international chains.

intervened in the economic system in an attempt to stabilize it, but this has led to higher deficits and more control of business activity.

THE CANADIAN MARKET ECONOMY

Understanding the complex nature of the Canadian economic system is essential to understanding Canadian business. In this section, we will examine the workings of our market economy, including markets, demand, supply, private enterprise, and degrees of competition.

Demand and Supply in a Market Economy

In economic terms, a **market** is not a specific place, like a supermarket, but an exchange process between buyers and sellers. Decisions about production in a market economy are the result of millions of exchanges. How much of what product a company offers for sale and who buys it depends on the laws of demand and supply (see Talking Business 2.2).

The Laws of Supply and Demand

In a market economy, decisions about what to buy and what to sell are determined primarily by the forces of demand and supply. **Demand** is the willingness and ability of buyers to purchase a product or service. **Supply** is the willingness and ability of producers to offer a good or service for sale. The **law of demand** states that buyers will purchase (demand) more of a product as its price drops. Conversely, the **law of supply** states that producers will offer (supply) more for sale as the price rises.

To optimize profits, therefore, all businesses must constantly seek the right combination of price charged and quantity supplied. This "right combination" is found at the equilibrium point.

Talking Business 2.2

Virtual Goods: An Emerging Market

Not too long ago, people doubted the commercial sales potential of bottled water because a perfectly good substitute was available for virtually no cost. At the time, many skeptics made comments like "What's next, are we going to sell air?" Today, consumers purchase approximately 200 billion litres of bottled water worldwide each year. The skeptics did not foresee an era dominated by the internet, smart phones, and social media.

At least bottled water is a physical product. But how much is an avatar worth? How much would you spend on a virtual good? If your answer is $0, you don't know what's going on in the virtual gaming world. Have you heard of Zynga? World of Warcraft? Mafia Wars? FarmVille? If you answered "no" to all these questions, you may be shocked to learn that, in 2010, virtual goods sales were expected to reach $1.6 billion in the U.S. alone, and are projected to grow to $3.6 billion by 2012.

As we've noted, a market is an exchange process between buyers and sellers of a particular good or service. This definition fits the evolving virtual goods world as well. Whether you are buying a potato to make French fries (to eat), or a virtual potato to plant in your own FarmVille virtual garden (for entertainment), you are involved in a market of buyers and sellers. Hard-core virtual gamers are willing to spend good money to ensure that they have the best gear available in games like World of Warcraft.

Facebook links people to the virtual world and has over 500 million users. The company is now trying to capitalize on its popularity by adding a new revenue stream. It plans to charge 30 percent on virtual game props (similar to Apple's approach to apps). It is also testing the extended use of its Facebook credits. If all goes as planned, Zynga (which has 120 million game users) may be forced to adopt this model. Facebook could collect as much as $500 million over the next three years from Zynga and other gaming companies, including Electronic Arts, CrowdStar, Slide, RockYou, and Digital Chocolate. One thing is certain, there is nothing virtual about the revenue potential.

Consider the following case of demand and supply.

Maple syrup is a quintessential Canadian commodity (we produce 80 percent of the total world's supply), but its price fluctuates because weather influences the supply. Unfavourable weather reduced the supply in 2008, but good weather in 2009 caused yields to increase by 85 percent over 2008.[10] Price fluctuations in several other commodities are described in Talking Business 2.3 entitled "The High Price of High Prices."[11]

Talking Business 2.3
The High Price of High Prices

Economic theory tells us that when demand for a commodity increases, its price goes up, and people try to find substitutes that are cheaper. For example, when the price of oil is high, companies use corn to make ethanol to add to gasoline, and palm oil is used to make diesel fuel (called biodiesel). But, as more producers start using corn or palm oil, the demand for those commodities goes up and so does their price. During 2006, for example, the price of palm oil rose from less than US$400 per metric tonne to more than US$500 per metric tonne.

When prices of commodities rise rapidly, there are usually some unanticipated outcomes. One of these is increased criminal activity. As the price of stainless steel and aluminum rose during the last few years, thieves began stealing items such as beer kegs, railway baggage carts, railroad tracks, light poles, and highway guardrails. These items were then sold to scrap yards for cash.

The impact of stealing is limited to lost revenue (it's only money), but sky-high prices for food can actually threaten people's lives. Global food prices increased 83 percent between 2005 and 2008, and that put a lot of stress on the world's poorest countries. In some countries, families are spending one-half their income just on food. One culprit, ironically, is the push to convert corn into biofuel. In countries like Haiti, Cameroon, Senegal, and Ethiopia, citizens have rioted over higher prices for important staple items such as beans and rice. In Pakistan and Thailand, army troops were deployed to prevent the theft of food from warehouses. The World Bank has identified 33 countries that are at risk for serious social upheaval because of high food prices. To cope with the problem, some countries are slashing import duties and imposing export duties. This is just the reverse of what countries normally do.

PRIVATE ENTERPRISE AND COMPETITION

Market economies rely on a **private enterprise** system—one that allows individuals to pursue their own interests with minimal government restriction. Private enterprise requires the presence of four elements: private property rights, freedom of choice, profits, and competition.

- *Private property.* Ownership of the resources used to create wealth is in the hands of individuals.[12]
- *Freedom of choice.* You can sell your labour to any employer you choose. You can also choose which products to buy, and producers can usually choose whom to hire and what to produce.
- *Profits.* The lure of profits (and freedom) leads some people to abandon the security of working for someone else and to assume the risks of entrepreneurship. Anticipated profits also influence individuals' choices of which goods or services to produce.
- *Competition.* Profits motivate individuals to start businesses, and competition motivates them to operate those businesses efficiently. **Competition** occurs when two or more businesses vie for the same resources or customers. To gain an advantage over competitors, a business must produce its goods or services efficiently and be able to sell at a reasonable profit. Competition forces all businesses to make products better or cheaper.

Degrees of Competition

Economists have identified four basic degrees of competition within a private enterprise system: perfect competition, monopolistic competition, oligopoly, and monopoly.

Perfect Competition

For **perfect competition** to exist, firms must be small in size (but large in number), the products of each firm are almost identical, both buyers and sellers know the price that others are paying and receiving in the marketplace, firms find it easy to enter or leave the market, prices are set by the forces of supply and demand, and no firm is powerful enough individually to influence the price of its product in the marketplace. Agriculture is usually considered to be a good example of pure competition in the Canadian economy. There are thousands of wheat farmers, the wheat produced on one farm is essentially the same as wheat produced on another farm, producers and buyers are well aware of prevailing market prices, and it is relatively easy to get started or to quit producing wheat.

Monopolistic Competition

In **monopolistic competition,** there are fewer sellers than in pure competition, but there are still many buyers. Sellers try to make their products appear to be at least slightly different from those of their competitors by tactics such as using brand names (Tide and Cheer), design or styling (Ralph Lauren and Izod clothes), and advertising (like that done by Coca-Cola and Pepsi). Monopolistically competitive businesses may be large or small, because it is relatively easy for a firm to enter or leave the market. For example, many small clothing manufacturers compete successfully with large apparel makers. Product differentiation also gives sellers some control over the price they charge. Thus, Ralph Lauren polo shirts can be priced with little regard for the price of shirts sold at the Bay, even though the Bay's shirts may have very similar styling (see Talking Business 2.4).

Oligopoly

When an industry has only a handful of very large sellers, an **oligopoly** exists. Competition is fierce because the actions of any one firm in an oligopolistic market can significantly affect the sales of all other firms.[13] Most oligopolistic firms avoid price competition because it reduces profits. For example, the four major cereal makers (Kellogg, General Mills, General Foods, and Quaker Oats) charge roughly the same price for their cereals. Rather than compete on price, they emphasize advertising, which claims that their cereals are better tasting or more nutritious than the competition's. Entry into an oligopolistic market is difficult because large capital investment is usually necessary. Thus, oligopolistic industries (such as the automobile, rubber, and steel industries) tend to stay oligopolistic. As the trend toward globalization continues, it is likely that more global oligopolies will come into being.[14]

Monopoly

When an industry or market has only one producer, a **monopoly** exists. Being the only supplier gives a firm complete control over the price of its product. Its only constraint is how much consumer demand will fall as its price rises. For centuries, wine bottles were sealed using natural cork made from tree bark. But a new technology allows wine bottles to be sealed with plastic corks that are cheaper and work just as well. The natural wine cork industry has lost its monopoly.[15] In Canada, laws such as the Competition Act forbid most monopolies. **Natural monopolies**—such as provincial electric utilities—are closely watched by provincial utilities boards, and the assumption that there is such a thing as a natural monopoly is increasingly being challenged. For example, the Royal Mail Group's 350-year monopoly of the British postal service ended in 2006, and rival companies are now allowed to compete with Royal mail.[16] In India, private couriers like FedEx and United Parcel Service now provide more than half the delivery business in that country after they were allowed to compete with Indian Post, which had a monopoly on mail delivery for several hundred years.[17]

Talking Business 2.4

Consumers often buy products under conditions of monopolistic competition. For example, there are few differences between various brands of toothpaste, cold tablets, detergents, canned goods, and soft drinks.

THE ECONOMIC ENVIRONMENT

The **economic environment** refers to the conditions of the economic system in which an organization operates.[18] For example, McDonald's Canadian operations are (as of this writing) functioning in an economic environment characterized by moderate growth, moderate unemployment, and low inflation. Moderate unemployment means that most people can afford to eat out, and low inflation means that McDonald's pays relatively constant prices for its supplies. But is also means that McDonald's can't easily increase the prices it charges because of competitive pressures from Burger King and Wendy's.

Economic Growth

At one time, about half the Canadian population was involved in producing the food that we eat. Today, less than 2.5 percent of the population works in agriculture because agricultural efficiency has improved so much that far fewer people are needed to produce the food we need. We can therefore say that agricultural production has *grown* because the total output of the agricultural sector has increased. We can apply the same idea to a nation's economic system, but the computations are much more complex, as we shall see.

Aggregate Output and the Standard of Living

How do we know whether or not an economic system is growing? The main measure of *growth* is **aggregate output**: the total quantity of goods and services produced by an economic system during a given period.[19] To put it simply, an increase in aggregate output is economic growth.[20] When output grows more quickly than the population, two things usually follow: output per capita (the quantity of goods and services per person) goes up and the system provides relatively more of the goods and services that people want.[21] And when these two things occur, people living in an economic system benefit from a higher **standard of living**—the total quantity and quality of goods and services that they can purchase with the currency used in their economic system.

The Business Cycle

The growth (and contraction) pattern of short-term ups and downs in an economy is called the **business cycle**. It has four recognizable phases: peak, recession, trough, and recovery (see Exhibit 2.4). A **recession** is usually defined as two consecutive quarters when the economy shrinks, but it is probably more helpful to say that a recession starts just after the peak of the business cycle is reached and ends when the trough is reached.[22] A **depression** occurs when the trough of the business cycle extends two or more years. Periods of expansion and contraction can vary from several months to several years. During the latter half of the 1990s, the Canadian economy was continuously expanding, leading some people to believe that the business cycle was a thing of the past. That belief was shattered twice in the last 10 years: in 2000, when the high-tech bubble burst, and in 2008, when a major financial crisis and worldwide recession occurred. Many economists predicted that the most recent recession would be long, and some compared it to the Great Depression of the 1930s.

Gross Domestic Product and Gross National Product

The term **gross domestic product (GDP)** refers to the total value of all goods and services produced within a given period by a national economy through domestic factors of production. If GDP is going up, the nation is experiencing economic growth. Canada's GDP in 2009 was $1.56 trillion.[23]

GDP measures all business activity within a nation's borders and it has widely replaced **gross national product (GNP),** which refers to the total value of all goods and services produced by a national economy within a given period regardless of where the factors of production are located. For example, the profits from a Canadian-owned manufacturing plant in Brazil are included in Canadian GNP—but not in GDP—

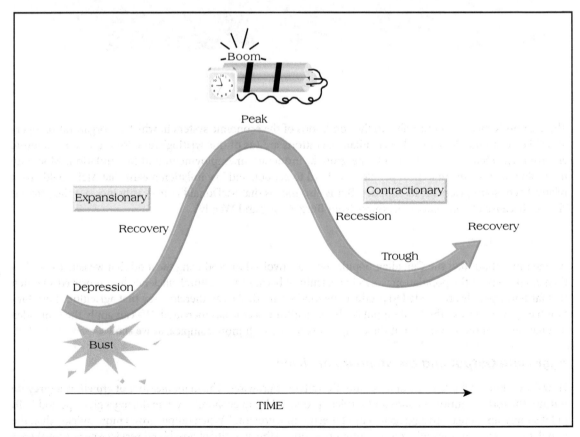

EXHIBIT 2.4   The business cycle.

because its output is not produced in Canada. Conversely, those profits are included in Brazil's GDP—but not GNP—because they are produced domestically (that is, in Brazil) but not by a Brazilian company.

Today, GDP is the key measure of economic growth because it tracks an economy's performance over time. However, some argue that such measures are flawed. A commission created by French president Nicolas Sarkozy and chaired by famous economist Joseph Stiglitz declared that our obsession with GDP helped contribute to the strength of the most recent recession. According to the findings, if a bit more attention had been paid to other indicators, like rising debt, governments may have reacted more cautiously. An article in *The Economist* magazine even referred to GDP as "grossly deceptive product."[24] An organization called Redefining Progress has proposed a more realistic measure to assess economic activity—the Genuine Progress Indicator (GPI). GPI treats activities that harm the environment or our quality of life as costs and gives them negative values. For example, in 2010, activities required to clean the mess from the BP Gulf of Mexico oil drilling disaster were included in measurements of economic growth. But the oil spill was not a good thing. The GPI measure shows that while GDP has been increasing for many years, GPI has been falling for over 30 years.[25]

Real Growth Rates   GDP is the preferred method of calculating national income and output. The *real growth rate of GDP*—the growth rate of GDP *adjusted for inflation and changes in the value of the country's currency*—is what counts. Remember that *growth depends on output increasing at a faster rate than population.* If growth rate of GDP exceeds the rate of population growth, then our standard of living should be improving.

GDP per Capita   **GDP per capita** means GDP per person. We get this figure by dividing total GDP by the total population of a country. As a measure of economic well-being of the average person, GDP per capita is a better measure than GDP. Norway has the highest GDP per capita of any country ($40 807), followed by the United States ($38 808), Ireland ($35 306), and Switzerland ($34 440). Canada ranked eighth at ($31 369).[26]

Real GDP   **Real GDP** means that GDP has been adjusted. To understand why adjustments are necessary, assume that pizza is the only product in an economy. Assume that in 2010, a pizza cost $10 and in 2011 it cost $11.

In both years, exactly 1000 pizzas were produced. In 2010, the GDP was $10 000 ($10 × 1000); in 2011, the GDP was $11 000 ($11 × 1000). Has the economy grown? No. Since 1000 pizzas were produced in both years, aggregate output remained the same. If GDP is not adjusted for 2011, it is called **nominal GDP**, that is, GDP measured in current dollars.[27]

Purchasing Power Parity   In our example, *current prices* would be 2011 prices. On the other hand, we calculate real GDP when we account for *changes in currency values and price changes.* When we make this adjustment, we account for both GDP and **purchasing power parity**—the principle that exchange rates are set so that the prices of similar products in different countries are about the same. Purchasing power parity gives us a much better idea of what people can actually buy. In other words, it gives us a better sense of standards of living across the globe.

Productivity

A major factor in the growth of an economic system is **productivity**, which is a measure of economic growth that compares how much a system produces with the resources needed to produce it. Let's say, for instance, that it takes one Canadian worker and one Canadian dollar to make 10 soccer balls in an eight-hour workday. Let's also say that it takes 1.2 Saudi workers and the equivalent of $1.2 (in riyals, the currency of Saudi Arabia) to make 10 soccer balls in the same eight-hour workday. We can say, then, that the Canadian soccer-ball industry is more *productive* than the Saudi soccer-ball industry.

The two factors of production in this extremely simple case are labour and capital. According to the Organisation for Economic Co-operation and Development (OECD) rankings, Canada stood in sixteenth place with a productivity ratio of 78.2 percent compared to the United States. Luxembourg was the most productive nation at 140.4 percent. Norway (136 percent) and the Netherlands (100.4 percent) were also classified above the benchmark U.S. statistics.[28]

If more products are being produced with fewer factors of production, what happens to the prices of these products? They go down. As a consumer, therefore, you would need less of your currency to purchase the same quantity of these products. Thus, your standard of living—at least with regard to these products—has improved. If your entire economic system increases its productivity, then your overall standard of living improves. In fact, the standard of living improves only through increases in productivity.[29]

The Balance of Trade and the National Debt

There are several factors that can help or hinder the growth of an economic system, but here we focus on just two of them: *balance of trade* and the *national debt*.

Balance of Trade   The **balance of trade** is the economic value of all the products that a country *exports* minus the economic value of its *imported* products. A negative balance of trade is commonly called a *trade deficit*, and a positive balance of trade is called a *trade surplus*. Canada traditionally has had a positive balance of trade. It is usually a *creditor nation* rather than a debtor nation. For example, Canada received $47 billion more from exports than it spent on imports in 2008, but in 2009 a long trend was reversed when Canada had a trade deficit of $4.8 billion.[30] The United States usually has a negative balance of trade; it spends more on imports than it receives for exports.[31] It is therefore a consistent *debtor nation*. A trade deficit negatively affects economic growth because the money that flows out of a country can't be used to invest in productive enterprises, either at home or overseas.

National Debt   A country's **national debt** is the amount of money that the government owes its creditors. Like a business, the government takes in revenues (e.g., taxes) and has expenses (e.g., military spending, social programs). For many years, the government of Canada incurred annual **budget deficits**, that is, it spent more money *each year* than it took in. These accumulated annual deficits have created a huge national debt (estimated above $600 billion by the end of 2010). A typical recession causes an 86 percent increase in the national debt.[32]

From Confederation (1867) to 1981, the *total* accumulated debt was only $85.7 billion, but in the period 1981–1994, *annual deficits* were in the $20- to $40-billion range. But from 1997 to 2008, Canada was the only highly industrialized county in the world that had annual budget surpluses. That all changed in 2009 when the government announced a deficit of $46.9 billion. The good news, if you can call it that, was that this figure was actually 12 percent lower than initially expected.[33] The bad news was that another $49 billion deficit was projected in 2010 as well as $27.6 billion in 2011 and $17.5 billion in 2012.[34] Big increases in annual deficits are also predicted for the United States because of the multibillion-dollar bailouts that were given to companies in the financial sector. In spite of this, the United States is still able to borrow large amounts of money from countries like China because the United States is seen as a strong economy and a safe haven in troubled economic times.[35]

How does then national debt affect economic growth? When the government of Canada sells bonds to individuals and organizations (both at home and overseas), this affects economic growth because the Canadian government competes with every other potential borrower—individuals, households, businesses, and other organization—for the available supply of loanable money. The more money the government borrows, the less money is available for the private borrowing and investment that increases productivity.

Economic Stability

A key goal of an economic system is **stability**: a condition in which the amount of money available in an economic system and the quantity of goods and services produced in it are growing at about the same rate. Several factors threaten stability—namely, *inflation, deflation,* and *unemployment.*

Inflation

Inflation is evident when the amount of money injected into an economic system outstrips the increase in actual output. When inflation occurs, people have more money to spend, but there will be the same quantity of products available for them to buy. As they compete with one another to buy available products, prices go up. Before long, high prices will erase the increase in the amount of money injected into the economy. Purchasing power, therefore, declines. Exhibit 2.5 shows how inflation has varied over the last 30 years in Canada.

Inflation varies widely across countries. One dramatic example occurred in Zimbabwe in 2008, when inflation reached an astonishing annual rate above 40 million percent (most countries have rates between 2 and 15 percent). One Zimbabwean dollar from 2005 would have been worth one trillion Zimbabwean dollars in 2008. Many workers simply stopped going to their jobs because their pay was not enough to cover their bus fare.[36] The problem was finally solved in 2009 when the government began allowing people to pay their bills using other currencies, like the U.S. dollar or the South African rand.[37]

Measuring Inflation: The CPI   The **consumer price index (CPI)** measures changes in the cost of a "basket" of goods and services that a typical family buys. What is included in the basket has changed over the years. For example, the first CPI in 1913 included items like coal, spirit vinegar, and fruit, while today the index includes bottom-freezer fridges, flat-screen TVs, energy-saving light bulbs, and laser eye surgery.[38] These changes in the CPI reflect changes that have occurred in the pattern of consumer purchases. For example, in

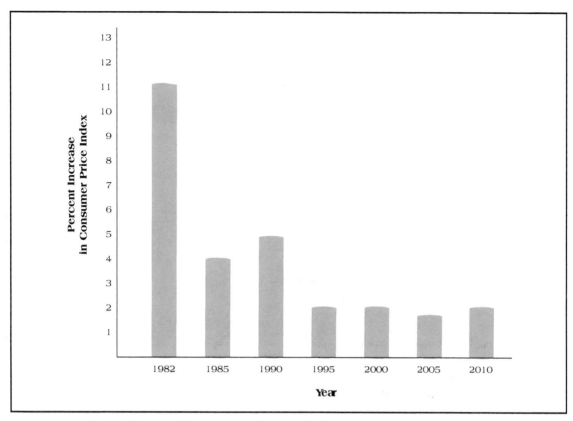

EXHIBIT 2.5 During the past fifteen years, the rate of price increases in Canada has been low and quite stable.

1961, about 53 percent of consumer spending went to necessities like food, housing, and clothing. By the turn of the century, only 40 percent of consumer spending went to necessities.[39]

Deflation

Deflation (falling prices) is evident when the amount of money injected into an economic system lags behind increases in actual output. Prices may fall because industrial productivity is increasing and cost saving are being passed on to consumers (this is good), or because consumers have high levels of debt and are therefore unwilling to buy very much (this is bad).

Unemployment

In 2009, there were 7.7 million men and 6.9 million women (over age 25) working in Canada's labour force.[40] But there were many additional people who wanted a job but could not get one. **Unemployment** is the level of joblessness among people actively seeking work. There are various types of unemployment: *frictional unemployment* (people are out of work temporarily while looking for a new job); *seasonal unemployment* (people are out of work because of the seasonal nature of their jobs); *cyclical unemployment* (people are out of work because of downturn in the business cycle); and *structural unemployment* (people are unemployed because they lack the skills needed to perform available jobs). Unemployment rates have varied greatly over the years, as Exhibit 2.6 shows, with the rates for men generally being higher than the rates for women. In June 2010, the Canadian unemployment rate stood at 8.1 percent, which was higher than the 6 to 7 percent average range for the previous decade, before the recession, but was better than the rate in the United States, which stood at 9.7 percent and the depressing 20.1 percent rate found in Spain at the time.[41]

When unemployment is low there is a shortage of labour available for businesses. As businesses compete with one another for the available supply of labour, they raise the wages they are willing to pay. Then, because higher labour costs eat into profit margins, businesses raise the prices of their products. If prices get too high, consumers will respond by buying less. Businesses will then reduce their workforces because they don't need to produce as much. But this causes unemployment to go up and the cycle starts all over again (see Talking Business 2.5).

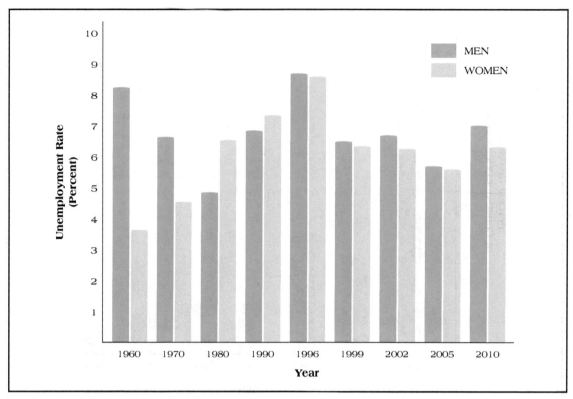

EXHIBIT 2.6 Historical unemployment rate. From 1970 to 1996, there was a steady upward trend in unemployment rates, but the rate began to decline in the late 1990s. The recession, which began in 2008, caused a clear increase in unemployment, as seen in the chart.

Talking Business 2.5

During the depression of the 1930s, unemployment was very high, with nearly one-quarter of the population unable to find work. Lines of unemployed workers outside soup kitchens were an unfortunate reality during those difficult economic times.

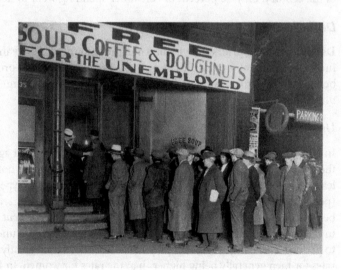

*CHAPTER SUMMARY

This chapter offered a basic introduction to the nature of economic systems. In addition to identifying the factors of production, we showed how demand and supply affect resource distribution in Canada. Elements of private enterprise were discussed, as well as the various degrees of competition in the Canadian economic system. We also defined key indicators of economic stability and growth.

*Chapter Summary by Len Karakowsky.

*CANADIAN ECONOMY LURES TARGET

As the pace of U.S. retailer expansion into Canada gains speed, we look at the contributing factors and ask, "What's next for Canadian retail?"

Not since Walmart's 1994 acquisition of Woolco stores has the topic of U.S. retailers' expansion into Canadian markets attracted so much attention. Despite the fact that U.S. retailers such as Best Buy, Sears, Home Depot and Costco have been operating in Canada for years, the formal announcement of Target acquiring 220 Zellers stores continues to be a huge story in Canadian retail—and it could continue to be the biggest story for a decade.

Strong Loonie

Target had been rumoured to be looking for opportunities to enter the Canadian market for several years, so why is it that they and a growing list of U.S. brands consider now to be the time to make the investment in Canada? One of the most compelling factors for U.S. retailers is the value of the Canadian dollar relative to the U.S. dollar. With a stronger Canadian dollar, it becomes increasingly worthwhile to establish Canadian stores rather than to sell only to those Canadian customers who shop online or on cross-border trips. For some U.S. retailers, Canada is the largest, closest and/or most similar market to the U.S., and represents a logical next move now that the economic conditions are right.

Sell to Canadians in $CDN

Aside from the currency advantage, establishing stores in Canada could keep Canadian shoppers north of the border and away from the sales, outlet stores and other price-based incentives consumers see across the U.S. as retailers try to entice recession-weary shoppers back into their stores. In Canada, total retail spending increased by a comfortable 5% from 2009 to 2010, and retailers have by and large not resorted to dramatic price-cutting to maintain sales volumes. U.S. retailers see the opportunity to open stores in Canada to sell merchandise at full sticker price, rather than at heavy discounts south of the border.

Retail spending per capita for Canada and the U.S., expressed in US dollars, are now equal. As recently as 2004, Canadians' retail sales per capita equated to $8,000 (US), while south of the border, Americans' spending power was 50% higher, at about $12,000 (US) per capita. While not all retailers are compelled by the same macro-economic factors (Walmart and others have been successfully operating Canadian divisions despite the currency difference), the exchange rate plays some part in the spate of recent announcements.

Target's announcement of their Canadian plans makes Kroger, Walgreen and CVS Caremark the only top 10 U.S. retailers that are either not in Canada or have not publicly announced northern expansion plans.

For a U.S. retailer not currently in Canada, expansion north can be a logical next step in its growth strategy. With an exchange rate that now favours the Canadian dollar, in terms of total retail market potential, Canada is only slightly smaller than California, the most populous state in the union. Within a 45-minute drive of Downtown Toronto, there are more than 5.8 million people—more than the population of Wisconsin, Minnesota or Colorado. It is estimated that more than 70% of Canada's population lives within 100 kilometers of the southern U.S./Canada border. Many U.S. retailers could supply a first phase of Canadian expansion using existing supply chains, which significantly reduces the investment (and risk) of entering Canada. However, Gord Cook, Colliers Executive Vice President, Brokerage in Toronto says, "The trend is for retailers to set up Canadian supply chain networks before opening retail stores. Target is looking at three distribution centres across the county."

More Opportunity in Canada

Compared to the U.S. retail market, Canada represents a bounty of untapped potential. Using national-level statistics, the United States has more than 23 square feet of shopping centre floor

(Continued)

area per capita,** compared to only 14 square feet per person in Canada. With hundreds of millions of square feet of vacant retail floor area in the U.S., there is no doubt the retail sector is over-built for the current U.S. economy, but nevertheless, the Canadian market as a whole is relatively under-served, and growing medium-to-large metropolitan centres offer the most compelling opportunities. If retailers can maintain their same cost structure and operational efficiency in Canadian stores as they do in U.S. stores, there is the potential for significantly greater profitability north of the border. With a strong Canadian currency and shopping centre sales averaging $580 per square foot in Canada compared to $309 in the U.S., there are opportunities for retailers and investor owners alike.

Competition Affects Retailers and Owners Differently

Target has attracted a lot of attention by planning to have 200+ stores in Canada and to reach $6 billion in sales in 6 years. In comparison, Loblaw Companies had sales of $31 billion in 2010, and Walmart had sales of $15 billion in 2010. This extra spending will come from somewhere, and it is not likely to come from induced demand (conversion of saving to spending). Much of the spending that Target will attract from Canadians will be transferred from other competing retailers. For Canadian retailers and property owners, the impact of Target's migration into Canada will last well beyond the initial store openings. Competitors will be investing in new locations and existing stores will be renovated to establish market position. Once Target stores are open, there could be additional acquisitions of Canadian brands that cannot compete head-to-head with both Walmart and Target. In general, the next five years will likely see a period of declining profit margins for large Canadian retailers, and revenue growth for retail property owners, as increased retailer competition impacts both parts of the retail economy differently.

The Next Wave

Canadians can expect to see some of their most familiar national chain stores disappear as foreign retailers will look for opportunities to enter the Canadian market quickly and easily through acquisition rather than store-by-store expansion. With the Canadian retail sector pushing forward at a sustainably healthy rate, demand for space in shopping centres and streetfronts will continue to get tighter, with a resultant increase in lease rates—particularly in growing urban markets (See Municipal Growth Stars in Canada). For retailers that need greater numbers of stores to maintain economies of scale entering Canada for the first time, the Walmart and Target approach of buying a chain with similar location and size preferences has many advantages—even for smaller retailers:

- It allows them to establish the banner across the country quickly.
- It allows them to launch operations in already familiar/tried and tested retail locations.
- They acquire existing leases with lower base rates than what they would pay if they signed new leases.

Some retail categories that could see foreign acquisitions as a way to enter the Canadian market include women's apparel, accessories, jewellery, men's apparel, home furnishings, home improvement and general merchandise. A couple of years from now, Canadians will have a different roster of tenants to choose from at their malls. Major brands rumoured or confirmed to enter the Canadian market include Express, Marshall's, J.C. Penney, Nordstrom, Topshop, J. Crew, Kohl's and Dick's Sporting Goods.

---

*Source: "Canadian Economy Lures International Retail Interests," Colliers International, *The Retail Report*.

**2009 data according to the international Council of Shopping Centres.

Questions:

1. What factors influenced Target to come to Canada?
2. What economic factors played a role?
3. What impact might Target have on the Canadian economy?

The Competitive Context*

Why do industry-leading firms sometimes lose their market position to rivals? Why do some entrepreneurial firms fail to survive and grow following early marketplace successes? These questions can be addressed through the study of industry evolution and change. Industries are an essential backdrop for the analysis of how competitive forces affect the viability and performance of organizations. An industry's stage of evolution is a critical determinant of the degree and type of competition faced by organizations.

LEARNING OBJECTIVES

By the end of the chapter, you should be able to:

1. Describe the different stages of the industry lifecycle model.
2. Identify the key drivers of industry evolution.
3. Explain how competitive forces change during the lifecycle.
4. Describe the key success factors for firms at each stage of the lifecycle.
5. Consider how and why competitors fall victim to downsizing.

THE BUSINESS WORLD

Biggest bookstore chain in U.S. files for bankruptcy

Michael S. Rosenwald

The story of Borders Group has apparently reached its climax.

The iconic United States bookstore chain, founded in 1971 by brothers Tom and Louis Borders, filed for Chapter 11 bankruptcy reorganization Wednesday, weighed down by more than $1 billion debt and unable to navigate rapid changes in consumer behaviour.

In: E-books downloaded whenever, wherever. Out: People buying books in Borders stores.

The Ann Arbor, Mich., company said in court filings that it will close about 30 per cent of its more than 600 stores. Thousands of employees will lose their jobs.

"This is the biggest bankruptcy in the history of the book business," said Albert Greco, senior researcher at the Institute for Publishing Research. "This is a really depressing day."

---

* I am grateful to Professor Eytan Lasry, York University, who co-authored this chapter.

(Continued)

Borders Bankruptcy and Our Changing World

Walter Riker

Yesterday I went to the only local Borders Bookstore and it is closing. It is kind of a sad thing to see because I for one loved my book stores. I would not only buy books I would sit in their coffee shops and read the books that I purchased (yes I did that, buy them that is). I would be the coffee shops for hours on end reading and sometimes writing. It was a far better place to do that than a Starbucks or a McDonald's.

What is happening to the bookstores is what is going to be happening to many other businesses unless current business models are revamped and in some cases thrown out.

I helped to put Borders into Bankruptcy—I now own a Kindle. I am doing the same to newspapers by getting my news on my computer, my Kindle as well as my phone. **Note:** I get the news *that I want to read.* It's kind of like my music. I buy the songs I want and not the albums with songs I do not want.

I heard someone say, "I still like the feel of the newspaper!" That person also watches the news on TV and one day (it won't take long) when they discover CNN or Google News (ABC, NBC, CBS) on their computer they will start that short slide over to the dark side.

Do we have to wait until all of the old line methods of operation go bankrupt or is it possible that some of these businesses begin to understand they must change.

Digital technology is not disruptive anymore—it is here!

How fast is this technology virus moving through the people? I can't grasp the speed however look around. Not only look at the devices look at the people that are using them—they are not all kids and they are intent on what they are doing.

From International Data Corporation (IDC) in September of 2010:

> The worldwide market for converged mobile devices (also commonly referred to as smartphones) is expected to grow 55.4% this year compared to 2009 amid greater-than-expected demand for the do-it-all devices.

A little further down in the report:

> For the first half of 2010, vendors shipped a total of 119.4 million units or 55.5% more than the 76.8 million units shipped during the first half of 2009.

Now let's look at the Apple iPad of which Apple sold almost 15 million in 9 months (April thru December) in 2010. When introduced I head from many sources say; "it's nice and perhaps they will sell 2 million but no one wants a tablet." "Microsoft has not been able to make this a success why would Apple succeed?" No one saw this coming.

One thing is for sure, we have accepted (well most of us) the digital world and are now going into it at full speed.

THE INDUSTRY LIFECYCLE MODEL

This chapter addresses important environment questions by taking a macro-level, long-term view of industries and their evolution. Industries both old and new are not static and change in dramatic ways over time. It is, therefore, critical to examine how some of the key competitive forces shape the external environment of organizations.

While it seems obvious to even the most casual observer that the nature and intensity of competition is quite specific to each industry, it is nonetheless remarkable how very different industries follow very similar and predictable paths in how competitive pressures evolve over time. Research in the fields of economics, strategic management and organization theory has highlighted how virtually all industries evolve along particular trajectories and through specific phases from their early emergence and growth to their eventual maturity and decline.

This is commonly known as the **industry lifecycle model**. Given a long enough period of observation, almost all industries exhibit an inverted U-shaped growth pattern, with the number of organizations rising initially up to a peak, and then declining as the industry ages (see Exhibit 3.1). The pace of an industry's evolution along its lifecycle is closely related to the evolution of technology within the industry. Technological innovations will often trigger the start of a new lifecycle or the creation of an entirely new industry.

The industry lifecycle model divides industry evolution into four distinct phases: *introduction, growth, maturity* and *decline*. According to the model, new industries tend to be highly fragmented (i.e., with many small competitors) and characterized by experimentation with novel technologies and business models. This *introductory* phase sees many entrepreneurial firms enter the industry, hoping to emerge as a market leader. As the industry coalesces around a particular approach and this dominant model is adopted by customers, suppliers and other key constituents, the firms whose approach does not conform to the emerging standard exit the industry during a shakeout. The widespread diffusion of an industry standard or *dominant design* is a critical step in facilitating an industry's transition to the *growth* phase.

Over time, the industry reaches the *mature* phase, where the market stabilizes and sales grow more slowly. Firms must then become more efficient producers to lower costs and compensate for slower revenue growth. This is often achieved through mergers and acquisitions that result in higher industry concentration. In the *decline* phase, aggregate sales drop and rivalry further heats up as the industry undergoes greater consolidation through more mergers and the exit of inefficient firms. Exhibit 3.2 shows the typical S-curve pattern of how sales volume grows, stabilizes and declines as an industry develops.

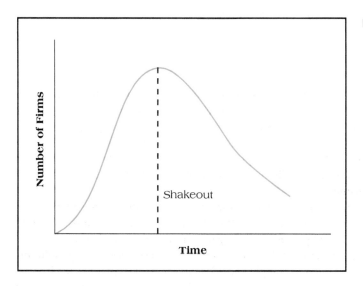

EXHIBIT 3.1 Industry growth.

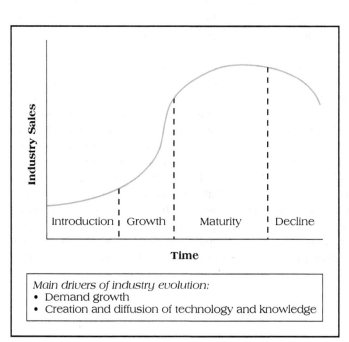

EXHIBIT 3.2 Industry lifecycle.

Understanding which phase of the lifecycle an industry is in is therefore critical for effective management at all levels of the organization. The lifecycle phase affects the degree of competition firms face, the type of organizational structure, the kind of strategy and the appropriate management approaches needed to survive and grow. The key success factors and sources of competitive advantage for firms are very different from one stage of the lifecycle to the next. Being successful when facing many small entrepreneurial competitors with no clear leader in a fast-growing and technologically innovative market requires a very different approach than being part of a highly concentrated industry with a few large, established incumbents and slow or declining growth. Different types of firms tend to be market leaders at different stages given the difficulties organizations experience when they must adapt to a different environment and make the transition from one type of organizational structure or strategy to another.

While different industries move along the lifecycle at a different pace, the remarkable regularity of the pattern across a very wide spectrum of different industries makes the lifecycle model a powerful tool for managers and entrepreneurs. In addition, the industry lifecycle is a complementary approach to Porter's five forces framework, presented in Chapter 9. The five forces framework is essentially a static model that provides a valuable snapshot of an industry's attractiveness *at a specific point in time*. The lifecycle model, however, is inherently dynamic and shows how evolution affects industry structure and thus the forces of rivalry, potential entrants, customer and supplier power and substitute products described in the Porter model. In conjunction, both models can provide managers with a more complete set of tools for analyzing industries and understanding the forces of competition. We will now examine each of the different phases of the lifecycle in greater detail.

THE INTRODUCTION PHASE: INDUSTRY EMERGENCE AND CREATION

New industries emerge as the result of changes (usually technological or regulatory) that create opportunities for entrepreneurs to leverage novel combinations of resources to develop innovative products, services or processes. These opportunities are not always exploited immediately and some remain untapped and unrecognized for many years until someone decides to start a new firm that will take advantage of the resources and create a new market. Some industries are the result of important technological breakthroughs such as the biotechnology industry that emerged following the discovery of recombinant DNA by scientists Stanley Cohen and Herbert Boyer. (See Talking Business 3.1.)

Some industries are the outcome of government regulation (or deregulation) that creates markets for new products or services. For example, the Environmental Protection Act and a variety of companion state laws enacted in the United States in 1970 specified guidelines for organizations' behaviour toward the environment. As a result, an industry of consultants, lawyers, lobbyists and even a market for trading pollution credits through brokers has emerged to enable firms to comply and adapt to the new legislation. In Canada, the Supreme Court's decision of June 9, 2005, overturned the ban on private health insurance in Quebec. Many analysts regard this ruling as opening the door to the creation of a private health care industry in Canada. Whether this will in fact happen, what this potential industry will look like and how it will operate remains, however, very unclear at this point.

The early years of an industry are generally a tumultuous period where there is tremendous uncertainty about the future of the market. There is no dominant technology or business model and it is far from certain that the market will ever grow sufficiently to provide attractive financial returns and growth opportunities. At the same time, this is also a period of unbridled optimism among entrepreneurs jockeying for position as the future of the market unfolds. Early entrants into an industry tend to be small entrepreneurial firms excited by the prospect and potential growth of a new market. Large, established firms tend to lag smaller ones in entering new industries for two reasons. First, a nascent market is usually too small and risky to justify the entry of large firms burdened with high overhead costs and the need to generate more certain, even if lower, financial returns. Second, older incumbent firms usually have bureaucratic organizational structures that inhibit their ability to move quickly and flexibly into new markets. Smaller and more nimble firms rely on simpler structures and lower startup costs to capture a first-mover advantage. Entrepreneurial startups are inherently more tolerant of ambiguity and risk because they have much less to lose than established firms and are therefore more willing to gamble in the hopes of generating a very large payoff.

Talking Business 3.1

The Birth of Biotech

The biotechnology industry was born of a scientific discovery made in 1973 by Herbert Boyer, professor at the University of California at San Francisco (UCSF), and Stanley Cohen of Stanford University. At the time, many scientists were working on the idea of recombinant DNA but Cohen and Boyer were the first to perfect a technique for snipping out DNA—the blueprint molecules that cells use to make proteins—and combining it with fragments of DNA from another organism.

A scientific breakthrough, no matter how important, is not itself sufficient to trigger the birth of a new industry. This requires entrepreneurs who have the dream and the drive to commercialize technological innovations and develop marketable products. This is where Robert Swanson, an ambitious 29-year-old venture capitalist, comes in. In 1976, Swanson wanted to commercialize a new way of engineering drugs based on splicing DNA from one organism into the genome of another so he called Boyer and dropped by his lab at UCSF. As the pair sketched out their business plan over beers in a San Francisco bar, they were about to change the drug industry forever by creating the field of commercial biotechnology.

To turn this invention into a business, Boyer and Swanson incorporated under the name Genentech Inc. In 1982, the company won Food & Drug Administration (FDA) approval for the first genetically engineered drug, human insulin. Soon many more entrepreneurial scientists created new biotechnology firms, using recombinant DNA techniques to develop drugs aimed at diagnosing and treating everything from anemia to cancer.

Herbert Boyer's fascination with James Watson and Francis Crick's groundbreaking 1953 revelation that DNA was a double helix is what led him to a career in biochemistry. "The whole structure was so beautiful, and it explained so much about genetics," he says. Boyer and Swanson, who studied chemistry and management at the Massachusetts Institute of Technology (MIT) and began his career as a venture capitalist, shared a great love of science. The pair made a perfect team and complemented each other perfectly in their roles as businessman and scientist. Swanson, the CEO, was the front man dealing with potential investors, strategic partners and clients while Boyer was the internal operations chief who supervised the scientists on staff. As an academic, Boyer understood the Genentech scientists' need to communicate and disseminate their discoveries and persuaded Swanson to let them publish their results, even at the risk of exposing the firm's trade secrets.

Today, Swanson and Boyer are widely recognized as the founding fathers of the global, multibillion dollar biotechnology industry. Genentech, which was started during that fateful meeting in 1976 and has since spawned a slew of competitors—1,400 firms in the United States alone—is now worth more than $100 billion. Boyer, who retired in 1991 as vice-president of Genentech and has remained on the board of directors ever since, says he and Swanson couldn't fathom the impact their innovation would have on the world. "When he walked into my office, it changed my life," he says, along with the lives of millions of people around the world. Just three years after retiring as chairman of Genentech's board in 1999, Swanson died of brain cancer at the age of 52.

Source: Based on "Robert Swanson and Herbert Boyer: Giving Birth to Biotech" in *Business Week* (October 18, 2004).

This introductory phase is one of great technical uncertainty where producers experiment with very different and novel combinations in the hopes of discovering a superior approach that will dominate those of other firms. Firms are intensely focused on research and development (R&D) activities during this period. This results in a high degree of product innovation with many different versions of products incorporating different features and technologies (see Talking Business 3.2). This also leads to confusion for customers and other stakeholders, which prevents the market from taking off into the growth phase. The types of customers who tend to purchase in the introduction phase of the lifecycle are early adopters willing to pay a premium for the privilege of owning a product before most anyone else, despite its early flaws and glitches. Conservative and price-conscious customers will usually wait until the mature stage before buying.

Talking Business 3.2

The Early Years of the Automobile Industry

While it is hard to imagine the modern automobile industry with its few large, established firms as a hotbed of entrepreneurial activity, the early years of the American auto industry were indeed very dynamic and entrepreneurial activity was rampant. Between 1899 and 1923, the industry experienced a large surge of market entry with over 3,000 recorded attempts at automobile production launched during this period. Many of these firms failed within a year of entering and over 68% exited the industry within two years. While perfectly consistent with the industry lifecycle theory, the sheer abundance and diversity of producers and early designs is quite astonishing in light of today's highly concentrated and standardized industry. Consider, for example, the following early cars and their makers:

- The Roberts Electric was a two-seat electric car powered by two 60-volt motors, one for each rear wheel, and was made in 1897 by C.E. Roberts of Chicago.
- Kent's Pacemaker, a steam-powered car with three rear wheels and a single wheel in front for steering, was made by the Colonial Automobile Co. of Boston from 1899 to 1901.
- The Luxor, a gasoline-powered vehicle that resembled a Roman chariot, was designed by C.R. Harris of Pennsylvania, who never managed to get it into production.
- The Cotta Steam was a steam automobile with four-wheel drive and steering. It was produced in very limited numbers by the Cotta Automobile Co. of Rockford, Illinois, in 1903.
- The Rotary, a gasoline-powered car with a single-cylinder engine and two crankshafts, was made in Boston by the Rotary Motor Vehicle Co. in 1904 and 1905.
- The Pratt was a car with four rear wheels and two front ones and was powered by a 75-horsepower engine. It was built by Pratt Chuck Works of Frankfurt, New York, in 1907.
- The Menkenns, a three-wheeled car powered by a front-mounted airplane propeller was made in 1937 by Willie Menkenns of Hillsboro, Oregon.

While many of these designs may seem bizarre today, they highlight the uncertainty faced by the pioneers of the automobile industry. It was far from clear at the turn of the century what basic features the successful car would have. For example, a critical decision involved the type of engine or propulsion system to use. Steam, electric and gasoline-powered engines were all potential candidates and many producers used technologies and fuel other than gasoline. In fact, many early analysts believed that steam was a superior technology to power car engines.

Around 1920 however, the dominant design of the automobile had emerged—an all-steel enclosed body mounted on a chassis and a gasoline-powered internal combustion engine. This is the fundamental architecture of a car that remains (save for material innovations in the steel body) unchanged to this day. The adoption of this dominant design for cars was accompanied by the failure of many car manufacturers and a dramatic reduction in the number of new entrants. From a peak of 350 car makers in the United States in 1915, there were fewer than 50 by 1930 and less than 20 by 1940 (see Fig. 10-5 Carroll and Hannan, 1995). Today there are only two car makers left in the United States (GM and Ford) and the global industry is highly concentrated with 10 manufacturers controlling more than 80% of the worldwide market.

The first cars produced were quite expensive and affordable only by the very rich. By 1923, however, 50% of U.S. households owned an automobile. The diffusion of the automobile was accelerated by Henry Ford's introduction of the Model T in 1908 for an affordable $850; and by Ford's development of one of the most significant industrial innovations of the 20th century—the moving assembly line in 1913. This revolutionary process brought the product to the workers for the first time rather than having workers moving around a factory to perform tasks. Inspired by Frederick Taylor's principles of specialization and standardization, Ford had workers perform a single repetitive task rather than whole portions of automobile assembly. The new Ford plant in Highland Park, Michigan, produced over 300,000 cars in one year, 1914—more than in the entire history of the company. The increases in productivity allowed Ford to continually drop the price of the Model T to as low as $290 in 1927, making cars truly affordable for the masses and paving the way for the massive changes brought on by the automotive industry we now know.

Source: Based on Glenn R. Carroll and Michael T. Hannan, *Organizations in Industry: Strategy, Structure & Selection* (New York, NY: Oxford University Press, 1995); and George Constable and Bob Somerville, *A Century of Innovation: Twenty Engineering Achievements that Transformed our Lives* (Washington, DC: Chapter Joseph Henry Press, 2003).

Despite (and partly because of) the uncertainty inherent in a new industry, the introduction phase of the lifecycle is a period of extraordinary creativity and innovation. An industry is rarely as vibrant as in its early years, when hope and optimism fuel the dreams of entrepreneurs and inventors. This period is the "gold rush" era of the industry where everyone can still make it big, given that nobody has yet.

In addition to the large upsurge in entry, new markets are extremely volatile. They may have no clear boundaries, and segments are not well defined. The market shares of the different producers are highly unstable and many entrants fail shortly after entering. It is nearly impossible to predict which firms will survive and grow, and it is often not all that obvious whether the industry itself will emerge as a viable entity able to sustain a group of producers. While we tend to study only those industries that did develop viable markets because we can observe the entire lifecycle, there are numerous examples of industries that began their lifecycle with much promise yet never made it past the introductory phase.

In the 1990s, several highly ambitious ventures planning to provide wireless telecommunications and broadband Internet services through satellite networks were launched with much fanfare. Iridium, backed by the wireless firm Motorola, and Teledesic, which was funded by McCaw Cellular and Microsoft owner Bill Gates, were two such ventures, along with Globalstar, ICO and others. Teledesic planned to blanket the earth's atmosphere with 288 low-earth orbit (LEO) satellites to build an "Internet in the sky." A combination of technical difficulties, financial troubles, mismanagement and slow customer adoption, due to the very high cost of satellite communications led to the demise of these ventures and of the nascent satellite communications industry—though not before they had lost billions of dollars in the process (more than $9 billion in Teledesic's case). Iridium filed for bankruptcy in 2001 after having launched 66 satellites into space at a cost of more than $6 billion. An Iridium satellite now hangs in the Smithsonian National Air and Space Museum as a testament to the technological ability (and commercial failure) of this venture. While some of these firms have emerged from bankruptcy protection in a different form, the satellite communications industry has clearly not lived up to the high expectations of its early pioneers. Perhaps the technology was ahead of its time and it will eventually take off and grow. Nevertheless, this case illustrates that new industries can suffer quite severe growing pains and may never develop into mature industries. There are other industries that are still in the early stages of development and currently struggling to make it into the growth phase.

The Quest for Legitimacy

Organization theorists studying industry emergence and evolution have focused on the institutional and social conditions that affect the changing nature of markets and competitive forces. One of the most important contributions to emerge concerns the concept of the legitimacy of new industries and organizational forms. Suchman defines organizational legitimacy as " . . . a generalized perception or assumption that the actions of an entity are desirable, proper, or appropriate within some socially constructed system of norms, values, beliefs, and definitions."[1] Other researchers have distinguished between two forms of legitimacy; sociopolitical and cognitive legitimacy.[2] **Sociopolitical legitimacy** refers to the endorsement of an industry, activity or organizational form by key stakeholders and institutions such as the state and government officials, opinion leaders or the general public. **Cognitive legitimacy** refers to the level of public knowledge of a new industry and its conformity to established norms and methods reflected in the extent to which it is taken for granted as a desirable and appropriate activity.

All organizations require legitimacy in order to acquire from external stakeholders the resources they need to survive and grow. Because organizations must extract resources from their environments, failure to conform to societal and institutionalized norms and beliefs results in a lack of legitimacy that will hinder their ability to recruit employees, obtain financial and material resources, sell products and services to customers, etc. There are many reasons why an organization's actions may not be perceived as desirable, proper or appropriate. Failure to comply to legal rules or to the ethical norms of society is one of them, as is pioneering a new type of firm or way of doing business.

Being new, small, unknown or unrecognized can cause a firm to lack legitimacy as it must prove to outsiders that it does conform to institutional norms. Even in existing industries, startup firms face higher risks of failure than incumbent firms with established track records and relationships with customers, suppliers and other stakeholders. In entirely new industries, the lack of legitimacy is even more pronounced, given how business models and organizational forms are novel and have yet to acquire sufficient legitimacy as desirable and appropriate entities. Entrepreneurs operate in a murky and ambiguous environment where there are few, if any, precedents available to determine what is considered a desirable and appropriate business activity. Stakeholders will therefore question the viability, not only of the specific venture, but of the nascent industry itself. Society's lack of understanding, acceptance and familiarity with the industry leads to even greater difficulties in marshalling resources so that new firms in new industries are even more likely to fail than new firms in established industries. (See Talking Business 3.3.)

To illustrate this idea, contrast the situations of an entrepreneur deciding to start a restaurant and another deciding to start a wireless text message advertising firm. A potential restaurateur need not convince external stakeholders of the virtue of the restaurant as a business model. It is a tried and true concept, and we have well-known templates for what they should look like. Everyone the entrepreneur speaks to will know what a restaurant is, how it will operate and make money. It is taken for granted that customers sit down and make choices from a menu, that food is prepared and served and that payment is tendered. With minor variations in menu, location or pricing, virtually all restaurants operate this way and have for hundreds of years. Entrepreneurs who conform to these institutional norms will have an easier time gathering the needed resources for their new venture. While the legitimacy of the individual venture needs to be overcome, the legitimacy of the restaurant industry is not an issue.

On the other hand, entrepreneurs launching a wireless text messaging advertising firm will need to explain to stakeholders exactly how this business will operate and generate revenues. They will also need to convince stakeholders of the potential viability of this concept as the text message advertising industry is still so new that, unlike restaurants, there are no institutional norms for how this business should be organized. It is not clear how and to whom ads should be sold and delivered. Will consumers accept them or find them intrusive and resent them? Is the technology proven? At the organizational level, entrepreneurs must establish the legitimacy of their specific venture, and at the industry level, they must collectively demonstrate that their novel organizational form or business model is desirable and appropriate.

Talking Business 3.3

Grey Goo and the Promising Future of the Nanotechnology Industry

Nanotechnology is the science and technology of building electronic circuits and devices from single atoms and molecules. These devices are typically less than 100 nanometers in size (one nanometer equals one millionth of a millimeter). This burgeoning industry is expected to make significant contributions to the fields of computer storage, semiconductors, biotechnology, manufacturing and energy. While the concept of nanotechnology was first introduced by the physicist Richard Feynman in 1959, advancements truly began to accelerate after Richard Smalley's discovery of carbon nanotubes won the 1996 Nobel Prize. In 2001, following large increases in U.S. government funding for nanotechnology research and the publication of an entire issue of the influential magazine *Scientific American* on the topic, the U.S. National Science Foundation predicted the newly defined "nanotechnology market" would grow to $1 trillion shortly.

These events triggered significant investments by venture capitalists and entrepreneurs in a variety of nanotech startups. According to some scientists, the future of nanotechnology is one of astonishing possibilities, where diseases will be wiped out and we will live for hundreds of years. Envisioned are all kinds of amazing products, including extraordinarily tiny computers that are very powerful, building materials that withstand earthquakes, advanced systems for drug delivery and custom-tailored pharmaceuticals as well as the elimination of invasive surgery (because repairs can be made from within the body). Nano-sized robots will be injected into the bloodstream and administer a drug directly to an infected cell. Because they are composed of biological elements such as DNA and proteins, the nanobots can easily be removed from the body.

The promise of a technological and industrial revolution of unprecedented magnitude based on the science of nanotechnology rests on many underlying assumptions of technical advances that, while theoretically possible, remain unproven. The emerging industry also has to contend with fears, stoked by science-fiction films and novels, that there are great risks involved with nanotechnology. One of these is that self-replicating nanobots run amok will devour the earth in three hours, turning it into "grey goo"—a phenomenon called global ecophagy. More realistic concerns point to the potential toxicity of certain nanosubstances that are so small they can penetrate cell walls and membranes and disturb the immune system. Nevertheless, the high degree of uncertainty and controversy has not deterred entrepreneurs from entering the fray in the hopes of eventually "cashing in" on the upcoming nanotech revolution.

While there may be intense technological competition between early entrants in an industry, there is also a high degree of collaboration for the greater good through the establishment of trade associations and standards-setting bodies that facilitate the pursuit of industry legitimacy. So-called "institutional entrepreneurs" play a critical role in helping to ensure the survival and growth of a fledgling industry by promoting its interests and coordinating efforts to gain institutional support and legitimacy. Linus Torvalds, the Finnish engineer who developed the Linux open source operating system, Jeff Bezos, the founder of Amazon.com, and Richard Smalley and Eric Drexler in the nanotechnology field are among the entrepreneurs who have become advocates and evangelists for the cause of the industry they pioneered in order to mobilize resources and legitimize it in the eyes of society. The collective action strategies pursued by institutional entrepreneurs often bear a striking resemblance to social movements. Successful institutional entrepreneurs are adept at presenting themselves as revolutionaries rebelling against the established order of large corporations, even though most of them actually aspire to grow their organizations and industry to replace the large firms.

In an industry's formative years, intra-industry rivalry is less intense as new organizations collaborate in the pursuit of legitimacy. New markets that have yet to achieve a sufficient degree of acceptance benefit from the endorsement of recognizable players. Smaller startups therefore often welcome the entry of established incumbents into the new market. When a large organization with a known track record enters the new industry, all firms benefit as this acts as an endorsement that signals the industry's viability and attractiveness, which helps it grow. This was the case when IBM entered the personal computer industry, for example, or when Wal-Mart entered the online retail market. When a large and successful retailer like Wal-Mart launches an e-commerce Web site, this signals to various stakeholders that the new market is important and worthy of Wal-Mart's attention. Wal-Mart's online presence attracts consumers to online shopping as well as attention from the media, the financial community and other stakeholders, all of which contribute to the establishment of cognitive legitimacy for the e-commerce industry.

THE GROWTH PHASE: DOMINANT DESIGNS AND SHAKEOUTS

In the introduction stage, the objective is to find the new industry's dominant model and get it accepted and institutionalized; although sales are important and contribute to the purpose, they are subordinate to the main goal of legitimization. As we will discuss, in the industry growth stage, the game becomes all about sales and market share. The growth stage begins when the market converges around a single dominant design or approach. A *dominant design* is defined by Anderson and Tushman as "a single architecture that establishes dominance in a product class."[3] In some cases, technical standards are specified and must be adhered to by all firms wishing to enter the market. When a standard is legally mandated and enforced by a government or standards organization, it is called a **de jure standard**. For example, the gauge of a railroad track, a light bulb socket, an electrical outlet, are all based on standards that have been explicitly specified by a standards organization—usually to ensure compatibility. A company wanting to produce light bulbs must make them to the correct specifications or they will be useless to consumers. A **de facto standard**, on the other hand, arises by virtue of common usage and is not officially sanctioned by any authority. It is a standard "in fact" or "in practice," rather than in law. Microsoft Windows is the *de facto* standard for personal computer operating systems because over 90% of the market uses Windows. Software developers must therefore write programs that are compatible with Windows if they want to reach the majority of the market.

As the standard or dominant model spreads across the industry, the producers that persist with a different approach usually exit the industry. This is one of the main causes of industry shakeouts. A **shakeout** in an industry is defined as a large number of exits from the market at the same time as the aggregate output of the industry increases. A large number of failures in a declining market is *not* a shakeout. A shakeout is a natural and healthy—albeit painful—process for an industry as it simply purges and weeds out the weaker competitors. The firms remaining after the shakeout emerge as strong competitors able to scale up production and serve the needs of a growing market. Nevertheless, there are cases of firms pursuing the path of a proprietary standard not in line with the rest of industry and remaining successful, though on a much smaller scale. Apple Computer, which pioneered the personal computer market, has been able to maintain its small share of loyal customers over the years. By not adhering to the Windows standard, Apple effectively restricted its market to small niches of graphic designers, academics and other consumers dissatisfied with Windows' quasi-monopoly. This, as Apple's troubles over the years can attest, is a very risky strategy. A firm must provide a significant benefit for a consumer to be willing to overcome the problems of incompatibility with 90% of the market.

Most other personal computer firms from the early 1980s, such as MITS, Commodore, and Tandy, did not survive. Prior to 1981, when IBM launched the IBM PC, and real commercial growth began, the different computer firms all had their own proprietary hardware and software platforms. Most of the exits from the industry occurred between 1987 and 1993. This period coincides with the introduction of Intel's 386 processor in 1986 and the release of Windows 3.0 in 1990, which had graphical interfaces that made computers more user-friendly. These versions of the Intel X86 line of microprocessors and of the Windows operating system firmly entrenched the so-called Wintel standard, which replaced the IBM PC as the dominant architecture for personal computers. Once this design was institutionalized as the standard, personal computers assembled and sold by clone manufacturers had to conform and include an Intel chip and Windows in order to be accepted by the market. When the vast majority of other users have a Wintel PC, few consumers are willing to deviate from the norm. Although there are newer versions of these components, the fundamental architecture of the PC with an Intel central processing unit (CPU) and Windows OS running application software has remained virtually unchanged for the past 15 years.

The adoption of a dominant design greatly accelerates the growth rate of new markets. As with automobiles, after about 20 years of industry evolution, 50% of U.S. households in 1999 owned a computer. Growth in demand is significantly related to the falling prices for products during the second phase of the lifecycle. The diffusion of a dominant industry model allows firms to standardize products and processes, resulting in dramatic costs savings that push prices lower. Standardization creates incentives for other firms to offer complementary products and services, such as software that runs on Windows or gas stations to fuel cars. The development of an industry infrastructure stimulates even more demand for the products in a cycle that leads to growth rates that increase during this stage. Products now appeal to a much wider mass market rather than just early technology adopters or the wealthy. As output grows further, economies of scale allow producers to generate more cost savings that drive prices even lower. This is another important cause of industry shakeouts. As product prices fall, inefficient producers come under significant competitive pressures and exit. Firms that are unable to match the economies of scale, production process improvements and lower prices of the most efficient producers will be driven out of the market. Also, high volume producers can afford to operate with lower profit margins while smaller firms are forced to exit.

Despite fierce competition and many exits, the high growth and reduction in uncertainty attracts many new entrants to the industry. Established firms from other industries that may have lagged the startups in entering now see the new industry as either potentially lucrative or threatening to their own assets and markets. They often enter by acquiring a firm already in the market rather than going through the trouble of starting a new division or subsidiary from scratch. Large firms bring tremendous resources to invest in distribution, marketing and advertising to capture a greater share of the market, as well as expertise in efficient production and the capacity to withstand fierce price competition. This is the case, for example, with many pharmaceutical firms that acquired promising biotech ventures rather than developing their own internal R&D capabilities in biotechnology.

In the introduction phase, product innovation and R&D were critical skills for organizations. After standardization, however, process innovation and sales and marketing become more important. This is a critical difference between the early and middle phases of the lifecycle and explains why large firms with greater resources and expertise in production processes and sales and marketing can displace entrepreneurial startups that fail to capture a meaningful first-mover advantage through property rights (e.g., patents, trademarks), customer loyalty or technological leadership. In the early market, organizations were more likely to collaborate to increase aggregate sales and achieve legitimacy. In the growth phase, rivalry is much more intense and firms try to build brand recognition and position themselves for when the market will cease to grow as rapidly.

THE MATURITY PHASE: A CRITICAL TRANSITION

In the mature stage, the third in the lifecycle, growth in aggregate demand begins to slow. Markets start to become saturated as there are fewer new adopters to attract and so competition intensifies even more. This can, nevertheless, be a very profitable period for the surviving firms as the industry enters a period of relative stability. For example, between 1980 and 2000, the U.S. beer brewing industry was in a mature phase and was dominated by three large firms that controlled over 80% of the market (Anheuser-Busch: 47%; Miller: 23%; Coors: 10%). Over the 20 year period, market shares were very stable, and no firm gained or lost more than about a single share point in any one year.

Despite the high degree of concentration in mature markets, rivalry is fierce. A single point of market share can mean millions of dollars in revenue so firms spend large amounts on advertising and sometimes enter into damaging price wars to lure customers from the competition. Because technological knowledge has diffused to the far corners of the industry and patents may have expired, firms focus their innovative efforts on incremental improvements to products. (See Talking Business 3.4 on the British chocolate bar market.) This is the era where firms market the "new and improved" versions and the 25 different scents and flavours in the hopes of differentiating their products ever so slightly from the competition's. Incremental innovations also provide opportunities to extend the lifecycle in order to delay the inevitable arrival of the decline stage. As consumers accumulate knowledge of the industry and its products over time, they become much more sophisticated and demanding buyers. This influences the industry's trend toward the **commoditization** of its products and makes consumers even more price conscious, which in turn forces firms to continuously squeeze out more cost savings from their production processes.

When there is very little product differentiation and consumers have become notoriously fickle, power once held by the manufacturers now shifts to the distribution channel firms that control access to the customer. This is why shelf space is so critical in mature packaged goods markets like laundry detergent. When customers see very little difference between Tide and the competition, they will essentially grab whatever they have access to or what happens to be on sale. Retailers who control and allocate shelf space have more bargaining

Talking Business 3.4

Block Chocolate—Breaking the Impasse

In a mature, largely commoditised market subject to heavy discounting by supermarkets and at odds with a preoccupation with healthy eating, block chocolate faces a battle for growth. Until last year, sales had been almost stagnant for five years, despite a short-term boost in 2002 following the launch of Nestle's premium chocolate Double Cream. The retail value of sales grew from $1.276 billion in 1998 to just $1.278 billion four years later, according to Euromonitor.

"We eat 2.5 kg of chocolate per person every year, and it would be hard—not to mention politically incorrect—to drive the market above that," says Datamonitor consumer analyst John Band. But the scale of the challenge hasn't stopped confectionery manufacturers looking for ways to boost value in their market. These include line extensions, premium launches, rebranding and refocusing promotional spend on the most successful brands.

In the UK block-chocolate market, Cadbury is the most successful player. It extended its lead over main rivals Nestle and Mars last year through a major relaunch of Cadbury's Dairy Milk, fuelling growth in the sector from $1.278 billion in 2002 to $1.456 billion—a rise of 14%. The relaunch brought products such as Fruit & Nut, Whole Nut, Wispa and Caramel Bar under the Dairy Milk umbrella, Variants, including Dairy Milk with mint chips and with crispy pieces, were added to the range, which has created a distinctive "purple patch" on supermarket shelves.

Sales of the line grew 13% last year, according to a Cadbury spokesman, and Euromonitor puts the company's market share at 53.1%, up from 50% last year. Of individual brands, Dairy Milk now has a commanding lead in share of the market, with 30.9%, well above its nearest rival, Masterfoods' Galaxy, which owns a 9.8% share.

Growing Pains

While Cadbury's success demonstrates there is scope to grow the block-chocolate market through new product development and innovation in branding, rivals have struggled to emulate it.

Mars relaunched Galaxy as a range, including products such as Minstrels and Ripple, with a $35 million campaign last year. Sales of Galaxy rose more than 10%, with Galaxy Milk Block sales soaring by 12% in the four months following its launch in September 2003. But an analyst from ACNielsen questions whether Galaxy's success is sustainable, given that it was achieved largely on the back of heavy promotional activity.

Nestle's strategy, meanwhile, has been to try to consolidate its position in the premium sector, with the recent launch of Double Cream: Double Chocolate and Double Berry. Double Cream, which contains Ecuadorian cocoa beans, was Nestle's first brand launch in five years, and aims to bridge the gap between Dairy Milk and Lindt by offering a hint of luxury at a price that is only marginally premium. [. . .] But sales of Double Cream, described by Nestle Rowntree managing director

(Continued)

Chris White as "a product that re-establishes Nestle's chocolate credentials," have so far been disappointing. Analysts are sceptical about the ability of manufacturers to change the tastes or price expectations of British consumers for whom Dairy Milk represents the taste, price and quality standard.

"There is not much scope for a premium market in the UK at the moment, and the big three producers' fortunes will depend largely on their success in promoting their core ranges," says Jeremy Cunnington, UK senior research analyst at Euromonitor.

Nevertheless, there is a discernible rise in sales of chocolate containing between 70% and 80% cocoa solids, such as Lindt and Green & Black's. "Sales of Lindt Excellence rose by about 15% last year, but are still worth less than $44 million," says Cunnington. Sales of Green & Black's, which has 90% of the total UK organic chocolate market, were up 70%, albeit from a low base, and the company owns 3% of the block-chocolate market.

Band says that even if Green & Black's does manage to convert consumers to stronger chocolate, its ethical credentials would curtail its ability to capitalise on growth, while its super-premium positioning prevents it from leveraging its name on "middlebrow" products.

It is a mistake the Day Chocolate Company, which dominates the market in fair trade chocolate, with brands such as Divine and Dubble, has been careful to avoid. Sales of fair trade chocolate and cocoa products rose from $2.2 million in 1998 to $24 million last year, according to the Fairtrade Foundation. [. . .]

Health Kick

Despite their small overall share of the block-chocolate market, organic and fair trade brands may capitalise on the trend toward healthier eating. A high proportion of the products are dark chocolate, with a lower milk content, while the high level of cocoa solids makes them richer and more difficult to consume in volume. "You can buy a bar of Green & Black's, eat a bit and put the rest in the fridge for another day," says marketing director Mark Palmer. "We are not a snack food, but a considered eat, and operate on the premise that less is more."

Maybe, but less chocolate also means less profit, and none of the manufacturers has a ready solution to the battle that exists with healthy eating. As the ACNielsen analyst puts it: "Obesity concerns are not good for the market." Band concludes: "If someone could come up with a cheap, tasty and healthy chocolate bar, it might do OK. But chocolate is obviously so indulgent that a healthy version is missing the point—like low-alcohol beer."

One of the main challenges facing chocolate manufacturers is aggressive pricing by the big supermarkets. Prices are lower than they have been for several years, and Asda and Tesco have been particularly aggressive by offering almost constant promotions.

The challenge is exacerbated by a fall in impulse sales, due mainly to the declining share of independent food stores as confectionery retailers. Supermarkets increased their share by 43% last year. The big grocers devote significant promotional space to confectionery, but prefer to sell lines popular enough to shift multipacks. This makes competition for shelf space tougher and encourages manufacturers to go for a cautious approach to product development.

The mixed fortunes of Nestle's Double Cream demonstrate how difficult it is to launch a product in the market. The high costs are difficult to justify when margins are so thin. And having to sell a "premium" chocolate at a discount undermines its positioning. By contrast, the launch of Kit Kat Chunky in 1999 was so successful because it already had high brand recognition. Not surprisingly, in a retail climate dictated by the big supermarkets, the most successful launches are those that extend well-known brands, as Cadbury's Dairy Milk did last year.

The good news is that the retailers have probably taken as many savings as they can out of the system. If they want a healthy range of products to sustain interest in the aisles, they know they can't squeeze manufacturers until their pips squeak. The pressure on prices won't go away, because supermarkets compete so hard on price, but they may start to relax a bit.

Source: Reproduced from *Marketing* (June 9, 2004), pp. 40–44, with the permission of the copyright owner, Haymarket Business Publications Limited.

power than they did in earlier phases where customers would seek out a particular product because it possessed features not shared by others.

Given the scale required to compete efficiently, there is very little, if any, entry at this stage of the lifecycle. The sources of competitive advantage for firms reside in process engineering to derive greater manufacturing and production efficiencies and reduce costs even more. This often means outsourcing and shedding activities that can be subcontracted more efficiently. In some industries, production will shift from advanced to developing countries during this stage in order to benefit from lower labour costs. In terms of the generic competitive strategies described in Chapter 9, whereas differentiation was the favoured approach in the earlier stages, organizations that adopt a cost leadership strategy in mature markets tend to outperform their peers.

The shift from a dynamic and technologically innovative environment with many small firms to a stable and cost-efficient market with few large rivals also requires a change in the type of organizational structure, as described in Chapter 4. In the high-flying and uncertain early market, entrepreneurial startups need to be innovative, dynamic and flexible. The organic structure, with its decentralized approach, limited hierarchy and low formalization, is better suited to the environment of the introduction and early growth phases. In a mature market where efficiency and cost-cutting matter more than innovation, the mechanistic structure, with its stricter rules, chain of command and narrow division of labour, is more appropriate. Making the transition from one structure to the next is very difficult when organizations have been conditioned to behave a certain way. This is the main reason why few firms are able to remain industry leaders throughout the entire lifecycle.

THE DECLINE PHASE: DIFFICULT CHOICES

An industry enters the decline stage when sales begin to fall. It is difficult to predict when this will happen, and the time it takes for industries to reach the decline stage varies widely. Nevertheless, industry sales typically decline as a result of one of the following:

1. *Changes in demographics:* e.g., Toward the end of the baby boom in the 1960s, demand for baby food dropped and rivalry among the leading firms—Gerber, Heinz, Beech-Nut—intensified considerably.
2. *Shifting consumer tastes and needs:* e.g., Social trends and health considerations have resulted in declining demand for cigarettes and tobacco products since the 1980s.
3. *Technological substitution:* e.g., Word processing software led to the decline of the typewriter industry; DVDs have replaced VHS cassette tapes as the medium of choice for movies, and sales of VHS tapes and video cassette recorders (VCR) are thus in decline.

Competition becomes especially fierce in the decline stage as firms face tough choices regarding the future. A decline, though, does not necessarily equal the demise or death of the industry, and there are a number of strategic options available to organizations for dealing with a declining market. These choices are often highly dependent on the actions of rivals, however. If many competitors decide to exit the industry and liquidate their assets, this may lead to profitable opportunities for the remaining firms. If other firms merge, however, their increased market power may reduce opportunities for the remaining competitors.

Organizations have five basic alternatives in the decline phase:

1. *Maintain a leadership stance:* This approach requires a firm to continue investing in marketing, support, and product development, hoping that competitors will eventually exit the market. Despite declining sales and profit margins, there may still be opportunities to generate above-average returns for firms that remain the industry leaders during this phase.
2. *Pursue a niche strategy:* The objective is to find a specific segment of the industry that may not decline as rapidly as the rest and where the firm can expect to possess some form of competitive advantage to discourage direct competition in the niche. For example, a tobacco firm facing declining cigarette sales may decide to focus exclusively on the more robust cigar market and defend that niche heavily against competitors by investing in marketing and sales support.

A firm can ultimately choose to switch to a harvest, exit or consolidation strategy after having pursued a leadership or niche approach; the reverse is not true.

3. *Harvest profits:* This strategy requires squeezing as much remaining profit as possible from the industry by drastically reducing costs. The firm must eliminate or severely restrict investments in the industry and take advantage of existing strengths to generate incremental sales. This strategy is ultimately followed by the firm's exit from the industry.

4. *Exit early:* This approach allows firms to recover some of their prior investments in the industry by exiting the market early in the decline phase, when assets may still be valuable to others and there is greater uncertainty concerning the speed of the decline. Some firms also choose to exit the industry during the mature phase to truly maximize the value from the sale of its assets. Once decline becomes evident, assets are worth much less to potential buyers, who are in stronger bargaining position. The risk of exiting so early is that an organization's forecast for decline will prove inaccurate.

An important point to remember is that just as there are barriers to entering an industry, there are also barriers to exiting a market. A firm may have specialized assets, such as plants and equipment, that cannot be easily redeployed by other businesses. This greatly diminishes their resale value and acts as an exit barrier. Firms may also face high costs due to labour settlements if they exit an industry. The social cost of closing a plant in a region that is economically dependent on the industry can also hinder a smooth exit. Finally, there are non-rational exit barriers linked to the cognitive and emotional barriers that managers face in divestment decisions. Exiting an industry can be perceived as a sign of failure, and managers that have a strong emotional identification and commitment to an industry are understandably reluctant to admit defeat when they have worked hard at being successful.

5. *Consolidate:* This strategy involves acquiring at a reasonable price the best of the remaining firms in the industry. This allows the acquirer to enhance its market power and generate economies of scale and synergies to further reduce costs and make up for declining demand. For example, in the online brokerage industry, sales and profits have been declining since the market crash of 2000. Fewer people are trading stocks online, putting pressure on companies like Ameritrade and Etrade to compensate. While Etrade has responded by entering the growing banking and mortgage markets to diversify its sources of revenue, Ameritrade has been on an acquisition binge. Starting with its 2001 acquisition of National Discount Brokers, Ameritrade has devoured several of its smaller competitors: Daytek in 2002; Mydiscountbroker. com and National Brokerage in 2003; Bidwell and J.B. Oxford in 2004; TD Waterhouse for $2.9 billion so far in 2005. Analysts claim that the only way for discount brokers to survive the decline in online trading—besides another unlikely stock market bubble—is to merge to generate economies of scale and become more efficient. Ameritrade is claiming that it can generate more than $500 million in savings by merging its operations with TD Waterhouse.

Exhibit 3.3 shows a summary of the key characteristics of the different industry lifecycle stages.

EXHIBIT 3.3   Characteristics of the industry lifecycle stages.

Characteristic	Stage			
	Introduction	**Growth**	**Maturity**	**Decline**
Market Growth	Slow	Very rapid	Moderate	Negative
Customers	Affluent, early technology adopters	Niche markets, increasing penetration	Price-conscious mass market, repeat buyers	Late adopters, knowledgeable users, residual segments
Rivalry	Low; technological competition	Increasing; entry and exit; shakeout	Intense; increased concentration; exit	Price wars; exit; mergers and acquisitions; asset liquidation
Critical Functional Areas	Research & Development	Sales and Marketing	Production and Manufacturing	General Management and Finance
Products	Very wide variety of designs	Standardization	Commoditization	Continued commoditization
Technological Development	Rapid product innovation	Product and process innovation	Incremental innovation	Very little innovation
Organizational Structure	Organic	Organic	Mechanistic	Mechanistic
Generic Strategies	Product differentiation	Product differentiation	Cost Leadership	Cost Leadership/Focus
Key Objectives	Increase awareness; achieve legitimacy; specify dominant design	Create demand; capture market share	Cost efficiency; extend lifecycle	Market or niche leadership; cost reduction; consolidation; exit

THE CHANGING COMPETITIVE LANDSCAPE: DOWNSIZING

In terms of business buzzwords, probably the most dreaded buzzword of the 1990s was the term *downsizing*. While the 1990s have been referred to as the "lean, mean 90s," the trend toward leanness via downsizing has not gone away in the new millennium. In recent years, across Canada thousands of workers have been losing their jobs.

In broad terms, **downsizing** refers to the planned reduction in the breadth of an organization's operations. Typically, it entails terminating relatively large numbers of employees and/or decreasing the number of products or services the organization provides. It seems that if you think of just about any large corporation, it has likely experienced some kind of downsizing: from AT&T to Bell Canada, to Air Canada, to IBM, to General Motors, to Northern Telecom—all have experienced massive cuts in their workforce. Consequently, most of us associate downsizing with the reduction of the workforce. However, we can be more specific, given that organizations can downsize in a variety of ways. For example, does reducing an organization's ownership of assets amount to downsizing? Does a reduction in the number of employees constitute downsizing?

> One definition of downsizing that has been offered is: "downsizing is a set of activities undertaken on the part of management and designed to improve organizational efficiency, productivity, and/ or competitiveness. It represents a strategy implemented by managers that affects the size of the firm's work force, the costs, and the work processes.[4]

Based on this definition, there are three fundamental types of strategies for downsizing: workforce reduction, work redesign and systematic change. Workforce reduction typically involves a short-term strategy that is aimed at reducing the number of employees through such programs as attrition, early retirement, voluntary severance packages, layoffs, or terminations. Downsizing approaches have largely been directed at workforce reduction rather than the more detailed and longer-term strategies of job redesign and systematic change.[5] Following, we can more clearly identify the common approaches to downsizing. That is, we can be more specific about what exactly an organizational downsizing may entail. This will allow us to briefly identify the potential benefits as well as potential pitfalls of an organizational downsizing.

Methods of Downsizing

The most common forms of downsizing include any one, or a combination, of the following strategies (the pros and cons of each of these approaches are shown in Exhibit 3.4):

1. **Across-the-board cutbacks.** Cutting a fixed percentage of the workforce across all departments or units.
2. **Early retirement and voluntary severance.** Those nearing retirement take early retirement, voluntarily as opposed to a forced leave—typically as the first stage in a downsizing process.
3. **De-layering—cutting a level or levels of the organization.** Termination or reassignment of the middle managers who are not replaced, flattening the organizational hierarchy by removing horizontal slices.
4. **Contracting Out (also referred to as outsourcing).** Lay off staff in areas that perform specialized functions and contracting out this work to agencies that can staff those areas with temporary workers. Types of activities that are typically contracted out include payroll, data entry, public relations and clerical work, as opposed to the core activities of the organization.
5. **Dropping product lines.** Discontinue some programs or product lines provided by the organization.

Consequences of Downsizing

The strategy of downsizing that started in the mid-1980s has now become commonplace. In the early stages, downsizing strategies were viewed as a panacea for the ills of organizations, providing organizations with a method of cost reduction, productivity and profitability improvement and, consequently, a higher competitive ability. Unfortunately, there is vast evidence that the anticipated benefits of corporate downsizing have largely failed to materialize. It is of interest to reconsider the anticipated benefits of downsizing and in what way these benefits have not been realized.

As the Wyatt report and numerous other studies have indicated, there are a host of benefits that organizations feel they can achieve through downsizing, including reduced bureaucracy, lower overhead costs,

---

EXHIBIT 3.4 **Potential benefits and risks of downsizing.**

Potential Benefits

1.	Across-the-Board Cuts.	"Shares the pain," spreading it across the organization—all levels are equally affected.
2.	Early Retirement and Voluntary Severance.	Concentrates the terminations among those who are willing to leave. • May help achieve the reduced cost objective by encouraging the more senior and highly paid staff to leave.
3.	De-layering.	Because the organization is cut horizontally, all areas are equally affected, and the "pain" is shared across all departments. • To the extent that decentralized decision making is desired, this approach allows the shift of responsibility to the lower and, perhaps, more appropriate levels in the organization.
4.	Contracting Out.	Immediate cost savings.
5.	Dropping Product Lines.	• Decide what areas may not be productive to continue to maintain. • A closer connection to long-term strategic planning compared to other approaches. • Concentrates the disruption in one or a few business units, as opposed to the entire organization.

Potential Risks

1.	Across-the-Board Cuts.	Efficient parts of organization are hurt. This form of downsizing ignores how well or how poorly the units are managed. • Typically conducted when there is no strategic plan—it simply cuts staff throughout the organization.
2.	Early Retirement and Voluntary Severance.	Not necessarily guided by a strategic plan. • Encourages voluntary exits from all parts of the organization. • "Loss of corporate memory"—that is, a company may lose highly experienced, valued members who have been an intrinsic part of what the organization is all about.
3.	De-layering.	A loss of corporate memory with the removal of middle managers. There may also be an overload of responsibility to top management, who now may need to fill the role of some middle management as well. • There may be significant costs attached to the transition from a taller organization to a flatter one where lower level employees must be trained to take on additional roles and responsibilities.
4.	Contracting Out.	Difficulties of dealing with the new suppliers of this labour and avoiding future cost increases. • The general loss of control with these temporary workers.
5.	Dropping Product Lines.	Pain is concentrated and not shared across the entire organization—a few people will carry the burden of this type of downsizing.

---

improved decision making, improvements in productivity and a stronger ability to innovate. But does downsizing contribute to a better "bottom line"? That is, does this activity enhance the organization's financial performance? There is research evidence that suggests that a downsizing or layoff announcement often leads to a drop in the organization's share price, particularly if that announcement was related to financial concerns or a massive and permanent cutback of employees.[6] There is also evidence to suggest that investors respond negatively to layoff announcements.[7]

Does downsizing improve organizational performance as measured by return on assets and common shares? There is research evidence indicating that organizations that engaged in an employee downsizing (i.e., termination of at least 5% of the workforce combined with little change in plant and equipment costs) did not outperform other organizations in their industry.[8] Similarly, a CSC Index survey found that less than 33% of all downsizing initiatives had achieved their anticipated productivity or profitability goals.

In a large-scale study conducted in Canada, data were collected from 1,907 Canadian organizations with at least 75 employees. This study examined how a permanent workforce reduction affects employer efficiency, employee satisfaction and employee–employer relations. The findings indicated that a permanent workforce reduction was associated with negative consequences. This echoes the findings in the United States and elsewhere, and underscores the consistent failure of downsizing to live up to its expectations.[9]

Added to the lacklustre results of downsizing is the wealth of evidence of the costs of downsizing in terms of human consequences. Needless to say, those individuals who are victims of a downsizing can be subjected to intense psychological trauma. However, there is ample research evidence to indicate that the *survivors* of a downsizing may also experience trauma. According to numerous studies conducted, survivors of a downsizing typically report greater levels of stress, burnout, reduced self-confidence and self-esteem and lower job satisfaction.[10] Studies have also found that a downsizing can have adverse effects on employee commitment to the organization, performance, customer and client needs, and reduced morale and trust.[11] See Talking Business 3.7.

Why Has Downsizing Failed to Achieve Anticipated Results?

If the cost reduction results are inconsistent, if there is no evidence that productivity, profitability and competitiveness improve as a result of downsizing, what is going wrong? There are at least three fundamental issues that have been repeatedly linked with the failure of downsizing. These issues reflect shortcomings in the planning for an execution of organizational downsizings, rather than an outright condemnation of the practice itself.

1. **Lack of strategic planning.** Many downsizings have not been guided by a long-range strategic plan, but rather have been a short-term response to environmental pressures. The poor performance of downsizing has been associated with the tendency of downsizing programs to be hastily formulated and not linked with the organization's strategic plans.[12] While downsizing is by no means going away, by the end of the 1990s organizations were looking more critically at downsizing as a method of organizational change, and many reconsidered its role without the broader framework of organizational planning. Moreover, a *Fortune* magazine article expressed the growing sentiment that downsizing by itself provides no answers for organizational ills without a strategic plan. That sentiment is reflected in the observation made in Talking Business 3.8.
2. **Lack of concern for, and involvement with, employees.** Many downsizings do not involve those who are affected in the planning stages. That is, those in charge of the downsizing do not expect to get objective feedback or advice from those who will potentially be terminated, and so many employees are cut off from the actual planning of the organizational downsizing. It is important to note that the adverse effects of a downsizing may be mitigated through suitable communication of the downsizing to employees,[13] employee participation in the planning of the downsizing, a thorough analysis of tasks and perceived employee support from the organization,[14] as well as through advanced planning and

Talking Business 3.7

The Cost of Downsizing

Downsizing is a fact of life. The question is will this phenomenon help or hinder the success of Canadian business in the long run?

> Downsizing strategies employed by cash-strapped governments and companies alike . . . have burdened Canada's health-care system with up to $14 billion a year in additional costs, a new federal study concludes.
>
> The Public Health Agency of Canada report said increased workload, or "role overload," has driven costs higher and said doctor visits could be cut by 25 per cent and hospital stays by 17 per cent if the issue was properly addressed. "These numbers are a wake-up call to employers and governments," the study said.
>
> "The data presented in this report paint a frightening picture of how inattention to workplace health and work-life issues is impacting Canada's health-care system."
>
> Whatever savings realized from reduced corporate and government payrolls may well have already been wiped out by substantial increases in costs for health benefits and by more employee absenteeism, it said.
>
> "Simply put, Canada's ability to be globally competitive in the future depends on our ability to address this issue." **

Source: ** Keith Leslie, "Increased workload burdens health care," Canadian Press (November 10, 2004).

Talking Business 3.8
Downsizing and Strategy?

It is true that the workforce is not what it was for our parents or grandparents. The boss who held their hands and guided them up the hierarchical ladder is now nearing extinction. As corporations struggle to survive in this worldwide competitive war, costs must be minimized, and labour expenses are just the way to do that.

Labour represents approximately 60% of overall company costs. Cost cutting is consequently often tied to cutting human resources. And therefore, downsizings continue to dominate business behaviour. For example, in an effort to increase measures of performance and compete with other car manufacturers like Toyota, Ford Motor Company has reduced the salaried workforce in North America in recent years, by 2,700. This is a fraction of Ford's future de-layering plans, which include the expansion of those cuts to approximately 10,500 people in the coming years.

All this begs the question—is downsizing really the answer to a company's performance "woes"? The answer depends on how closely these downsizing plans are matched with a proper strategic plan. In the case of companies like Ford, only time will tell whether downsizing was a rational or non-rational response to external forces faced by the company.

Sources: M. Belcourt, G. Bohlander, S. Snell & A. Sherman. (2004). *Managing Human Resources,* 4th Canadian Ed., Chapter 6: Training and Development. Toronto, Ont.: Nelson Canada; CBS News, "Ford Cuts Yearly Outlook, Plans New" (2005, August 19). Available online: http://www.cbsnews.com/stories/2005/06/22/ap/business/mainD8ASCP2G1.shtml [Retrieved: August 20, 2005]; N. Shirouzu. (2005, July 22). "Ford job cuts may be deeper than expected: White-collar staff warned 30% could go," *The Globe and Mail,* p. B9.

coordination of outplacement services.[15] Attention needs to be given to both the terminated employees and those remaining. However, research evidence has suggested that insufficient attention has been given to the survivors of a downsizing.

3. **Careless removal of corporate memory.** Downsizings can eliminate individuals who are a central part of the organization's knowledge base—the notion of corporate memory. While intangible, the cost of corporate memory loss to an organization can be very significant. This can go beyond simply losing the expertise of a valued, experienced employee. This significance has been expressed by many observers:

> Downsizing devastates social networks. When a person is laid off, an entire personal network of internal and external relationships is lost as well. Downsizing destroys informal bridges between departments, disrupts the information grapevine, severs ties with customers, and eliminates the friendships that bond people to the workplace.[16]

It has also been suggested that the loss of corporate memory can be particularly devastating to the organization's ability to innovate.

For better or worse, downsizings continue to reshape the corporate landscape; and, given that they are unlikely to disappear in the very near future, one can only hope that they will be planned carefully in order to bring about some of the improvements for which they are intended. To this point, the results of downsizing do not appear to be largely positive for many organizations, and yet we have witnessed the pervasive acceptance of downsizing as a legitimate organizational practice. The question naturally arises: Why have so many organizations agreed to adopt a practice that is not proven to be effective? If there is no significant proof that downsizing offers the results organizations are struggling to achieve, the question arises, Why do companies continue to downsize? In order to make sense of why organizations engage in restructuring themselves, it is useful to consider why organizations adopt such trends as downsizing. In terms of a rational explanation, the evidence is weak. Consequently, researchers have also considered non-rational approaches to explaining the phenomenon of downsizing. This requires an understanding of how non-rationality can influence organizational structure. See Talking Business 3.9.

Talking Business 3.9

Mintzberg on Downsizing

Question: You've criticized the "lean and mean" philosophy of job cuts. What are the consequences of a decade of downsizing?

Mintzberg: All the productivity gains by business may turn out to be productivity losses, because those gains came from firing people left and right. Say you're running a company and you have a warehouse full of stock; you fire everybody and then ship inventory for the next year. The productivity figures look really good, because you're getting all these sales with no employees. And within a year you'll close down.

It takes time for a business to train people, to gain people who believe in you. There is a contract between employers and employees. All these things are destroyed by downsizing. And, by the way, customer satisfaction indexes are going down because customers are being badly treated.

Question: Isn't downsizing the only hope for struggling companies. . .?

Mintzberg: There's been a lot of downsizing that wasn't driven by losses. In the telecom sector, they have been, but in other sectors, a lot of it was just because they didn't meet their earnings targets for a quarter. It's mindless.

Source: McGill News, Fall 2002 <http://www.mcgill.ca/news/2002/fall/mintzberg/>.

Downsizing as a Non-rational Approach to Organizational Structure

How can organizational structure be non-rational? A perspective of organizations called **institutional theory** argues that organizations are driven to incorporate practices and procedures defined by current concepts of work and those accepted or institutionalized in society. Institutional acts, or the rules that govern organizational activity, are simply taken-for-granted means of "getting things done." They represent shared norms or expectations within or across industries. These rules dominate thinking with regard to how organizations should be designed. The implications are that accepted norms or rules, rather than a set of rational reasons based on clearly identifiable and measurable objectives, can encourage the creation or maintenance of organizational structures and processes. Institutional rules have little to do with efficiency, but they give organizations that conform to them a sense of legitimacy. That is, organizations can have, embedded in their structure, elements that are simply taken-for-granted ways of doing things—which may not, in fact, be accomplishing any specific organizational goals.

According to institutional theory, organizations may conform to institutionalized beliefs as a means to achieve legitimacy, resources and survival capabilities. The shared beliefs provide order through their institutionalization into organizational procedures and their direct influence on the behaviour of individuals. Consider such diverse organizations as IBM, Ben & Jerry's, McDonald's, Procter and Gamble and Bell Canada. All these organizations have risen within society. They have gained success and longevity through their ability to adapt their operations to the needs of society. Specifically, the organization becomes filled with various cultural forces: e.g., political rules, occupational groups and professional knowledge. In other words, as these organizations have grown, they have instituted acceptable ways of conducting business.

The ideas generated from institutional theory draw attention to the notion of the forces that act on an organization and encourage the adoption and maintenance of those activities that are viewed as legitimate. This perspective suggests that organizational structures and processes can arise not simply due to rational objectives for control and coordination, but because of adherence to non-rational, but institutional or socially accepted, rules. Meyer and Scott described a "continuum"—from organizations dominated by technical criteria (e g., manufacturing organizations) to those dominated by institutional criteria (e.g., schools). What we have seen since the mid-1980s is a questioning of many of the fundamental institutional rules governing how organizations should be designed. In other words, at one time, the machine bureaucracy was the socially accepted structure for most organizations. Recently, this rule has been called into question, and increasingly the phenomenon of re-engineering, downsizing and going virtual seem to be the established trend in organizational design.

The continued use of downsizing by organizations, even though it has not lived up to its reputation, appears to be non-rational. Organizations do not, in fact, always act purely rationally. Institutional theory asserts that organizational structures and policies can become institutionalized and persist, even when they are no longer efficient.[17] This theory emphasizes the fact that an organization's functions can become established or embedded in social networks. These functions, whether they are how organizations are designed or simply how they behave, are affected by the pressures of conformity and legitimacy, which arise from the organization's environment.[18] Meyer and Rowan[19] defined institutionalization as "the processes by which social processes, obligations, or actualities come to take on a rule-like status in social thought and action."

The notion of downsizing has come to represent more than a reduction in an organization's workforce. It has come to reflect a longer term, organizational evolution. Numerous organizations, by the 1990s, felt obligated to downsize given the intrinsic connection between being "lean and mean" and being highly competitive. Institutional theory offers some insight. Such institutional theorists suggest that the spread of corporate downsizing has been facilitated through: conforming to institutional rules that define legitimate structures and management practices; copying the actions of industry leaders; and responding to the legitimization of downsizing practices as accepted management practices via the media and popular press.[20] Why do organizations persist in conforming to the "rules" of downsizing?

Addressing this question can be accomplished through addressing the question of why organizations conform to institutional rules. At least three social factors have been cited. These factors include the notions of **constraining, cloning** and **learning**. We can briefly consider each factor in order to get a better understanding of how they influence adherence to the institutional rule of downsizing. In this regard, we can understand how these factors can make organizations follow rules or ideas that are not necessarily rational.

1. Constraining Forces

These forces represent those practices that come to define what are perceived as legitimate management structures and activities and that consequently place pressure on organizations to conform to these institutional rules. An example given[21] involves the relationship between large U.S. corporations and the stock market. Interestingly, studies have found that layoff announcements made by large corporations that were undergoing restructuring and consolidation were followed by increases in share prices. In other words, we have seen the tendency for public reactions to downsizings to be favourable—the notion of becoming "leaner and meaner" has become an accepted business strategy, and one apparently favoured by shareholders. Consequently, since the markets respond positively to such news, organizations have become constrained to perceive downsizing as a positive outcome and one to be sought. Of more interest is the finding that this constraining force was found to be even stronger when executives' compensation packages and bonuses were linked to share values.

2. Cloning Forces

These are forces or pressure for organizations to imitate the behaviours of industry leaders. Revisiting the downsizing example, some observers have suggested that organizations have been "jumping on the bandwagon." That is, many organizations downsize to demonstrate they are in tune with modern business trends, and consequently downsizing has been viewed as a way of "keeping up with the corporate Joneses."[22] This action represents a clear reduction in rationality—i.e., a move away from objectively defined criteria for downsizing and toward strict adherence to institutional rules. It has also been found that downsizing among industry members is more likely to occur when industry leaders downsize. The risks of failure are obvious given that this approach lacks a careful evaluation of the costs and benefits of this strategy.

3. Learning Forces

These forces are the result of institutionalized management practices. The lessons we teach future managers and businesses leaders are embedded in the courses taught in universities and professional associations. As an example of the biases generated in business schools, researchers like McKinley and his colleagues point out the case of cost-accounting techniques used in business strategy education.[23] From a purely cost-accounting perspective, the practice of outsourcing appears infinitely superior to maintaining a full-time workforce. Specifically, the method of allocating overhead costs clearly draws attention to the cost efficiencies gained by outsourcing; and, by definition, those units remaining as a permanent fixture for the organization appear more costly. According to McKinley, this perceived cost reduction gained from outsourcing increases the preference to outsource and can, consequently, become the driving force for a series of outsourcings and downsizings. This, then, is an example of how an emphasis on certain approaches toward business strategy that are spread through business education can come to play a role in rationalizing downsizing as a legitimate activity.

CHAPTER SUMMARY

Competitive processes evolve in a remarkably predictable manner in most industries. Understanding what to expect and what drives evolution along the lifecycle of an industry is critical for managers needing to steer their organizations through turbulent times. In this chapter, we have identified the major phases and milestones that mark an industry's evolutionary path from introduction and growth to maturity and decline. At each stage of the industry lifecycle, the skills and capabilities needed to survive and grow change in significant ways. We have examined the nature of these changes as competition evolves in markets that go from fragmented and fast-growing to concentrated and declining. Finally, in terms of industry decline, we examined how downsizing can affect the competitive landscape.

CONCEPT APPLICATION

†THE DECLINE OF THE NEWSPAPER INDUSTRY

The newspaper industry, particularly in the US, is going through an unexpectedly sharp contraction. It is losing readers and advertisements significantly.

The average daily circulation of US newspapers declined 7% in the six-month period, ending March 31, according to the latest data from the Audit Bureau of Circulations. The data indicate that a shift in consumer behaviour has led more people to get their news and information online.

Newspapers have also lost the lion's share of classified advertisement to the internet. To make things worse, a depressed economy has compelled more readers to cancel their newspaper subscriptions, and business companies to cut their advertisement budget as part of overall cost-cutting measurements. As a result, closures of newspapers, bankruptcy, job cuts and salary cuts are widespread.

Citing losses of $18.9 million per year, the *Christian Science Monitor* stopped printing daily and, instead, started printing weekly editions from April. The *Rocky Mountain News* in Denver published its last print edition on April 3, after 149 years of publication. It was losing $1.5 million a month. The 144-year old *San Francisco Chronicle* is under threat of closure. Its owner, Hearst Corporation, threatened to close the newspaper unless staff agreed to massive cutbacks. The paper's loss was more than $50 million in 2008.

The Tribune Company filed for bankruptcy in December 2008 with $13 billion debt. Another big paper—*The New York Times*—is struggling with a debt of some $400 million. And the list goes on. A BBC report rightly questioned: "If the economic crisis goes on much longer will there be any newspapers left in the US to write about it?"

It seems that newspapers are in severe difficulty and moving gradually towards death. Many have already started to calculate when the last newspaper will be published in the western world. It is hard to believe, but the existing scenario leads to this end.

Who is responsible for the anticipated death of print journalism? Is it Google and Yahoo who provide free contents to users? Or, has the print media failed to adapt to changing journalism in the internet era?

Yes, Google aggregates news contents and people are increasingly turning to the Internet. But, blaming Google for the demise of the newspaper industry is not right in many senses. Google doesn't generate any content. It works just like a newsstand, where titles are displayed and readers decide what to pick. Once readers choose their titles, Google directs them to the story's original website.

It is not Google or any other news aggregator, but the failure of newspaper managers to understand the new media. The existing business model of newspapers has proved its ineffectiveness in making profit in the digital age, and at the same time their web versions failed to generate revenue. It is not an easy task to make money online by selling information when users have already become habituated to free contents.

(Continued)

Developing nations have not been affected so far by this changing trend of journalism—thanks to low penetration of the internet. But, the blow is coming. As David Bell said: "Newspapers have to be very creative in thinking about the future challenges and opportunities."

†*Source:* "Is the Newspaper Industry at Death's Door?" Shameem Mahmud, *The Daily Star.*
Shameem Mahmud is a Lecturer at Mass Communication and Journalism, University of Dhaka, and post-graduate student at the University of Amsterdam.

‡The truth is the US newspaper industry has been in slow decline since 1987 with circulation hitting an all time low in 2009, its lowest in seven decades when papers lost 10.6 percent of their paying readers from April through September compared to the previous year.

With the development of the internet, newspapers have continued to face growing competition for readers' attention and advertising dollars. As consumers continue to move in droves from the printed page to the internet, newspapers have created online editions in an attempt to keep pace with the changing habits of their readers. It's involved a major transformation, not only how print papers have offered up the news but in how they've had to compete to maintain those advertising dollars. The problem is that there's not a lot of money to be made in newspaper ads on the internet as compared to their ink and paper counterpart. The transition has not exactly been a success story.

Now with the proliferation of daily deal and group buying sites such as Groupon and Living Social completely changing the way many people shop, newspapers have once again been taking a hard hit in an already very tough market. From News & Tech on Gilbert's speech:

> Gilbert said emerging competitors, such as Groupon, threaten to do a lot more damage to newspapers, much like Craigslist all but evaporated the industry's classified ad base. To defend their turfs successfully, Gilbert said newspapers have to re-examine every aspect of their operation, including pinpointing the costs of doing business.

This past fall, Paul Beebe of *The Salt Lake Tribune* talked about Gilbert and how he believed newspapers viewed the internet, at least initially.

> Even though newspaper executives saw the Internet coming, most could only think about the damage it would do, Gilbert said.
> "The desire to defend the traditional business kept them from seizing a new business. And this was both on the product side and the business model side," he said. "Protecting the tradition caused them to miss the future."
> "The survival rate of [companies] overcoming a disruptive innovation is about 9 percent. But of the 9 percent that made it through, 100 percent set up a separate group to focus on the digital innovation."

We once relied on newspapers to not only deliver the day's local, national and international news but they also told us about local retailers in the form of ads and brought those popular cents off coupons. Now daily deal sites, most notably Groupon, are taking over the landscape that once belonged to the local newspapers. Whether those that survive can reinvent themselves as Gilbert says they need to do is yet to be seen. The internet alone was enough to cause a downward spiral of the newspaper industry but with the arrival of Groupon, the printed paper as we once knew it may be on a slippery slope of no return.

†*Source:* "Groupon is Hastening the Demise of the Newspaper Industry," Kris Ashton, *Daily Deal Media.*

Questions

1. What stage in the lifecycle is the newspaper industry in? Please explain and justify.
2. What strategies are available to the newspaper industry for dealing with declining sales and what do you recommend?
3. Do you think the industry will die? Why? Why not?

The Technological Context*

What is the role of technology in the evolution of industries? How can technology "make" or "break" an industry? Technological innovation is a key driver of industry evolution. History tells us that radically new innovations or technologies can create entirely new industries or seriously disrupt existing ones. This chapter explains the role of technology in organizations. In addition, we will examine how organizations can radically re-design themselves with the assistance of technology.

LEARNING OBJECTIVES

By the end of the chapter, you should be able to:

1. Identify different types of innovation.
2. Understand the relationship between technological evolution and industry evolution.
3. Describe the key features of technology lifecycle models.
4. Discuss the concept of technological S-curves.
5. Examine business process redesign and its connection to technology.

THE BUSINESS WORLD

Print me a Stradivarius:
How a new manufacturing technology will change the world

The industrial revolution of the late 18th century made possible the mass production of goods, thereby creating economies of scale which changed the economy—and society—in ways that nobody could have imagined at the time. Now a new manufacturing technology has emerged which does the opposite. Three-dimensional printing makes it as cheap to create single items as it is to produce thousands and thus undermines economies of scale. It may have as profound an impact on the world as the coming of the factory did.

(Continued)

---

* I am grateful to Professor Eytan Lasry, York University, who co-authored this chapter.

It works like this. First you call up a blueprint on your computer screen and tinker with its shape and colour where necessary. Then you press print. A machine nearby whirrs into life and builds up the object gradually, either by depositing material from a nozzle, or by selectively solidifying a thin layer of plastic or metal dust using tiny drops of glue or a tightly focused beam. Products are thus built up by progressively adding material, one layer at a time: hence the technology's other name, additive manufacturing. Eventually the object in question—a spare part for your car, a lampshade, a violin—pops out. The beauty of the technology is that it does not need to happen in a factory. Small items can be made by a machine like a desktop printer, in the corner of an office, a shop or even a house; big items—bicycle frames, panels for cars, aircraft parts—need a larger machine, and a bit more space.

At the moment the process is possible only with certain materials (plastics, resins and metals) and with a precision of around a tenth of a millimetre. As with computing in the late 1970s, it is currently the preserve of hobbyists and workers in a few academic and industrial niches. But like computing before it, 3D printing is spreading fast as the technology improves and costs fall. A basic 3D printer, also known as a fabricator or "fabber", now costs less than a laser printer did in 1985.

Just Press Print

The additive approach to manufacturing has several big advantages over the conventional one. It cuts costs by getting rid of production lines. It reduces waste enormously, requiring as little as one-tenth of the amount of material. It allows the creation of parts in shapes that conventional techniques cannot achieve, resulting in new, much more efficient designs in aircraft wings or heat exchangers, for example. It enables the production of a single item quickly and cheaply—and then another one after the design has been refined.

For many years 3D printers were used in this way for prototyping, mainly in the aerospace, medical and automotive industries. Once a design was finalised, a production line would be set up and parts would be manufactured and assembled using conventional methods. But 3D printing has now improved to the point that it is starting to be used to produce the finished items themselves. It is already competitive with plastic injection-moulding for runs of around 1,000 items, and this figure will rise as the technology matures. And because each item is created individually, rather than from a single mould, each can be made slightly differently at almost no extra cost. Mass production could, in short, give way to mass customisation for all kinds of products, from shoes to spectacles to kitchenware.

By reducing the barriers to entry for manufacturing, 3D printing should also promote innovation. If you can design a shape on a computer, you can turn it into an object. You can print a dozen, see if there is a market for them, and print 50 more if there is, modifying the design using feedback from early users. This will be a boon to inventors and start-ups, because trying out new products will become less risky and expensive. And just as open-source programmers collaborate by sharing software code, engineers are already starting to collaborate on open-source designs for objects and hardware.

The Jobless Technology

A technological change so profound will reset the economics of manufacturing. Some believe it will decentralise the business completely, reversing the urbanisation that accompanies industrialisation. There will be no need for factories, goes the logic, when every village has a fabricator that can produce items when needed. Up to a point, perhaps. But the economic and social benefits of cities go far beyond their ability to attract workers to man assembly lines.

Others maintain that, by reducing the need for factory workers, 3D printing will undermine the advantage of low-cost, low-wage countries and thus repatriate manufacturing capacity to the rich world. It might; but Asian manufacturers are just as well placed as anyone else to adopt the technology. And even if 3D printing does bring manufacturing back to developed countries, it may not create many jobs, since it is less labour-intensive than standard manufacturing. . . .

. . . Just as nobody could have predicted the impact of the steam engine in 1750—or the printing press in 1450, or the transistor in 1950—it is impossible to foresee the long-term impact of 3D printing. But the technology is coming, and it is likely to disrupt every field it touches. Companies, regulators and entrepreneurs should start thinking about it now. One thing, at least, seems clear: although 3D printing will create winners and losers in the short term, in the long run it will expand the realm of industry—and imagination.

INNOVATION AND TECHNOLOGY

Types of Innovation

As our discussion of industry lifecycles suggested, technological innovation is a key driver of industry evolution. Radically new innovations or *technological discontinuities* can create entirely new industries as automobiles or wireless phones have done, or seriously disrupt existing ones such as jet engines in the aircraft industry or digital cameras in the photography industry. *Radical or breakthrough innovations* embody significantly new technical knowledge and represent a major departure from existing practices. They are often referred to as discontinuous (as opposed to continuous) innovations, given that they build on a new base of knowledge that discontinues the previous technological regime. The shift to jet engines in aircrafts did not build on or continue along the same technological trajectory laid out by propeller-based engines; it thrust the aircraft industry on an entirely new path. Digital cameras are discontinuous innovations in photography because they do not build on existing chemical photography technology and threaten to render obsolete the technological infrastructure of the industry based on film processing. *Incremental innovations*, on the other hand, make relatively minor changes or adjustments to existing practices. For example, having a larger, higher resolution colour screen on a cell phone represents an incremental improvement to the current technology. Making internal combustion engines in cars more fuel-efficient is another example.

Another way to classify innovations relates to the systemic nature of products and how their components interact. Most products can be thought of as a system of components that interact based on an architectural design in order to achieve a desired purpose. There are thus two aspects of systems here, the type and nature of the components, and how they are organized—the system's architecture. Innovations that involve changes to the product's components but leave the overall configuration of the system relatively intact are called *component or modular innovations*. Changes in the materials used in automobile bodies from steel to lighter-weight aluminum composites are component innovations. An innovation that alters the system's architecture or how the components interact and are linked with each other is an *architectural innovation*. Most architectural innovations, however, also require changes in the modules or components. A laptop computer is an architectural innovation given that it changes the standard configuration of a personal computer by making it portable, yet the components—microchip, operating system, keyboard, screen—remain essentially the same. Researchers have shown that organizations have a much more difficult time integrating and adapting to architectural innovations compared to modular innovations.

From an organizational perspective, it is useful to think of innovations in relation to an organization's skills and competencies. Technological innovations that build on a firm's existing knowledge and skills in certain areas are called *competence-enhancing*. Conversely, a *competence-destroying innovation* is one that renders obsolete an organization's technical skills and capabilities. A key point to remember is that whether a technological discontinuity is competence-enhancing or -destroying is often a matter of perspective. The same innovation can be competence-destroying to one organization and competence-enhancing to another, depending on their current knowledge base. Electronic calculators replaced slide rules as the tool of choice for engineers and mathematicians in the 1970s. This discontinuous innovation did not build on the knowledge of making slide rules and forced the largest U.S. slide rule manufacturer, Keuffel & Esser, out of the market. The calculator did, however, build on the electronics capabilities of firms like Hewlett-Packard (HP) and Texas Instruments (TI) that came to dominate the market. The calculator was thus competence-destroying for slide rule makers yet competence-enhancing for firms like HP and TI.

The Evolution of Technology

Joseph Schumpeter (1883–1950), an Austrian economist and professor at Harvard, was among the first to emphasize the role of technical progress and entrepreneurship as the driving forces of capitalist economies. In his work, he stressed the evolutionary and cyclical nature of industries that were periodically disrupted by the introduction of revolutionary innovations. In his most popular book, *Capitalism, Socialism and Democracy*, he coined the colourful, and now famous, expression of **creative destruction** to explain how innovations swept away old technologies, skills, products, ideas and industries and replaced them with new ones:

> …this process…that incessantly revolutionizes the economic structure from within, incessantly destroying the old one, incessantly creating a new one. This process of Creative Destruction is the essential fact about capitalism. It is what capitalism consists in and what every capitalist concern has got to live in.

In recent years, researchers have built on Schumpeter's ideas to further understand the process of technological innovation and evolution. The Abernathy-Utterback model, based primarily on their study of the automobile industry, forms the basis for most of the work that has followed on the technology lifecycle concept.[1] It states that technologies evolve from a fluid phase through a transitional phase to a specific phase (see Exhibit 4.1). When a new technology is initially introduced, it is still in a state of flux and there are a lot of technical as well as marketplace uncertainties. As the industry grows, a dominant design emerges and competition shifts from introducing new product features to meeting the needs of specific customers, which are by then well understood. A dominant design allows the standardization of parts and the optimization of organizational processes for volume and efficiency; therefore, in the specific phase, competition is based more on price than product features.

Anderson and Tushman build on this model to introduce the evolutionary notion of **punctuated equilibrium** to the study of industry evolution.[2] They study several industries over long periods and show that technological discontinuities tend to appear at rare and irregular intervals. These discontinuities trigger an *era of ferment*, a period of substantial product-class variation that ends with the emergence of a dominant design. Once a dominant design emerges, future technical progress consists of incremental improvements

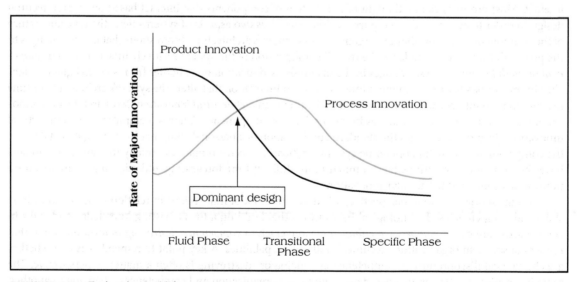

EXHIBIT 4.1 Technological lifecycle.

Source: Based on William J. Abernathy and James M. Utterback "Patterns of Industrial Innovation," *Technology Review* 80(7) (1978): 40–47.

elaborating the standard. The *era of incremental change* (usually coinciding with the industry maturity stage) is a much longer period of relative stability and equilibrium. These long periods of incremental change are punctuated by technological discontinuities, hence the reference to a punctuated equilibrium (see Exhibit 4.2).

Technological Forecasting

One of the problems with the Abernathy-Utterback and Anderson-Tushman models is that, while useful descriptions of technological evolution, they do not help in predicting when a discontinuity will occur. Although it is virtually impossible to accurately predict when a technological discontinuity will appear, we can make more informed analyses of technological trajectories using **S-curves**. Foster introduced the concept of the S-curve to explain the rate of advance of a technology.[3] (See Exhibit 4.3.) When a new technology emerges, progress starts off slowly, then increases very rapidly as the technology is better understood and firms pour more efforts into research and development. As the physical limits of the technology are reached and the returns to engineering efforts start to decrease, the rate of technical progress begins to diminish. A new technology able to overcome the physical limits of the old one will then trigger a new s-curve so that performance keeps improving with successive generations of S-curves. (See Exhibit 4.4).

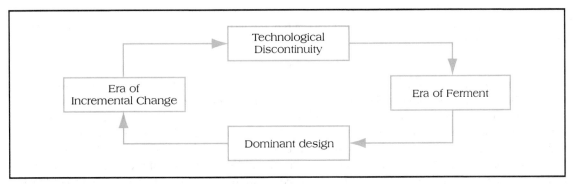

EXHIBIT 4.2   A cyclical model of technological change.

Source: Based on Phillip A. Anderson and Michael Tushman, "Technological discontinuities and dominant designs: A cyclical model of technological change," *Administrative Science Quarterly* 35 (1990): 604–633.

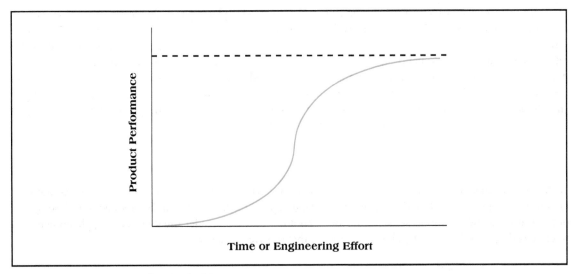

EXHIBIT 4.3   Foster's technological S-curve.

Source: Based on R. Foster, "The S-curve: A New Forecasting Tool," *Innovation, The Attacker's Advantage* (New York, N.Y.: Summit Books, Simon and Schuster, 1986), pp. 88–111.

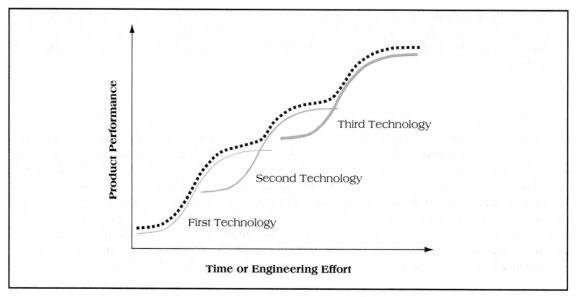

EXHIBIT 4.4 Successive S-curves.

Source: From Clayton M. Christensen, "Exploring the Limits of the Technology S-Curve," *Production and Operations Management* (1), 1992.

Technological progress of the last 30 years in the computer industry has been driven in large part by what has become known as Moore's law, for Intel co-founder Gordon Moore. In 1965, Moore predicted that the power and performance of microchips would double every 18 months as a function of semiconductor manufacturers' ability to double the number of transistors on a chip. This prediction has proven fairly accurate, and the rate of technical advance in microprocessor technology has in fact been exponential. These technological achievements are based on a strategy of continually shrinking the size of the transistors on chips so that electrons have less distance to travel, thereby speeding up the processing of data. As circuits get packed closer and closer on chips, however, they begin to overheat and performance suffers. This drop in performance signals that the current microchip technology is reaching the peak of its S-curve as the physical limits to shrinking transistor sizes are attained. In order for semiconductor firms like Intel and AMD to continue to generate performance improvements in line with Moore's law, a new technological discontinuity will have to replace the current strategy of miniaturization.

Several innovations are already in the works. One involves replacing a single high-speed processor with two or three that don't need to be as speedy, linked together on the same chip. A second, even more radical innovation entails stacking circuits in a three-dimensional manner and arranging chip functions vertically, rather than in a flat, horizontal design as current chips are configured. This technique promises to generate dramatic performance gains—some claim quantum leaps—and even reduce power consumption. Even though these innovations will require overhauling all the software running on chips and devising new methods for chip design and assembly, they may ultimately allow manufacturers to make the jump to the next technological S-curve and resume the phenomenal progress of Moore's law.

TECHNOLOGY & RE-ENGINEERING

Technology changes everything. If ever that statement was true, it is true for the world of business and how organizations operate. Much of the changes in the landscape of organizations can be credited to technology. In order to understand the fundamental power of technology, we can consider the longstanding phenomenon of re-engineering—a well entrenched business practice that is driven by technology.

What is Business Process Re-Engineering?

Re-engineering is a business buzzword that has been around for a long time. However, don't let that fool you. The ideology behind re-engineering continues to guide many business strategies. Where did this all start?

RE-ENGINEERING

A management consultant by the name of James Champy was asked to observe the operations of an insurance company in an effort to improve its efficiency. Among his observations, Champy discovered that it took 24 days to obtain a policy after the client purchased it. Champy was curious to understand what work was done on these insurance policies during the 24 days it took to reach the purchaser. After following the trail of these policies, Champy found that only about 10 minutes of work was actually performed on these policies during that 24-day period. The additional time arose because the policies were transferred through 14 different departments. Was this necessary? Champy discovered that while there was no real need for policies to travel through this long and winding road, it nevertheless had become a tradition: "This is how we do things here." There had been no assessment, however, of whether, indeed, this method was still necessary.

James Champy and one of his colleagues, Michael Hammer, engaged in many more observations of different types of organizations, and they, along with a number of other experts, advocated a rethinking of organizational design, detailed in their best-selling book, *Reengineering the Corporation*. Re-engineering became one of the hottest business buzzwords of the 1990s; but what exactly is it? Fundamentally, re-engineering asks the question, If I were creating this company today, if I could start over, given what I know and given current technology, what would it look like? A more systematic definition includes the following elements:

> The fundamental rethinking and radical redesigning of business processes to achieve dramatic improvements in measures of performance (cost, quality, service, speed).[4]

In examining the definition of *re-engineering,* we can understand its essence and its basic contributions to organizational design. Let's consider each element of this definition.

1. **Fundamental rethinking of the organization's structure and functions.** Re-engineering involves a critical examination of the traditional method of structuring work. An organization will examine how it performs its functions in order to assess whether, indeed, this method makes the most sense. This examination of work processes is done with a focus on how to best serve customer needs. Two fundamental questions that any re-engineering effort must ask are: "How do we improve quality of our product/service?" and "How can we reduce costs?" One central aim is to eliminate any company practice that is not adding value to the process of generating a product or service for the customer. The notion of focusing on the company's "core competencies" implies that the aim is to concentrate on what the company does best and eliminate unnecessary functions or practices.

2. **Radical redesign of organization processes and structure.** The thrust of re-engineering is to "re-invent" the organization according to the current objectives. Hammer and Champy suggested that a lot of organizations that claim they are making changes to become more efficient are really just trying to do "worthless tasks" more efficiently. What re-engineering advocates is a "quantum leap." However, it is important to note that while the radical redesign of an organization is the fundamental rationale behind re-engineering, it is difficult to achieve in practice.

Accomplishing the goal of redesign typically involves organizing around process rather than around functions. For much of the 20th century, beliefs about organizing focused on specializing jobs, compartmentalizing them into the simplest elements, therefore ensuring work was standardized (as advocated in scientific management and Weber's notion of bureaucracy). Re-engineering advocates the collection of individual tasks into more whole jobs. This relates to the distinction between process and functions. It is reflected in the notion of moving away from a focus on specialized tasks to a focus on process. Consider an example offered by Hammer and Champy, the case of a credit agency, in Talking Business 4.1.

The illustration reflects the notion of organization around process—in other words, designing the organization in a way that considers the actual jobs that need to be performed. This is in contrast to a blanket approach to organizational design that would simply advocate the creation of different departments that jobs will be organized in. Often the bureaucratic structure becomes preoccupied with administrative levels of hierarchy, rules and regulations. The machine bureaucracy and the professional bureaucracy are examples of these popular forms of organizational design. What re-engineering advocates is to move away from a preoccupation with organizing work based on tasks, jobs, departments and administrative levels of hierarchy, and instead to focus on processes—the activities required to transform inputs into outputs. This fundamental logic

Talking Business 4.1

The Credit Agency

This organization found that the task of processing a credit application was extremely slow and inefficient, taking anywhere from six days to two weeks to complete. After a credit request was received by phone it was recorded on a piece of paper. This paper was then passed along to credit checkers, pricers (who determined what interest rate to charge), and to many other individuals who performed single, compartmentalized tasks. Credit applications typically were bounced around to different areas before they were properly completed. Now after much scrutiny, it was discovered that the time actually required to complete such an application shouldn't take more than 90 minutes! Consequently, it was time to re-engineer—"scrap" the traditional method organized around specialized, compartmentalized tasks and redesign the work around the process itself of completing a credit application. This did not require numerous specialists but simply required a few generalists. That is, one person could process an entire application without passing it on to others. So this work was re-engineered, resulting in a decrease in the four-hour application time, an enormous increase in the number of applications processed and fewer employees required to do the job.

of re-engineering was recently observed, as shown in Talking Business 4.2, by management scholar William Kettinger.

With regard to the nature of the job, re-engineering also advocates combining several jobs into one. This, too, was reflected in the credit agency example above. This is akin to the notion of job enrichment: that is, enriching the responsibility and challenge of jobs by allowing workers to do more of the task rather than one narrow, highly specialized piece of the work. Certainly technology has helped facilitate the integration of jobs and the ability of fewer people to perform a greater variety of tasks. In fact, it has been observed that among the leading factors contributing to the proliferation of re-engineering activity in the early 1990s were

Talking Business 4.2

Lessons in Re-Engineering

Typically in an early lecture in one of my classes, I ask a student to come to the board and draw a picture of a company where she or he has worked. Inevitably, they draw a hierarchical organization chart—the student is typically on the bottom, and the bosses are on top. I respond that if this is a picture of a company, then where are the customers, and how do products and services get produced, delivered, and improved? This pushes them to draw a horizontal, or process-based representation, of the company which explains these relationships. Soon the board is covered with every conceivable business process—order fulfillment, product development, quality assurance, and on and on. These students quickly see that a business process is nothing more than logically related tasks that use the resources of a company to achieve a defined business outcome. This is a simple, but powerful, concept! Within a few classes, these students have internalized a process view (or "process think," as we refer to it) that helps them conceptualize new ways to improve operations, satisfy customers, and make the best use of the latest information technologies. Similar to the way these students learn process thinking, employees at all levels have grown to incorporate a process view into all aspects of their work. As process thinking has become mainstream, re-engineering has lost its radical tone. We have seen reconciliation with more incremental process change methods such as TQM. Today we recognize that we must broaden the business change tent to accommodate radical business objectives, incremental implementations, and both top-down-driven and bottom-up-driven process change.

Source: Reproduced with permission from Varun Grover, William J. Kettinger, and James T.C. Teng, "Business process change in the 21st century" *Business and Economic Review* (Jan.–Mar. 2000) 46(2): 14–18.

advances in information technology. Technologies including shared databases, client-server architecture and imaging could be efficiently applied to facilitate processes that cross different functional departments.[5]

The above suggests that re-engineering may result in the view that work can be performed efficiently with fewer employees. Typically, re-engineering means *cutting* the size of the workforce, and often involves flattening the organizational hierarchy. Examples abound, including organizations like Pepsi-Cola North America, which cut seven layers of its hierarchy to four in order to focus on designing itself around serving customers rather than simply maintaining a hierarchical bureaucracy. This also presents a major challenge for organizations attempting to re-engineer: the threat of job loss for many employees. Management scholar Varun Grover recently observed the following:

> Perhaps the biggest challenge associated with the success of the re-engineering phenomenon may be that of selling such a major change to the employees of the organization and getting them to "buy into" the strategic changes that must be undertaken for the firm to survive and prosper. For example, outsourcing activities that don't contribute to core competencies or technology to other firms that can perform them better may be a legitimate outcome of a good re-engineering effort. It would lead to work force reduction, but only with the purpose of making the firm leaner and more responsive. Time-based competition and the creation of "agile" corporations may not even be possible without such changes in work force size and composition. As companies emphasize the notion of capturing and leveraging "knowledge" as a source of value, a broader focus on process change management may perhaps be the only way to avoid skill obsolescence of employees and encourage horizontal career paths. The extent to which top level management can sell such a vision of change and its impact on the employees is critical. We found that often information technology problems are considered critical before the project, but it's the management of people and change that really makes the difference.[6]

TOWARD A VIRTUAL ORGANIZATION

If downsizing has become one of the most feared business buzzwords in recent years, a much more benevolent yet popular buzzword is the *virtual organization*. How does an organization become virtual? And equally important, Why would an organization want to become virtual? The virtual organization underscores how far we have come from the traditional notion of organizations. According to our old philosophy, the bureaucratic structure is typically large. The virtual organization, on the other hand, is not dependent on size for its functions. In fact, the virtual organization attempts to maximize its fluidity, flatness and integratedness with the environment—i.e., building off many of the structural trends we identified earlier. Let's consider the ways a virtual organization attempts to achieve these characteristics.

Outsourcing

Outsourcing (or contracting out) involves hiring external organizations to conduct work in certain functions of the company. For example, payroll, accounting and legal work can be assigned to outsourced staff. The organization typically will retain its core functions or competencies—that is, those areas that it is in business to conduct. In other words, it sticks to what it does best and outsources functions that it doesn't wish to focus on. While the buzzword *outsourcing* may seem relatively recent, the practice of outsourcing has, in fact, been with us for many years. Consider the extensive list of "suppliers" of expertise to industry—lawyers, public accountants, independent insurance adjusters, contractors, appraisers, health care professionals and independent medical specialists. Perhaps what is also more recent is the trend toward building businesses with a consideration of which activities are required "in-house" and which functions can simply be outsourced. For example, CIBC outsourced a major portion of its human resource administrative functions to Electronic Data Services (EDS). The move is consistent with the philosophy of outsourcing: shedding business activities that do not reflect the organization's core competencies. Obviously, managing human resource functions, such as payroll or pension plans, are not part of CIBC's core competencies. These functions can be outsourced to a company whose core competency is in such areas. EDS specializes in these areas. CIBC gains by having an expert company deal with these functions, and at the same time the company has cut costs through the elimination of almost half its human resources department.[7]

A good example of the potential benefits and, often, necessity of outsourcing is found in the popular trend of outsourcing the payroll function. There are a variety of reasons for choosing to outsource the payroll function, including dealing with increased human resource demands that may be caused by employee population growth, mergers, acquisitions, spinoffs, consolidations and downsizing. As Heather Erickson points out in a recent article, outsourcing can often be used to help in special or unique circumstances. As an illustration, Erickson offers a number of possible circumstances that have encouraged the outsourcing of the payroll function in Exhibit 4.5.

Networking

We have increasingly been observing organizations limiting themselves to fewer activities in which they have expertise and assigning specialists to handle all other functions. This is also associated with the notion of integrated or networked organizations that we identified earlier. That is, organizations can engage in co-operative relationships with suppliers, distributors or competitors. The aim is to improve their efficiency and flexibility in meeting new consumer needs. For example, a close relationship with a distributor might offer the supplier company more information about the changing needs of customers. The Japanese version of networked organizations called *keiretsu* could, in fact, really be considered the first form of the virtual organization.

Typically, a *keiretsu* involves a large bank or financial institution, a large industrial organization and a number of smaller firms. This integrated network of relationships allows the large industrial organization to produce the product with financial assistance from the bank. The role of the smaller firms may be to supply parts to the manufacturer, conduct research or, perhaps, distribute the final product. What we observe in virtual organizations are only those activities that are central—they are kept in-house, so to speak, and all other functions are outsourced to separate companies or individuals who are typically coordinated by a small head office. Or, each company is simply involved in some kind of network where each brings its own expertise to the collection of companies.

Shed Non-Core Functions

The outsourcing aspect, again, is a central feature of the virtual organization. Clearly, organizations can become more "virtual" by shedding some of their non-core functions and outsourcing these to affiliated organizations. Companies that use information technology (IT) need to become as flexible as the virtual organizations, given the rapidly changing face of technology and its applications. For organizations whose core competency is not IT or all its elements, there is much to be gained from partnering with other organizations, in the virtual sense.

---

1. **Mergers:** Following consolidation, the payroll function may be outsourced in order to permit the HR function and accounting function to focus on making changes that reflect the pay and benefit policies of the new corporation.
2. **Foreign acquisitions:** When a foreign buyer acquires a Canadian company, the unique nature of tax laws may not mix well with the new parent company's payroll system. Outsourcing the Canadian subsidiary payroll function avoids this conflict.
3. **Closing down a division:** In cases where a company is shutting down a division, complex severance packages paid over an extended period of time to a diverse group of former employees may be required. The demanding nature of these packages may not be efficiently dealt with by the internal payroll function, but may be better served by being outsourced to an external party while allowing the internal payroll department to focus on existing employee accounts.
4. **Confidentiality:** Salaries are typically a sensitive issue requiring high security. Some organizations may prefer to outsource the work done on particularly high security salaries, such as for senior executives, and on performance and incentive compensation plans in order to ensure that no organizational member becomes privy to this information.
5. **Entrepreneurial firms:** Small companies that are experiencing rapid growth in numbers of employees may find that outsourcing can offer a faster, more cost-effective way to manage the increasing demands of payroll. The outsourcing of the payroll function allows the business managers to focus on managing business growth and the core functions of the business rather than becoming preoccupied with the peripheral yet demanding function of payroll. For example, a small business that grows rapidly from three employees to 150 in 12 months found that when there were only the three owners to pay, writing cheques was easy. On the other hand, at 150 employees, the owners realized it was a function they no longer had time to manage. By outsourcing, the owners avoided hiring a full-time payroll person, and consequently the cost was much less than the cost of salary and benefits for a new full-time employee.

EXHIBIT 4.5 Outsourcing payroll: Why?

Source: Based on Heather Erickson, "Maybe organizational insider: Outsource payroll? Makes sense" *Canadian HR Reporter* (September 10, 2001) 14(15): G8.

A growing number of IT departments are considering outsourcing models to address all or part of their needs. "Small component" or discrete outsourcing service providers include such specialized offerings as storage and Web hosting. Application management has become a high-growth area in outsourcing service markets in Canada. Those seeking such services have a range of services to choose for outsourcing, including desktop or infrastructure services to various business functions. Network management can be outsourced, along with backup and recovery, as well as data centre services. Such examples are noted in Talking Business 4.3.

Talking Business 4.3

Outsourcing: You Can't Afford Not To

Matthew von Teichman

It's a Thursday morning, your business is a few months old, you've just made your first sales and things are looking bright.

You've got calls to make and deals to close. But you've also got bookkeeping to catch up on and mountains of administrative work. How do you prioritize?

Entrepreneurs have a tendency to tackle too much, to fulfill that overarching desire to make a new business succeed. A lack of capital to hire people, a fledgling idea and a stern resolve are all motivations to handle everything yourself.

But there is an alternative: Focus on what you're good at, and outsource everything else. That's right, outsource.

Most people are exceptional at certain functions, whether it be sales, administration, accounting or programming. But very few entrepreneurs are good at all of these things, or even most of them. Consider outsourcing non-core elements of the business to people who excel at them. You might think, "I can't afford to pay someone to manage my books," but the truth is you can't afford not to.

Your business will suffer if you spend your waking hours working on tasks you're neither interested in, nor good at. How much time do you waste trying to figure out how to use new accounting software when you could be out there developing your idea? Too much.

Try this: Establish a value for your time—let's say $40 an hour for the sake of argument. Then figure out how long it takes you to perform non-core elements of your business, in this case let's say 20 hours a week. In our example, that means you're wasting $800 a week on unproductive aspects of your business, elements that you hate.

How long do you think it would take an expert, and what would her rate be? Let's say she could do it in half the time but for twice as much money—it's the same variable cost outlay, right? Wrong. Think of the extra item you have to put into the core elements of your business, the elements you like to do. In an average week, you could have a far greater impact on your company by outsourcing a few functions, paying that $800, while driving the business forward by doing what you're good at.

And consider how much better and more productive you'll feel at the end of the week when you're only working on things you like to do. It's worth the $800 for your positive state of mind alone.

When I started my current business, I sat down and prioritized what I felt were core elements of the business that I should not outsource, such as product development, quality assurance and key account sales. Then I tried to outsource everything else. I ended up outsourcing manufacturing (a big one), storage, transportation, accounting and distribution. And to tell you the truth, it was easy.

Nowadays, there are specialists for just about everything you need, and they are not only ready to assist, that's all they do. I decided to use government resources (our tax dollars put to good use) to help me source some companies that could assist me. I was put in touch with food processors that could make my products, I was provided a list of transportation companies, public warehouses and distributors.

I used the web to find outsourced bookkeeping and other services I felt I would need. For the first two years, I was a team of one—with a lot of help from my wife—and a lot of outsourced brainpower and brawn. It took me a full two years to hire my first employee, and even now, I only have five full-time staff.

Building a business is hard enough. Don't bog yourself down by working on things you're not good at and don't like. Focus on your core competency and find good companies to expertly look after what you're weak in, and your business will be far better off, as will your state of mind.

A virtual organization might be composed of simply a small group of business executives who form the core of the organization. Their responsibility is to oversee and coordinate the activities that might be done in-house as well as those functions that are outsourced—which might involve coordinating relationships among the companies that develop, manufacture, market and sell their products. Many more companies have found that they can become quite profitable without actually having to own their entire operation. Certainly, the traditional bureaucracy is structured so that production occurs in company-owned plants; research and development are conducted by in-house experts; sales and marketing are performed by the company's own sales and marketing department. This is not the case for the virtual organization, which doesn't believe you need to own everything. For example, Dell Computer owns no plants, and simply assembles computers from parts whose manufacture has been outsourced. Similarly, Apple Computer subcontracted the manufacture of its first Notebook to Sony as a means to speed entry into the market. Companies like Nike and Reebok have achieved success by focusing on what they do best—designing and marketing their products. They outsource almost all their footwear manufacturing to outside suppliers. Obviously, the virtual organization doesn't just outsource the peripheral function of the company; it outsources whatever costs less than conducting it in-house. (See Talking Business 4.4.)

Talking Business 4.4

Yahoo's New Core Competency Seems to Be Outsourcing to Others

Matthew Ingram

Yahoo CEO Carol Bartz, after more than a year of looking at the company's operations, seems to have settled on a new business model—namely, outsourcing various parts of its sprawling web empire to other companies. Today saw two similar announcements: one has online dating site Match.com taking over Yahoo's personal classifieds service, and the second has mobile giant Nokia assuming command of a joint venture involving the web company's mobile email, chat and mapping services. In similar moves made earlier this year, Yahoo merged much of the operation of its health site with Healthline Networks and management of its online shopping service was effectively handed over to PriceGrabber.

In the Match.com pairing—the value of which wasn't disclosed by the companies—users of Yahoo's personals site will gradually be transitioned to something called "Match.com on Yahoo." The web service had been expected by some to sell the personals business outright, with analysts giving the unit an estimated value of $500 million. In the Nokia deal, meanwhile, the Finland-based mobile handset company will provide its mobile mapping technology for use in all of Yahoo's services, while Yahoo's email and chat will become the engine behind Nokia's new Ovi email and chat features.

On the one hand, outsourcing and partnering with others around some of its business units makes sense for Yahoo, where Bartz has been trying hard to rationalize its sprawling empire by cutting costs and improving its return on investment. At the same time, however, many of these deals seem to fall into the category of "too little, too late," as Kevin noted in his analysis of the Nokia deal. Like the company's most substantial outsourcing attempt of all—the multibillion-dollar deal with Microsoft to partner on search—they seem to be an admission that Yahoo has failed to make much of these businesses on its own, and is satisfied to simply take a small share of someone else's business in return.

So if it's no longer interested in trying to dominate search (at least, not by itself), and it doesn't want to own mobile in a major way, or be a controlling force in many of the things it used to want to do online (shopping, dating, health, etc.), then what does Yahoo want to do? It seems that the company has its heart set on doing the same thing that AOL—another former web star that has seen better days—wants to do: become a major media company. Yahoo, which has been hiring dozens of high-profile journalists to write for its expanding blog network and just bought a content company called Associated Content for $100 million, says it is now "the world's largest media company" and is betting its future on that status.

That may be an ambitious goal, but at least the company seems to know what it wants to be when it grows up, which is a start—although Bartz seemed less than precise about it in her interview with Mike Arrington at TechCrunch's Disrupt conference, in which she answered the question "What is Yahoo?" by saying it's a "great company that is very, very strong in content for its users. . . . it's a place where you can just get it together." What Bartz needs to do now is to find a way to put some meat on those bones, and to do that she's going to need more than just a talent for using expletives.

There are a number of *gains* potentially achieved by going virtual:

1. **The cost savings are significant.** A virtual organization need not own its own plants, nor employ its own research and development teams, nor hire its own sales staff. This means the virtual organization also doesn't need to hire the extra staff to support all these functions—such as personnel specialists, company lawyers, accountants, etc. The virtual organization can outsource most of these functions, and focus on what it does best. So there is little, if any, administrative overhead, so to speak, because work activities are largely contracted. Costs savings arise in areas such as training, purchasing of work-related tools, benefits, downtime and educational requirements. All of these requirements are typically obtained with the arrival of the external or "outsourced" experts.
2. **The virtual organization is a great alternative for entrepreneurs.** That is, individuals seeking to start up a new business or venture may face huge startup costs. The network of arrangements can exploit the expertise of different companies while not requiring the initiator of the business to buy everything and start a business from scratch.
3. **For a mature company, going virtual can be a fast way to develop and market new products.** Relying on the expertise of partners means that no huge investment is required to enter a new product or service territory.
4. **Fast and flexible are adjectives to describe the virtual organization.** The flexible arrangements of those parties involved can be of a temporary nature to produce a good or service. Resources can be quickly arranged and rearranged to meet changing demands and best serve customers. Management isn't getting bogged down in peripheral functions, but is simply focusing only on central functions.

Among the *risks and challenges* of becoming virtual are the following:

1. **Probably the biggest sacrifice is the notion of control.** Control has traditionally been a key goal of any organization. The structure of the bureaucratic organization is fundamentally based on the notion of control—control through standardization of work, control through hierarchy of authority, control through rules and regulations, control through clear division of labour. However, the virtual organization doesn't provide such control. Think of it—how can you monitor all activity when it may not even be occurring within the walls of one building? Among the fears of going virtual and outsourcing is that we are "hollowing out" the organization and making it extremely dependent on external sources. The employees are not all ours; outsourcing to independent contractors doesn't carry with it the same level of control as staffing our own employees to do the work. Difficulties in control can particularly occur when a variety of subcontractors are involved in the work. This lack of control may also generate a lack of control over costs—once a company becomes dependent on a supplier, it may be unable to refuse an increase in the supplier's prices.
2. **Another potential disadvantage is the lack of employee loyalty.** If our organization is largely composed of temporary workers and subcontractors, who is really committed to perpetuating the goals of this company? Can a virtual organization really develop a sense of identity or culture that is the "glue" that binds everyone to a common purpose? This is an issue that virtual organizations must deal with. In fact, turnover in many virtual organizations tends to be high, because employees are committed only to the task for which they are hired, and in addition, employees may be working under temporary contractual arrangements and could be dismissed in favour of another contractor.
3. **A final significant risk in going virtual is the potential to sacrifice competitive learning opportunities.** Outsourcing involves the strategic decision to "let go" of some aspect of the organization—the decision could be to permit the manufacture of the footwear, as in the case of Nike, while retaining the core competencies (such as the marketing function, also, as in the case of Nike). The question is, Is there a danger in "letting go" of functions that may currently appear peripheral, but could become important functions of the organization should the organization's strategy change in the future? Clearly, if a function is outsourced, the experience or learning of this function as a skill is lost to the internal organization. Is there an inherent danger in such a situation? That is, Is there a danger in outsourcing, given the risk of losing key skills that could be needed for future competitiveness? Read Talking Business 4.5 for the risks of outsourcing.

Talking Business 4.5

The Hidden Dangers of Outsourcing

Freek Vermeulen

Outsourcing is one of those words that have become hideously fashionable in corporate lingo in the last 5 to 10 years. A business cynic—which obviously I am not!—might conjecture that perhaps it is popular because it appeals to some fundamental human desires for shirking and procrastination, finally telling managers "to stop doing certain stuff" rather than always pushing them "to do more". I, as a more thoughtful business observer, on the contrary, think that outsourcing often makes sense, simply because you cannot, and should not try to do everything yourself. Other companies can sometimes do a particular thing better and more efficiently than you, if alone because they can bundle and specialise in it, and then you're better off buying it from them.

Some companies take it a bit far though… Some time ago I was talking to a senior executive of a major airline and they actually had the idea that in the future they might be able to get rid of all their staff, facilities, pilots, planes, and so forth, and concentrate on "being the director of the chain"; that is, not actually do anything but tie together all the activities conducted by others. Hence, outsource everything except for the coordination between all the parts. Well… here is my opinion: You can forget about that. Try that, and it won't be long before nobody needs you anymore.

The classic example of that is IBM's PC in the 1980s. It was IBM's plan to outsource everything, add its brand name and just one little microchip connecting all the PC's ingredients. They outsourced the PC's microprocessors to some geeky guys who owned one of those founded-in-a-garage little companies in Palo Alto (the little company's name was Intel) and the operating system to yet another geeky guy with big glasses heading a founded-in-a-garage little company in Seattle (the geeky guy's name was Billy Gates), in the process provoking the genesis of the most powerful alliance the world of business has ever witnessed: Wintel (Windows and Intel).

Because following in IBM's footsteps towards Palo Alto and Seattle were all the other computer manufacturers which copied the PC; hence buying their microprocessors from Intel and their operating system from Microsoft. And not for long, Intel, Microsoft and end users alike could not quite remember why they needed IBM in the first place and completely "disintermediated" them. It was Intel and Microsoft that reaped the great big benefits of the booming computer market and not grandfather Big Blue IBM, which ended up in a severe crisis as a result of it.

Hence, be careful with outsourcing; giving up control might get you more than you bargained for (especially if it concerns geeky guys in a garage).

Source: The Hidden Dangers of Outsourcing, www.freekvermeulen.com.

TECHNOLOGY AND THE CHANGING WORKPLACE: IMPLICATIONS FOR THE JOB CONTEXT

The relationship of employees and organizations has been undergoing tremendous change and will continue to do so. A number of authors, including Jeremy Rifkin in his book entitled *The End of Work*, have talked about how the nature of work itself is changing. That is, the nature of work or the type of work we will perform in the future may be dramatically different from that we did for most of the 20th century. It is argued that the job itself is becoming an artifact, and the task of organizations is to create the "post-job" organization.

How will the job disappear, and why should organizations shift away from jobs? Well, though this sounds mystifying, much of this can be understood in the context within which we have explained many of the changes to organizational design. To clarify, the authors are not actually referring to disappearing jobs in terms of the number of jobs lost or job losses in certain industries, but rather the very notion of the job itself is becoming outdated. In the future, certainly, people will continue to work, but not within the familiar envelopes that we call jobs. And in fact, many organizations are already becoming "de-jobbed" (see Talking Business 4.6).

Rifkin argues that what we think of as a job is really a social artifact. That is, it is based on an idea that emerged in the late 19th century to package the work that needed to be done in the growing factories and

Talking Business 4.6

Nothing to Fear From Teleworking

Danny Bradbury

How many people today work entirely in the office on a 9–5 basis? As mobile data services enable workers to plug into their office from anywhere, more of us are beginning to work on the road, or from home. The challenge for organizations lies in ensuring we can do it properly, deliver on our goals and avoid losing control of employees.

According to the latest Statistics Canada data, 1.4 million employees in this country work at home at least part of the time. Hopefully, as mobile data plans from Canadian carriers become more liberal that will increase, but it already represents a significant portion of the population.

"Mobile work is here to stay. It goes hand in hand with the revolution in information technology," says Robert Fortier, president of the Canadian Telework Association. "Until someone destroys all things digital, it will continue to grow."

Mr. Fortier argues that the benefits to teleworking far outweigh the potential challenges. "By improving their capability to attract employees who look for flexible work, it helps organizations on the recruitment side, and it also helps avoid turnover," he says.

Then, there are the potential business continuity benefits involved in teleworking. If an epidemic such as SARS or H1N1 flu hits us again, and forces people to stay at home for health reasons, then they may be able to continue operating the business successfully from their homes. For companies that have effectively implemented teleworking as best practice, transit strikes will present no significant problems for corporate productivity.

However, a whole generation of middle management is used to a "line of sight" approach, where they can see a worker is at their desk. The idea of managing teleworkers remotely can be daunting. It can seem like they are relinquishing control. If a worker is out of the office, then how do you know they are working?

"A manager that has not been properly briefed or assessed can do a lot of harm to a pilot program," warns Linda Russell, managing partner of Telecommuting Consultants International, which helps clients implement telework and virtual office programs.

It is important to pick those managers and workers that are open to the idea at the start, she says. "Anywhere between five and seven managers in 10 can be reasonably comfortable with members of their staff teleworking at the start, and if it works out well, then a significant proportion can start to do it."

For companies already operating their business in a sophisticated way, the transition to teleworking shouldn't be too painful. Ideally, companies will not be measuring productivity by how many hours an employee spends at his desk. Rather, they will be applying more meaningful productivity metrics. How many customers did that employee help satisfactorily on the phone that day? How many Web forms did they process?

Measuring the basics that you would measure with any worker—quality, quantity and output—should be enough to show how productive teleworking staff are, Ms. Russell says. It is important not to let fear of losing control force managers and workers into untenable positions. "You can measure these things, but sometimes what happens is teleworkers end up getting measures to within an inch of their lives."

Generally, teleworking is not an all-or-nothing practice, Mr. Fortier says. In an ideal situation, teleworkers work from home or on the road a set number of hours a week, but come into the office to work and interact with managers for the rest of the time. This gives them a healthy balance, as well as the flexibility they crave while ensuring they don't feel too isolated. It can also lead to a situation where companies need less rented office space, because not all of their employees will be in the office all the time.

That gentler approach to teleworking, in which employees maintain regular physical contact with the office, could be a reassuring model for the more wary managers who are used to facetime with staff. And of course, managers would themselves be expected to practice what they preach. Somehow, managing a distributed workforce might seem all the more attractive when you do it at least a couple of days a week from home, checking in online over toast and coffee, rather than enduring the regular morning commute.

bureaucracies of industrialized societies. Before that time, people worked just as hard, but at shifting clusters of tasks, depending on the needs of the day. In a sense, Taylor and scientific management helped build our concept of jobs—as compartmentalized, specialized tasks that we are trained to perform. However, the conditions that created this notion of the job have changed dramatically over 200 years: mass production and large bureaucratic organizations are vanishing.

Technology allows us to automate the assembly line, so masses of unskilled labour are much less needed. Large firms are outsourcing much of their activities, as we discussed earlier. So, given that the conditions under which jobs were created have changed, we are redefining not just organizational structure, but also how work should be performed—not in the traditional jobs that led our thinking for most of the 20th century.

If you consider some of the issues we identified in this chapter, virtual organizations, re-engineering, outsourcing—it is understandable that with so much change occurring around us, clearly the very nature of the type of work we perform within these organizations must also somehow be changing! For example, in place of full-time jobs, we are seeing more and more temporary and part-time work situations. That is simply one manifestation of a greater underlying change: the fact is, organizations are essentially moving away from a structure built for the performance of jobs into simply a field of work needing to be done. In other words, the specialization or division of labour encouraged us to become preoccupied with filling jobs and positions rather than simply focusing on performing the work that needs to be done.

In a relatively stable environment, rigid jobs are fine for performing the work; however, the increasingly dynamic nature of our environment seems to almost continuously require new skills and new combinations of work; a philosophy that is wedded to a "jobs mentality" is simply too slow to adapt. This is the new, post-job, world.

Fast-moving organizations like Google, Microsoft and Intel understand the need for flexibility. Here, an individual is hired and assigned to a project. This project changes over time and, consequently, the person's responsibilities and work change with it. Of course, this person may also be assigned to other projects requiring other responsibilities and skills. Getting work done efficiently within these evolving projects requires skilled project teams, not a formal hierarchy of authority with masses of workers who are working under a formal job description. No supervisor, nor any job description, can sufficiently guide a worker through these continually changing projects.

CHAPTER SUMMARY

We have considered the role played by technological innovation in the shaping of industry evolution. We have identified different models for the evolution of technology and discussed some tools for predicting the path of technological progress. This chapter also examined a significant consequence of technology on business process. Specifically, we discussed business process re-engineering and how it has been re-shaping the nature of business and work for many years now.

CONCEPT APPLICATION

P&G AND HP OUTSOURCING

Outsourcing Deal Gives P&G Clout with HP

Patrick Thibodeau

When executives at The Procter & Gamble Co. seek answers from the company's IT outsourcer, Hewlett-Packard Co., they don't have to deal with help desks, trouble tickets or support tiers.

Instead, they most likely work directly with someone in the top levels of HP's executive ranks.

The Cincinnati-based consumer product maker's clout with HP might make some of the latter's other customers a bit jealous, but the two corporations are in the midst of a 10-year, $3 billion mega-outsourcing deal that carries high stakes for the bottom lines of both parties.

The contract, signed in 2003, called for HP to take over P&G's IT infrastructure and hire some 2,000 of the company's IT workers.

In a presentation at *Computerworld's* Premier 100 IT Leaders Conference here earlier this month, Jim Fortner, vice president of IT development and operations at P&G's business services division, said constant communication between executive suites is imperative in such large and costly deals.

For instance, Ann Livermore, executive vice president of HP's enterprise business, travels to P&G headquarters about six times a year to take part in a joint review of the vendor's performance. HP CEO Mark Hurd attends those meetings about twice a year.

"[HP executives] are wired into our business," Fortner said. "When you have the CEO of a company sitting across the table saying, 'We're going to deliver this,' you know they're going to deliver."

Maintaining close relationships with all of its IT vendors has long benefited P&G, particularly when it bought Gillette in 2005 for $57 billion. Within two weeks, P&G's partners had assembled a team to start integrating Gillette's IT systems.

Robert Joslin, an analyst at Everest Group, a Dallas-based outsourcing research and consulting firm, said having access to top executives is "extremely critical to the success of an outsourcing relationship." In fact, the contract should stipulate that specific executives of the service provider will meet regularly with senior managers from the client firm.

The level of access to a vendor's senior executives will depend to some extent on the size of the contract and its strategic importance to both parties, but "you do try to go up as high as you can," said Joslin.

Top-level access "increases the probability that it will be a successful relationship for both parties," he noted.

Therefore, he contended, you should make decisions about when meetings will be held and who should attend before a contract is signed.

At P&G, having HP manage the IT infrastructure allows data center personnel to focus on other tasks. They're currently developing tools designed to simulate the in-store tendencies of potential customers. Simulation "is really big for us," said Fortner.

For example, the company has created a Second Life-like environment where users can interact virtually with simulated displays of products on store shelves; they can even take items off the shelves and read their labels. The simulations are coupled with back-end analytics to assess the impact of changes to displays.

Questions:

1. Discuss core competencies of P&G and HP, and which roles these companies play in outsourcing.
2. What are the potential benefits and risks of P&G in this outsourcing arrangement?
3. What are other ways P&G can become more "virtual"?

The Labour Context

What do you know about the nature of the labour pool in Canada? Are you familiar with how it has been changing? Do you know how the interests of the labour pool can be protected in the workplace? These questions are addressed in a two-fold manner in this chapter. First, we will examine the issue of demographic diversity in the workplace and the fundamental issues it raises. Second, given that many businesses operate within a unionized context, it is important to understand the role and function of labour unions. Consequently, this chapter also explores the issue of industrial relations and specifically how unions can impact both organizations and society.

LEARNING OBJECTIVES

By the end of this chapter, you should be able to:

1. Consider the influence of diversity on business.
2. Discuss the rationale behind and the implications of the identification of designated groups.
3. Describe the workings of employment equity.
4. Identify different kinds of union actions.
5. Examine the impact of unions on business and society.

THE BUSINESS WORLD

Canada's labour pool

Canada's labour pool can be a strange beast for the country's employers. During the recent recession, unemployment and a lack of hiring was the main concern as businesses struggled to cut costs. However, with the recovery taking hold globally, an old problem is creeping back: labour shortages.

"The labour shortage dipped after the recession, and the availability of labour improved," said Dan Kelly, senior vice-president of legislative affairs for the Canadian Federation of Independent

Business. "But even in the depths of the recession, a third of small and medium-sized businesses said they struggled to find the employees needed to put out their products and services."

That was the bottom in 2009, but since then labour shortage concerns have steadily been creeping up, Mr. Kelly said. He expects companies will likely see the return of a slew of labour shortage worries that plagued many in 2007 and 2008. "Many of the patterns we saw then are starting to re-emerge," he said.

Before the financial crash that sent global stocks tumbling, Canadian businesses had gone on a hiring spree. The phenomenon was particularly pronounced in Alberta, where energy giants increasingly expanded their operations, and began hiring more and more workers. And for good reason. Oil was rushing to a record price of US$147 a barrel in the summer of 2008, and companies were scrambling to pump out more of it.

Small businesses, which are often sources of jobs for new entry workers, found more experienced and skilled workers leaving for the oil sands and large energy companies.

Many Atlantic provinces, in particular, saw their youth head west, creating a labour vacuum in the process.

Some businesses have adapted to Canada's ever-changing labour realities. Ganong Bros. Ltd. for example, looked to overseas labour pools to fill its employee shortage. In 2005, management at the chocolate maker's factory in St. Stephen, N.B.—a town just shy of 5,000 people— realized they needed about 30 additional employees after a year of big contracts.

First, Ganong attempted to make working at the company more appealing by increasing hourly wages. It even created a workplace survey to gauge satisfaction. But, it soon became apparent the labour realities of the region they were in were too complex to be solved with perks.

Sherri Deveau, human resources director for Ganong, said the idea for bringing in foreign workers was first suggested by the provincial government's Population Growth Secretariat. "They suggested we look to Romania as a potential source of new employees, given that there were many similarities between New Brunswick and that country," she said. "The climate was similar, the religion was similar, and many Romanians learn English as a second language."

A few months later, Ms. Deveau flew to Romania to interview 100 candidates, eventually hiring 30. And while the subsequent relocation and adjustment to foreign workers was not easy—Ganong helped each of them find homes in the community—the experiment has been a huge success for the company.

Nicole Picot, assistant deputy minister for the New Brunswick Population Growth Secretariat, said other companies in the province are looking to Ganong's success and have expressed a desire to mimic its model. "We go to other countries as well, but there has been some success in co-operating with Romania," she said.

Anil Verma, professor of industrial relations and human resource management at the University of Toronto, contends Canada's labour problems go far beyond labour shortage. In many cases, businesses can't bring in overseas workers to fix their problems.

In such cases, he said, the onus might be on the employer to make sure they are fostering the kind of work environment people want to work in.

"Employers need to do more—you can't just sit at your desk and expect people will be lined up outside begging for jobs," he said.

Vancouver-based Kloth recently moved its manufacturing facility to Port Alberni, B.C., a resource-based community wracked by wood mill closures. And while its presence hasn't solved all of Port Alberni's problems, the idea behind a business taking advantage of an excess labour pool by moving shop could have legs.

(Continued)

Fashion designer Lara Presber chose to sign a contract with Kloth to manufacture her line of clothing at the Port Alberni facility, because the company's model fit her idea of sustainable, locally produced products.

"I love what they are doing because it aligns with my personal and company values and am so happy to be a part of it," she said.

CFIB's Mr. Kelly said the businesses he has spoken to all have different suggestions to tackling labour issues in Canada, many of which fall in between the approaches taken by Ganong and Kloth.

He said the key is to ensure that a multi-faceted approach is taken to address the problem.

"None of the answers are easy," he said. "But there are a few we think are important. One of those is to provide some form of skillbuilding credit under employment insurance, so we're actually advocating a hiring and training credit for small and mediumsized companies."

Mr. Kelly also said the CFIB strongly believes that using the temporary worker system for businesses in Canada could provide one of the biggest overall solutions in tackling labour challenges like shortages.

"This is absolutely something we should be leveraging," he said.

UNDERSTANDING THE IMPLICATIONS OF A DIVERSE WORKFORCE

Canadian business operates within a diverse society. The Canadian population reflects a multitude of cultures and demographic backgrounds. Women comprise a significant component of the Canadian labour force and account for about half of both the employed work force and all union members. Visible minorities and people with disabilities, together with women, make up over 60 percent of Canada's labour force. Recent census figures provided by Statistics Canada show that over 5 million Canadian citizens were foreign-born, comprising nearly 20 percent of the total population. This diversity is increasingly reflected in the Canadian labour pool.

Diversity in our work force is also reflected in the growing presence of older workers. At the start of the twenty-first century, Canadians 37–55 years old made up about 47 percent of the labour force. Given the existence of an aging society and forecast labour shortages in almost every sector across Canada, recruiting workers from all groups of society is critical. Consequently, it is clear that organizations must attend to the rights of a diverse group of individuals.

Immigrants who came to Canada in the 1990s have accounted for approximately 70 percent of the total growth of the labour force in recent years. Dr. Jelena Zikic, Professor of Human Resource Management at York University, has extensively researched issues surrounding the immigrant labour pool and its implications for business and society. Below is an outline of some of the key findings.

The Immigrant Labour Pool

Recent immigrants have accounted for 70% of Canada's net growth in the labour force during the past decade. It is expected that within the next few years all net labour force growth will come from immigration. Canada is seen as the model nation for highly skilled immigrant policies, offering all potential newcomers access through human capital-based evaluations of their immigrant applications. Those admitted are further supported by Canada's progressive, diverse and multicultural society. Canada's selection of skilled migrants derived from human capital theory favours individuals who are thought to be adaptable and so who have general skills and experience (i.e., certain level of education/credentials) as opposed to looking for specific skills in market demand.

This recent wave of immigration is becoming vitally important for Canada's economic growth, particularly for the growth of Ontario where almost half of the immigrants end up residing. The government faces, however, a major associated challenge, as many of these immigrants encounter serious issues and barriers in their search for employment and successful pursuit and continuation of their careers in Canada.

Immigrant workers are less likely to experience continued career success because they face longer periods of unemployment than Canadian born workers and when employed, they are often underemployed, working at jobs below their skill levels, and earning lower wages than the Canadian-borns. Moreover, underutilization of immigrant professionals (IPs) as a result of non-recognition of their credentials and discounting of their foreign experience also imposes significant costs upon the Canadian economy.

Ironically, immigrants with more foreign labor market experience tend to work in lower-paying occupations. Labour economists in particular suspect that this is due to local employers' being unsure how to value the foreign experience. These kinds of barriers not only prevent individual immigrants from finding satisfactory employment and pursuing successful careers, they also entail specific psychological problems and adaptation difficulties for immigrants and their families.

Local government and related institutions are becoming more concerned for the underemployment of immigrants and the associated costs to Canadian economy. As a result, various local institutional and governmental agencies and services have been put in place to help newcomers in the adjustment and career transition to Canada. In Canada for example, different levels of government are asked to establish coordination between each other and provide information and support in immigrant job search. Several such partnerships have been created to bring together various stakeholders and to focus on addressing underemployment of immigrant professionals. Many of these local institutions can potentially alleviate the barriers to labour market entry, and start informing and educating potential migrants even prior to their arrival.

In regards to language training, the government has been promoting general language training for some time. However, there is a call to provide language and cultural communication training, focusing more on understanding cultural differences in communication. Furthermore, training programs, especially those which include some form of mentoring, bridging, apprenticeships, or internships are found to be making a positive impact on individuals career transition. Many of these programs, in addition to bringing migrants closer to potential jobs in their field, are intended to help achieve more effective job search as well. Bridging programs and internships are also geared towards allowing for better and faster socialization into a particular occupation in Canada.

DIVERSITY AS STRATEGY

Given the diversity of the population, organizations have come to realize that diverse workplaces are also "good business". For example, consider the case of IBM. Today it is the role model of diversity but this was not always the case. Part of IBM's successful turnaround, led by CEO Lou Gerstner (see Talking Business 5.1), in the 1990's was due to a greater recognition of the value of diversity.

As one writer noted:

When most of us think of Lou Gerstner and the turnaround of IBM, we see a great business story. A less-told but integral part of that success is a people story—one that has dramatically altered the composition of an already diverse corporation and created millions of dollars in new business. By the time Gerstner took the helm in 1993, IBM already had a long history of progressive management when it came to civil rights and equal employment. Indeed, few of the company's executives would have identified workforce diversity as an area of strategic focus. But when Gerstner took a look at his senior executive team, he felt it didn't reflect the diversity of the market for talent or IBM's customers and employees. To rectify the imbalance, in 1995 Gerstner launched a diversity task-force initiative that became a cornerstone of IBM's HR strategy. . . . By deliberately seeking ways to more effectively reach a broader range of customers, IBM has seen significant bottom-line results. For example, the work of the women's task force and other constituencies led IBM to establish its Market Development organization, a group focused on growing the market of multicultural and women-owned businesses in the United States.[1]

Talking Business 5.1

Global Giant IBM Corporation Remains a Diversity and Inclusion Trailblazer

Michael Rainey

IBM, a multinational computer, technology and IT consulting corporation, stands as one of the world's largest technology companies and ranks as one of the top global brands (some recent surveys have IBM as No. 1). In addition to being a leader in the technology industry, IBM has also been a leader in its commitment to diversity and inclusion and its implementation of such policies long before Affirmative Action laws were enacted in the 1960s. In fact, IBM hired its first female employee in 1899, its first African-American employee just a few years later, and its first employee with a disability in 1914. To say that the company was ahead of the curve on these issues would be a gross understatement.

Lisa Gable is a 22-year IBM veteran who was recently named U.S. Diversity Recruiting Manager. Prior to this role, Gable was the IBM Global Women's Initiatives Program Manager, responsible for the development and advancement of women throughout the IBM Corporation. I spoke with her on the second day of her new position and she was in the process of expanding her knowledge of what IBM is doing in the recruiting space. Her initial plan is to step back and look at what the company is doing today and then go over the numbers and objectives to see if there's anything else that can be done to help the company reach its goals as they pertain to diversity hiring.

Gable was quite successful in her previous role as the Global Women's Initiatives Program Manager. She is proud of the fact that 29 percent of IBM's total workforce is comprised of women, although she still sees room for improvement in that number. Gable hopes to put her expertise in developing initiatives to use in helping increase the overall diversity at IBM within the United States.

"We have a wide array of diversity initiatives in place already, and we work with a number of external organizations in addition to our internal efforts," Gable said. "In my new role I intend to see if we can better marry the two as it pertains to recruiting. We source talent from all over the globe and we have a very diverse workplace already. Our intent is to continue to grow IBM's diverse workforce."

There is no doubt today that most businesses recognize the need to harness the power of a diverse work force in order to succeed. And understanding the diverse nature of the working population, must consider the different dimensions of diversity (see Talking Business 5.2). In addition to race, ethnicity, gender, there are other dimensions such as age.

Over the next 30 years, people aged over 60 will grow by 50% and the number of adults between the ages of 20 years–59 years will fall by 6%. Specifically, the numbers of those aged 20–29 will decrease by nine million. All this indicates that there will be a constant decrease of the working population coinciding with the ageing workforce.[2] Statistics Canada reported that in 2006, the median age of the workforce surpassed the 40-year mark for the first time with about two million workers between the ages of 55 and 64.

What are some of the implications for business regarding these changes in the labour context? Clearly, as the population ages, employers will need to retain older members for a longer period of time. As early as 2005, reports such as that generated by the American Association of Retired Persons (AARP) indicated that two thirds of workers plan to keep working part-time or full-time beyond age 65.[3] Given the increased economic challenges since that time, this trend has certainly taken off.[4] This pattern will be further propelled by shifts in retirement policies and the abolition of mandatory retirement in many industrialized countries.

The need to retain older workers will have many implications for workplace policy and practice. One fundamental change will occur in management attitudes—specifically the need to abolish the practice of age discrimination or ageism. While advocates of diversity have long argued for the benefits of an integrated diverse workplace, employers have nonetheless been typically reluctant to hire older workers. It appears this resistance to age diversity will need to change.

Talking Business 5.2

Bombardier: Giving Women Wings

Gail Johnson

Bombardier Aerospace is one of the world's largest producers of civil aircraft, with nearly 17,000 full-time employees in Canada. But its areas of engineering and manufacturing traditionally haven't attracted many women.

The company is out to change that.

"We've broadened our strategy to increase diversity, with having more women throughout the organization as a top priority," says Elisabeth Bussé, director of leadership development and talent management at the Dorval, Que.-based organization, a division of Montreal's Bombardier Inc. BBD.B-T. "Increasing diversity is a business strategy: We want our employees to be representative of the community in which we do business."

Women have made up two-thirds of the recent growth in the Canadian work force, climbing from 35 per cent in the 1970s to 50 per cent in 2005, according to the book *Organizational Behavior: Managing People and Organizations.* Following its inaugural two-day Women in Leadership Forum in Montreal in 2010, Bombardier Aerospace set a goal to increase the percentage of women in management positions from the current 16 per cent to 25 per cent by next year.

Expanding diversity while recruiting top talent with specialized skills is a challenge for any company. But Bombardier Aerospace has turned an obstacle into opportunity by taking a diverse approach.

For example, its Women in Leadership Program, which aims to get women into the company's talent acceleration pool (TAP). The proportion of women in the TAP program reached 30 per cent in 2010.

To continue to broaden the scope of an inclusive workplace—Bombardier Aerospace employees currently represent 40 nationalities—it collaborates with PROMIS (Promotion, Intégration, société nouvelle), a non-profit organization that promotes the integration of immigrants and refugees into Quebec society.

Then there is the common-sense marketing strategy of raising the profile of female leaders such as Julie Brulotte, an aerospace mechanical engineer and project manager of the C-Series, a new commercial aircraft. She and others participate in career fairs at universities, colleges and even high schools.

"We want to show young women that working as an engineer at Bombardier doesn't have to just be a dream but is a reality," says Stephane Pelletier, senior director of talent acquisition and human resources.

Ms. Brulotte acknowledges she has a role in encouraging more women to pursue a career in engineering. And although she's far outnumbered by her male peers, she's never felt in any way a minority.

"If you're competent, that's all that matters," says Ms. Brulotte, a mother of three whose father was an engineer. "It's important to lead by example, for young women to see for themselves that they don't have to make a choice between having a family and being an engineer. . . ."

Source: *The Globe and Mail.*

THE LEGAL CONTEXT FOR DIVERSE WORKPLACES

A significant portion of our valued labour pool is derived from members of **designated groups** whose participation in the workplace contributes to the success of an organization. With regard to past discrimination, there are four groups in Canada that traditionally have not received equitable treatment in employment: women, Aboriginal peoples, visible minorities, and people with disabilities. Exhibit 5.1 identifies their relative presence in the population and the labour pool. Ironically, while these groups represent 60 percent of the total work force, they have historically been denied fair treatment at work. These designated groups have faced significant obstacles related to their status in the labour force, including high unemployment, occupational segregation, pay inequities, and limited opportunities for career advancement. We have come to expect that organizations will help address the challenges faced by these groups.

EXHIBIT 5.1 Fact sheet on members of designated groups, Canada, 2006.

	Both Sexes	Males	Females
Total Population	31,241,030	15,326,265	15,914,760
Population Representation	100.0%	49.1%	50.9%
15 years and over	25,664,220	12,470,770	13,193,430
Workforce	18,418,100	9,599,250	8,818,855
Workforce Representation	100.0%	52.1%	47.9%
In Labour Force	17,146,135	9,020,595	8,125,540
Participation Rate	66.8%	72.3%	61.6%
Unemployment Rate	6.6%	6.5%	6.6%
Employment/Population Ratio	62.4%	67.6%	57.5%
Earnings (Full-Time, Full-Year)	$ 51,221	$ 58,537	$ 41,331
Earnings (Female/Male)	N/A	N/A	70.6%
Visible Minorities			
Total—Visible Minorities	5,068,090	2,464,025	2,604,065
Population Representation	16.2%	7.9%	8.3%
15 years and over	3,922,695	1,880,550	2,042,150
Workforce	2,811,390	1,451,265	1,360,125
Workforce Representation	15.3%	7.9%	7.4%
In Labour Force	2,639,520	1,374,015	1,265,505
Participation Rate	67.3%	73.1%	62.0%
Unemployment Rate	8.6%	7.8%	9.3%
Employment/Population Ratio	61.5%	67.3%	56.2%
Earnings (Full-Time, Full-Year)	$ 43,979	$ 48,631	$ 37,932
Earnings (Female/Male)	N/A	N/A	78.0%
Aboriginal Peoples			
Total—Aboriginal Peoples	1,172,785	572,095	600,695
Population Representation	3.8%	1.8%	1.9%
15 years and over	823,890	393,685	430,205
Workforce	568,195	285,695	282,500
Workforce Representation	3.1%	1.6%	1.5%
In Labour Force	519,255	264,980	254,270
Participation Rate	63.0%	67.3%	59.1%
Unemployment Rate	14.8%	16.1%	13.5%
Employment/Population Ratio	53.7%	56.5%	51.1%
Earnings (Full-Time, Full-Year)	$ 39,942	$ 44,605	$ 34,712
Earnings (Female/Male)	N/A	N/A	77.8%

(continued)

EXHIBIT 5.1 **Fact sheet on members of designated groups, Canada, 2006. *(Continued)***

	Both Sexes	Males	Females
Persons with Disabilities (Employment Equity Defined)			
Total—Persons with Disabilities (EE Defined)	999,640	473,650	525,990
Population Representation	4.6%	2.2%	2.4%
Workforce	874,700	425,210	449,490
Workforce Representation	4.9%	2.4%	2.5%
In Labour Force	689,100	342,030	347,070
Participation Rate	68.9%	72.2%	66.0%
Unemployment Rate	11.9%	13.6%	10.3%
Employment/Population Ratio	60.7%	62.4%	59.2%
Earnings (Full-Time, Full-Year)	$ 42,727	$ 47,630	$ 36,662
Earnings (Female/Male)	N/A	N/A	77.0%

Represents % Designated groups in the Labour Force
N/A = Not Applicable Totals may not equal the sum of components due to rounding and suppression.
"-" = Data too unreliable to publish.
Date: January 2009
Prepared by: Data Development Section, Labour Standards and Workplace Equity Division Operations
Directorate, Labour Program, Human Resources and Skills Development Canada

Source: Unpublished data, 2006 Census of Canada (20% sample data), 2006 Participation and Activity Limitation
Survey (PALS). Date Modified: 2009-11-06.

The Four Designated Groups

Women

Traditionally, women have been segregated in occupations that are accorded both lower status and lower pay. According to a report by Statistics Canada, while women represented 48 percent of the total work force, they are clearly not equally represented across occupations. For example, women have been underrepresented in such areas as semiprofessional occupations, management and board positions, supervisors in crafts and trades, and sales and service personnel. The failure of women to achieve higher-level corporate positions has been attributed to a variety of sources, including lack of mentoring opportunities, lack of female role models, stereotyping and preconceptions of women's roles and abilities, exclusion from informal networks of communication, and failure of senior leaders to assume accountability for women's advancement.

In a report commissioned by the Women's Executive Network (WEN) in Canada, the majority of women executives surveyed believe they have to work twice as hard as men to achieve success. Respondents also indicated that they continuously find themselves hitting the "glass ceiling," and are not accepted into the executive-level culture, which includes participation in "the boys club." The findings also revealed a concern that women continue to face more barriers to career advancement than men with the same qualifications, and are often presented with fewer opportunities. Among the greatest career barriers identified was "the lack of comfort on the part of men in dealing with women on a professional level." Gender-based stereotyping was also indicated as a career barrier. In addition, many respondents felt that they are paid less than men with similar qualifications and they receive less credit and recognition for accomplishments.

Aboriginal or First Nations People

Aboriginals make up about 3 percent of the population. They represent one of the fastest growing populations in Canada but remain vastly underrepresented in the work force. Researchers have estimated that the Aboriginal population "baby boom" will result in 350,000 Native people reaching working age by the next few years, and this underscores the growing need for Canada to absorb more Native people into its work force. However, as researcher Stelios Loizedes of the Conference Board of Canada observed:

> A major difficulty in achieving this goal is that most of this large cohort of Native Canadians coming of working age will have insufficient education and limited job experience, restricting their ability to compete for jobs. . . . Native communities and the private and public sectors will have to implement creative solutions to narrow the education and employment gaps. The educational challenge has proven to be a significant barrier with Aboriginal populations experiencing a high-school drop-out rate of 70 percent. In addition, the lack of job experience, and language and cultural barriers have made the plight of this group often appear bleak. Another barrier to improved employment is the geographical distribution of the Native community. Employment opportunities on or near the Aboriginal reserves are limited. In addition, while over half the Aboriginal population live in the four western provinces, these provinces account for a relatively small percentage of the total jobs in Canada, compared to Quebec and Ontario. Sadly, in many urban contexts, Aboriginal workers have typically been largely segregated in low-wage, unstable employment.

Among the biggest barriers faced by the Aboriginal community may be perception—with many Aboriginal Canadians feeling that they do not "fit" with the corporate environment. As one expert observed:

> That's a problem for both the First Nations community and corporate Canada to address. Aboriginal Canadians have been prevented from playing a part in the modern corporate world for so long that many now feel that exclusion is normal.

Individuals with Disabilities

Individuals with disabilities have faced a variety of employment obstacles. Typically, this group has experienced a higher unemployment rate compared to the national average. Among the challenges faced are attitudinal barriers in the workplace, physical demands unrelated to the job requirements, and inadequate access to the technical and human support systems. The Canadian Health Network, a national, nonprofit, Web-based health information service, clearly notes the importance of acknowledging this segment of the population and of the labour pool:

> In the coming decades, people with a disability will comprise a larger percentage of the population in Canada than ever before. The math is pretty straightforward. As the baby boom generation grows older, the overall age of the population will increase. And because the incidence of disabilities is strongly correlated to age, these numbers will rise together. The degree of accessibility available to this aging population will play a key role in determining their level of health or of hardship, just as it plays a critical role in the daily lives of the more than four million people currently living with a disability in Canada.

A major challenge faced by persons with disabilities is the issue of accessibility. This can entail a variety of obstacles. While physical barriers may be the most visible obstacle to full accessibility, economic barriers, social discrimination, and obstacles to communication can all prevent someone from having equal access to a building, a service, or a job.

Visible Minorities

This group makes up a rapidly growing segment of the population. In the last decade, almost 70 percent of the growth in the labour force was accounted for by newcomers who arrived in the 1990s. In addition, as the baby boom generation retires, immigrant workers will play a greater role in the labour pool. New immigrants comprise most of the labour force growth.

Workplace obstacles faced by visible minorities include culturally biased aptitude tests, lack of recognition of foreign credentials, and excessively high language requirements. Recent statistics indicate that while visible minorities are well educated, they experience the highest unemployment rates, with recent estimates at roughly twice as high as that for the Canadian-born population.

A study released by the Canadian Race Relations Foundation indicated that desirable jobs and promotions elude many visible minorities and Aboriginal people who believe that subtle forms of racism permeate the workplace. The report, prepared by Jean Lock Kunz, Anne Milan, and Sylvain Schetagne from the Canadian Council on Social Development (CCSD), examined the experiences of visible minorities and Aboriginal peoples in cities across Canada. Among the findings were the following:

- Aboriginal peoples, visible minorities, and immigrants to Canada encounter more challenges in finding employment in all regions in Canada.
- Foreign-born visible minorities experience the greatest difficulty finding desirable work, and only half of those with a university education have high-skill jobs.
- Compared to white Canadians, visible minorities and Aboriginals who possess a university education are less likely to hold managerial and professional jobs. Among those visible minorities who do hold managerial jobs, over 50 percent are self-employed, compared with only 30 percent of white Canadians.
- Higher education appears to yield fewer benefits for minorities and Aboriginals in terms of employment and income. Given the same level of education, white Canadians (both foreign-born and Canadian-born) are three times as likely as Aboriginals and about twice as likely as foreign-born visible minorities to rank among the top 20 percent of income earners.

GUARDING AGAINST DISCRIMINATION

Legal Protection

The Department of Justice defines discrimination as occurring "when a law, program or policy—expressly or by effect—creates a distinction between groups of individuals which disadvantages one group based on shared personal characteristics of members of that group in a manner inconsistent with human dignity."

There are a number of legal sources aimed at protecting individuals against discrimination, including the Charter of Rights and Freedoms and the federal Canadian Human Rights Act. In this section we will also consider employment equity legislation.

Canadian Charter of Rights and Freedoms

A central principle behind human rights legislation in Canada is to balance individual and collective rights. Consequently, courts have traditionally upheld restrictions to individual rights in order to protect vulnerable groups in society. For example, while individuals have a right to free speech, there are also laws that place limits on this freedom if such speech threatens other groups. The Constitution Act of 1982, which contains the Canadian Charter of Rights and Freedoms, is the central legislation governing human rights in Canada. It protects the fundamental rights of all Canadians, including:

- Fundamental freedoms that comprise the standard rights of freedom of speech, press, assembly, association, and religion
- Democratic rights
- Mobility rights regarding the right to move freely from province to province for the purposes of residence or employment
- Legal rights, which provide standard procedural rights in criminal proceedings
- Equality rights, which guarantee no discrimination by law on grounds of race, ethnic origin, colour, religion, sex, age, or mental and physical ability
- Language rights

The Charter only applies to activities and institutions controlled by the government and, consequently, it does not protect individual rights against private businesses or individuals. Therefore, rights are additionally protected via other federal and provincial human rights legislation, as discussed below. With the increasing number of cases of alleged human rights violations perpetrated by employers, it is critical that management understand their responsibilities under the legislation, and consider that damages can be awarded for bad faith if there is noncompliance with the law.

The Canadian Human Rights Act

In 1977, Parliament passed the Canadian Human Rights Act. This act is aimed at ensuring equality of opportunity and freedom from discrimination in the federal jurisdiction. The spirit of the act reflects the view that individuals should not be disadvantaged or discriminated against simply because of their membership in any of the following categories:

- Race
- Colour
- National or ethnic origin
- Religion
- Age
- Sex (including pregnancy and childbearing)
- Marital status
- Family status
- Physical or mental disability (including dependence on alcohol or drugs)
- Pardoned criminal conviction
- Sexual orientation

The act protects the rights of Canadians but applies to a specific class of organizations: all federal government departments and agencies; Crown corporations; and other businesses and industries under federal jurisdiction, such as banks, airlines, railway companies, and insurance and communications companies. An organization that doesn't fall into one of these categories will be governed by one or more of the provincial or territorial human rights acts or codes. Therefore, organizations not covered under the federal jurisdiction will be covered under provincial human rights laws. For example, if a company has offices in Nova Scotia and Alberta, then the codes from both of those provinces will apply.

The Canadian Human Rights Act and each of the provincial human rights codes govern human rights issues and provide detailed procedures for investigation and resolution. Provincial laws are similar to federal laws, and the provisions of most provincial codes are largely identical. For example, each provincial jurisdiction or territory has a human rights act or code. In addition, all codes contain a blanket provision that outlaws discrimination based on disability and provisions that specifically relate to discrimination in employment.

The Canadian Human Rights Commission

At the federal level, the Canadian Human Rights Commission (CHRC) is granted authority under the Canadian Human Rights Act to prohibit employment discrimination in federally regulated businesses, including such areas as race, religion, sex, age, national or ethnic origin, physical handicap, and marital status. Each of the provincial human rights codes also enforces fundamental freedoms and governs human rights issues.

The role of the CHRC is to examine allegations of discrimination (addressed by the Canadian Human Rights Act) and to assist in the establishment of greater equality of opportunity. The CHRC describes its mandate as follows:

- To provide effective and timely means for resolving individual complaints.
- To promote knowledge of human rights in Canada and to encourage people to follow principles of equality.
- To help reduce barriers to equality in employment and access to services.

Individuals have a right to file a complaint if they feel they have been the target of discrimination. The complainant is first required to complete a written report describing the discriminatory action. A CHRC representative assesses the facts and determines whether the claim is legitimate. After a complaint has been accepted by the CHRC, an investigator is assigned the task of gathering more facts, and a report is subsequently submitted to the CHRC recommending a finding of either substantiation or nonsubstantiation of the allegation. Once a claim is substantiated, the parties may choose to attempt to settle the matter in the course of the investigation. However, if the parties cannot reach an agreement, a human rights tribunal may be appointed to further investigate. The tribunal has the power to seek damages for the victim, in the event that the accused is found guilty of a discriminatory practice. The enforcement of human rights through commissions can occur at both the federal and provincial levels.

In her article in the *Canadian HR Reporter*, Natalie McDonald made the following observation:

> With the growing number of cases alleging human rights violations in the courts, it is critical that all employees at the management level understand the legislation under which they are governed

and the duty to comply with the legislation, particularly given the damages which can be awarded for bad faith if there is non-compliance.

Employment Equity

The Department of Justice Canada defines equity as focusing on "treating people fairly by recognizing that different individuals and groups require different measures to ensure fair and comparable results." In layperson's terms, the notion of equity is equated with fairness and impartiality. **Employment equity** refers to the treatment of employees in a fair and nonbiased manner. This term was developed by Judge Rosalie Silberman Abella, Commissioner of the Royal Commission on Equality in Employment (1984) to reflect a distinct Canadian process for achieving equality in all areas of employment. In addition, the term was intended to distinguish the process from the U.S. notion of "affirmative action," as well as to move beyond the "equal opportunity" measures that were available in Canada at that time.

Under the authority of the Commission, a process was developed to deal with systemic discrimination in the workplace. According to the Commission, "systemic discrimination" was responsible for most of the inequality found in employment. Employment equity was designed as an ongoing planning process used by an employer to accomplish a number of objectives, including:

- Eliminating employment barriers for the four designated groups identified in the Employment Equity Act—women, persons with disabilities, Aboriginal people, and members of visible minorities.
- Redressing past discrimination in employment opportunities and preventing future barriers.
- Improving access for the designated groups and increasing their distribution throughout all occupations and at all levels.
- Fostering a climate of equity in the organization.
- Implementing positive policies and practices to ensure the effects of systemic barriers are eliminated.

Employment equity is an issue for all individuals regardless of their sex, religion, age, national origin, colour, or position in an organization.

The Legal Basis of Employment Equity Act

The notion of employment equity is derived from the wording of federal and provincial employment standards legislation, human rights codes, and the Canadian Charter of Rights and Freedoms. Employment equity encompasses a number of activities, including identifying and removing systemic barriers to employment opportunities that adversely affect the four designated groups and implementing special measures to remove any barriers and provide reasonable accommodation.

The Employment Equity Act was passed in 1986. Its purpose includes the following mandate:

> . . . to achieve equality in the workplace so that no person shall be denied employment opportunities or benefits for reasons unrelated to ability and, in the fulfillment of the goals, to correct the conditions of disadvantage in employment experienced by women, Aboriginal peoples, persons with disabilities, and visible minority people by giving effect to the principle that employment equity means more than treating persons in the same way but also requires special measures and the accommodation of differences.

The second Employment Equity Act received royal assent in 1995 and came into force on October 24, 1996. It built upon the earlier legislation and clarifies and enforces employer obligations as outlined in the act. The act governs private sector employers under federal jurisdiction as well as almost all employees of the federal government.

The Employment Equity Act (1995) requires employers and Crown corporations that have 100 employees or more and that are regulated under the Canada Labour Code to implement employment equity and report on their results. Under the act, the employer must:

- Distribute to employees a questionnaire that allows them to indicate whether they belong to one of the four designated groups.
- Identify jobs in which the percentage of members of designated groups is below their relative representation in the labour market.

- Disseminate information on employment equity to employees, and consult with employee representatives.
- Scrutinize the current employment system in order to assess whether any barriers exist which may limit the employment opportunities of members of designated groups.
- Generate an employment equity plan directed at promoting an equitable workplace.
- Endeavour to implement the employment equity plan.
- Monitor, assess, and revise the plan in a timely fashion.
- Complete an annual report on the company's employment equity status and activities.

Today critics have raised a number of questions regarding the utility of the Employment Equity Act (see Talking Business 5.3).

More and more businesses have begun to recognize that employment equity is "good for business," and Canada continues to strengthen its programs in order to exploit the strength of an increasingly diverse workforce. Among the numerous organizations that focus on employee equity is the Bank of Montreal Group of Companies (BMO). BMO has received accolades from the Conference Board of Canada for their employment equity and diversity initiatives, including its employee-led diversity action teams, internal

Talking Business 5.3

Employment Equity Policy: One Size Doesn't Fit All

Frances Woolley

Greek women are not officially part of a visible minority, but they earn less than many women who are, with a 7 per cent wage penalty relative to those reporting British origins.

For men, Pendakur and Pendakur found a larger visible minority disadvantage. *All else being equal*, Canadian-born Chinese men earn 8 per cent less than British-origin men, South Asian men 19 per cent less and self-described Blacks 40 per cent less.

Canadian-born Greek men earn about the same as a typical member of a visible minority, even though they are not counted as such—18 per cent less than similarly qualified men of British origin. (These comparisons are for the Canadian-born only, not immigrants.)

Members of visible minorities are defined by Statistics Canada as "persons, other than Aboriginal peoples, who are non-Caucasian in race or non-white in colour."

But no living person's skin tone matches the "ultra white" shade in a paint colour fan deck. Deciding whether paint is off-white or beige is a judgment call. So is determining which ethnic groups are visible minorities. Statistics Canada considers the following ethnic groups to be visible minorities: Chinese, South Asian, Black, Arab, West Asian, Filipino, Southeast Asian, Latin American, Japanese and Korean.

Greeks aren't on the visible minority list, even though, according to Pendakur and Pendakur's research, they struggle more in the labour market than do Chinese Canadians, and experience challenges similar to those faced by South Asian Canadians.

Canada's employment equity policy was inspired by a 1984 report written by Justice Rosalie Abella. The report contains these words:

> "Although it is unquestionably true that many non-whites face employment discrimination, the degree to which different minorities suffer employment and economic disadvantages varies significantly by group and by region. To combine all non-whites together as visible minorities for the purpose of devising systems to improve their equitable participation, without making distinctions to assist those groups in particular need, may deflect attention from where the problems are greatest."

Canada's current employment equity policy inspires anger and resentment, as evidenced by 1106 comments on The Globe and Mail website. As long as it ensures equity in employment for some designated groups—instead of all Canadians—it will continue to do so.

employee assistance program, and its recently launched project to help identify workplace barriers among persons with disabilities.

Many businesses have also stepped up their efforts to assist the Aboriginal community in gaining greater self-sufficiency and participation in the work force. There are a number of companies that have been actively involved in boosting the presence of Aboriginals in the workplace. Many businesses have proven that they can work with Aboriginal communities, educational institutions, and government to enhance employment prospects for Aboriginals. A typical recruitment method for companies is to offer support for educational institutions, training initiatives, and scholarships for Aboriginal students. For example, 3M Canada contributes to bursaries given through the Department of Indian and Northern Affairs Canada for Aboriginal students who are pursuing careers in fields related to health care. In addition, recruitment strategies that reach out to Aboriginal communities and organizations are also employed.

Dating back to 1990, the federal government formally recognizes federally regulated companies for achievements in implementing employment equity and addressing the needs of a diverse work force. Employment Equity Awards have been given to those organizations deemed as models in the establishment and implementation of equity practices. The Vision Award is presented to those organizations that exhibited outstanding approaches to the implementation of equity, diversity, and inclusiveness in the workplace. The Certificate of Merit is presented to organizations for their sustained efforts towards attaining a representative work force.

Awards have been presented to such high achievers in equity and diversity as Pelmorex Inc., the company that runs the Weather Network. Employee surveys conducted at Pelmorex indicated that more than 90 percent of employees feel the company highly values equity. This company also offers training on nondiscriminatory interviewing techniques, integrating new employees into the workplace, and accommodation strategies. Interestingly, the company rewards managers for their support of the company's efforts—annual bonuses for managers are linked to promoting equity.

The Saskatoon-based trucking company Yanke Group was another award winner. It was recognized for its involvement with community organizations in order to facilitate the hiring of people with disabilities and Aboriginals. In addition, Yanke Group was applauded for its practice of generating employment equity benchmarks, which are reviewed quarterly. Talking Business 5.4 lists other recipients of these government awards.

Talking Business 5.4
Employment Equity in IBM and Shell Canada

- In 2003, IBM launched the Canadian Women's Leadership Council, involving the participation of women executives and senior leaders to become active in the development of high-potential women in IBM Canada. This program mirrors the goals of a similar body created in 2002 to increase development of visible minorities.
- For the past five years, IBM Canada's visually impaired employees have mentored students at the Canadian National Institute for the Blind's Summer Camp to acquaint them with technology.
- Shell Canada provides diversity awareness training to all employees, including management, and has implemented an Ombuds office to facilitate fair and equitable resolution of workplace issues.
- In 2001, Shell completed a review of their progress related to diversity and implemented various initiatives, including hiring a full-time diversity advisor and developing a diversity gap analysis to help identify priority areas of action.
- The company offers a disability management program to assist ill or injured employees.
- Shell Canada supports the recruitment and retention of Aboriginal employees through participation in Aboriginal community outreach programs, funding of educational initiatives, and offering scholarships through the National Aboriginal Achievement Foundation.

Source: Government of Canada, http://info.load-otea.hrdc-drhc.gc.ca/workplace_equity/fcp/merit_awards/2003/

*UNION MEMBERSHIP AND STRUCTURE

Unions are the organizations most directly responsible for representing the interests of Canada's working people.

Unions have been defined as workers' associations formed to enhance their power in dealings with employers, particularly in negotiating the terms and conditions under which work is performed and in handling workers' grievances; however, while collective bargaining and grievance-handling may be their core functions, Canadian unions do many other things as well. In Canada, as in most other countries, many unions are heavily involved in political action, which is often aimed at passing legislation that will advance the interests of all working people, whether union members or not. Many unions also serve on joint union–employer industry panels aimed at advancing the interests of a particular industry. Beyond that, union political activities may include joining coalitions with other organizations, such as community groups, women's groups, anti-poverty groups, groups focused on equity rights for gays and lesbians, and other equity-seeking organizations.

In recent years, unions have also become increasingly involved in publicity campaigns of various kinds—some focused on mobilizing support for specific bargaining items, others designed to call public attention to social justice issues or problems of a more general nature, such as ongoing cutbacks in the federal and provincial governments, the problems associated with the increasing number of Canadian children living in poverty, and the need for a national daycare system. Finally, many unions provide assistance to non-profit and humanitarian projects both in Canada and abroad. The Canadian Autoworkers' Social Justice Fund (SJF) and the United Steelworkers' Humanity Fund contribute to a variety of causes such as emergency relief following natural disasters, human development and anti-poverty activities in Latin American and Africa, housing and training projects for homeless youth, the removal of landmines in formerly war-torn regions, and a variety of community development projects both nationally and internationally. Thus, unions are far more than organizations aimed at improving the terms and conditions of employment for their members. **Social unionism**, the pursuit of broad "social and political strategies on behalf of the working class in general," has long been an important aspect of the Canadian labour movement—certainly more so than its American counterpart, which focuses more primarily on the economic function of unions.

UNION MEMBERSHIP

Why have union membership and density rates risen and fallen as they have?

The most important factor behind the recent stagnation in union growth and decline in union density is most likely the loss of hundreds of thousands of manufacturing jobs, most in heavily unionized sectors, coupled with job growth in sectors, such as the private service sector, where unionization rates tend to be quite low. Organizing the service sector has presented a major challenge to unions and their successes have lagged significantly behind the growth of employment in this sector. Yet despite severe losses in traditional manufacturing strongholds, the Canadian labour movement as a whole has fared significantly better than those of many other industrialized countries, such as Britain, Japan, Australia, and the United States, all of which have experienced significant declines in union density since 1980.

As has been the case for some time, the public sector continues to be far more heavily unionized than the private sector. In 2003, more than 70 percent of Canadian public sector workers were unionized, as opposed to just 18 percent of the country's private sector workers. The extremely high unionization rates, in such sectors as education, public administration, and health care explains why 53 percent of the country's union members come from the public sector, even though fewer than one-quarter of all Canadians are employed there.

As has also been the case for some time, part-time workers are significantly less likely to be union members than full-timers. However, consistent with trends in employment, part-time workers' share of union membership rose from 8 to 14 percent between 1984 and 2003 and their union density rose from 18 to 23 percent. Meanwhile, full-timers' share of union membership declined from 92 to 86 percent and their union density rate fell from 39 to 32 percent. Also consistent with overall employment trends, unionization rates have decreased slightly for permanent employees while for non-permanent employees rates rose from 22.7 percent in 1997 to 25.1 percent in 2003. Finally, between 1997 and 2003, union density fell

---

*Unless otherwise credited, all content from here to the end of this chapter is taken from *Canadian Industrial Relations*, Third Edition, by John Peirce and Karen Joy Bentham.

3.9 percentage points within large firms of over 500 employees and rose 0.7 per centage points within firms of fewer than 20 employees.

Generally, union membership rates do not appear to be very strongly affected by an individual's age or educational attainment, except that very young workers (those aged 15 to 24) are far less likely than others to be union members. The likeliest explanations for the low density rate among young workers are the high proportion that work part-time and the frequency with which young people tend to change jobs.

Canadian versus American Union Membership Rates

In 1965, American union density was just slightly higher than that of Canada, both being around 30 percent. By 1980, the Canadian rate had risen to almost 36 percent, or more than half again greater than the US rate of just over 23 percent. Since 1986, the Canadian rate has invariably been more than twice that of the United States. Industrial relations scholars have put forward a variety of explanations for the growing divergence in the two countries' membership rates. One is differing public labour policy. In Canada, such policy has generally been more supportive of unions than it has in the United States.

UNION ACTIONS

The question of the methods or actions that unions use to achieve their objectives has been of interest to industrial relations experts for more than 100 years. In a classic 1897 work entitled *Industrial Democracy*, Sidney and Beatrice Webb suggest that unions rely primarily on three methods: mutual insurance, collective bargaining, and legal enactment.[5]

The mutual insurance function of unions was extremely important in the days before unemployment insurance, publicly funded health care, and sick and disability leave. Union benefit funds could help tide unemployed workers over periods of cyclical depression and support the families of workers killed or injured at work, or incapacitated due to illness. By representing themselves as "mutual benefit societies" or "friendly societies," unions were also able to get around harsh nineteenth-century legislation banning them as criminal conspiracies in restraint of trade. Much of the unions' traditional mutual insurance function has been taken over by government. However, some elements of it survive, such as the Supplementary Unemployment Benefits contained in some collective agreements, which top up government EI payments to a level near the worker's normal wage. A number of unions also now provide their members with such benefits as lower-priced auto and disability insurance.

Unions' collective bargaining activities are still generally carried on more or less as the Webbs envisaged, though the range of issues brought to the table is now often considerably greater. As for legal enactment, unions have been among the strongest supporters of higher minimum wages, health and safety legislation, anti-discrimination laws, and a broad range of social programs of benefit to all working people—not just union members. Again, this emphasis on working on behalf of all working people is in line with the Webbs' original emphasis.

Even today, the Webbs' three methods are at the core of what most unions spend a good deal of their time doing. But the range of union activity has expanded a good deal over the past century and to some degree its character has also changed. In the area of collective bargaining, for example, while most bargaining continues to be adversarial, a growing number of unions have entered into more co-operative arrangements with management. In some cases, unions have taken on what amounts to something approaching joint governance of the workplace—a role that would have been totally foreign to the unionist of 50 years ago and that continues to arouse considerable controversy within the Canadian labour movement even now.[6] In the political arena, unions have also expanded their role, moving beyond support for specific pieces of labour-related legislation to more or less permanent alliances with parties such as the NDP and less formal arrangements with women's, environmental, anti-poverty, and church groups and other progressive organizations, as well as the creation of "humanity" or "justice" funds to support specific causes. They have also become adept at using publicity campaigns to help achieve their objectives and at using their members' savings and pension funds to promote local and regional development and job creation through a broad range of labour-sponsored venture capital corporations and pension pools. Finally, Canadian unions have long been and continue to be involved in a broad range of educational ventures.

Thus, while their general objectives remain the same as those of unions in the past, today's unions tend to operate within a far broader context. They also have available to them strategies and technologies that the unionists of, for example, the 1940s could only dream about.

Collective Bargaining

Overall, the Canadian industrial relations system can fairly be described as voluntarist. This means that in unionized workplaces, most outcomes are left to be negotiated between the union and management—rather than being established through legislation, as is the case in some European countries such as France. As a result, collective bargaining is, almost by definition, a core activity for virtually all Canadian unions.

First, collective bargaining now addresses a far broader range of issues than it generally did early in the century, when agreements might be just one or two pages long and were usually limited to such core issues as wages, hours of work, holiday and overtime pay, and union security provisions. During the early post-war period, unions began to negotiate a broad range of employee benefits such as paid vacations, sick leave, pensions, and medical and hospitalization insurance. More recently, demands from an increasingly diverse workforce containing growing numbers of women have caused unions to negotiate maternity and paternity leave provisions, flexible schedules, workplace daycare centres, and in some cases anti-discrimination and anti-harassment provisions that go beyond the requirements of human rights legislation. At the same time, the introduction of labour-saving technology into workplaces has caused unions to seek (albeit often unsuccessfully) to negotiate protection against job or income loss resulting from such technology. The introduction of new chemicals and other potentially hazardous substances has led to the negotiation of clauses regarding their use, as well as the employer's responsibility to provide appropriate safety equipment and training in the handling of such substances. Finally, growing concern for members' well-being both on and off the job has led unions to negotiate employee assistance programs to help employees with drug, alcohol, financial, or other personal problems, and in some cases wellness programs to provide employees with improved access to fitness facilities. The addition of this broad range of issues to such core issues as wages and hours of work has tended to make bargaining a longer and more complex process than it was in the past.

Second, while most collective bargaining continues to be adversarial, a growing proportion of it is now more problem-solving in nature. A problem-solving approach is most obviously useful in cases involving clear "win-win" issues, such as health and safety; however, this type of bargaining has sometimes been more widely applied, even in cases involving monetary issues.

Joint Union–Management Ventures at the Workplace

The same types of challenges posed by a shift from adversarial bargaining to a problem-solving approach apply, to an even greater degree, to unions' participation in joint ventures with management designed to increase worker morale and productivity. Such ventures can range from single-issue labour–management committees to broad **gainsharing plans** such as the Scanlon Plan. They can also include quality circles, self-directed work teams, and employee stock ownership plans.

In a few cases, unions and management have negotiated joint governance arrangements whereby the union becomes, in effect, a full partner in management of the organization. These arrangements, which have been much more common in Quebec than elsewhere in Canada, entail a radical transformation of the union's role, from that of workers' advocate to that of administrator and perhaps even manager of discontent. They also open up far greater possibilities for direct communication between management and employees—possibilities that run the risk of reducing the union's influence in the workplace and may even conflict with its advocacy role. If, for example, in its role as co-manager, a union has agreed with management on the need to cut costs, but rank-and-file members are pushing hard for immediate, up-front wage increases, what will union negotiators do at the bargaining table, and how will the demand for wage increases affect the union's continued participation in the joint governance scheme?

Moreover, participation in such schemes often requires union members and officials to learn new skills. Traditionally, motivational and political skills were most important for union leaders. But if a union is co-managing an organization, its officials and those of its members involved in joint governance committees will also need to learn business-related skills such as finance, economics, and accounting.

Union participation in joint co-operation and employee involvement schemes has often proved quite controversial, within individual unions, in the Canadian labour movement as a whole, and among IR academics. Some regard increased employee involvement as inevitable, given globalization and increased competitiveness. Such writers argue that unions have no choice other than to participate in employee involvement programs. If unions don't participate, they suggest, management will introduce the programs anyway, and the interests of neither individual workers nor the union will have been well-served.[7] Others are more skeptical, while still others oppose any union participation in such ventures outright—on the grounds that for a union to assume any significant co-management role amounts to a conflict of interest with its core role as the workers' advocate. Within the labour movement, some unions have adopted policies of outright opposition to joint co-operation schemes, while some of the schemes' strongest supporters, such as the CEP and Steelworkers, have insisted on being given a major role as a condition of participation.[8] The economic environment of the past 15 years, which has seen many large-scale layoffs even in highly profitable organizations, has arguably made such joint ventures a dicier business from the unions' perspective. When large-scale layoffs occur despite unions' best efforts to increase productivity, even former supporters may wonder what the benefit of the schemes is for workers; at a minimum such layoffs serve to strengthen the hand of union "hawks" opposed to co-operation (see Talking Business 5.5).

Political Action

Almost all unions engage in some kind of political action. This is because, to a large extent, unions' ability to achieve their objectives depends on the types of legislation and government policies in place. They can't possibly hope to influence legislation or government policy without in some way becoming involved in the political process, whether through lobbying government on specific issues or through more formal connection with a political party.

Most Canadian unions are explicitly committed to social unionism, a type of unionism that believes that the role of unions is to further workers' well-being as a whole, outside the workplace as well as within it. Almost by definition, a commitment to social unionism entails some kind of affiliation with a political party, since acting on behalf of the working class as a whole necessitates winning passage of a broad range of legislation that will benefit workers and lower-income Canadians. This is something that's extremely difficult to do through ad hoc lobbying on specific issues. While affiliation with a political party is no guarantee of success, it does arguably improve unions' chances, by providing them with an experienced partner to assist them in their political ventures on a steady basis.

Talking Business 5.5

Working to Protect Workers against Bankruptcy

Bankruptcies are a common feature of economic life in Canada. Over the past five years, an average of about 10 000 firms per year have declared bankruptcy. During the first half of 2004 alone, the figure was 4980, with roughly 10 percent of these coming from the manufacturing sector.

Unfortunately, under current bankruptcy legislation, workers are last in line when a firm goes under. A company's taxes, lenders, and even its suppliers all get paid before its workers do. The result is that thousands of workers each year lose not only their jobs but their vacation pay, termination and severance pay, and even back wages for work they've already done. In addition, they lose their group insurance benefits. And if, as is often the case, the employer hasn't fully funded the pension plan, current workers and retirees will face cutbacks in their pension benefits as well.

The United Steelworkers of America (USWA) is a union whose members have been hard-hit by corporate bankruptcies in recent years. When the Fonderie Canadienne D'Acier in Montreal went bankrupt, the company's secured creditors recovered the $5 million owed them, but there was nothing left to cover an unfunded $260 000 pension fund liability, which meant pension benefits were cut.

Similarly, when Toronto's Ontario Store Fixtures went bankrupt twice in 2002–2003, over 1200 unionized employees lost their jobs. These employees were owed $800 000 in unpaid vacation pay and $11 million in statutory severance and termination pay. After lengthy negotiations with the firm's directors, the union won an agreement to pay the unpaid vacation claim and a small portion of the amount owed for severance and termination pay. But over $9 million owed to the firm's workers will never be paid.

For years, the USWA has been pushing to provide Canadian workers with better protection against bankruptcies. Now it appears their efforts may be about to bear some fruit, in the form of legislation which would put workers first in the event of corporate bankruptcies.

In English Canada, the labour movement has most often chosen the NDP or its forerunner party, the CCF, as its political partner. Unions are allowed a given number of delegate slots at NDP conventions and many choose to affiliate directly to the party, a decision that allows them to play an active role in formulating its policy. In Quebec, most labour activists support the Parti Québécois, or the federal Bloc Québécois party.

Unions' Expanded Scope of Action

Canadian unions have greatly expanded their scope of action beyond such core activities as negotiating collective agreements, handling members' grievances, and seeking to achieve passage of pro-labour legislation. To begin with, they have entered into a broad range of partnerships with management, both within workplaces and beyond the workplace. Politically, their sphere of interest has widened, to encompass coalitions with anti-poverty and other social justice groups at home and with foreign unions and Canadian NGOs promoting economic development and human and labour rights overseas. And particularly over the past 15 years, many have entered the world of business, learning how to use available funds such as pension monies to promote job creation, community development, affordable housing, and other social objectives.

The areas into which a union or labour federation chooses to expand will depend on a variety of factors, including the organization's traditions and history, its membership composition, its members' interests, and the economic pressures facing the industry in which it operates. Some may wish (or need) to expand into more "new" areas than others. But in today's highly volatile economic and political environment, few if any unions can afford the luxury of simply burying their heads in the sand and concentrating solely on "minding the shop." While Canadian union membership rates have not declined anywhere near as sharply as those in the United States have, the pressures on Canadian union membership are nonetheless real. In the coming decades, the ability to mount effective publicity campaigns and to use members' accumulated funds to create or save jobs may become increasingly critical to a union's survival. Our prediction, therefore, is that the scope of union action will continue to expand to meet the even stiffer challenges unions are likely to face in the coming decades.

UNION IMPACTS

Not surprisingly, given the broad range of activities in which we have just seen that they engage, unions have an equally broad range of impacts on their members' wages and working conditions, on the productivity and overall performance of the firms in which their members work, and on the Canadian economy and Canadian society as a whole.

Union Impact on Productivity

There is considerable disagreement within the industrial relations profession as to whether, on balance, unions serve to increase or decrease firms' productivity.

Neoclassicists and others primarily interested in unions' economic impacts argue that unions reduce productivity by raising wages above competitive levels, by reducing output through the strikes they call, and by forcing management to agree to restrictive work rules. Institutionalists and others primarily interested in workplace equity or equity within society as a whole argue that far from reducing productivity, unions often have positive effects on it. These include reduced quit rates and improved morale and worker–management co-operation resulting from union grievance processes and other mechanisms that give workers a sense that they have some say in what goes on in the workplace. Unions can also induce management to use more efficient production methods and even, perhaps, more effective personnel policies. In addition, they can increase productivity by collecting information about the preferences of all workers, information that can help the firm select better personnel policies and a more appropriate mix of wages and employee benefits. For their part, managerialists as well as some institutionalists argue that unions can have either positive or negative productivity effects, since what is most important is whether a union helps or hurts relations between workers and management. From this perspective, what may be of greatest interest are management's policy towards unions and the union's willingness to enter into a co-operative relationship with management. For example, if a union opposes an employee involvement initiative, the program's chances of success will clearly be reduced.

Which position is closest to the truth? The one thing almost everyone can agree on is that the question is an extremely difficult one to answer. As the previous discussion has suggested, some union effects are clearly positive, while others are clearly negative, and still others can be either positive or negative depending on the particular situation. Complicating matters still further is the fact that in many situations, particularly where what is being "produced" is a service rather than a tangible good, it may be extremely difficult if not impossible to measure productivity as such. In such cases, asking whether unions increase or decrease productivity may not be at all useful. Here (assuming we were trying to determine the effects of unionization in a recently unionized establishment), it might be far more useful to start by asking workers whether they found they were getting along better or worse with their supervisor than they were before the union came in, or whether they felt more or less confident than before about their ability to do their job. Even where productivity can be measured, the union's impact on the labour–management relationship may still be the most important factor. Where this is positive, it can lead not just to improved bargaining and communications, but to a broad range of problem-solving behaviour in all areas of workplace life, which in turn can result in reduced accident and illness rates, lower grievance and strike rates, and even reduced down time and spoilage.

Conversely, where the union's impact on the labour–management relationship is negative, the results can include greatly increased sickness, accident, and industrial conflict rates and increased down time and spoilage. At the end of the day, both positive and negative impacts of the less tangible variety described here may turn out to be more important than the generally modest union wage impacts discussed earlier.

Union Impacts on Management of the Organization

People from all different perspectives on IR agree that union impacts on the management of organizations are substantial. Where they disagree is on whether such impacts are beneficial. From a comparative perspective, these impacts appear to be greater in North America, with its detailed collective agreements regulating many different aspects of workplace behaviour, than in Europe, where agreements are apt to be more general and unions do not generally have a significant effect on firms' day-to-day operations, a fact that may help explain North American managers' greater opposition to unions. It is also worth noting that in many European countries, alternative mechanisms, such as works councils, are available to handle day-to-day problems on the shop floor.

In North America, unionization constitutes a significant limitation on management's freedom to run the enterprise as it sees fit. Here, management authority is specifically limited by any collective agreement provision; to counter such limitations, almost all management organizations insist that collective agreements contain management rights clauses, which generally have the effect of referring to management any matter not specifically addressed in the agreement. In Canada, unionization invariably brings with it a grievance process, since all jurisdictions' labour legislation requires collective agreements to include a process for the handling of disputes arising over the interpretation of the agreement.

Unions' most important impacts on the management of firms come through the aforementioned grievance processes, work rules laid out in collective agreements, and joint participation with management on various committees. For the average worker, and perhaps for management as well, it's the grievance process that is of greatest importance. Most significantly, the grievance process offers an avenue of redress for any worker who feels she or he has been unjustly dismissed. The chances of reinstatement following a dismissal grievance are more than 50 percent, whereas the non-unionized worker has no chance of reinstatement, except in the few jurisdictions offering the equivalent of a dismissal grievance process to certain non-unionized workers. The wish to avoid a costly and possibly embarrassing dismissal grievance process undoubtedly deters many managers from engaging in arbitrary dismissals. If managers are unduly timid, fear of a dismissal grievance may even keep them from firing people who should be let go. In lesser matters, as well, the grievance process serves as a brake on what might otherwise be capricious or arbitrary management behaviour.

Indeed, the threat of possible grievances typically causes management to operate in a very different way in a unionized establishment than it would in a non-unionized one. Now it must operate in accordance with two sets of rules: company policy and the collective agreement. This makes the whole process of managing more formal and more legalistic. To the extent that the collective agreement brings a degree of certainty to what might otherwise be a confused, chaotic management process, the firm will likely benefit. To the extent that its work rules stifle creativity and innovation and cause people to become more concerned about legalistic observance of the contract than about doing their jobs better, the firm is likely to suffer.

No theory can tell us whether the positive or negative effects are more likely to prevail; the only way to tell is to go to individual workplaces and do detailed case studies. Here again, the nature of the individual labour–management relationship may be pivotal. Where there is a positive relationship, both sides may be willing to exercise some discretion in interpreting the collective agreement. Where the relationship is bad, both sides are more apt to "go by the book" in almost every instance, a process that can prove extremely counterproductive or even paralyzing if carried to extremes.

The work rules contained in collective agreements address a broad range of issues. Unless limited by legislation (as in the case of many public sector organizations) or by management rights provisions stating that layoffs and promotions are totally within management's discretion, collective agreement provisions are apt to use **seniority** as one of the criteria for promotion, and reverse seniority as the primary criterion for layoffs. Unions generally like seniority-based promotion and layoff provisions because they prevent management from promoting or laying people off in an arbitrary fashion. Without seniority provisions, employers facing an economic downturn might lay off more senior workers, because they would normally be earning higher wages, or might simply lay off any workers management didn't like. While the use of seniority to govern promotions is more controversial, relatively few collective agreements use seniority as the sole basis for promotion; much more common are provisions that state that seniority will be one criterion along with skills and ability.

Other union work rules may apply more specifically to the work process. In some cases, workload itself may be limited. More recently, it has often been the case with agreements in education. Public schoolteachers' agreements have sometimes limited class size; university professors' agreements have sometimes stipulated a normal or maximum number of courses a professor will be expected to teach.

Another important group of work rules has to do with procedures governing workforce reduction. In addition to provisions requiring that layoffs be in reverse order of seniority, unions may negotiate total or partial restrictions on management's ability to contract out work to outside firms. They may also negotiate restrictions on management's ability to implement technological change, such as requirements that the union be given a period of advance notice or that affected workers be provided with retraining opportunities. Finally, contracts may provide for a layoff notice period greater than that required by employment standards legislation or for training, job search assistance, or other benefits for employees facing layoff. In the federal public service, many agreements contain a separate workforce adjustment appendix outlining detailed procedures to be used in the event of large-scale reorganization or restructuring.

In addition to the impacts resulting from grievance procedures and the work rules contained in collective agreements, unions also affect the management of organizations through their joint participation, with management, in a number of committees or other forms of joint governance mechanism. The most important of these committees are the joint health and safety committees required in all jurisdictions. Here, unions often play a key role, both by educating and informing workers on the issues and by helping to ensure that the committee is not just a token. Unions also play an important role in the pay equity process through their involvement in job-evaluation procedures. Beyond that, collective agreements often provide for a variety of labour–management committees. While the scope and powers of these committees vary greatly, they do involve a good many workers, at least to some degree, in the day-to-day management of the organization—a development that most industrial relationists and many managers would probably regard as healthy.

Union Impacts on Society as a Whole

The previous discussion suggests that within the workplace, unions can have both positive and negative effects. For society as a whole, the situation is rather more clear-cut. Here, particularly in the social and political spheres, the impacts appear to have been almost entirely positive. It is largely thanks to unions, through their participation in politics, that Canadians have publicly funded medical care, unemployment insurance, public pensions, and other worthwhile social programs. Note here that the labour movement could not have achieved these results without a political partner (today the NDP, formerly the CCF), nor could the NDP or CCF have achieved them without the labour movement's active support. Earlier, we noted that the CCF and NDP have not only passed legislation providing for pro-labour legislation and social programs when they have been in government, they have also forced governments from other parties to pass such legislation when they have held the balance of power in minority governments, or when there has been a serious threat that those governments would lose to the CCF or NDP in the next election. It's important to note as well that the CCF, in particular, did not really get off the ground until it started attracting strong support from unionists during the Second World War. More recently, the NDP was strengthened by the increased support it started receiving from the CLC and affiliated unions beginning with the 1979 federal election. In the four federal elections held starting in 1979, the party posted some of the best results it had ever achieved. The critical role played by the labour movement within the NDP is also shown, in a negative way, by the party's relatively poor showing in all federal and Ontario elections since 1993 (the year of the social contract debacle), particularly in Ontario.

Without strong, steady support from the labour movement, the NDP has little chance of remaining viable as a national political party.

The labour movement has made other important contributions to Canadian society. Over the years, it has done a great deal to raise the profile of health and safety issues, educating members, managers, and the general public alike. While Canadian workplaces are still far from safe, they are safer than they would be without the work of unions, which have played a particularly important role in the joint health and safety committees required in all Canadian jurisdictions. Unions have also worked to bring in affirmative action, pay equity, and anti-discrimination legislation, and other human-rights measures benefiting all Canadians. Overall, we can only agree with Desmond Morton, that "[m]uch that has made Canada a humane and civilized society has come from the social vision of its labour movement."

ARE UNIONS STILL NEEDED?

Often, one hears the argument that while unions were very much needed in the late nineteenth and early twentieth centuries, when most workers were wretchedly paid and forced to work under appalling conditions, they have outlived their usefulness. Today, so the argument goes, almost all workers are well-paid, management has become totally enlightened, and working conditions everywhere are first-rate, thus making unions essentially redundant (see Talking Business 5.6).

Talking Business 5.6

Trade Unions in Canada: All Struck Out

Weaker Than They Look

These are hard times for Canada's trade unions. When car plants and factories close, union jobs go. The public has turned hostile, even in traditional blue-collar towns. When municipal workers in Toronto and Windsor went on strike this summer, leaving rubbish piled up in the streets and head-high weeds in parks, residents had little sympathy. Some have lost their own jobs, or their savings. The union's image was further harmed when a striker in Windsor was caught on video dumping rubbish and berating a family picking up litter in a park. In an opinion poll taken in Toronto during the strike by the Strategic Counsel, a survey firm, only 13% of respondents supported it.

Conservative pundits are proclaiming the death of unions. In fact some 30% of Canadian workers were union members in 2008. That is down from 38% in 1981, but still higher than in many other rich countries. But the overall membership conceals a discrepancy: whereas 71% of public-sector workers are unionised, only 16% of those in the private sector are. That is partly because in Canada—as in the United States, but unlike in Europe—unions negotiate by workplace rather than across an industry. So government and big manufacturing plants are attractive to union organisers; banks, retailers and service industries, with branches scattered across the country, are not.

Union supporters hope that the stagnation of average wages will eventually produce public pressure to change the law so as to make organising easier. Conservatives think that market forces will make that unnecessary. If the workforce shrinks as baby-boomers retire, individual workers will be in a stronger position to secure wage rises, argues Charles Cirtwill of the Atlantic Institute for Market Studies, a think-tank based in Halifax.

To survive, unions need to sell themselves more actively, says Elaine Bernard, a labour specialist at Harvard University. They should be reminding people of the benefits they bring, such as a stable workforce in communities with high unemployment, or the broader standards they have set that all workers enjoy, such as paid holidays and a five-day week. "People are asking, and not just in Canada, what do unions do? The answer has to be something that appeals to the individual worker, provides some service to the employer, and promotes a collective or community good," Ms. Bernard says.

That message was hard to find on the picket line at DriveTest this week. Not surprisingly, the strikers were preoccupied with regaining their jobs and keeping their system of seniority. That is unlikely to win the broader public support that the unions need.

Source: *The Economist.*

other authoritarian regimes and military dictatorships generally do not allow unions at all, or at the very least constrain their activities severely; while in Communist countries, such as the former Soviet Union, unions have most typically been absorbed into the larger state apparatus and given no independent role of their own in the IR system. Quite simply, it would appear that free trade unions go hand-in-hand with democracy.

As for what Canadian society would be like without unions, the most immediate and obvious differences would be noticed at the workplace. To start with, many fewer Canadians would enjoy any real protection against dismissal or other arbitrary action by their employers. And many fewer would have any part in setting the terms and conditions of their employment. This would become a privilege enjoyed only by a select group of professionals, athletes, and middle- to upper-level managers. Health and safety laws would be less strictly enforced, even if the laws themselves did not change; the same would likely be true for human rights laws. Moreover, the already strong trend towards less secure work and more part-time, temporary, and contractual work would very likely accelerate without the brake now placed on it by union collective agreement provisions.

In addition to losing unions' workplace representation, working people would also lose political representation, since the one national party pledged to advance their interests, the NDP, would almost certainly cease to exist without a labour movement to support it. Publicly-funded health care might not disappear immediately, but support for it would certainly diminish, as would support for EI, social assistance, and other social programs, and public arts funding. Supporters of health care and public arts funding would definitely find their job much harder if they were forced to operate without the labour movement's financial support and the NDP's political support.

In a more general way, the question is perhaps best answered by two more. If there were no Canadian labour movement, what other group in contemporary Canadian society would be big enough and strong enough to provide a significant check to the economic and political clout of big business and the political right? And what other group would be in a position to advance the economic and political interests of the broad spectrum of ordinary working Canadians? Such questions are, admittedly, far from new or original. Expanded only slightly, they form much of the basis of the institutionalist perspective on industrial relations described earlier. They are nonetheless worth asking, given that the advocates of a union-free society have thus far had little to say in response to either one.

Fortunately, such questions are likely to remain purely hypothetical. As we pointed out earlier, the practical need for unions appears if anything to be increasing, rather than decreasing. From a broader perspective, a society without free unions would almost certainly be one in which few Canadians would care to live.

CHAPTER SUMMARY

We examined the issue of demographic diversity at work. The potential opportunities and responsibilities raised by the immigrant labour pool were addressed. We identified the four designated groups and discussed related responsibilities of employment equity and human rights protection. Second, this chapter explored the role of unions and their influence on business.

CONCEPT APPLICATION

THE NEAR COLLAPSE OF THE AUTO INDUSTRY—ARE UNIONS TO BLAME?

*MAYBE!

A Brown

According to the Indianapolis Star, in the year ending 2007, the average base wage for a GM blue-collar employee was just under $28 an hour. GM officials say that average reaches $39.68 an hour, when you consider base pay, cost-of-living adjustments, night-shift premiums, overtime, holiday and vacation pay. Health-care, pension and other benefits average another $33.58 an hour. This brings the total average cost of employing a single GM worker to an astounding $73.26 per hour.

Compare these outrageous hourly numbers to those of our Mexican counterparts. In June of 2008, Ford Motor Company announced that their Union had agreed to cut wages for new hires, to about half of the current wage of $4.50 per hour. Starting wages at some plants in Mexico are as paltry as $1.50 per hour with a lot less of the related pension and health care costs of U.S. workers. The total cost to employ a worker in China is even less than the cost in Mexico. There is no need to dissect those numbers, as I believe the point has been made quite clear.

The entire North American auto industry is on the brink of collapse and we wonder how in the world this could happen. The answer is quite obvious. North America can simply not compete with the foreign auto manufacturers. Certainly not at these hourly labor rates. The Unions have been holding a knife at the throat of the manufacturers for far too long. Greed in its purest form has broken the back of the auto industry. The Union is unrepentant as they have already spoken out and declared that they refuse to make any form of concession even during the industries' darkest hour.

Leadership on behalf of the Union is largely responsible. The shepherds of the cattle if you will, who advise and direct their herd to fight to the bitter end in order to get what they want. They have no regard for the economics of their demands. Their stance has consistently been, give us what we want or we will take our ball and go home. In other words they will go on strike. Once again, holding the industry hostage. . . .

. . . Congress, it would seem, is negotiating with the wrong people. They need to sit down with the United Autoworkers Union and provide them with a simple ultimatum. Either accept some very deep cuts not only to your wages but to your benefits and pension as well or the Government will break the Union and start anew. Then and only then should the Government consider providing financial aid to this troubled industry. . . .

**MAYBE NOT!

Eric Peters

I am not a huge fan of the UAW. . . .

. . . But the idea that the collapse of General Motors and Chrysler Corp. is the fault of the unions is swill of the worst sort. Because not only is it false, if accepted it will simply mean that taxpayers are made to shovel more money down the gullet of companies that won't make the necessary changes to their business model because they haven't been forced to confront the fact that their problems have not been caused by "the unions"—the braying mantra they've been falling back on for years now.

Point Number One:

While almost everyone in the media and elsewhere is talking about the failure of the industry, note that Ford is not in trouble like GM and Chrysler are in trouble. It is GM and Chrysler that are on the verge of bankruptcy. Ford itself is healthy—and only in danger of being dragged along with GM and Chrysler because the collapse of those two would have a catastrophic ripple effect across the entire industry. Toyota, Honda and all the others would be gut-shot, too.

And yet, Ford uses UAW labor just like GM and Chrysler. But Ford somehow makes money—or at any rate, loses less than GM and Chrysler have. What to make of this? Could it be that perhaps Ford's business model is—dare it be said—more attuned to market realities and better set up than GM's and Chrysler's?

Point Number Two:

GM and Chrysler claim the core problem is so-called "legacy costs"—meaning the pension and health-care obligations they owe current and retired UAW workers. There is an element of

(Continued)

truth to this; the Japanese automakers don't have to worry about health care costs because the Japanese have national health care (which means everyone pays, instead of just the automakers).

Fair enough.

But to pin GM and Chrysler's current debacle on "legacy costs" is at best a half-truth. A quarter-truth, really. The real problem—in Chrysler's case—is an obsolete, unattractive product line. Not all of its cars—but enough to gum up the works very badly indeed. Chrysler failed to produce a successful successor to the formerly hot-selling Neon economy car; the PT Cruiser (also once a big seller) is now seriously dated; the Magnum and Pacifica wagons were huge belly flops—as have been the Jeep Patriot and Compass and Commander. The list goes on. . . .

In GM's case, it is a divisional structure that should have been completely redone at least 20 years ago. It is absurd that an automaker whose total market share is only 20-something percent continues to try to sell cars through six full-line divisions (Chevy, Saturn, GMC, Pontiac, Buick, Cadillac—plus Hummer) and hawks often as many as three or even four rebadged versions of the same basic car.

Whose fault is *this?* The unions? . . .

. . . Bottom line, the problems besetting GM and Ford are systemic and structural. The unions may not *be helping,* but the idea that they are the *cause* and that if only GM and Chrysler could cut their pay and rid themselves of the obligations they have to current and former workers, all would be well—is rank nonsense of the first order.

But it looks like the taxpayers are on the hook—because the federal government has fallen for the bait. On Friday, it was announced that some $17 billion would be made available to the ailing automakers. If the money is not conditioned on more than just forcing UAW concessions, but on addressing some of the much more cancerous problems laid out above, all we'll get is a brief "time out" before we're right back to where we were . . . about six–eight months from now.

Source: "The Collapse of the Auto Industry—Are Unions to Blame?" A. Brown, *EzineArticles.com.*

**Source:* "Are the Unions to Blame?" Eric Peters, *The American Spectator.*

Questions:

1. Why should unions be blamed for the near collapse of the North American car industry?
2. Why should unions *not* be blamed?
3. What lessons can be gained from this?

The Global Context

What are some of the fundamental sources of influence on the decision to engage in global business? In addition to addressing this question, this chapter will identify the different types of global business activity. We will examine one of the central controversies of globalization: the multinational corporation. This chapter will also explain why nations desire, or do not desire, to promote international trade, including an examination of the pros and cons of Canada's free trade agreement with the United States.

LEARNING OBJECTIVES

By the end of this chapter, you should be able to:

1. Identify factors that have encouraged the globalization of business.
2. Describe the central channels or forms of global business activity.
3. Discuss the importance and consequences of multinational and borderless corporations.
4. Explain the purpose of protectionism and its relationship with international trade.
5. Identify the types of regional economic integration.

THE BUSINESS WORLD

With Target, Canada's retail landscape set for massive makeover

Marina Strauss, Jacquie McNish

> U.S. department store chain Target has been searching for a way into Canada for years. When it appeared competitors were eyeing a bid for Zellers, the company moved fast. In just 30 days, the $1.8-billion deal was done, and now the retail landscape of this country is set for a massive makeover

Less than three years after Richard Baker bought a struggling Hudson's Bay Co. from the widow of its former owner, the New York investor is set to pocket close to $2-billion in a deal that accelerates Target Corp.'s entry into Canada.

(Continued)

HBC sold the bulk of its weakest chain, Zellers Inc., to the U.S. retail giant. Target will assume control of up to 220 Zellers stores and said it will spend more than $1-billion to convert 100 to 150 of them to its own banner within the next two to three years.

The move, which comes after years of rumours and discussion about Target's desire to acquire space in Canada, will dramatically reshape the domestic retail landscape.

It underscores the growing demand by foreign retailers for Canadian locations to take advantage of the country's relatively healthy economy. It also opens the door to other U.S. chains, such as Kohl's Corp., which are believed to be interested in Canadian expansion and are now expected to examine some of the Zellers locations that Target doesn't want.

Mr. Baker owes much of his windfall to a vibrant Canadian retail sector and brisk consumer spending activity. According to sources, the interest from popular U.S. chains is so great that when word leaked out last fall that Mr. Baker's private equity fund NRDC Equity Partners might consider a sale of Zellers, a number of U.S. players expressed interest.

The most ardent suitor was Target Corp., which had quietly been eyeing a Canadian perch for a decade.

The popular retail chain has never operated outside the United States, but sources familiar with the discussions said Target pushed its search into high gear in November by entering talks with Mr. Baker when it learned that competitors were also stalking Zellers.

"They didn't want to get beat out by other parties," Mr. Baker said in an interview Thursday.

Zellers, which has struggled since the mid-1990s, entered what could be its last chapter in its 70-year history last week in Target's headquarters in Minneapolis, Minn., where Mr. Baker travelled to negotiate an agreement.

The deal relieves Hudson's Bay of the burden of a tired retail chain that was losing ground to bigger U.S. competitors, particularly discount giant Wal-Mart Stores Inc.

The deal ultimately was done in about 30 days, Mr. Baker said, opening the way for the cheap-chic U.S. discounter, often referred to as Tar-zhay by the style-savvy, to launch its first outlets in Canada by 2013.

And it will undoubtedly change retail dynamics, providing solid competition to Wal-Mart, which was also at the table with Mr. Baker, looking to pick up Zellers stores. "Wal-Mart Canada should be concerned about the Target entry," said Rick Pennycooke, president of the retail real estate consultancy Lakeshore Group. "There will definitely be an impact on their stores, at least in the short term."

The sale is a financial coup for Mr. Baker. He acquired HBC in 2008 for roughly $1.1-billion; now he's set to collect more than $1.8-billion in the agreement, plus "hundreds of millions of dollars" for an estimated $800-million worth of Zellers inventory that will be divested, sources said.

In addition, Mr. Baker is sitting on more than $1-billion worth of real estate that HBC owns, including its downtown Toronto flagship Bay store and the connecting office tower.

The deal provides Target with 240 days to select the Zellers stores it wants to occupy. The company expects to eventually have more than 200 outlets in Canada over the next decade, said Gregg Steinhafel, chairman and chief executive officer of Target.

Nevertheless, Target still faces some hurdles in its Zellers deal. It has to negotiate terms of each lease with an array of Canadian mall owners. "We have a lot of work ahead of us, property by property," Mr. Steinhafel acknowledged.

However, landlords generally are keen about getting Target—or another new retailer—into its sites.

RioCan Real Estate Investment Trust, the largest Zellers landlord, hasn't ruled out allowing current leases to stand—at $6 a square foot they are all below the market average of $14, said CEO Edward Sonshine. But he said he's not willing to rubber stamp the deal without more research.

"I think it's going to be a question of the individual properties," said Mr. Sonshine. "We're not helpless here—and at the same time they have a lot of power too. It's a pretty level playing field. In some places we'll say if they leave, we're screwed so let's give them what they want. But at another location, we may say they can like it or lump it."

Meanwhile, Target may have a fight on its hands. Toronto fashion merchant Isaac Benitah has owned the rights to the Target name in Canada for almost a decade but now the U.S. discounter has challenged his right to use the name before federal trademark authorities. Mr. Benitah is pressing on with plans to expand his Target Apparel chain by adding at least a dozen of the superstores in the next couple of years, a source has said.

Mr. Baker said he'll use the proceeds of the Zellers sale to reduce debt and invest $500-million over the next three to four years in his other chains, including the Bay and U.S. department store retailer Lord & Taylor. Later this year, he plans to take the company public.

"I really wanted to fix Zellers and turn it into its own version of Target," he said. "We were just offered too much money to pass this opportunity up."

_____

WHAT IS GLOBALIZATION?

"The Business World" highlights the global context—one that involves many more players than local business and its domestic market. Business in the global context involves many stakeholders, including domestic and foreign competitors, workers, industries, governments, national cultures and economies. How business is conducted in light of trade agreements and the global arrangements is a key issue for our entire society. And this is a theme we will explore more fully in this chapter.

While you may have heard or read about this popular buzzword, many of you may not be completely familiar with what it represents and its implications. What is globalization? While there is no one, universal definition, it is useful to consider this concept as a process.

Globalization is a process involving the integration of world economics. The presence of trade blocs reflects the accelerating pace with which nations are integrating their economies. For example, NAFTA, the North American Free Trade Agreement, discussed later in this chapter, is a free-trade bloc consisting of Canada, the United States and Mexico. The EU (European Union) groups 25 countries, while APEC (Asian Pacific Economic Cooperation) consists of 21 nations forming a free-trade zone around the Pacific.

Globalization is a process involving the integration of world markets. This reflects the notion that consumer preferences are converging around the world. Whether it is for products made by McDonald's, Sony, Gap or Nike, organizations are increasingly marketing their goods and services worldwide. Though local modifications may be made to tailor the product to the local consumers, there is a push toward global products. On the other side, production is increasingly becoming a global affair. Businesses will set up operations wherever it is least costly to do so.

In sum, the recurrent themes raised in any discussion of globalization tend to include elements of the following:

- Globalization can be considered a process that is expanding the degree and forms of cross-border transactions among people, assets, goods and services.
- Globalization refers to the growth in direct foreign investment in regions across the world.
- Globalization reflects the shift toward increasing economic interdependence: the process of generating one, single, world economic system or a global economy.

SOURCES ENCOURAGING GLOBAL BUSINESS ACTIVITY

Why have we witnessed a tremendous surge in business activity on an international scale? From giant multinational corporations to small businesses, in recent years the drive toward global business has accelerated. A number of fundamental factors have encouraged the move to "go global." Some factors can be considered **pull factors**, and are the reasons a business would gain from entering the international context. Other factors are **push factors**—these are forces that act upon all businesses to create an environment where competing successfully means competing globally. (See Exhibit 6.1).

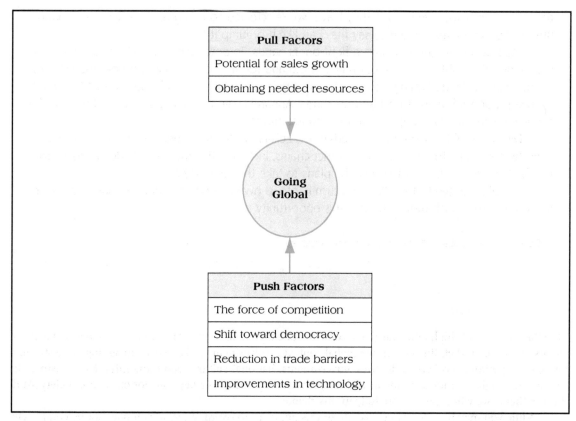

EXHIBIT 6.1 The impetus to "go global."

Pull Factors

Potential for Sales Growth

A fundamental reason for engaging in global operation is to help a business expand its markets. Increased sales are typically the central aim behind a company's expansion into international business. A significant portion of sales among the world's largest firms are generated from outside the home country. For example, U.S.-based specialty coffee chain, Starbucks Corp., began expanding operations in Europe almost a decade ago (especially in Vienna). The potential for increased sales was clearly a pull factor, a key question was, Would consumers in this European culture be attracted to these American business? Starbucks' aim was to provide a more modern version of the relaxed atmosphere of the Viennese café in order to attract this new consumer segment. Clearly, having the world as your market offers almost limitless potential beyond domestic consumers. Having access to foreign consumers also may mitigate the negative effects of domestic downturns in demand for the businesses' product of service. Consider, for example, the case of Avon Products Inc. This organization faced declining sales in North American markets, largely due to its traditional marketing channel (door-to-door sales), which failed to address the increased entry of women into the workplace and away from the home. On the other hand, Avon was able to successfully transfer its approach globally to over 20 emerging markets, including China, Brazil, South Africa and Mexico.

Obtaining Needed Resources

Businesses may choose to engage in global business activity in order to obtain resources that are either unavailable or too costly within the domestic borders. Acquiring foreign imports is a case of obtaining needed resources. It could be the case that a textile manufacturer imports its raw materials from a foreign supplier because these materials are not available locally. As well, the decision to locate businesses or plants in developing or underdeveloped nations may be a means to access inexpensive labour. For example, to access less expensive energy resources, a number of Japanese businesses have located in China, Mexico and Taiwan, where energy costs are not as high. Both Canadian and U.S. firms continue to expand their operations overseas because they can achieve higher rates of return on their investments, largely due to lower labour costs. (See Talking Business 6.1.)

Push Factors

The Force of Competition

Many domestic economies have become inundated with competing products or services. Typically, a business that seeks to grow needs to consider the markets beyond its domestic borders: this is where new, and potentially untapped, market opportunities still exist. Ironically, domestic economies are increasingly being filled with foreign competitors in many industries. The fact is, a business may find that it must compete against not merely domestic competitors, but foreign competitors as well. By default, a business may be *pushed* into becoming a global business by the simple fact that it is forced to compete with a foreign competitor. Moreover, for some businesses it seems foolhardy not to combat the foreign competition by attempting to go after the competitor's market overseas. In other words, the drive to "go global" may be a response to competitors' actions.

In addition, other domestic competitors may be expanding their markets overseas, which creates additional incentive for the business to follow suit. The notion of **first mover advantage** is a philosophy that underscores the benefits of being among the first to establish strong positions in important world markets. Later entrants into a foreign market may have more difficulty establishing themselves, and may even be effectively blocked by competitors.

Shift Toward Democracy

The shift toward democracy among many societies that were formerly economically and politically repressed has contributed to the creation of new market opportunities. Numerous totalitarian regimes have been transformed in Eastern Europe and Asia, for example, which has created new economic opportunities for businesses in other parts of the world. Countries like Russia and Poland have shifted toward a more capitalistic and democratic approach. Perhaps one symbol of this acceptance was the success of the North American McDonald's in entering the Russian marketplace years ago. Similarly, there has been a great interest in foreign investment in China since its move toward privatization—reduction in government ownership—in many areas.

Talking Business 6.1

Made in China

China's role is increasingly important in the world economy, and its growing role raises questions for the country itself and the world. China sees globalization as a key to its economic development and a better future for its people. Rapid growth has had a dramatic impact on the lives of millions of Chinese citizens. The success can be measured by tens of millions of people who have escaped poverty in China in the past decade or more. China's sheer size, coupled with its rapid growth, makes it a major player in the global economy. In nominal terms, China currently accounts for almost 4% of world output. By the end of 2004, China had attracted a total of $562.1 billion in foreign direct investment, approved the establishment of more than 500,000 foreign-funded enterprises in China, and created a huge import market of about $560 billion annually. Consequently, both the United States and Canada have to come to terms with the emergence of China as a major nation. China's fast development has brought not only great opportunities for China but challenges for the rest of the world. Some producers see Chinese competition as a threat. They worry about competitive Chinese exports flooding their markets and destroying jobs. However, this is what globalization is about: a major realignment of power and capacities in the world, as not only China but other countries become more important, and more influential. The world's economies are becoming increasingly interdependent.

Reduction in Trade Barriers

In recent years it has been observed that global business activities have been growing at a faster rate than in previous years, and in comparison to growth in domestic business. This acceleration may be largely due to the general push toward freer trade. In fact, probably the most powerful source of influence encouraging increased international business is the reduction in trade and investment restrictions. For example, the North American Free Trade Agreement (NAFTA) was established as an agreement to remove trade barriers between Canada, the United States and Mexico. This agreement essentially aimed to produce a common market among the members. Later in this chapter we will consider in more detail the nature of NAFTA, as well as a number of other important trade agreements.

Improvements in Technology

Another fundamental source of influence on globalization has been technology. Advancements in technology have more efficiently facilitated cross-border transactions. Innovations in information technology, as well as advances in transportation, have made it increasingly easy to transfer information, products, services, capital and human resources around the world. E-mail, the Internet, teleconferencing, faxing and transatlantic supersonic travel were among the activities that were not available until the late part of the 20th century.

Electronic commerce, or e-commerce, has been relatively free from government control, and this flexibility has contributed to the rate of globalization and the generation of virtual global organizations. Virtual organizations increasingly exist at the global level, where the geographic sources of the product or service and the location of the workforce are unimportant.

CHANNELS OF GLOBAL BUSINESS ACTIVITY

There are a variety of ways that businesses engage in global business. While practically any connection a business has with a foreign country essentially constitutes a form of global business, the degree of involvement of a business with a foreign country can vary. Below, we highlight various channels or forms within which businesses operate in the global sense. At a lower level of interconnectedness, a business can simply export or import goods or services to or from other countries. At a somewhat higher level, a company may choose to outsource some aspect of its business operations; it may choose to license some aspect or, perhaps, even arrange for franchise operations in foreign territory. Forming a strategic alliance or creating a joint venture with a foreign company requires the business to become more fully entrenched in the global context via directly investing in a foreign country. This can take the form of a merger, acquisition, the creation of a subsidiary or some other forms of direct investment in foreign operations. Each of these possible channels is discussed following. (See Exhibit 6.2.)

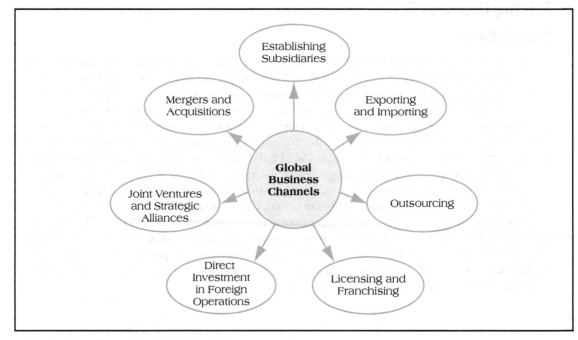

EXHIBIT 6.2 Channels of global activity.

Exporting and Importing

Businesses that engage in international business are more likely to be involved in importing and exporting than in any other type of global business activity. In addition to selling our goods or services to other countries, Canadian businesses may also purchase goods or services from foreign countries for resale to Canadians. Merchandise exports are tangible goods transferred out of the country, while merchandise imports are goods brought into the country. On the other hand, businesses might deal in service exports or imports of services. For example, banking, insurance or management services can be performed at an international level. Another type of service export or import can involve the use of a company's assets, including things like patents, trademarks, copyrights or expertise. The use of such assets constitutes a service rather than the provision of a tangible good, and is typically arranged through a licensing agreement. We discuss this channel of global business later on.

Exporting certainly offers much additional profitable activity for businesses, and the business opportunities available through exporting are significant. While there are about 30 million potential customers within our Canadian borders, there are over 6 billion potential customers across the world, increasing by about 95 million people annually. Many Canadian businesses have taken advantage of the benefits of exporting. Canada exports over 40% of our production, making us a major trading nation. (See Exhibits 6.3 and 6.4 for recent trade patterns.)

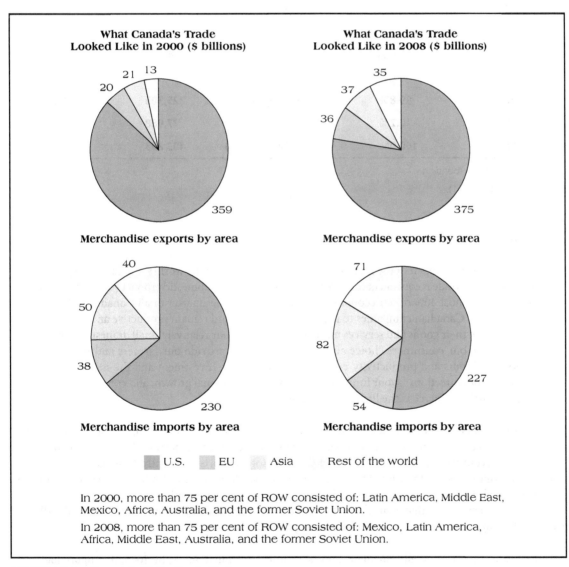

EXHIBIT 6.3 Canada's Major Trade Partners.

Source: Industry Canada Trade Data Online (TDO), from the Conference Board of Canada Report *Re-Energizing Canada's International Trade* (Feb. 2010). Find this report and other Conference Board research at www.e-library.ca.

EXHIBIT 6.4   Canada is a trading nation.

Canada's Major Trade Partners—By Country

Canada trades with the world but its main trading partner is the U.S., accounting for roughly two-thirds of trade and the majority of capital moving in and out of Canada.

Canada's Top 10 Export Markets by Country, 2010			Canada's Top 10 Import Markets by Country, 2010		
Country	Total Exports ($CAD millions)	% Share of	Country	Total Exports ($CAD millions)	% Share of
United States	298,524	74.9%	United States	203,152	50.9%
United Kingdom	16,396	4.1%	China	44,464	11.1%
China	13,232	3.3%	Mexico	22,105	5.5%
Japan	9,194	2.3%	Japan	13,411	3.4%
Mexico	5,008	1.3%	Germany	11,281	2.8%
Germany	3,938	1.0%	United Kingdom	10,697	2.7%
South Korea	3,709	0.9%	South Korea	6,148	1.5%
Netherlands	3,245	0.8%	France	5,429	1.4%
Brazil	2,567	0.6%	Italy	4,647	1.2%
Norway	2,529	0.6%	Taiwan	3,970	1.0%
Total of Top 10	**358,342**	**89.8%**	**Total of Top 10**	**325,305**	**81.6%**
Others	**40,484**	**10.2%**	**Others**	**77,988**	**19.6%**
Total (All Countries)	**398,826**	**100.0%**	**Total (All Countries)**	**403,293**	**100.0%**

Note: Numbers may not add to totals due to rounding.

Source: Industry Canada, April 2011 (5/2011).

According to International Trade Canada:

> Canada is the most open of the globe's major economies. We are the world's fifth largest exporter and importer—trade is equivalent to more than 70% of our gross domestic product (GDP). Exports account for almost 40% of our economy, and are linked to one-quarter of all Canadian jobs . . . Exports allow Canadian companies to keep generating jobs and remain productive and competitive by selling their goods and services more broadly than in our relatively small domestic market. Imports give our consumers choice and reduce costs, and provide our farmers and manufacturers with inputs and productivity-enhancing technologies. Investment and the movement of people in both directions favour innovation, business and personal growth, and competitiveness. International commerce is the lifeblood of our economy.[1]

Statistics Canada reports indicate that Canada is the United States' most important trading partner, and for many years, the United States has been Canada's largest trading partner. By the 21st century, the United States accounted for between 75–80% of Canada's total exports. Currently, Canada exports more of its manufacturing output to the United States than it consumes domestically. While Mexico still accounts for a relatively small share of our trade, trade with that country has grown greatly.

Observers have noted that while the bulk of our exports continue to go to the United States, distributing patterns of change have emerged. As a *Maclean's* magazine report noted:

> In 1993, 74 per cent of all Canadian exports went to the United States; by 2005, that figure had risen to 84 per cent. And yet . . . even as our U.S.-bound exports have gone up, their profile has been

changing, and not for the better: we are becoming more hewers of wood and drawers of water, not less so. We are sending the Americans more and more raw commodities (oil, natural gas, metals and other resources) and a smaller proportion of manufactured goods. Trade in services (everything from call centres to financial services), never strong to begin with, has also seen a relative decline. This trend is particularly worrisome: the services sector now makes up two-thirds of our domestic economy, yet we haven't figured out how to export it. A whole segment of potential export growth and wealth creation is going unfulfilled.[2]

In 2009, the economic downturn in global economies damaged Canada's international trade. However, since that time economies have improved including Canada's. Nonetheless, Canada must continue to improve its export status (see Talking Business 6.2).

Talking Business 6.2
A Fundamental Shift in Canada's Export Mix

In 1992, Canada's export profile was dominated by the auto and auto parts segment, which represented roughly three times the value of the next largest export group. By 2000, merchandise trade had expanded across the board, although the signs of decline in some sectors, notably paper and textiles, were becoming evident.

Between 2000 and 2008, overall merchandise export growth was minimal. But the trade mix changed significantly. (See chart.) Oil and gas replaced autos and auto parts at the top of the exports list as Canada went from being a net auto exporter to a net importer. Computers and electronics declined sharply following the tech bust. Paper continued to fall. And wood dropped out of the top 10.

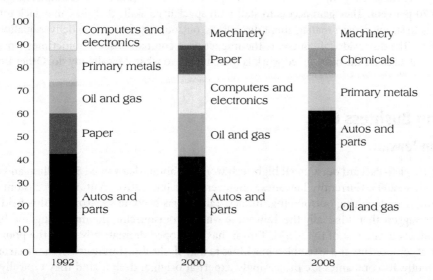

Canada's Shifting Merchandise Export Mix
(top five exports, per cent)

Note: The top five exports represented 37 per cent of total exports in 1992, 45 per cent in 2000, and 49 per cent in 2008.

Sources: The Conference Board of Canada; Statistics Canada.

Source: The Conference Board of Canada Report Feb. 2010, *Re-Energizing Canada's Internal Trade;* Statistics Canada; Industry Canada.

Outsourcing/Offshoring

As you may recall, outsourcing involves hiring external organizations to conduct work in certain functions of the company: so, for example, payroll, accounting, and legal work can be assigned to outsourced staff. The organization typically will retain its core functions or competencies: that is, those areas that it is in business to conduct. Nike is well-known for its use of outsourcing on an international basis. Nike has typically entered into contractual arrangements with manufacturers in developing nations to produce its footwear while it focuses largely on marketing its product. In fact, this has been a major underlying source of controversy with regard to businesses "going global"—the fear that relatively higher-paying North American jobs will be lost as business decides to outsource manufacturing functions to cheaply paid labour in Third World countries. (See Talking Business 6.3.) Countries can be contracted for the production of finished goods or component parts, and these goods or parts can subsequently be imported to the home country or to other countries for further assembly or sale.

India is one example cited as a major offshore or outsourced location. As observed by one writer:

> Globalization has played a significant role in India's rise as an economic force. It is also the foundation behind the country's success in the outsourcing industry ... One of the biggest beneficiaries of this "openness" is the outsourcing industry. Today, no company with outsourcing plans does not have India on its laundry list. India was able to achieve self-sufficiency not by closing its doors to the world. Rather, it spread the word across the world of how easy it is to do business in India.[3]

Offshoring and Canada

The following *Globe and Mail* article by David Ticoll offers an interesting and disturbing insight into outsourcing in Canada:

> It looks like Canada may soon join the growing political firestorm raised by the transfer of information technology jobs to places such as India and the Philippines.
>
> Companies elect to go with outsourcing—and offshore outsourcing in particular—for good business reasons. They enjoy cost savings on application development, for example, ranging from 35 to 70 per cent. They gain access to staff with specialized skills that they may lack internally. Thanks to strong project management disciplines, outsourcing firms often deliver quality results, and fast. The downside, of course, is the impact on a company's staff. Sometimes workers are protected, because the outsourced work is incremental to what they already do. Other times, the

Talking Business 6.3

Made In Taiwan

Dell and Hewlett-Packard outsourced high-tech work to Taiwan that valued $10 billion and $21 billion respectively in 2005. Currently, Taiwanese engineers offer innovative solutions for customers seeking design and manufacturing outsourcing. In fact, Taiwan has become so strong in this field that some observers suggest that it is really the Taiwanese who are outsourcing the marketing and branding of their products to the rest of the world. Taiwan has developed dramatically from the poor and lowly provider of components and assembled machines to that of a leading innovator in the electronics industry. Currently, its companies are increasingly expert at original design, and they typically dominate manufacturing in central categories such as notebook computers. Taiwan's success has been attributed to several sources, including its lower pay scales. For example, its engineering costs are approximately one third of comparable services in the United States. However, many observers are quick to point out that Taiwan's strength is not simply based on cheap labour but on its entrepreneurial culture combined with effective government involvement. Taiwan has grown from a provider of cheap labour and products to one of the most talented sources of high-tech expertise in the world.

Source: Based on Bruce Einhorn, with Matt Kovac in Taipei, Pete Engardio in New York, Dexter Roberts in Beijing, "Why Taiwan Matters" *Business Week* (May 16, 2005) 3933: 76.

outsourcing firm hires a company's staff as part of the deal. But there are also times when people lose their jobs.

Consulting and technical support by IT firms has consistently been a growth business. Never before have so many IT services jobs vanished, nor have such losses occurred over such an extended period.

Industry Canada analysts aren't sure why. But they suspect offshoring may have something to do with it.

If this theory turns out to be true, it will be striking evidence. After all, most jobs that migrate offshore aren't exported by IT firms, but by their clients in other sectors—banking, manufacturing, and so on. A bank, for example, concludes it can save call centre costs in India. It hires a North American or Indian IT services firm to handle it.

. . . What's the right thing to do? The answer is neither simple nor obvious. The anti-offshoring camp decries firms for caring only about profit. They shamelessly dump loyal employees. They submit them to the humiliation of training their own replacements. On a larger scale, the argument goes, we moved manufacturing jobs to China based on the theory that our economy needs more knowledge-intensive professions. Now that such jobs are moving offshore, it looks scary. We may all end up working at Wal-Mart.

The pro-offshoring camp has answers. Offshoring delivers a multiple return on investment. This creates capital for more promising ventures and demand for the next wave of innovative jobs. Consumers will pay less for goods and services. Places such as India prosper and grow as export markets for North American goods. Another line of argument says: Hey—why should rich countries have all the good jobs? Offshoring is a step in the direction of global justice. This is free trade at its best . . .[4]

Licensing and Franchising Arrangements

The licensing agreement is an arrangement whereby the owner of a product or process is paid a fee or royalty from another company in return for granting permission to produce or distribute the product or process. How could this be a type of global business activity? For example, a Canadian company might grant a foreign company permission to produce its product; or conversely, perhaps a Canadian company wishes to distribute a foreign-made product in Canada and requires a licensing agreement.

Why might a business enter into licensing agreements? Essentially, companies that don't wish to set up actual production or marketing operations overseas can let the foreign business conduct these activities and simply collect royalties. Whether it is for licensing fees or for management consulting services between two companies from different countries, the fees paid to foreign firms in return for the performance of a service would constitute service imports. Fees earned by businesses through providing such services would constitute service exports.

Franchising shares some of the advantages of licensing, in that both are relatively lower risk forms of global business. Franchising is, of course, a common type of business activity in Canada and elsewhere. This becomes a global business activity when the franchises are scattered in different locations around the world. (See Exhibit 6.5 for a list of global franchises.) While franchising is discussed elsewhere in this book, it is sufficient to note here that franchising involves drafting a contract between a supplier (franchiser) and a dealer (franchisee) that stipulates how the supplier's product or service will be sold. The franchisee is the dealer (usually the owner of a small business), who is permitted to sell the goods/services of the franchiser (the supplier) in exchange for some payment (e.g., flat fee, future royalties/commissions, future advertising fees). Probably one of the best-known international franchises is McDonald's, which licenses its trademark, its fast-food products and operating principles to franchisees worldwide in return for an initial fee and ongoing royalties. In return, McDonald's franchisees receive the benefit of McDonald's reputation, its management and marketing expertise. As one observer noted:

Franchising has proven to be one of the best marketing and expansion methods ever created. And while American franchises may be seen by a few as symbols of American greed, the majority still associates franchise brands with business success and economic development—even hope—worldwide. Why the popularity of international franchising? . . . More than simply liking the concepts, these franchisees desire the advantages U.S. franchises provide. "The consumer perception gives the international franchisee a better base to start with, as many American brands enjoy universal brand recognition" . . .[5]

EXHIBIT 6.5   The top 10 global franchises.

Franchise	2011 Rank	2010 Rank
Subway	1	2
McDonald's	2	1
KFC	3	3
7-Eleven	4	5
Burger King	5	4
Snap-On Tools	6	8
Pizza Hut	7	7
Wyndham Hotel Group*	8	N/A
ServiceMaster Clean	9	11
Choice Hotels**	10	N/A

*Brands of Wyndham Hotel Group were under consideration as individual entities in previous years
**New to this year's ranking

Note: Based upon an objective methodology that incorporates a host of criterion which includes, but is not limited to:

> System size, based on number of units
> Sales revenue for the company
> Number of years in franchising
> Stability and growth
> Support for prospective and current franchisees
> Environmental policies
> Corporate citizenship

Direct Investment in Foreign Operations

Foreign direct investment (FDI) involves the purchase of physical assets or an amount of ownership in a company from another country in order to gain a measure of management control. Capital can be invested in factories, inventories and capital goods or other assets. Control of a company can be achieved without necessarily owning 100%, or even 50%, interest. A direct investment can be done through acquisition of an already existing business in the host country or through a startup built "from scratch," so to speak. The choice may be dependent on a number of factors, including the availability of suitable businesses in the host country. If a suitable business already exists in the host country, it may prove more efficient than starting up a business there from scratch. It is no surprise that the vast majority (about 90%) of all FDI stems from developed countries, given that business in these countries will more likely have sufficient resources to invest overseas. Foreign direct investment in Canada is the second highest in the G7 as a share of GDP. (See Talking Business 6.4 regarding Canada's relationship with the United States.) In addition, Canadian investments abroad are the third largest in the G7 as a share of GDP.[6] (See Exhibit 6.6 for an illustration of foreign direct investment in Canada.)

Throughout the 1990s, we observed a growth in foreign ownership in the Canadian business context. Toward the end of the 1990s, foreign firms controlled about 22% of assets in Canada, which is a modest growth from 20.5% in 1994. By 2007, foreign controlled firms accounted for about 30% of all corporate operating revenues.

Why would businesses wish to engage in foreign direct investment? Controlling companies can obtain access to a larger market or needed resources via the FDI. Earlier in the process of globalization, direct investment was, in a sense, a substitute for trade. That is, while companies traded commodities that they had in abundance or that they could produce more competitively, they would also directly invest in countries where they needed to secure their source of raw materials or to manufacture their products inside the domestic market and, thereby, avoid tariffs or other import barriers. In that way, foreign investment occurred as a substitute for trade. More recently, however, with the liberalization of trade, foreign investment exists alongside trade. This is clearly seen in the fact that about one-third of world trade is conducted between members of the same

Talking Business 6.4

Canada/U.S. Trade and Investment

4 February 2011

Washington, D.C.

Canada and the United States enjoy one of the largest commercial relationships in the world with trade in goods and services totaling nearly $600 billion in 2009. Some $1.6 billion worth of goods and services cross the Canada-U.S. border each and every day.

The bilateral commercial relationship is critical to the economic prosperity and standard of living of people in both countries. About eight million jobs in the United States are linked to trade with Canada, while it is estimated that up to one in five jobs in Canada is linked to trade with the U.S.

The two economies are highly integrated, and Canada and the U.S. are each other's largest export markets. In fact, Canada is the number one foreign market for goods exports for 34 of the 50 states.

Key Statistics:

- In 2009, 47.1 million cars crossed the border and 39.3 million trips were made by Canadians to the U.S.
- In 2009, approximately three-quarters of Canada's merchandise exports went to the United States and one-half of our imports came from the United States. In turn, approximately one-fifth of the United States' goods exports went to Canada, and one-seventh of its goods imports came from Canada.
- More trade flows between Windsor, Ontario and Detroit, Michigan than through any other border crossing in the world.
- Over 20 million American travellers spend about $7 billion in Canada every year.
- Travellers from the United States represent 83 per cent of arrivals into Canada.
- The United States is the largest foreign investor in Canada and the most popular destination for Canadian investment.
- A truck carrying goods crosses the border every 2-3 seconds.

Source: Canada/U.S. Trade and Investment—Prime Minister of Canada.

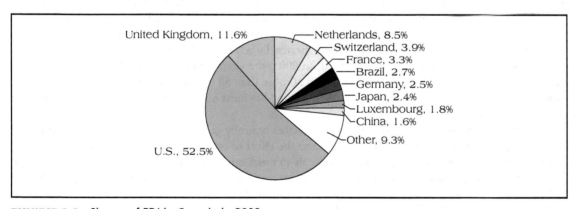

EXHIBIT 6.6 Shares of FDI in Canada in 2009.

Data: Statistics Canada.

organizations—i.e., between a parent company and its subsidiary, and between two subsidiaries of the same company. For example, a foreign subsidiary may require resources or supplies from the home country and, consequently, will import them.

Consequently, although FDI increases in a country, employment levels do not necessarily rise because of this increased investment. For example, mergers often result in the consolidation and elimination of some common functions: this can entail layoffs and, therefore, reduced employment levels. This relates to a more general concern about FDI: Does it benefit, or harm, the host country? That question continues to be debated. According to the recent report *Canada's State of Trade* (2010):

> FDI provides benefits to Canadian firms through the transfer of knowledge, technology and skills, and increased trade related to the investment, all of which enhance Canada's productivity and competitiveness. FDI is also one of the ways in which Canadian companies can integrate into global value chains.

Joint Ventures, Strategic Alliances

A joint venture involves an arrangement between two or more companies from different countries to produce a product or service together, or to collaborate in the research, development, or marketing of this product or service. This relationship has also been referred to as a strategic network. These organizations develop an arrangement whereby they share managerial control over a specific venture, such as seeking to develop a new technology, gaining access to a new market, etc. For example, Sony Ericsson is a mobile phone maker that is a joint venture between L.M. Ericsson of Sweden and Sony of Japan. Strategic alliances often aim to: extend or enhance the core competencies of the businesses involved; obtain access to the expertise of another organization; and generate new market opportunities for all parties involved. The level of ownership and specific responsibilities can be unique to that particular joint venture created among the partners. It has been observed that a high number of international joint ventures have failed largely due to the inability of the partners to find a proper "fit" with regard to their approaches and managerial styles. As in any relationship among partners, it must be given special attention, particularly when the partners are culturally diverse.

A typical arrangement may exist between a multinational corporation (MNC) and a local partner, since this facilitates the MNC's quick entry into a new foreign market through the joint venture with an already established local business. Consequently, the international joint venture has proven to be an efficient way of entering foreign markets rapidly and easing entry where local requirements have been implemented with regard to a degree of domestic ownership and participation in the production or distribution of the good or service.

Mergers and Acquisitions

A Canadian-owned company could actually merge with a foreign-owned company and create a new jointly owned enterprise that operates in at least two countries. The newspapers have been littered with reports of mergers and acquisitions on a global scale. It makes sense that, to the extent that globalization is a process of increasing the connectedness among economies, there is a further consolidation of markets and companies. For example, the Montreal-based commercial printing and book-publishing business, Quebecor World Inc., was able to expand rapidly in Latin America, largely through acquisitions and partnerships with local companies in Argentina, Chile and Peru. In 2004, the Canadian brewery Molson merged with U.S. Adolph Coors Co. in a "merger of equals" valued at more than $8 billion, creating a new "Canadian–U.S." company called Molson Coors Brewing Co. (See Talking Business 6.5 for a discussion of Canadian mergers and acquisitions.)

Why do such mergers occur? A number of factors typically generate the drive to merge, including the goal of obtaining new markets for the business and the effort to obtain new knowledge and expertise in an industry. The notion of achieving economics of scale in production may also be a source of influence on the decision to merge. Companies that merge on a global scale may be doing so in order to generate world-scale volume in a more cost effective way. Specifically, economies of scale in production are obtained when higher levels of output spread fixed costs (overhead, plant, equipment, etc.) over more produced units and, consequently, reduce the per unit cost. It is, in a sense, the ability to achieve cost efficiency through larger-scale production that is made possible through the creation of a bigger organization.

Establishment of Subsidiaries

Another well-known type of global business activity is the creation of subsidiaries or branch operations in foreign countries, through which the enterprise can market goods and services. Where possible, a business may choose to maintain total control of its product or service by either establishing a wholly owned subsidiary or by purchasing an existing firm in the host country. Acquisitions of local companies have become increasingly popular. These types of acquisitions allow efficient entry into a market with already well-known products

Talking Business 6.5

Is Canada Being "Hollowed Out" by Foreign Takeovers? Putting M&As in Historical Perspective

Public concerns that Canada is "up for sale" were fuelled by a series of high-profile mergers and acquisitions (M&As) in the 2006–07 period, involving such national icons as the Hudson's Bay Company, Fairmont Hotels, Inco, Falconbridge, and Alcan.

Recent Conference Board analysis shows that these takeovers are an exception to Canada's longer-term investment trend. Canadian companies have actually been more active in M&A activity abroad over the last decade and a half, than have been foreign companies in Canada. Mostly smaller in value, these takeovers attracted less attention (although they also involved some mega-deals—notably the acquisition of Reuters Group by Thomson Corp., which was the largest takeover of a foreign company in Canadian history).

Why the recent spike in large and expensive Canadian acquisitions? (See chart.) Analysis shows a strong link between M&A activity and record corporate profits in the U.S. and Canada, as well as with lower interest rates. The spike may also be part of a global phenomenon. In an era when China, India, Brazil, and others have emerged as major exporters and destinations for FDI, many companies need to expand in size in order to become more efficient and be able to compete against these lower-cost economies.

M&A activity in Canada is highly cyclical and is expected to slow over the near term due to tightening U.S. lending standards, a stronger Canadian dollar, and slower growth in U.S. corporate profitability. Given growing global competitiveness, however, the long-term trend for M&A is likely in an upward direction.

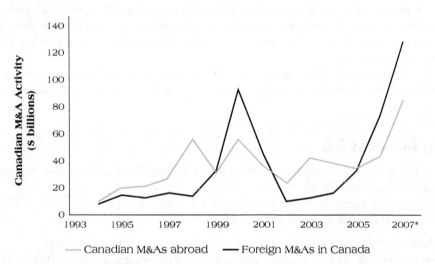

* up to third quarter of 2007

Source: Financial Post Crosbie: Mergers & Acquisitions in Canada.

Source: Thériault and Beckman, *Trends in Foreign Direct Investment.* See also Bloom and Grant, *"Hollowing Out"— Myth and Reality.*

Conference Board of Canada, *Re-Energizing Canada International Trade,* Feb. 2010.

and distribution networks. On the other hand, establishing a subsidiary from scratch in the host country may also be a viable option. For example, shortly following the import quota placed on Japanese cars in the 1980s, Japanese-based car manufacturers set up operations in North America and captured an even greater segment of the consumer market. Toyota, Honda and Nissan are among the companies that have successfully employed this strategy.

What are the benefits of such types of global arrangements? If the foreign country is a high source of sales for the enterprise, it may make sense to establish a presence in that country, in order to be more responsive to local consumer needs. Among the risks is the fact that much more is at stake when the company has invested in a wholly owned subsidiary: they have invested time, effort and expense to create this operation. Subsidiaries may face the threat of political instability, as evidenced in the past in places like China or South Africa. Subsidiaries may also face adverse environments that might turn hostile toward foreign ownership. For example, Toyota's presence in Canada has not been without controversy. In recent years Toyota's Canadian subsidiary argued that it was being unfairly slapped with import tariffs on parts, making it more difficult to compete with North American-based car manufacturers. Acquiring a Canadian business effectively transforms it into a "subsidiary" of the acquiring company. (See Talking Business 6.6.)

THE MULTINATIONAL CORPORATION

In terms of global types of business activity, the multinational corporation is a type of global business that has been receiving increasing attention, for better or worse. What is a multinational corporation, and why are we seeing its presence increasing across the globe? Observers have noted that such corporations are breaking down borders among countries and creating, in essence, borderless corporations. What are the implications of multinationals in terms of the costs and benefits they bring to the countries in which they set up business? We will address these questions in this section.

The first place to start is to offer a definition. What exactly are multinational corporations, and in what way are they "global business"? A global business is a business that engages directly in some form of international business activity, including such activities as exporting, importing or international production. A business that has direct investments (whether in the form of marketing or manufacturing facilities) in at least two different countries is specifically referred to as a multinational corporation (MNC). In other words, multinational organizations, or MNCs, are business enterprises that control assets, factories, etc., operated either as branch offices or affiliates in two or more foreign countries. An MNC generates products or services through its affiliates in several countries, and it maintains control over the operations of those affiliates, and manages from a global perspective. MNCs may also be referred to as global companies when they operate in myriad countries across the world.

Typically, MNCs are very large organizations and, in terms of their relative role in the world setting, it has been estimated that the 600 largest MNCs account for about one-quarter of the activity of the world's

Talking Business 6.6

More recently, a spate of high-profile acquisitions of well-known Canadian companies by foreign interests re-ignited the takeover debate.

Here's a list of some of the big-name Canadian companies that have fallen under foreign control in the past two years (or are due to become foreign-owned):

- Falconbridge of Sudbury, Ont., is acquired by Swiss-based Xstrata for $18 billion.
- Houston-based Kinder Morgan Inc. buys Vancouver-based utility company Terasen Inc. for $6.9 billion.
- Hamilton steelmaker Dofasco is bought for $4.7 billion by Luxembourg-based Arcelor SA.
- Graphics chip-maker ATI Technologies of Markham, Ont., is sold to California-based Advanced Micro Devices Inc. for $5.34 billion US.
- The Fairmont Hotel chain (the Chateau Frontenac, the Banff Springs hotel among others) is bought for $3.24 billion by an investors group led by a Saudi prince.
- Intrawest, owner of B.C.'s famed Whistler resort, is sold to a New York firm for $1.8 billion U.S.
- Vincor, Canada's largest winemaker, sold to N.Y.-based Constellation Brands for $1.1 billion.
- The Hudson's Bay Co., owner of the Bay and Zellers, taken private by South Carolina investor Jerry Zucker for $860 million.
- Sleeman Breweries of Guelph, Ont., bought by Japan's Sapporo Breweries for $400 million.
- Four Seasons Hotels agrees to $3.7-billion US takeover bid from Bill Gates's Cascade Investments and Kingdom Hotels International.
- Facing two competing foreign takeover bids, Inco finally agrees to $19.8-billion offer from Brazil's CVRD.
- Montreal-based paper-maker Domtar has agreed to a $3.3-billion merger with a unit of U.S. paper giant Weyerhaeuser.

economies. Technically, it may be more accurate to refer to such organizations as MNEs (enterprises), given that such organizations could, in fact, possess partnership status, for example, rather than being incorporated: a business can be multinational without being a corporation per se. Further, MNEs can be divided between those businesses that are globally integrated and those that are multi-domestic. Globally integrated companies are companies that integrate their geographically diverse operations through decisions centralized at head office. Consequently, all areas might be given the task of developing and selling a single global product; or perhaps each region is contributing to the manufacture of a certain product. A multi-domestic company, on the other hand, permits its geographically diverse components to operate relatively autonomously. (See Talking Business 6.7 for another example.)

So who, exactly, creates these organizations? Most MNCs have headquarters in developed countries—the *home* country. More specifically, over half of the MNCs have headquarters in the United States. France, Germany, the United Kingdom and Japan are among the other countries that are home to headquarters for most of the remaining MNCs. MNCs maintain branch plants or subsidiaries in two or more foreign countries—these are the *host* countries, and they are either developed, developing or Third World countries. (See Talking Business 6.8.) Among some of Canada's well-known MNCs are Bata Corp., which operates footwear manufacturing and distribution facilities in about 60 countries, and Bombardier Inc., which similarly is very much a part of the global market. This company has operations that include transportation equipment and aircraft production. While its head office is in Montreal, nearly 90% of its sales are in markets outside of Canada. It has production facilities in locations including Canada, the United States, France and Austria; and it markets products on five different continents.

Talking Business 6.7

China's Big Move into Alberta

Shawn McCarthy

Beijing Flexes Financial Muscle With Play for Oil Sands Trophy Asset

State-controlled Sinopec is spending $4.65-billion (U.S.) to become the first Chinese multinational to buy a direct stake in a major producing oil sands project, paying a rich premium for ConocoPhillips Co.'s 9-percent stake in Syncrude Canada Ltd. The deal represents the next stage in Chinese investment in the oil sands, as Beijing-controlled companies scour the globe for energy resources and look to diversify the country's growing imports away from the Middle East.

China's growing presence in the oil sands is likely to add momentum to the effort by pipeline giant Enbridge Inc. to build the Gateway pipeline to Kitimat, B.C., and provide Alberta oil producers with access to Pacific Rim markets.

The proposed pipeline, however, faces opposition by environmentalists and West Coast native groups, who have vowed to block Gateway, saying it would bring undue risks to an ecologically sensitive region.

Enbridge is in the process of lining up producers to supply the pipeline. The company has not publicly identified them yet, a spokeswoman said.

Syncrude is the trophy asset of Canada's oil sands, producing 350,000 barrels a day (with a substantial expansion in the works), and reserves of at least 5 billion barrels that ensure decades of future production. It was the first mega-project in the Alberta oil sands, dating back to development starting in 1973.

Until now, Beijing-controlled companies have purchased interests in proposed projects, or minority stakes in companies that have interests in oil sands production.

Sinopec, a subsidiary of China Petroleum & Chemical Corp., first arrived in Canada in 2008 with the purchase of a 40-percent interest in the proposed Northern Lights project north of Fort McMurray, Alta. It has since added to that stake and is now a 50-50 partner with France's Total SA.

Chinese multinational energy companies, however, have been increasingly aggressive buying into oil development in the Americas, including Canada, Venezuela, Brazil and Argentina, said Steve Lewis, a China-watcher at Houston's Rice University. . . .

Source: The Globe and Mail.

Talking Business 6.8
What's the Third World?

With regard to the globalization debate, it is useful to note that the term *Third World* was originally intended to describe the poor or developing nations of the world. In contrast, the first and second worlds were composed of the advanced or industrialized countries. The developed worlds were viewed as including the United States, Canada, and most of the countries of Eastern and Western Europe, as well as Australia, New Zealand and Japan. Within the broad territory described as the Third World, there are actually countries that are developing either rapidly (e.g., Brazil, Hong Kong, Israel, Mexico, Singapore, South Africa, South Korea and Taiwan) or modestly (including many countries of Africa, Asia and Latin America, in addition to India, Indonesia, Malaysia, and China) and others that have remained underdeveloped (e.g., Somalia, Sudan, sub-Sahara Africa). According to recent estimates, the Third World contributes most to the world's population growth, but is able to provide only about 20% of the world's economic production. A major controversy with regard to global business revolves around the fate of these underdeveloped nations: will they be purely exploited for the economic gain of MNCs, or will they benefit from the presence of increased industry?

The Borderless Corporation

Anthony Spaeth commented in a *Time Magazine* article: "The machinery of globalization is already integrating financial systems, dismantling territorial frontiers and bringing people closer together."[7] This comment is perhaps best illustrated in the new term for MNCs—*borderless corporations.*

Borderless corporation refers to the increasing ability of MNCs to ignore international boundaries and set up business just about anywhere. In fact, more and more MNCs are taking on the appearance of borderless corporations. Many of today's organizations that operate globally are, perhaps, less accurately referred to as MNCs than as TNCs, or transnational corporations; and in fact, these two terms are often used interchangeably. The term *TNC*, as well as the term *borderless corporation,* is also being applied to MNCs, given the increasing tendency of not simply setting up branch plants in foreign countries but of organizing management, investment, production and distribution as if the world were one country.

The term *multinational* is a bit inaccurate, given that many of these companies do not claim any specific nationality but, in fact, gear their planning and decision making to global markets. For example, goods could be designed in one country, raw material obtained from a second country, manufactured in a third country and shipped to consumers in a fourth country. Consequently, top management can be composed of international members, reflecting the international composition of the organization. The headquarters of MNCs can often be quite irrelevant. For example, while Nestle Food Corp. is headquartered in Switzerland, fewer than 5,000 of its over 200,000 workforce are actually working in the home country. Nestle has manufacturing facilities in over 50 countries and owns suppliers and distributors all over the world. Other similar examples of borderless or stateless corporations would include Coca-Cola, which, although headquartered in the United States, operates independent facilities around the world. In fact, Coca-Cola has seen the bulk of its profits generated in the Pacific and in Eastern Europe rather than in the United States, as have companies like General Motors. Other companies are equally transnational and almost borderless: Phillips, Nissan and Canada's Northern Telecom (Nortel), which has increasingly moved beyond the title of being a "Canadian business." (See Talking Business 6.9.)

The term *borderless corporation,* as opposed to *multinational,* emphasizes the notion that an enterprise can be a global company without any clear nationality. Often, the company has international ownership and international management. Headquarters do not necessarily belong to one home country.

Borderless companies are very mobile across borders with regard to the transfer of financial capital, materials and other resources. They set up business where it is profitable, rather than creating a branch plant whose head office is in another corner of the world. Decision making is local and decentralized. This underscores their focus in addressing the local needs of the market within which they operate.

Reduction in trade barriers is said to give rise to borderless corporations. However, borderless corporations can be equally effective in circumventing any trade barriers. Borderless corporations typically pledge

Talking Business 6.9

Think Global, Act Local

There is no better way of serving the needs of a geographically diverse market than by locating in the different geographical regions. This is reflected in the motto well-known among today's MNCs: "Think global, act local!" It has been suggested that many MNCs, such as Coca-Cola, Sony, Motorola and Nestle, have decentralized decision making among their geographically dispersed locations. For example, in IBM each subsidiary has its own local management, its own culture and its unique market focus. What this does is ensure that, for example, a Canadian client of IBM Canada sees the company as, indeed, IBM Canada, and not as simply a subsidiary of another U.S. MNC. This same philosophy is increasingly being employed by just about every MNC. Consider Nestle, which is headquartered in Switzerland, and yet which seems to many to be a U.S. company. Consider also the car industry—is a Ford car an American car? Well, not exactly, if you can imagine that it might be assembled in Brazil with parts from Europe and the United States. Like many other MNCs, in the new global economy the idea is to think global but act local. Regardless of where they operate, MNCs aim to reflect the local market tastes.

no allegiance to any one country or location; business is simply set up wherever profits can be maximized. Consequently, countries refusing to conduct trade with another country may not view a borderless corporation as a problem.

Currently the rapid rise of these MNCs, or TNCs, or borderless corporations, is raising many questions and concerns. For example, at a time when many countries are concerned with their competitiveness in the international market and their status in terms of trade, should we be concerned with who is generating the bulk of our exports? Does it matter what a company's nationality is, as long as it is providing jobs? Which government, and whose set of rules, will govern the behaviour of MNCs, or borderless corporations? Critics view the globalization of business as bringing with it as many threats as it does opportunities. (See Exhibit 6.7.)

Potential Benefits

- Encourages economic development.
- Offers management expertise.
- Introduces new technologies.
- Provides financial support to underdeveloped regions of the world.
- Creates employment.
- Encourages international trade through a company's access to different markets: it is relatively easy to produce goods in one country and distribute them in another country through a subsidiary or foreign affiliate.
- Brings different countries closer together.
- Facilitates global co-operation and worldwide economic development.

Potential Threats

- MNCs do not have any particular allegiance or commitment to their host country.
- Profits made by an MNC do not necessarily remain within the host country but may be transferred out to other locations depending on where the MNC feels the funds are most needed.
- Decision making and other key functions of MNCs may be highly centralized in the home country, so that even though other operations are performed in the host country, they do not necessarily include things like research and development and strategic planning.
- Difficulty in the ability to control and hold MNCs accountable can create serious ethical concerns for the host country. (See Talking Business 6.8.)

EXHIBIT 6.7   **The potential benefits and threats of MNCs.**

INTERNATIONAL TRADE

The globalization of business may be a relatively new buzzword, but one of its fundamental forms has been around for a long time: the notion of international trade. International trade essentially involves the purchase, sale or exchange of goods or services across countries. This can be distinguished from domestic trade, which involves trade between provinces, cities or regions within a country.

Certainly, the trend of globalization has included the gradual reduction in trade barriers among many nations of the world as a means to promote greater international trade. You have probably heard about the Free Trade Agreement and the debates surrounding it, but perhaps you are not very familiar with the issues. What are the implications of promoting freer trade across nations, and what are the implications of barriers to trade?

In order to understand some of the critical implications of free trade, it is useful to consider the nature of international trade. Why might countries want to trade? Why might countries want to engage in protectionism? Below, we will consider a brief history with regard to the issue of international trade.

The Logic of Trade

One fundamental argument is that since some countries can produce certain goods or services more efficiently than others, global efficiency and, hence, wealth can be improved through free trade. Clearly, it is not advantageous for citizens of a country to be forced to buy an inferior quality, higher-priced domestic good if they can purchase a superior, lower-priced, foreign-produced import. Consistent with this view is the belief that trade should be permitted to continue according to market forces and not artificially restricted through trade barriers. Freer trade would allow countries to trade as they deemed appropriate, rather than trying to produce all goods domestically. Consequently, each country can specialize or focus on producing those goods or services in which it maintains an absolute advantage, and simply trade with other countries to obtain goods or services that are required, but not produced by domestic suppliers.

Free trade is based on the objective of open markets, where a level playing field is created for businesses in one country to compete fairly against businesses in other countries for the sale of their products or services. The aim reflects the fundamental principles of comparative advantage. Each country expects to take advantage of each other's strengths, and thereby be permitted to focus on their own strengths. In simplistic terms, it is relatively inefficient for Canada to try to grow coffee beans or bananas, given the climate. Rather than wasting effort and money, these items can be imported from countries more suited to such endeavours, while Canadians can focus their efforts in areas where they can produce relatively more efficiently.

Mercantilism

The trade theory underlying economic thinking from the period ranging from about 1500 to 1800 is referred to as **mercantilism**. Specifically, the fundamental view was that a country's wealth depended on its holdings of treasure, typically in the form of gold. Mercantilism, essentially, is the economic policy of accumulating this financial wealth through trade surpluses. **Trade surpluses** come about when a country's exports exceed its imports and, consequently, more money is entering the country (from foreign consumers buying these exports) than is leaving the country (from domestic consumers buying foreign imports). This policy was particularly popular in Europe from about the late 1500s to the late 1700s, with the most dominant mercantilist nations including Britain, France, Spain and the Netherlands.

Countries implemented this policy of mercantilism in a number of ways. Foremost, the government would intervene to ensure a trade surplus by imposing tariffs or quotas, or by outright banning of some foreign imported commodities. Typically, the governments would also subsidize domestic industries in order to encourage growth in their exports. Another strategy employed by mercantilist nations was colonialization: acquiring less developed regions around the world as sources of inexpensive raw materials (such as sugar, cotton, rubber, tobacco). These colonies would also serve as markets for finished products. Trade between mercantilist countries and their colonies resulted in large profits, given that the colonies typically were paid little for their raw materials but were forced to pay high prices to purchase the final products. Obviously, the colonial powers benefited to the detriment of the colonies. In addition, mercantilist countries aimed to become as self-sufficient as possible with regard to domestic production of goods and services. This also served to minimize reliance on foreign imports.

Given this brief historical description, it is easy to see why, today, countries that endeavour to maintain a trade surplus and expand their wealth at the expense of other countries are accused of practising mercantilism or neo-mercantilism. Japan has often been viewed as a mercantilist country because of its typically high trade surplus with a number of industrial nations, including the United States.

Trade Protectionism

Essentially, **trade protectionism** is about protecting a country's domestic economy and businesses through restriction on imports. Why might imports be a threat to a country's business and economy? Two fundamental reasons can be considered:

1. Low-priced foreign goods that enter the country could compete with goods already produced here and, in effect, take business away from domestic producers. The ultimate consequence may be loss of sales and loss of jobs for domestic industries that are unable to compete with these lower-priced imports.
2. A country that imports more than it exports will have a negative balance of trade, or a trade deficit—which often results in more money flowing out of the country (to buy the imported goods) than flowing in (for our exports).

Among the best-known government responses to address these potential risks are the imposition of tariffs and import quotas. A **tariff** is essentially a tax placed on goods entering a country. Specifically, protective tariffs are intended to raise the price of imported products in order to ensure that they are not less expensive than domestically produced goods. This, of course, discourages domestic consumers from buying these foreign imports by making them more expensive to purchase.

Another common form of trade barrier or restriction is the **import quota**, which limits the amount of a product that can be imported. The reasons for this restriction are the same: to help ensure that domestic producers retain an adequate share of consumer demand for this product. For example, in the 1980s, both the U.S. and Canadian governments were concerned with the growing popularity of Japanese-made cars in Canada and the United States. These cars were higher quality and less expensive than the "Big Three" North American car manufacturers. After pressure from the automakers, both the U.S. and Canadian governments negotiated deals with the Japanese government and the Japanese automakers to "voluntarily" restrict the number of vehicles they would export to Canada and the United States for the following three years. Ironically, this strategy was short-lived, given that Japanese automakers eventually built auto plants in Canada and the United States and achieved an even greater share of the North American market.

As trade agreements continue to expand, countries are becoming increasingly critical of "protectionism." (See Talking Business 6.10.)

Talking Business 6.10

Protectionism in Canada? Nah . . . Couldn't Be

Kelly McParland

Canada's concerns about the dangers of protectionism are shared by many governments worried that their products and services will be blocked as governments put up barriers in ill-advised efforts to protect domestic business.

Business 24/7, in the United Arab Emirates, printed an article warning about the dangers of such short-sightedness, and citing Canadian airline policy as an example:

> At present, Canada limits Emirates to just three flights a week. That is three flights total—not just to each city. Emirates would like to increase its Toronto to Dubai service from three times a week to daily but is not allowed to do so. And what about services to Montreal or Vancouver? Sorry, that is not allowed either.
>
> This is absurd. The Canadian government does not limit the number of companies allowed to sell computers or cars so should it restrict consumers' ability to buy plane tickets. I suspect that the answer lies in the Canadian government's desire to protect Air Canada by forcing passengers bound to the Middle East to transfer in Europe so they can fly via the flag carrier's extensive transatlantic network. That might be good for Air Canada and its trade unions but is bad for any business that wants to expand its links with the rapidly growing Gulf.

What's Wrong with Mercantilism and Protectionism?

A trade surplus, as opposed to a trade deficit, certainly seems like a desirable aim, and is, in many respects, a benefit for any nation. The issue, though, is whether a policy of mercantilism is feasible, given its dependence on restriction of foreign imports. Perhaps the most significant criticism of mercantilism is that the central assumption upon which this policy is largely based is inherently flawed. Mercantilism assumes that trade involves a **zero-sum gain**—that is, the world's wealth is a fixed pie, and a nation can only increase its share of the pie by forcing other nations to reduce their shares of the pie. Based on this logic, one can understand the drive to minimize imports while maximizing exports. The flaw in this logic, however, is readily apparent. The practice creates a "one-way street" of trade, so to speak. That is, a mercantilist country aims to maximize the goods/services it sells to other countries, yet it expects to restrict the goods/services that these same countries attempt to sell to it. Even in the time of colonialism, the policy was ultimately self-defeating: colonies that received little payment for their raw material exports could not accumulate sufficient wealth to afford the high-priced imports that the mercantilists offered. (See Talking Business 6.11.)

Promoting International Trade

Whether it is tariffs, or quotas, or other forms of protectionism, we have seen a gradual lifting of trade restrictions as part of the wave of globalization. Most countries are endeavouring to eliminate trade barriers.

One of the most ambitious programs designed to encourage free trade was established way back in 1948 with the founding of GATT (the General Agreement on Tariffs & Trade), which was an agreement among approximately 100 countries to reduce the level of tariffs on a worldwide basis. And it did encourage a gradual reduction in trade barriers. In 1995 the World Trade Organization (WTO), in effect, took over the management of the global trade system from GATT. Its mandate is, essentially, to develop and administer agreed-upon rules for world trade, and discourage protectionist laws that restrict international trade.

Other organizations exist whose purpose is also to assist nations or the global economy. For example, the International Monetary Fund (IMF) was established after World War II to provide short-term assistance in the form of low-interest loans to countries conducting international trade and in need of financial assistance. The World Bank was established at the same time to provide long-term loans to countries for economic development projects. Typically, the World Bank will borrow funds from the more developed countries and offer low-interest loans to underdeveloped Third World nations. So, both these organizations, by assisting less prosperous nations, help to facilitate trade and investment between countries.

Countries themselves have been pursuing trading blocs and other forms of economic integration as part of the general thrust toward a more integrated world economy. This means opening doors to more foreign competition as well as more foreign ownership. This issue of economic integration is discussed below.

Facilitating Global Business: Regional Economic Integration

Regional economic integration means bringing different countries closer together by the reduction or elimination of obstacles to the international movement of capital, labour, and products or services. A collection of countries within such an integrated region is typically referred to as a regional trading bloc. Why do countries endeavour to integrate? It is, largely, a logical conclusion to maximizing the benefits of international trade,

Talking Business 6.11

The Futility of Protectionism

Restrictions on imports can be self-defeating, given that other countries will act in a similar manner and reduce their imports. Consider the case of Canada, where a large portion of our raw materials are exported. Can it restrict imports from countries who are similarly purchasing our exports?

The Great Depression of the 1930s was largely due to the protectionist policy passed by the U.S. government at that time. The government placed tariffs on many goods entering the United States in order to protect U.S. industry. However, the result was that many other countries raised their tariffs and caused a sharp drop in U.S. exports and, in fact, hurt trade among almost all countries.

as discussed earlier, with regard to greater availability of products, lower prices and increased efficiency or productivity. Trading blocs increase international trade and investment, with the central aim of improving their economy and living standards for their citizens.

Regional integration can occur at different levels of intensity, so to speak. These include, from the lowest to the highest levels of integration, free trade areas, customs union, common market and economic union. It is worthwhile to briefly examine each form.

1. **Free trade area.** This form of economic integration involves the removal of tariffs and non-tariff trade barriers (i.e., subsidies and quotas) on international trade in goods and services among the member countries. Given that this form involves the lowest degree of regional economic integration, there is greater member autonomy with regard to such issues as how it chooses to deal with non-members and what types of barriers it should construct against non-member countries. Examples of this form are the North American Free Trade Agreement and APEC, both of which are discussed later in this chapter.

2. **Customs union.** This form of economic integration involves the removal of trade barriers on international trade in goods and services among the member countries. However, given that this form involves a somewhat greater degree of economic integration, there is less member autonomy with regard to such issues as how it chooses to deal with non-members, and what types of barriers it should construct against non-member countries. Members will typically generate a uniform policy regarding treatment of non-members. One example of this type of integration is the MERCOSUR customs union, which is a major trade group in South America. This customs union was established in 1991, and its partners include Argentina, Brazil, Uruguay and Paraguay; it grants associate status to Chile and Bolivia. By 1996 the members had eliminated tariffs on goods accounting for 90% of trade between the member countries and, eventually, largely abolished trade barriers. In 1995 MERCOSUR implemented a common external tariff: which, by definition, makes it a more highly integrated trading bloc than NAFTA. These countries represent an attractive market for foreign companies because of the large population and high proportion of middle-class consumers. However, tariffs for non-members have ranged from 16% to 32% and, consequently, have made it challenging for outsiders. Countries like Canada and the United States are awaiting further agreements like the FTAA (the Free Trade Area of the Americas) that would allow greater access to the Latin American markets for North American exports.

3. **Common market.** This form of economic integration builds on the elements of the two previous forms, including the removal of trade barriers and the implementation of a common trade policy regarding non-members. In addition, members of a common market will typically also generate a freer flow of labour and capital across their borders. Given the requirement of co-operation in economic and labour policy, this level of economic integration is, consequently, more difficult to achieve than the previous two levels. The European Union, discussed below, is one such example of a common market arrangement.

4. **Economic union.** This form of economic integration builds on the previous three forms and, in addition, involves a coordination of economic policies among the member countries. It requires a higher level of integration than a common market, because it involves the harmonization of fiscal, monetary and tax policies. In addition, it often includes the creation of a common currency. Consequently, member countries in such an arrangement maintain much less autonomy compared to the lesser forms of economic integration. In the following discussion of the EU, it can be noted that the members are moving toward greater integration of economic and political policies, which would, essentially, move them closer to a genuine economic union.

A significant portion of total world trade occurs within three regional trading blocs, also referred to as the Triad market of North America, Europe and Asia. Given the importance of these trading blocs, it is worthwhile to highlight each. Following is a relatively brief description of the trading blocs in Europe and Asia, followed by a lengthier discussion of the North American trade agreement and its implications for the Canadian business environment.

European Union (EU)

In 1992, 12 nations of Europe established a common market, called the European Community (EC); and in 1994, after adding several new members, it became known as the European Union (EU). The European Union is a common market with a single currency, a free flow of money, people, products and services within it member countries. Currently, there are 27 member states within the EU, with some members also adopting a common currency (the Euro) and monetary policy. The members include Austria, Belgium, Denmark, Germany, Greece, Ireland, Italy, Portugal and the United Kingdom, among others. In total, the EU is currently the largest integrated common market in the world, with approximately 500 million consumers.

Common market is a term that refers to a group of countries who remove all tariff and non-tariff barriers to trade. Indeed, the aim of the EU is to create a borderless Europe, so to speak. In fact, the bulk of the advanced regions of Europe exist in essentially one giant market, with the free movement of goods and services, as well as people and financial capital. Businesses that operate outside the boundaries of the EU can achieve the benefits of membership if they have a subsidiary in at least one member country. For example, U.S.-based companies like 3M, Hewlett-Packard and GE have already established a European presence, and consequently enjoy the same benefits as businesses who are part of the member European countries. Those not yet established in Europe are developing strategies to exploit this large market.

The EU can be a double-edged sword for non-members. It can generate protectionist policies for its members, like tariffs or quotas, to bar the United States or Japan from entry, for example. On the other hand, the EU could also create opportunities for non-members—they comprise a huge market for North American exports, for example. A number of U.S.-based companies have chosen to engage in joint ventures with European-based companies as a means of obtaining some kind of presence in the European market.

Does this common market matter to Canada? It certainly does. The EU is one of Canada's most important trading partners. Clearly, this large market cannot be ignored. Aside from the United States, five of Canada's top ten export markets are in Europe. Consequently, observers view Europe as a potentially strong market for Canadian goods, if tariff and non-tariff barriers can be reduced. In addition, many critics feel that there is currently too high a reliance on one market (the United States) for Canadian exports and increased trade with other markets is preferable.

Asian Trading Bloc

Another region of growing importance to Canada has been the Asia-Pacific region. This region has a total population of about two billion—approximately twice that of the European community. In addition to the drive for greater economic integration and free trade in Europe and North and South America, Asia has also sought to create trading blocs. Singapore, Hong Kong, Taiwan and South Korea (also referred to as the Four Tigers), together with the relatively dominant partner, Japan, have grown to become an increasingly integrated economic region.

ASEAN   The Association of South-East Asian Nations (ASEAN) was established in 1967 and became the first major free-trade bloc in Asia. Its aim was to promote greater co-operation in areas such as industry and trade among the members, including Singapore, Malaysia, Indonesia, Thailand, Vietnam, the Philippines, Brunei, Cambodia, Laos and Myanmar. At the same time, member countries are protected by trade barriers from non-members. There is a move to create a greater East Asian trade and economic grouping, consisting of the Association of Southeast Asian Nations (ASEAN) countries, plus Japan, China and South Korea.[8] The process of creating a trading bloc has been slower in Asia partly because, unlike NAFTA and the EU, there is a very wide disparity between the economic infrastructures and the GDPs of Japan, South Korea and China. While disparities exist among members in the EU, they are not as great. For example, a number of current EU members, like Portugal and Greece, have remained behind such members as Germany, France and Britain. In addition, much of Mexico's southern region lives in essentially Third World conditions. However, the disparities in the economics of China, South Korea and Japan are much greater. All this contributes to a greater difficulty in integrating the regions for trade purposes.

APEC   The Asia-Pacific region has also set out to facilitate greater economic cooperation and freer trade through the establishment of the Asia-Pacific Economic Cooperation (or APEC), formed in 1989. Among the members of APEC are the People's Republic of China, Hong Kong, Japan, Indonesia, Malaysia, South Korea, Canada and the United States, to name some of the 21 members. It is viewed as a significant economic force, given that its members generate over 50% of the global output and about 50% of its merchandise trade. APEC was established to promote economic co-operation among members in the areas of trade and investment. Its relatively diverse mix of countries is, in effect, an effort to counter the narrower regionalism of such arrangements as the EU and NAFTA. In fact, APEC includes three of the traditionally largest economies—the United

States, China and Japan. NAFTA was included in APEC largely as a means to forge stronger economic links between North America and Asia.

How important is APEC to Canada? Canada's central aim in joining APEC was to expand trade opportunities with the region. This region has a total population of about two billion—approximately twice that of the European community. This represents a large market for Canadian exports. Next to the United States, Japan has been one of Canada's largest trading partners; and Japan, along with other member nations, represents a high potential as consumers for our exports. The suggestion is not necessarily to decrease the level of trade and investment that Canada has established with the United States; but rather to pursue similar levels of access to other major regions, such as Asia. As business writer David Crane observed:

> Globalization in the 21st century is more likely to have an Asian face than an American one, as China and India boost their investments in education and research and development, building their own multinationals and expanding their economic reach. What will this mean for Canada? . . . Canada's capacity to play the global role that Canadians aspire to will depend on many factors, including creating and allocating the resources that allow it to do so. This means Canada has to be an economic, social and environmental success at home. In particular, Canada has to make the transition to a knowledge-based society, with a high level of literacy and capacity for innovation.[9]

North American Trading Bloc and NAFTA

The Canada–U.S. Free Trade Agreement (FTA) came into effect January 1, 1989, and was largely aimed at reducing, and eventually eliminating, tariff barriers on almost all goods and services traded between Canada and the United States, as well as at further facilitating cross-country investments. Among the other provisions of the agreements are rules regarding government subsidies, the imposition of countervailing duties, standards of health and safety, and the environment. Essentially, for Canadian exporters this agreement offered better access to the huge American market for Canadian goods and services. In 1994, the North American Free Trade Agreement (NAFTA) was established and this, similarly, was an agreement to remove trade barriers between Canada, the United States and Mexico. This agreement, which replaced the FTA, essentially aimed to produce a common market among the members. There has been much written regarding the impact that NAFTA has had on Mexico, the United States and Canada. Before we identify some of the major arguments supporting or condemning free trade, let's consider some of the areas that have been impacted by this free trade agreement: Trade, employment and business, culture, competitiveness and the consumer (see Exhibit 6.8).

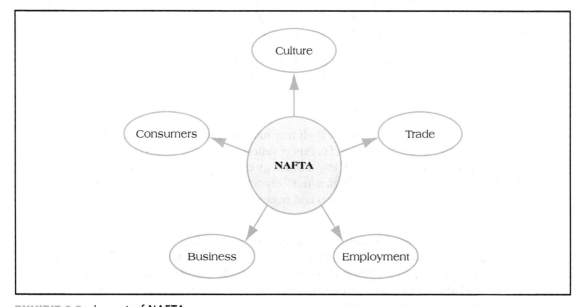

EXHIBIT 6.8 Impact of NAFTA.

Advocates of free trade say:

- NAFTA achieved its most fundamental objective: to increase the level of trade between Canada and the United States. Canada and U.S. trade increased by about 75% since the establishment of the FTA. Of course, the United States continues to be Canada's major trading partner, accounting for almost 80% of Canada's total trade.

- Canada's merchandise trade with the United States increased by 80% in the first five years of the NAFTA, and Canada's trade with Mexico increased by 65%, reaching $271.5 billion and $1.4 billion, respectively, in 1998.

- One measure of the relative significance of trade to a country is to observe the volume of an economy's trade relative to its total output (percentage of GDP). Exports of Canadian goods to the United States were approximately 17% of GDP in the 1980s, prior to NAFTA. With the implementation of NAFTA, exports and imports grew significantly over the period from 1990 to 1999. Specifically, as a proportion of GDP, exports grew from 25.7% to 43.2%, while imports grew from 25.7% to 40.3%. In contrast, for the 10 years prior to the Free Trade Agreement, exports and imports as a proportion of GDP were practically constant. Total Canada–U.S. trade in both goods and services rose from $425 billion in 1995 to $700 billion in 1999.

- The Government of Canada Web site has underscored what it views as many positive consequences of NAFTA, including the following:

  > NAFTA has helped transform the three economics while creating synergies that go far beyond economic prosperity. As with any trade liberalization initiative or other economic change, NAFTA affected some sectors positively and others adversely, but there is little doubt that on the whole, the agreement produced real net benefits for workers and consumers of the three countries . . . some 70 million passengers cross the US–Canada border each year (twice the population of Canada), along with 7 million commercial trucks, and 1.3 million rail containers. Since NAFTA's implementation in 1994, total merchandise trade between the US and Canada has grown by over 120%, and when you include trade in services, the growth has been closer to 140%. US trade with Mexico has shown even more significant growth (nearly tripled) over the same period. United States exports to Canada and Mexico have surged 85% from $142 billion to $263 billion in the same period, significantly higher than the 41% increase of United States exports to the rest of the world.[10]

Critics of free trade say:

- Any trade improvements witnessed over the last decade may be more attributable to Canada's then relatively low dollar than due to the results of NAFTA. The fact that for years, the U.S. dollar was stronger than the Canadian dollar may have been a stronger help for Canadian exports. As one writer observed:

  > Much has been made of Canada's NAFTA-driven trade success, but the reality does not live up to the hype. Canada's merchandise trade surplus with the U.S. is less than meets the eye . . . a federal Industry Department study found that by far the largest factor—accounting for 90% of the 1990s export surge—was the low Canadian dollar.[11]

- While the quantity of Canada–U.S trade itself may have improved, there have not been any improvements in the quality or nature of Canada's export patterns. As noted earlier, Canada had been far too reliant on exporting of raw materials ("low-technology exports"), in relatively unprocessed form, to the United States. More "added-value," "higher-tech" exports need to be generated so that we can become stronger in more valuable types of exports and engage in more research and development in order to do so. As one critic indicated:

  > Although there was an increase in some high-tech sectors, notably telecommunications and aerospace, the trade deficit in high-tech products remains high . . . and Canada's poor record in private sector R&D persists. Relative to GDP, Canada's exports of higher value-added products—including autos, machinery and equipment, and consumer goods—have fallen by one-quarter since 1999. . . .[12]

- NAFTA has encouraged us to become too dependent on trade with the United States. This point is driven home by such observations as the following:

    > Meanwhile, outside NAFTA, the world economy has undergone a vast metamorphosis. China has grown into a trading giant. India is becoming a global leader in the services trade. The European Union is bringing growth to once-perennial underperformers such as eastern Europe and Spain; the latter's economy has grown to roughly the same size as Canada's. The United States has made a higher priority of trading bilaterally with emerging players, and some of their trade agreements may prove more comprehensive than NAFTA, putting Canada's preferred status in the United States at risk. Indeed, China will soon supplant us as America's top trading partner.[13]

- We need to expand trade with other nations rather than relying solely on NAFTA. NAFTA may have caused Canada to become too complacent in the global market. Consequently, many observers note the need for Canada to place much greater effort on establishing strong trade ties with other countries. As Phillip Preville commented in his recent *Maclean's* report:

    > Our share of global exports and investment to China has actually been on the decline, and we are no longer among China's top 10 trading partners. . . . Trade policy should be geared towards facilitating exports of services, and also importing components to reduce the cost of goods manufactured in Canada—a way of making China's manufacturing prowess work for us. . . . also recommends pursuing trade with India and other emerging nations in Asia and Latin America, as well as renewing relationships with old partners in Europe and Japan.[14]

NAFTA's Impact on Canadian Employment and Business   NAFTA's impact on employment and wages has not been clearly determined to date. Different groups have offered different information as to whether jobs have been lost or created as a result of free trade. The key controversy surrounding NAFTA is the issue of jobs. Do open trade and increases in foreign presence in a country result in job creation or job loss? If countries allow products or services to freely enter their borders, what happens to the domestic producers of such products or services?

Advocates of free trade say:

- Foreign competition forces domestic businesses to improve their operations and improve their products or services.
- Protecting domestic business amounts to discouraging competitiveness and innovation and, ultimately, will lead to job losses, given the inability to remain competitive in world markets.
- Free trade encourages countries to abort inefficient operations and focus on the relatively stronger commodities or services in which they have a competitive or comparative advantage.

Critics of free trade say:

- Many Canadian manufacturers cannot compete with U.S. imports, and are forced out of business.
- Job losses arise from U.S. companies deciding to shut down their Canadian subsidiaries and exporting their tariff-free goods to Canada.
- Many manufacturing jobs are lost to Mexico, given that country's relatively cheaper labour and, hence, lower-priced goods.

    > Free trade was sold as a solution to Canada's persistent unemployment problem. Though there are other factors at play, the record does not bear this out. Average unemployment during the last 15 years has remained about the same as the average rate during the previous 15 years. Nor has the promise of increased employment quality—high skill, high-wage jobs—under free trade materialized. On the contrary, displaced workers in the trade sectors have moved to lower-skill, lower-wage jobs in the services sector. Precarious forms of employment (part-time, temporary, and self-employment) have also increased. . . .[15]

NAFTA's Impact on Canadian Culture

Advocates of free trade say:

- The agreement is not signing away Canada's cultural heritage, any more than the European Community forced European nations to lose their individual cultures.

- According to Statistics Canada, Canadian cultural exports exceed $4.5 billion, and more royalty money for music is coming into Canada than is leaving.

Critics of free trade say:

- Free trade will encourage the destruction of a unique Canadian culture.
- Increasing foreign domination of the Canadian economy will transform Canada into a pure economic subsidiary of the United States.
- Publishing and broadcasting industries are threatened by American competitors and the increasing presence of American-based media.
- The presence of the United States in areas like the Canadian entertainment industry would pose a serious threat to the transmission of Canadian culture.

NAFTA's Impact on Canadian Competitiveness and the Canadian Consumer

Advocates of free trade say:

- One of the central objectives of the FTA was to encourage Canadian businesses to become more competitive through exposing Canadian businesses to greater competition from American business.
- Canadian consumers are given more choice and are exposed to competitive products with free trade. That is, they will have access to potentially less expensive goods or services—whether they come from the United States, or from increasingly competitive Canadian businesses.
- Canadian companies that require inputs from U.S. businesses can now obtain them more cheaply, and pass these savings on to the consumer.
- Canada cannot afford to ignore the U.S. market. If Canadian companies wish to become more competitive, they also need to serve a larger market—and the United States certainly offers a huge market for Canadian goods. Free trade gives Canada greater access to selling goods and services to this market through the reduction of trade barriers.

Critics of free trade say:

- NAFTA has not encouraged any increase in productivity. Canadians have been unable to match U.S. productivity rates for the past 20 years, and have produced at rates that are equal to about 80% of the output of workers in the United States.
- NAFTA has not reduced the productivity gap between Canada and the United States:

> As for the productivity gap with the U.S. that was, according to proponents, supposed to narrow under free trade, it has instead widened. Canadian labour productivity (GDP per hour worked) rose steadily in relation to U.S. productivity during the 1960s and 1970s, peaking at 92% of the U.S. level in 1984. Thereafter, it slid to 89% in 1989 and by 2005 had fallen to just 82% of U.S. productivity—below where it was in 1961.[16]

- Our good record of exports has come about largely because the relatively low value of the Canadian dollar has made our goods cheaper in the past. In other words, it is not that we were producing cost-efficient goods, but rather it is an artificial reduction in the value of our dollar that has made them cheaper on foreign markets. Consequently, a higher Canadian dollar results in decreased export. What is needed, arguably, is real improvements in productivity coming from things like updating equipment, retraining workers and building competitiveness.

WHERE IS CANADA HEADED?

NAFTA, like other trade agreements, facilitates globalization—the mobility of resources across borders, the freer flow of goods and service, the increase in foreign investment and the growing interdependence of economies. Such instruments bring potential benefits and threats. While many observers see dangers in the outcomes of freer trade, only time will tell us whether Canada ultimately gains or loses. Talking Business 6.12 presents excerpts from the recent popular press that also attempt to identify the pros and cons of Canada embracing freer trade and foreign investment.

Talking Business 6.12

Was NAFTA a Good Thing?

Praising NAFTA*

In supermarkets and department stores from coast to coast, Canadian consumers are faced with almost endless choices. But few are likely to be aware that both the range and affordability of products are linked to Canada's membership in the world's largest trading agreement.

That's been increasingly so in the decade since Canada, Mexico and the United States entered into the landmark North American Free Trade Agreement, or NAFTA.

With a combined gross domestic product of US$11 trillion among its members, representing about 30 percent of the world's total, NAFTA ranks as an economic and diplomatic success. The access it has provided to the vast U.S. market has made Canada the envy of trading nations around the world.

... Both agreements have eliminated tariffs on most merchandise, set out clear-cut trading rules and created a larger, more integrated market. This makes North America one of the most efficient regions in the world in which to conduct business. Among the biggest winners of all have been Canadian consumers.

"Canadian shoppers win two ways," says John Curtis, the senior economist with International Trade Canada. "First, they have more choice because more goods and services are being imported. Second, prices are lower because NAFTA has made all three trading partners more competitive."

But it's not only consumers who benefit from freer flowing trade: it's the economy overall. Through NAFTA, Canada has consolidated its position as the largest trading partner of the U.S. In 2003, nearly 80 percent of Canada's total exports went south of the border, up from 71 percent in 1989. The importance of the U.S. as an export market has increased for most Canadian provinces and nearly every industry.

Consumer boon: NAFTA has eliminated tariffs on most merchandise, set out clear-cut trading rules and created a larger, more integrated market, making North America one of the most efficient regions in the world in which to conduct business.

"NAFTA has been a powerful force for Canadian manufacturers," says Perrin Beatty, President of the Canadian Manufacturers & Exporters, adding that predictable trade rules and the elimination of tariffs have created greater demand in the U.S. for Canadian-made parts and merchandise. "While there was a period of adjustment for manufacturers, NAFTA on balance has been enormously positive for Canada and has proven that we can compete."

Spurred on by NAFTA's success, Canada has been pursuing further trade opportunities throughout the hemisphere and beyond. Bilateral free trade agreements took effect in 1997 with Chile and in 2003 with Costa Rica. Canada is currently negotiating agreements with El Salvador, Guatemala, Honduras and Nicaragua. As well, Canada, Mexico, the U.S. and the other 31 democratic countries of the hemisphere are now working toward establishing a Free Trade Area of the Americas.

Such agreements can only be good for Canada, with its relatively small population and the importance of trade for its economic prosperity.

"There is very little doubt that our country's fiscal health is linked to freer international trade and investment," Curtis adds.

The Perils of Freer Trade**

Not too long ago, the Investment Review Division of Industry Canada reported a record number of foreign takeovers of Canadian companies in the same year.

After the House of Commons Industry Committee recently proposed dropping restrictions on foreign ownership of telecommunications and cable companies, our two national newspapers and some of the Asper dailies bubbled over with lavish praise. That this is happening in a country that already has such a terribly high degree of foreign ownership and foreign control is not only difficult to comprehend, but dismaying for those of us who value Canadian sovereignty and independence.

Even more dismaying is the likelihood that ... the sale of Canada to foreign owners will accelerate. Today, over thirty-five per cent of corporate profits in Canada already go to foreign companies.... At what point would you say that enough is enough? And then, exactly what would you do about it? Of course, you do recognize ... that under the investment provisions of NAFTA we must continue allowing Americans to buy up our country, whether we like it or not. What would you then do about NAFTA ...?

(Continued)

Today, most manufacturing and oil and natural gas operating revenues in Canada already go to foreign owners. Dozens of key sectors of the Canadian economy are majority foreign-owned and controlled. As I have indicated in the past, in the United States there's not one single industry majority foreign owned. Not one!

Why do virtually all other developed countries resist massive foreign ownership of their economies? Here's a quick and very partial short list. Foreign corporations employ sophisticated transfer pricing and debt-loading schemes to transfer profits to their own countries or to tax havens before they are taxable in the host country. Foreign firms import much higher levels of parts, components and services than equivalent domestic companies. As a result, employment ratios to sales are invariably well below that for domestic firms. (One recent study showed that foreign firms in Canada import five times as much as domestic firms on a comparative basis.)

Excessive foreign ownership leads to hollowing out. . . . Head office jobs transferred out of the country result in truncated management, and key corporate decisions are made by people who live in another country and care little if at all about the welfare of the host country.

No self-respecting country would allow foreign corporations to control so many industries and so much of their economy as we do in Canada. The greatest irony of all continues to be that our own banks, pension funds and other financial institutions have for years been putting up most of the money that foreigners use to buy up our country.

. . . [O]f all the hundreds of billions of dollars of foreign direct investment monitored by Industry Canada, 96.6 percent has been for takeovers and only a pathetic 3.4 percent has been for new business investment. During this period just under 10,500 companies in Canada have been taken over by foreign buyers.

Welcome to what will soon be the colony of Canada.

Sources:

* From "A decade after the North American Free Trade Agreement was signed, its effects are being felt throughout Canada's economy—and supermarkets," *Canada World View,* Issue 24, Winter 2005, Foreign Affairs Canada. Reproduced with the permission of Her Majesty the Queen in Right of Canada, represented by the Minister of Foreign Affairs, 2005. <http://www.dfait-maeci.gc.ca/canada-magazine/issue24/06-title-en.asp>

** Reproduced with permission from Mel Hurtig, "Welcome to what will soon be the colony of Canada," *ABC theorists* (May 22, 2003) <http://canadianleaders.abctheorists.com/modules.php?op=modload&name=News&file=article&sid=50&mode=thread&order=0&thold=0>

Grappling with NAFTA

Though it has been about two decades since NAFTA has been in effect, its members are still struggling to understand and deal with a number of controversies that NAFTA has presented. For many critics, the benefits of NAFTA accrue largely to corporations rather than to individuals. As one observer comments:

. . . the North American Free Trade Agreement was sold to the people of the United States, Mexico and Canada as a simple treaty eliminating tariffs on goods crossing the three countries' borders. But NAFTA is much more: It is the constitution of an emerging continental economy that recognizes one citizen—the business corporation. It gives corporations extraordinary protections from government policies that might limit future profits, and extraordinary rights to force the privatization of virtually all civilian public services. Disputes are settled by secret tribunals of experts, many of whom are employed privately as corporate lawyers and consultants. At the same time, NAFTA excludes protections for workers, the environment and the public that are part of the social contract established through long political struggle in each of the countries.[17]

The concern that the rights of corporations are paramount in NAFTA is clearly illustrated in the growing number of lawsuits aimed at governments accused of discriminating against foreign-owned corporations. A case in point was that of UPS versus the Canadian Government (see Talking Business 6.13). Specifically, this

Talking Business 6.13

UPS versus the Canadian Government

Why was UPS Suing the Canadian Government?*

UPS claims that Canada's publicly funded network of mailboxes and post offices gives Canada Post an unfair advantage over private sector courier companies. It claims that Canada Post is unfairly subsidizing its competitive courier and express services by using a network that was built to provide its letter service. In fact, the post office is legally mandated to provide a broad range of postal services to everyone in the country, no matter where they live.

UPS wants Canadians to pay $160 million US in damages over its complaint involving Canada Post. If this weren't scary enough, the case could set a dangerous precedent. Most Crown corporations and public agencies deliver some services that are in competition with the private sector. The suit that UPS has launched could just as easily be launched over public education or health care.

Going Postal on NAFTA**

That's the problem with trade laws. No matter how nefarious they may be, all those clauses, numbers and government suits (not to mention the complete absence of any splashy 6 o'clock news villains) make us yearn for nap time. Or MTV.

An American corporation is using Chapter 11 to go after one of our public service pillars, Canada Post. It's something activists take very seriously, warning that if the company in question, United Parcel Service (UPS), wins its case (the first-ever NAFTA suit against a public service in this country), the fallout could be devastating.

The details sound fairly run-of-the-mail: UPS sues the Canadian government because Canada Post has somehow taken advantage of its letter mail monopoly to fund its parcel and courier services. The case is still pending. But if UPS wins, Deborah Bourque, national president of the Canadian Union of Postal Workers (CUPW), says the government will likely order Canada Post to get out of the parcel delivery biz, as the European Union's antitrust watchdog basically ordered Germany's national postal service to do after UPS successfully sued it back in 1994. "The problem," says Bourque, "is that Canada Post needs the profits it gets from the parcel business to ensure it can provide universal [letter] service in rural communities," something UPS obviously does not offer.

So What Happened? Canada Post Wins NAFTA Challenge Launched by UPS†

Tara Brautigam

Canada Post has defeated a NAFTA challenge from United Parcel Service of America Inc., that alleged the Crown corporation engaged in unfair competition, bringing an end to a seven year-old dispute between the two delivery companies.

UPS, the world's largest package delivery firm, launched a claim for $160 million (U.S.) against the Canadian government in April 2000 under the North American Free Trade Agreement.

UPS contended Canada Post has an unfair advantage because its services such as Express Post and Priority Courier draw on an infrastructure of sorting facilities, mailboxes and post offices that private firms must provide for themselves.

But Canada Post CEO Moya Greene told the company's annual meeting yesterday that the NAFTA tribunal hearing the challenge had dismissed it.

"So any thought that we were using the small little bit of the reserved market that we have in Canada to improperly subsidize our competitive businesses, that is now gone," Greene said.

Greg Kane, a spokesperson with UPS, said NAFTA's decision was disappointing.

"Obviously we had hoped for a better result, but we still respect the NAFTA dispute resolution process and the decision," Kane said.

"Our primary motivation in this whole case was to develop and promote a level playing field here in Canada along the lines of the courier market. We're still striving to do that."

(Continued)

The company, which has been operating in Canada for more than 30 years, is still reviewing the decision, Kane said.

Officials with NAFTA, the International Trade Department and the two companies said copies of the decision weren't yet publicly available.

Union officials representing Canada Post workers said the case represented the first time Ottawa was being pressured to withdraw from an established government program or service. If it had succeeded, they said it might have forced the company to get out of the courier business altogether.

Earlier at the Canada Post meeting, Greene said the company will likely raise postage rates next year for certain categories such as parcel delivery.

"In terms of the basic letter mail, that depends on where inflation goes during the year," she said.

"But in other categories of mail, for example some of our parcel business and some of our direct marketing mail, I think you can expect that we will keep up with the market and where we think we're adding value, we will obviously be very reasonable and respectful of our customers."

A decision on whether postage rates will change for letter mail is expected by the end of the month.

Canada Post generated $7.3 billion in operating revenue last year, up 4.6 per cent from the previous year, and had net profit of $119 million in net income, down 40 per cent from 2005.

Sources:

* Excerpts, reproduced with permission from Canadian Union of Postal Workers Web site (May 10, 2002) <http://www.cupw.ca/pages/document_eng.php?Doc_ID=250>

**By Adria Vasil in *NOW Magazine* Online Edition, 24(1) (January 20–26, 2005) <http://www.nowtoronto.com/issues/2005-01-20/news_feature.php>. © 2005 Now Communications Inc.

†"Canada Post Wins NAFTA Challenge Launched by UPS," Tara Brantigam, *Canadian Press*.

controversy largely stemmed from one section of NAFTA legislation referred to as Chapter 11. Chapter 11 of NAFTA asserts that foreign corporations are permitted to sue the federal government for compensation if that government's legislation, policy, or the deliver of public services interferes with present or future profits of the foreign corporation.

CHAPTER SUMMARY

There is little doubt that the phenomenon of globalization will have profound effects on businesses and societies across the world. In this chapter we tried to make sense of this phenomenon—what it entails and what its implications are. Specifically, we considered why organizations may "go global," and we identified the different types of global business activity. We examined the significance of multinational and borderless corporations. We also considered why nations desire, or do not desire, to promote international trade, including an examination of the pros and cons of Canada's free trade agreement with the United States. Is all this good or bad? That is, will the trend toward an increasingly integrated world economy benefit societies, or generate greater harm? What are the challenges and opportunities for managers in the global workplace? It is hoped that the material in this chapter has encouraged you to think more critically about these questions.

CONCEPT APPLICATION

AMAZON IN CANADA

‡Good News?

Ottawa said it will allow U.S. on-line bookseller Amazon.com Inc. to set up its own distribution centre in Canada, a second major move in recent months by the federal government to effectively override foreign-ownership rules.

The ruling allows the Seattle-based firm to cut its costs significantly, prompting heavy criticism by local booksellers who say it will allow Amazon to price Canadian businesses out of the market.

Until now, Amazon.ca has had to use a Canada Post subsidiary to ship goods in Canada in order to avoid violating cultural protection rules.

"This signals a government of Canada policy change confirming that a company no longer needs to be Canadian-owned to sell books in Canada," said Heather Reisman, chief executive officer of Indigo Books & Music Inc. . . .

. . . Instead, the Conservative government secured a number of "commitments" from Amazon in exchange for approving the distribution centre.

According to Heritage Minister James Moore, those "commitments" include a $20 million investment in Canada, $1.5-million of which will go to "cultural events and awards in Canada and the promotion of Canadian-authored books internationally." Amazon has also agreed to run a summer internship program for Canadian postsecondary students.

"Our government is committed to strengthening Canada's economy through all its sectors, especially arts and culture," Mr. Moore said in a statement. "Amazon has shown its willingness to promote Canadian cultural products, and we are pleased it is continuing to demonstrate this through this new investment." . . .

±Bad News?

. . . Since the early 1970s, the federal government has been committed to strengthening Canadian control of the book industry. Like other regulated cultural industries such as broadcasting, books are central to the nation's identity. As Hugh Faulkner, a Trudeau-era cabinet minister, put it, "Canadian books and magazines are too important to the cultural and intellectual life of this country to come completely under foreign control, however sympathetic and benign."

The federal government was then responding to a rash of American takeovers of Canadian publishing companies. In order to keep at least some of the industry in Canadian hands, the feds created regulation leaving existing foreign-controlled subsidiaries in place but requiring new publishing or bookselling ventures to be majority controlled by Canadians. The government also made financing available to Canadian-controlled firms publishing Canadian authors. . . .

. . . That's the story in publishing. In bookselling, another field where it's tough to make money as an independent, the landscape is dominated by Indigo Books & Music, which owns Chapters. Indigo is, in a sense, a creature of federal book policy. In 1996, Heather Reisman, the company's CEO, tried to partner with the U.S.-based chain Borders. But the venture was disallowed since it was de facto foreign-controlled, so Ms. Reisman worked within the policy's parameters. She started Indigo, acquired the rival Chapters chain five years later and became Canada's most successful bookseller.

Which brings us back to Amazon. It's already the major competition for Ms. Reisman and every other Canadian bookseller. Eight years ago, the government ruled that Amazon.ca didn't contravene the foreign-investment policy because it was operating from cyberspace, without a physical presence in Canada. But if the government were now to allow Amazon to incorporate in Canada and operate from its own physical plant, it would create a precedent that would shatter the policy.

Ms. Reisman would then be entirely within her rights to say, as she did recently in this newspaper: "Supposing I should decide three years from now that . . . I'd like to partner up with a foreign company? I do not want to be disadvantaged." Any bookseller or publisher would have the right to sell to non-Canadians, putting the commanding heights of the book industry in foreign hands. High-powered multinationals would move into both publishing and bookselling, driving companies specializing in Canadian authors further to the margins, or out of business altogether.

Decades of public investment in the industry would be lost. And for what?

(Continued)

Abandoning the book industry to the free play of market forces would result in Wal-Martization, the law of lowest cost, lowest common denominator. This would be portrayed as a victory for the consumer but would, in fact, be the very opposite. Readers would be able to buy all the imported bestsellers they wanted, very cheaply, but would be deprived of the current rich choice of Canadian and international titles.

And if the domestic publishing and bookselling sectors were decimated, there would be little incentive for foreign multinationals to assume their role by publishing and selling a wide range of Canadian authors. It simply wouldn't fit their business model.

The losers would be our writers and readers—our country. Canadians would go from being owners of their own literary house to mere renters. And why would the government allow that? Everyone knows that, once the family home and furniture and silverware are sold, you can't get 'em back.

---

‡*Source:* "Amazon Given Green Light to Set Up Shop in Canada," Omar El Akkad and Marina Strauss, *Globe and Mail.*

±*Source:* "Canada Would Be Renting, Not Owning its Literary House," Roy MacSkimming, *Globe and Mail.*

Questions:

1. How is the notion of globalization present in this case? Refer to the definition of globalization and the forms of global business.
2. What are the potential risks and benefits of this move?
3. How are the implications of this event similar to other cases discussed in this chapter? What is unique here?

The Political Context

Should the Canadian government take a more active role in the welfare of Canadian industry? The traditional relationship between government and business is clearly undergoing change. In this chapter, we will examine how government can intervene in business activity while fulfilling its role as both guardian of society and guardian of business. We will consider current and critically important trends regarding the shift toward reduced government involvement in the business sector. Specific attention will be paid to the issues of deregulation and privatization.

LEARNING OBJECTIVES

By the end of the chapter, you should be able to:

1. Discuss government's relationship with business with reference to government's guardianship of society.
2. Identify the purpose of Crown corporations.
3. Explain the notion of government as guardian of the private business sector.
4. Discuss government's role with regard to global business.
5. Describe the objectives and consequences of deregulation and privatization.

THE BUSINESS WORLD

*Corporate "welfare" more than $200 billion over 13 years

Vancouver Sun

Bailouts and subsidies to businesses by Canadian governments surpassed $200 billion between 1994 and 2007, adding up to $15,126 per taxpayer, according to a report Friday from the Fraser Institute.

"Unfortunately for Canadian taxpayers, our governments have a long history of spending public money on corporate welfare in attempts to pick winners and losers among various business sectors," said Mark Milke, author of the report.

In 2007 alone, Canadians paid $1,244 per taxpayer.

(Continued)

Milke paid special attention to the auto sector in his report, saying the $15.3 billion pumped into the sector—with General Motors and Chrysler being the biggest beneficiaries—between April and June of 2009 did not save jobs and in fact hurt other auto manufacturers.

"Insofar as governments picked winners, they made losers out of the shareholders and employees of Ford, Toyota, Honda, Hyundai, Volkswagen and others who also manufacture and sell cars and trucks in North America," said Milke, the research director for the Frontier Centre for Public Policy think-tank, and a lecturer in political science at the University of Calgary.

"The illusion of corporate welfare directed to the automotive industry in 2009 was the illusion that jobs were being saved. No, they were not. Instead of jobs being cut at General Motors or Chrysler, they were simply cut elsewhere or prevented from being created at other automotive companies that would have increased production to meet market demand in the absence of GM or Chrysler in the marketplace."

Milke's data is gleaned from the most recent Statistics Canada surveys, which show aid to corporations reaching $202 billion from 1994 through 2007.

He also tracked corporate announcements through 2008 and 2009, which suggest the figure climbed by up to $15 billion—or $217 billion—once aid to the auto sector is factored in. His figures do not include aid to other industries.

**It's time to end Canada's billion-dollar handout to big oil and coal

Cheryl McNamara

Meanwhile, the federal government subsidizes oil companies to the tune of $1.4 billion every year, according to the International Institute for Sustainable Development (IISD). It's more if you factor in other fossil fuels such as coal.

It's not as if fossil fuel companies need public handouts, which together with provincial subsidies amount to $2.84 billion. According to the Climate Action Network Canada, companies with tar sands investments have combined annual revenues of more than $1.2 trillion. Of these revenues, more than $1.1 trillion belong to foreign-owned companies. In 2010, Fortune magazine ranked five of these companies as being among the top 10 largest in the world.

The bulk of these subsidies come in the form of special tax breaks and royalty reductions. The rest include loan guarantees and indemnification programs, as well as footing the bill for infrastructure that supports the industry.

According to a recent IISD report, government balances are actually worse off with the subsidies which are intended to increase exploration. The reason for this imbalance is that the subsidies have a negligible effect on job creation. While government support for the industry generates revenue from corporate taxes there is very little in the way of labour taxes, a major source of government income. As a result, the federal government's balance is lower by one per cent.

While contributing to Canada's massive debt, these subsidies lead to massive ecological damage as well. In addition to destroyed ecosystems and polluted fresh water and air, the subsidies alone will contribute to a two percent increase in Canada's greenhouse gases by 2020, according to the IISD.

Imagine rather than supporting rich oil companies, the government continued with the now defunct EcoENERGY Retrofit—Homes program, which offered grants to homeowners who weatherized their drafty houses. The federal government's approximate $460-million investment in this four-year-old program generated hundreds of thousands of grants in support of participants who had their homes insulated and EnerGuide windows and doors and solar hot water heaters installed.

Source: Vancouver Sun.
**Source: Calgary Beacon.*

THE CANADIAN BUSINESS ENTERPRISE SYSTEM: FUNDAMENTAL FEATURES

"The Business World" example highlights the importance of understanding the boundaries of what constitutes a legitimate relationship between business and government. What role should government play in business?

Historically, the government has played a critical role in the Canadian economy. From our very beginning as a nation, the government has taken responsibility for the success of business. It is useful to briefly consider the nature of our economic or business enterprise system, within which all business operates. The Canadian economic system has been described as a mixed system. This refers to the notion that while we possess a capitalist economy, government nonetheless plays an important role.

All developed countries have some sort of economic or **business enterprise system** that essentially determines the following:

1. what goods and services are produced and distributed to society.
2. how the goods and services are produced and distributed to society.

What kind of business enterprise system we have determines how or by whom these decisions are made. For example, the two decisions above might be made purely by business, or they might be determined by government, or perhaps by a combination of the two. To understand the basis of our Canadian business enterprise system, it is necessary to understand the nature of capitalist economic systems. So let's briefly explain what capitalism is.

Capitalism is a type of economic system that is based on a number of fundamental principles, including the following:

1. **Rights of the individual.** The notion of capitalism is based on the view that it is the individual who takes precedence in society, as opposed to institutions or the overall society. This implies that individuals have every right to pursue their own self-interest, which includes seeking to make profits from business enterprises. The notion of the individual as the most important element of society is not entirely representative of the ideology present in Canadian society. There are limits placed on individuals' right to pursue their self-interest. Government regulations enforce rules that affect how business owners conduct their affairs. For example, government guidelines regarding job candidate selection criteria may affect who is hired for a job, and may place emphasis on certain groups in society over others.
2. **Rights of private property.** As opposed to state ownership, capitalism asserts that individuals have the right to own land, labour and capital. In Canada, certainly, individuals are permitted to own their means of production, whether it is land, labour or capital. However, because there has been an uneven distribution of wealth in society, the government has intervened in a number of ways. For example, taxation is one approach that can be partly aimed at redistributing wealth among members of society. Much of the natural resources in Canada have still been retained by federal or provincial governments. The government may also decide that where a product or service is of a national interest, this product or service should be nationalized—e.g., government control of health care.
3. **Competition.** Capitalism advocates competition. The belief is that sufficient competition among business enterprises will ensure that business provides the goods and services required by society at a fair cost. Competition is the "invisible hand" (in the words of economist Adam Smith) that ensures the market works in this manner. In Canada, the notion of "perfect competition" does not exist in practice—there is no guarantee that an adequate supply of competitors exists across all industries.
4. **The role of government.** The view of government is reflected in the French term *laissez faire,* which means "let people do as they choose." This suggests minimal government interference in the business enterprise system. This notion of capitalism has also been referred to as the "free enterprise system," reflecting the notion of the right to private ownership of property, competition, and restricted government involvement.

Of course, the polar extreme of capitalism is another economic system referred to as **communism**. Whereas the capitalist system allows individuals or businesses the responsibility for the allocation of resources, the communist system places the responsibility for the allocation of society's resources into the hands of the government. There really are no societies today that are either purely capitalist or communist. In Canada, government does intervene in the affairs of business. Business is not left entirely to conduct its own affairs. When Canada first came into existence as a country, the federal government was granted the power to "regulate trade and commerce." And the fact is, throughout our history, the government has played a major role in fostering industrial development and continues to provide significant support to the business sector.

GOVERNMENT AS GUARDIAN OF SOCIETY

Exhibit 7.1 illustrates the variety of ways government can influence business activity, issues that we explore in the following sections.

The Tax Collector Role

Government plays many roles in relation to business. The most obvious role, and perhaps the least popular one, is that of government as tax collector, whether it is at the federal, provincial or local level. There are two broad forms of taxes: revenue taxes and regulatory or restrictive taxes. The intent of revenue taxes is to collect money in order to help fund government services and programs. *Revenue taxes* include individual taxes as well as corporate income tax, along with property tax and sales tax. *Individual income taxes* have provided the largest source of revenue for the federal and provincial governments. Individual income tax is levied on the income of individuals or on the net profits of proprietorships and partnerships. *Corporate income tax* has provided the second largest source of revenue for the federal government. Corporations are taxed on their net profit at a combined federal and provincial rate that can vary among provinces, and are subject to change based on government policy. Government policy may include an agenda of manipulating taxation to stimulate government investment or to raise more revenues.

Sales taxes are an important source of revenue for most provinces, as well as for the federal government. This tax is paid through retail stores, which act as collection agents when they sell their goods to consumers. The Goods and Services Tax (GST) that came into effect in 1991 provides substantial funds to the federal government. It is a value-added tax—a tax that is paid at each step of the manufacturing process. Consider, for example: a producer buys raw materials from a supplier, and the GST is charged by the supplier. The producer may then work on the raw materials and produce a part for sale to a manufacturer, who is then charged GST on that purchase. Everyone involved in the goods or services production pays GST, but only the final consumer, obviously, cannot pass the tax on to another party.

Finally, another well-known form of taxation is *property taxes,* which have been the largest revenue source for municipal governments. The revenue gained from this form of tax is typically used to fund the operating costs of the municipal government and the services that it generates.

As mentioned earlier, the second broad form of taxation is referred to as **restrictive or regulatory taxes**. There are two main types of regulatory taxes, referred to as excise taxes and customs duties or tariffs. Restrictive taxes are primarily aimed at controlling or curbing the use of specific products or services. *Excise taxes* typically are applied to goods or services that the government desires to restrict, such as products deemed to be potentially harmful (including tobacco and alcohol products). Excise taxes have been used as a deterrent to potential excesses—in fact, back in 1976, the federal government actually levied an additional tax on gasoline to discourage overuse in order to help conserve what was then a product in very short supply. Whatever the source, excise taxes are, essentially, selective sales taxes. **Tariffs** are also a form of restrictive tax, the purpose of which is detailed elsewhere in this book.

The Business Owner Role: Crown Corporations

What is a Crown corporation? A **Crown corporation** or public enterprise is an organization accountable, through a minister, to parliament for its operations. Crown corporations may be federal (e.g., Canada Post, the Canadian Broadcasting Corporation [CBC], the Canadian Wheat Board) or provincial (e.g., the Liquor Control Board of Ontario [LCBO]). (See Exhibit 7.2.)

Government as Guardian of Society	Government as Guardian of Business

• Collecting taxes from businesses
• Acting as business owners
• Regulating the business sector
• Safeguarding Canadian interests in the global context
	• Spending money on private business
	• Assisting private business
	  — bailouts
	  — subsidies
	• Safeguarding Canadian business in the global context

EXHIBIT 7.1 The guardian roles.

EXHIBIT 7.2 Rankings for federal and provincial crown corporations.

Federal Crown Corporations			Provincial Crown Corporations		
Rank	Company	Revenue	Rank	Company	Revenue
1	Canada Mortgage and Housing	13,164,000	1	Hydro-Quebec	12,360,000
2	Canada Post	7,341,000	2	Ontario Power Generation	6,302,000
3	Canadian Commercial	1,898,750	3	Insurance Corp. of B.C.	4,758,000
4	Export Development Canada	1,612,000	4	Hydro One	4,748,000
5	Farm Credit Canada	948,922	5	B.C. Hydro & Power	4,358,000
6	Business Development Bank of Canada	824,962	6	Manitoba Hydro-Electric Board	2,413,000
7	Canadian Broadcasting Corp.	646,390	7	Saskatchewan Power	1,557,000
8	Via Rail Canada	550,511	8	ATB Financial	1,454,669
9	Atomic Energy of Canada	514,786	9	Saskatchewan Telecommunications	1,163,464
10	Canadian Air Transport Security	477,396	10	SGF du Quebec	1,016,168

Source: Report on Business Magazine.

Whether federal or provincial, why are Crown corporations established? Governments establish Crown corporations for a number of possible reasons:

- **To implement public policy that includes protecting or safeguarding national interests.** For example, federal Crown corporations, such as Air Canada and Petro-Canada, helped facilitate government policy in the area of cross-Canada transportation and Canadian ownership in the domestic oil industry.
- **To protect industries deemed to be vital to the economy.** The Canadian Radio Broadcasting Commission was established by the Canadian government in 1932 to administer a national broadcasting service in order to prevent Canadian broadcasting becoming inundated with material originating in the United States. Similarly, this was a reason for taking control of the Canadian National Railways. The CNR originated in 1919 in order to "safeguard the government's large investment in the railways" and "to protect Canada's image in foreign capital markets."[1] While few municipal governments have traditionally held significant corporate holdings, they have been owners of public transit systems, recreational centres and other facilities that are intended to enhance the quality of life in society.
- **To provide special services that could not otherwise be made available by private business.** For example, Trans Canada Airlines (Air Canada) was established in the 1930s, after observing that no private business was willing or able to provide domestic air services. Consider also the Bank of Canada. The Bank of Canada, created in 1935, was established to first serve as a control agent for the chartered banks: for example, requiring the banks to report regularly on their operations and to hold deposit reserves with the Bank of Canada. Second, the Bank of Canada is responsible for developing monetary policy and regulating monetary operations in Canada.
- **To nationalize industries that were considered to be "natural monopolies," including the generation and distribution of electricity.** It is not hard to imagine that in the early days of Canadian society the private sector was too small to undertake the creation of a national electricity supply grid. On the other hand, government was capable of raising the necessary capital, and, consequently, it took on the establishment of public utilities, including things like water supply, sewage treatment plants and electricity-generating plants, in addition to road construction and the like. In some cases, there were companies capable of building their own private utilities, which then became subject to government regulation, as we will discuss further.

Each Crown corporation is a legally distinct entity wholly owned by the Crown, and each is managed by a board of directors. The recent range of Crown corporations has been relatively diverse, with corporations operating in a variety of areas of the economy. Naturally, the corporations differ with regard to their public policy purpose, as well as in their size and in their relative need for government financial support.

Many observers suggested that, traditionally, there has been a great reliance on Crown corporations in the Canadian context. For example, by the late 1980s there were 53 parent Crown corporations (at the federal level) and 114 wholly owned subsidiaries, employing about 180,000 people, and maintaining assets worth approximately $60 billion.

The Liquor Control Board of Ontario (LCBO) is a provincial Crown corporation in the sense that it is owned by the province of Ontario. Technically, it is also an agency of the Ministry of Consumer and Commercial Relations. It receives its purchasing directives from the Cabinet's Management Board Secretariat, and it abides by the same regulations, laws and trade agreements that govern purchasing for all provincial government departments. For many years, the LCBO has been the largest single retailer (and the largest buyer) of alcoholic beverages in the world. By 2000 it had established five regional warehouses and was supplying 602 stores across Ontario with over 7,000 products.

The state-owned liquor outlet of the Société des Alcohols du Québec receives the same type of praise and criticism as the LCBO. It has been viewed as a well-managed business with excellent customer service. (See Talking Business 7.1.) On the other hand, critics also argue that private food retailers would like to be allowed to enter the alcohol sales industry more fully, given that the potential for profits is very lucrative. This sentiment also argues for privatization—the expansion of private industry into what has traditionally been the domain of the public sector.

There are other examples, globally, of state-owned corporations that are struggling to avoid privatization as well as to compete with private businesses. For example, according to recent reports,[2] European post offices are making great efforts to upgrade themselves because their two basic businesses—delivering letters and delivering parcels—are both threatened by e-mail and competition from U.S. market leaders Federal Express Corp. and United Parcel Service Inc. At stake is the state post office's concern for control of Europe's $27-billion fast-growing parcel service. Observers note that Europe's big postal bureaucracies have continued to lose ground, and are also losing their domestic letter monopolies in 2003 because of European Union deregulation. Next, we will discuss in more detail the issue of privatization and deregulation.

Talking Business 7.1

Kelly McParland

LCBO employees work for a well-run operation that last year *handed over* a $1.4 billion "dividend" to the province yet is still trying to cut costs. The union's main gripes are reasonable enough: almost 60% are part-timers who are paid adequately but get no sick days, benefits or vacations, and can be called in to work at a moment's notice. They're trying to fend off management that works for the government but does its best to imitate private enterprise.

The danger to Ontario's alcohol monopoly is the constant threat of privatization. It has been called for any number of times, and every once in a while some politician comes along pledging to sell off the LCBO. Once they're safely in office and get their hands on that fat dividend, they quickly forget having ever said any such a foolish thing, but you never know . . . some zealot may actually get elected and follow through on the threat.

So the liquor board has been doing its best to make so much money that even zealots have to think twice. The facilities have been vastly upgraded, the selection has increased, marketing novelties such as "tastings" and "sales" have been introduced—just like in the real world—and staff trained to say something other than; "I don't know, find it for yourself." Bright, attractive Booze-o-ramas have opened in strategic locations; if you can't find what you want they'll scout out a store that does and have them set it aside. No one can claim this is a monopoly that doesn't care.

True, it's not the same as privatization. Prices could be lower if so much wasn't poured into marketing, promotion and atmospherics. Other than a few aficionados peeved that $90 Scotch can be had for $80 in Alberta, Ontarians don't seem all that concerned. The first shelves emptied in Tuesday's rush were the ones selling $8–12 wine. Maybe a privatized LCBO could knock a buck off the price. Big deal.

The problem for the union is that its members are providing the service without benefiting from the result. The stores get nicer, the service gets better, the province's dividend keeps going up, but the employees get dirty looks when they ask for a week off.

Source: "Keep the LCBO monopoly; privatize Toronto," Kelly McParland. June 24, 2009.

The Regulator Role

Government economic regulation has been defined as "the imposition of constraints, backed by the authority of a government, that are intended to modify economic behaviour in the private sector significantly."[3] As Exhibit 7.3 indicates, there has been a relatively wide scope for government regulation in business activity:

EXHIBIT 7.3   The scope of federal regulation in Canada—by sector.

Major Federally Regulated Sectors	Scope
Financial, commercial and government information; regulations affecting business operations in all sectors	• Banking • Financial transactions • Marketplace, trade and investment • Weights and measures • Incorporation, ownership, investment, competition (e.g., telecommunications) and licensing • Life and health insurance (shared with provinces) • Bankruptcy and insolvency; patents, copyright and trademarks • GST, HST, excise, T4, T2, payroll, record of employment • Government business surveys • Procurement, contracting (i.e., selling to government) • Temporary foreign workers
Broadcasting, Telecommunications, Radio Frequency Spectrum	• Issuing, renewing and amending broadcasting licences • Decisions on mergers, acquisitions and changes of ownership in broadcasting • Tariffs and certain agreements for the telecommunications industry • Competition • Licences for international telecommunications services (for incoming and outgoing calls to and from Canada) • Radio frequency spectrum allocation, utilization and services
Transportation	• Safety, security and environmental sustainability of air, marine, road and rail transportation • Interprovincial transportation • Safe and accessible waterways
Environment	• Preserving and enhancing the quality of the natural environment, including water, air, soil, flora and fauna • Protecting the environment and human health (e.g., toxic substances, species at risk) • Coordinating environmental policies and programs for the federal government • Healthy and productive aquatic ecosystems • Sustainable fisheries and aquaculture
Food and Agriculture	• Food safety, seeds and marketing • Public health risks associated with the food supply and transmission of animal disease to humans • Achieving a safe and sustainable plant and animal resource base • Consumer protection and market access based on the application of science and standards • Packaging and labeling
Health	• Drug approvals, product safety, pesticides and chemicals • Approvals of the use of products, including biologics, consumer goods, foods, medical devices, natural health products, pesticides, pharmaceuticals and toxic substances • Prevention and reduction of risks to individual health and the overall environment • Promotion of healthier lifestyles and help for Canadians to make informed health decisions
Energy and Natural Resources	• Nuclear energy, pipelines, mines, fisheries and forestry • Responsible development and use of Canada's natural resources and the competitiveness of Canada's resource products • Protection of the health, safety and security of Canadians and the environment related to nuclear energy projects • International and interprovincial aspects of the oil, gas and electric utility industries

Source: Public Works and Government Services Canada.

for example, regulation focused on consumer protection, regulation aimed at environmental protection and regulation regarding the nature of competition. One obvious set of regulations exists fundamentally to protect the consumer, and the Canadian government has initiated a number of programs designed for consumer protection, many of which are administered by the Department of Consumer and Corporate Affairs—a body that plays a major role in regulating business in Canada. Among the numerous regulations, there is, for example, the Food and Drug Act, which was designed to protect the public from potential risks to health as well as from fraud or deception as it relates to food, drugs, cosmetics and the like. Similarly, the Hazardous Products Act serves to protect public safety by either banning products because they are deemed dangerous or requiring warning labels on products that might be considered hazardous. Ecological regulations are designed to protect the environment, and include things like the Environmental Contaminants Act, which creates regulations to limit any dangerous by-products of industrial production that could be harmful to individuals' health.

Why does the government need to intervene in the functioning of the business enterprise system? Consider the notions of competition and the public interest, discussed next. (See Talking Business 7.2, about critics of government regulation.)

Imperfect Competition

One fundamental shortcoming in the market system—the presence of imperfect, as opposed to perfect, competition—suggests the need for government involvement. If you recall our earlier discussion of the nature of the business enterprise system, we identified it as a system that essentially determines what goods and services are produced and distributed to society, and how they are produced and distributed. Ideally, such a system produces all the goods and services a society wants at a fair price. In very basic terms, on the demand side, decisions are made by individuals regarding their tastes or preferences for certain goods or services. On the supply side, businesses aim to meet the demands they face. The "invisible hand" of competition transforms these decisions of demand and supply into a system that uses scarce resources in the most efficient manner. In other words, business supply will be responsive to consumer demand: those products and services that are needed most will demand increased production, while those no longer in demand can only be sold with a drop in price; or, ultimately, businesses that do not serve any demand would go bankrupt. If a resource becomes scarce, its price will increase, and this may lead consumers to shift their preferences to a less costly alternative. In this sense, by allowing individuals and businesses to follow self-interest, the market system is responsive to consumer needs and to the capability of the environment. However, the system does not work flawlessly and, in fact, there are challenges to the effective functioning of this system. One such challenge is the notion of **imperfect competition**.

Generally, businesses aim to reduce competition as a means of succeeding and prospering. The fewer the competitors, the more secure a business becomes. Of course, on the consumer's side, the ideal scenario is perfect competition: where, essentially, there is an optimal number of competitors in any given industry to ensure fair pricing and distribution of the goods or services at the highest possible level of quality. In such a situation, those businesses unable to compete will be replaced by more efficient competitors. Imperfect competition occurs when fewer than the optimal number of competitors exist to ensure this type of situation. Where there are an insufficient number of competitors, there is less pressure on businesses to offer the best possible good or service at the lowest possible price. Businesses that are not worried about competition are also not worried about innovating, managing their operations at peak efficiency, improving product/service quality or offering their product/service at competitive prices. Consequently, inefficient businesses will remain, and consumers will be forced to accept those types of products or services, at prices dictated by those businesses. Overall, then, society is offered fewer of the goods and services citizens really want, as opposed to a situation where competition was stronger. This also leads to a less efficient use of society's resources, particularly compared to perfect competition, where resources are divided among various activities in a manner that generates the optimal combination of goods and services desired by consumers. For example, industries that lack sufficient competition may choose to restrict their output as a means to maintain higher prices, as opposed to the case of perfect competition, where businesses must accept prices determined by the market.

It is relatively easy to see, with an understanding of the notion of imperfect competition, that the market system itself will not necessarily guarantee the best and most efficient use of resources to generate the optimal mix of products and services for consumers at fair prices. Consequently, this is one fundamental rationale for government intervention in business (see Talking Business 7.2).

Talking Business 7.2

Used Car Buyers Are Protected

Monique Savin

Used-car buyers in Ontario will be able to shop with more confidence in the wake of tougher industry regulations enacted by the province.

Key changes to the Ontario Motor Vehicle Dealers Act deal with key areas such as advertising, cancellation rights and vehicle history to make dealers more honest about the cars they sell, and strengthen used-car buyers' rights.

"Whenever the economy goes through a rough period consumers want to ensure they get the very best value and they are somewhat more selective about the purchases they make," Ontario Minister of Consumer Services Ted McMeekin said.

The amendments were developed to bolster consumer confidence in the used car industry. Used car consumers will be more willing to buy knowing they have enhanced protection to make purchases than before these new laws came into effect and the motor vehicle industry hopes that will stimulate business, he added.

Here's how consumers will be protected:

Advertising Practices

As to promotion, dealers are required to offer one-price advertising that must include all fees. GST and PST do not need to be included if the ad states that taxes are not included.

Ads for used current or previous model year vehicles must clearly indicate that it is used.

Ads must state if the vehicle was previously owned by a consumer or other business, that is not a dealer, such as a daily rental, police cruiser, taxi and limousine.

If an extended warranty is included in the advertised price of a vehicle, the ad must state terms of the warranty and maximum individual claim limits. For example, an ad should read: Used 2009 BMW 328xi, loaded, 12,238 km, $38,550, one year warranty, $2,000 maximum single claim, plus taxes.

Cancellation Policies

A consumer will now be able to cancel a contract within 90-days for a full refund if certain information is not disclosed.

"If three of 22 items are not disclosed, if the odometer reading, for example, is less than 1,000 of exact reading, if the contract did not state prior use, if incorrect description of make, model or year, or if contract states the vehicle is branded, salvaged or rebuilt, a consumer can cancel," says Bob Pierce, director of the Used Car Dealers Association of Ontario.

Where a deal is cancelled, a consumer will be returned to the position as if the sale had not taken place. This includes financing arrangements, any extended warranty, insurance, PST and GST, or any other product that was part of the sale. . . .

. . . Sales and Car Dealers Accountable

For used-car buyers, the new regulations are making the dealers more accountable, putting information upfront in writing and making it mandatory.

Salespeople are now personally responsible for disclosing the true condition and history of pre-owned vehicles. A common complaint used-car buyers have about dealerships is a failure to disclose the history of a vehicle, which can lead to big repair costs in the future. That shift in accountability from company to both salesperson and dealership should bolster consumer trust. . . .

. . . However, the new regulations do not apply to unregistered private sales.

"The worse thing is going into the marketplace and buying privately," says Pierce, who was previously registrar for motor vehicle dealers at the ministry of consumer and commercial relations, "because consumers who purchase vehicles through curbsiders are not protected by provincial legislation." . . .

. . . Stiffer Penalties

In January a curbsider received a one-year sentence and the company was fined $375,000, the maximum under the previous Motor Vehicle Dealer Act 2002. The new regulations will double maximum jail time and increase fines to $2,500 per count. . . .

The Public Interest

One of the central objectives of government regulation is to protect the public interest. Instead of having to establish its own public enterprise, government can control the operations of a private enterprise through regulations. Consequently, what we see in some areas of business is government regulation of businesses through commissions, tribunals, agencies and boards. National regulators include the Canadian Transport Commission, which judges route and rate applications for commercial air and railway companies. In terms of provincial regulatory bodies, like the provincial liquor boards, for example, provincial boards or commissions will assess and judge proposals from private business. Liquor boards, for example, are responsible for approving any price changes proposed by breweries within their province. The Canadian Radio-television and Telecommunications Commission (CRTC), under the auspices of the Department of Communications, regulates the telecommunications industry and its carriers, such as Bell Canada, and its traditional responsibilities have included accepting or refusing requests for rate increases among these carriers.

The government has also established a competition policy to control the nature of competition in the business sector. Earlier, we identified the importance of competition in our economy, given its ability to encourage the production and distribution of goods and services at the lowest possible cost. Consequently, the competition policy, set out in the Competition Act, is intended to stimulate open competition and eliminate any restrictive business practices with the aim of encouraging maximum production, distribution and employment opportunities. The role of the Competition Bureau is discussed in Talking Business 7.3.

We have, for example, government regulation in the area of public utilities, such as an electric power company or a telephone company. The government has regulated this industry because there has traditionally been an absence of competition there. Consequently, the public utilities boards or commission that regulates the industry will monitor the company's performance, as well as assess requests for rate increases and changes in the types of services provided. Consider, for example, the CRTC, which, among other things, regulates the Canadian broadcasting system. The CRTC is responsible for issuing broadcasting licences, and can require companies seeking such a licence to conform with standards regarding the type or content of programming they will provide. The CRTC's responsibilities extend far beyond broadcasting, however, and also govern the nature of competition in the telecommunications and media industries. For example, in the telecommunications industry, there are regulations regarding the permissible amount of foreign ownership.

Talking Business 7.3

The Role of the Competition Bureau

What Is the Competition Bureau?

The Competition Bureau is an independent law enforcement agency responsible for the administration and enforcement of the *Competition Act*, the *Consumer Packaging and Labelling Act*, the *Textile Labelling Act* and the *Precious Metals Marking Act*. Its role is to promote and maintain fair competition so that all Canadians can benefit from competitive prices, product choice and quality services. Headed by the Commissioner of Competition, the organization investigates anti-competitive practices and promotes compliance with the laws under its jurisdiction.

The basic operating assumption of the Competition Bureau is that competition is good for both business and consumers.

Fair Competition

- makes the economy work more efficiently;
- strengthens businesses' ability to adapt and compete in global markets;
- gives small and medium businesses an equitable chance to compete and participate in the economy;
- provides consumers with competitive prices, product choices and the information they need to make informed purchasing decisions; and
- balances the interests of consumers and producers, wholesalers and retailers, dominant players and minor players, the public interest and the private interest.

The types of anti-competitive activities investigated by the Bureau include:

Price fixing: When competitors agree on the prices that they will charge their customers.

Bid-rigging: When, in response to a call or request for bids or tenders, one or more bidders agree not to submit a bid, or two or more bidders agree to submit bids that have been prearranged among themselves.

False or misleading representations: When materially false or misleading representations are made knowingly or recklessly to the public.

Deceptive notice of winning a prize: When a notice, sent by any means, gives a recipient the impression of winning a prize and requires the recipient to incur a cost to obtain the prize.

Abuse of dominant position: When a dominant firm engages in anti-competitive practices that substantially lessen competition in a market, or are likely to do so.

Exclusive Dealing, Tied Selling and Market Restrictions: When a supplier requires or induces a customer to deal only, or mostly, in certain products; requires or induces a customer to buy a second product as a condition of supplying a particular product; requires a customer to sell specified products in a defined market.

Refusal to deal: When someone is substantially affected in his or her business, or is unable to carry on business, because of the inability to obtain adequate supplies of a product on usual trade terms.

Mergers: When all or part of one business is acquired by another. The Bureau has the authority to review any merger, regardless of its size. However, the Bureau must be notified in advance of proposed transactions when the value of the assets or the target firm exceeds $50 million or the value of the amalgamated company exceeds $70 million, and when the combined dollar value of the parties and their respective affiliates exceeds $400 million.

Multi-level Marketing Plans and Schemes of Pyramid Selling: Multi-level marketing, when it operates within the limits set by the *Competition Act,* is a legal business activity, while a scheme of pyramid selling is illegal as defined by the law.

Deceptive Telemarketing: When a product's representation is false or misleading while promoting the supply of a product or a business interest during person-to-person telephone calls.

Deceptive marketing practices: When a product is advertised at a bargain price and is not supplied in reasonable quantities; when a product is supplied at a price above the advertised price; when retailers make "regular price" claims without selling a substantial volume of the product, or offering the product, at that price or a higher price in good faith for a substantial period of time; or when a contest, lottery, or game of chance or skill is conducted without making adequate and fair disclosure of facts that affect the chances of winning.

Source: Reproduced with permission from Competition Bureau Canada, 2005 <http://www.competitionbureau. gc.ca/internet/index.cfm?itemID=18&lg=e>. The reproduction is not represented as an official version of the materials reproduced.

GOVERNMENT AS GUARDIAN OF THE PRIVATE BUSINESS SECTOR

Government Assistance to Private Business

In Canada, we have a long history of government involvement in business in the sense of promoting and protecting our industries. For example, tariff and non-tariff barriers on imported goods were designed to protect our domestic business by making foreign goods more expensive relative to Canadian goods. In fact, we could argue that a large portion of Canada's industrial development is due to protectionism through tariffs first imposed in 1879 by Sir John A. Macdonald's National Policy. Eventually, the government also offered direct incentives for industrial and resource development. Incentive programs were established to encourage managers to conduct business in a manner desired by the government. For example, it may be desirable for managers to invest in a new product development, or engage in greater export activities, or locate in an underdeveloped region. Consequently, incentives will be offered to engage in such activities. Receiving government financial support or reward for such activities would influence decisions to engage in these activities.

For example, provincial and municipal governments can encourage new employment opportunities by offering incentives to industry for locating in their areas. The municipal government might offer property tax incentives to attract industry to its jurisdiction, and the provincial government might even offer an outright grant to attract large-scale industry. Governments at all levels have provided both direct and indirect assistance for businesses in the form of grants, loans, information, consulting advice, and bailouts (as discussed below).

The government has offered assistance to those industries deemed to be of particular importance. Industries with leading-edge technology, or those providing highly skilled jobs, or oriented toward exports, might be among the more likely recipients of government aid. The federal and provincial governments have also provided financial incentives in an effort to dissuade companies from moving their operations outside of Canada. For example, Pratt & Whitney Canada Corp. was given an $11 million loan from the federal government to encourage the company to retain the development of a new aircraft component within Canada. More recently, Pratt & Whitney received a $300 million government loan for research and development. (See Talking Business 7.4.)

Talking Business 7.4

Ottawa Loans Pratt & Whitney $300 Million to Help "Create and Maintain" Jobs

The federal government is lending $300 million to aircraft engine and parts maker Pratt & Whitney Canada as the company boosts its research and development with a $1-billion investment.

Industry Minister Tony Clement said Monday the government believes the project could "create and maintain" more than 700 jobs during the project work phase and more than 2,000 jobs during the 15-year benefits phase.

The company said it is currently looking to add 200 new engineers to the 1,500 it employs in Canada.

"(This) investment . . . will help this company make the technological improvements across its entire line of aircraft engines," Clement said at a press conference in Mississauga, Ont.

"The associated research and development . . . will lead to lighter engines that generate more power that have better fuel consumption and improved durability."

John Saabas, president of Pratt & Whitney Canada, said the investment will help to develop the next generation of high-performance aircraft engines and position the company for long-term growth.

"This major investment will enable us to sustain our engineering centres of excellence in Ontario and Quebec and reinforce our position as a leader in the global aerospace industry," he said.

The $300-million loan is made through the Strategic Aerospace and Defence Initiative (SADI), which supports industrial research and pre-competitive development projects in the aerospace, defence, space and security industries.

"SADI contributes to technologies that focus on the next generation of services, it helps spur innovation in the Canadian aerospace industry, ensuring that Canadian companies continue to compete with other world leaders in the field," Clement said.

"This is a program created by our government to support industrial research and pre-competitive development projects in the aerospace defence space and security industries."

The project's research and development work will take place in Longueuil, Que., and Mississauga, Ont.

The aerospace industry was especially hard hit during the recession as consumers cut back on air travel.

Pratt & Whitney Canada announced last year it would cut 250 jobs by the end of 2009 and an additional 160 jobs by the end of 2010, when it closes its Auvergne Street plant in Longueuil, Que., a community just south of Montreal.

Saabas has said the company could gradually recall some laid-off workers within the next six to eight months if the engine maker can ride an improving outlook to contract wins. The Montreal-based company has so far brought back about 10 workers with specialized skills of the 1,000 laid off at its Canadian operations.

Pratt & Whitney Canada has more than 6,200 employees at facilities in Alberta, Manitoba, Ontario, Quebec and Nova Scotia and is owned by United Technologies, a Connecticut-based diversified manufacturing company.

United Technologies weathered the recession by cutting costs and axing jobs. The restructuring helped blunt the impact of the downturn on subsidiaries such as Pratt & Whitney and Hamilton Sundstrand, which are exposed to weaknesses in the airline industry.

Bailouts

The term "bailout" refers to government assistance given to prevent an organization or industry from financial collapse. A bailout is when a bankrupt, or nearly bankrupt, business (e.g., bank or corporation) is given more "liquidity" in order to meet its financial obligations. Liquidity refers to cash flow. Typically the business may have a short-term cash flow problem but it possesses sufficient assets. Consequently, the government provides it with funds until it is in a stable financial condition again.

A government would usually enter into a bailout if the failing company is very large company and consequently whose failure would cause negative repercussions for the economy. Some critics are opposed to government bailouts based on the view that there is a reason the company has failed and therefore it should not be "artificially" sustained. In other words, when the government bails a company out, it can be viewed as overriding the functioning of the market.

Bailouts may involve a one-time financial assistance to combat significant financial troubles that a business may be experiencing. This financial assistance could also take the form of a loan or loan guarantee, for example. Bailouts were relatively common in the 1980s, involving such companies as Dome Petroleum, Chrysler Canada and Massey Ferguson. By the 1990s, while complete bailouts became rare, the government nevertheless did not refuse to offer some assistance in a bailout arrangement, as evidenced in the 1992 bailout of Algoma Steel, which involved government loan guarantees. More recently, there have been a number of significant bailouts in Canada and the U.S.

In 2008, the U.S. government bailed out financial institutions in the midst of a *mortgage crisis*. This industry is an important one for the economy since healthy credit markets are required for a smooth-operating market place. Banks use the credit markets to fund their activities. When the credit market is restricted, less money is available for banks to loan to individuals and businesses. This damages economic activities, like home buyers trying to obtain a mortgage. If the banking industry were to collapse the economy would be in shambles. Consequently, many of the U.S.'s top financial institutions were bailed out, including: Citigroup, JPMorgan Chase, Bank of America, Goldman Sachs, and Merrill Lynch. The bailout plan was called the *Emergency Economic Stabilization Act of 2008*. In total, the U.S. government gave that industry a $700 billion bailout package. This helped to restore liquidity to the financial markets and helped improve the economy. Other recent bailouts include the U.S. and Canadian government bailout of the auto industry, discussed in the next section.

*Auto Bailouts: Good or Bad Idea? For the past decade or so, Chrysler and General Motors (GM) have been experiencing increasing difficulties. Their market shares have declined because they did not produce cars that captured the interest of enough consumers. Chrysler's market share, for example, dropped from about 17 percent in 1998 to 8.5 percent in 2009, and its workforce dropped from 17,000 in 2000 to 8,200 in 2009. With the decline in market share came rapidly increasing financial problems, and in April 2009 Chrysler filed for Chapter 11 bankruptcy in the U.S. During the six weeks Chrysler spent in bankruptcy protection, it shut down its production facilities. It reopened its manufacturing plants in Brampton and Windsor in late June 2009. Chrysler is now controlled by Fiat, a company that is more adept at producing technically advanced small cars.

GM filed for bankruptcy in June 2009. Its biggest problem was a $7 billion shortfall in its pension plan. There is only one active GM worker for every six retired workers (at Chrysler, there is one active worker for every two retired workers). After emerging from bankruptcy, GM planned to produce the Volt (a "green" electric car), but doesn't know when it will be profitable.

The U.S. and Canadian governments required GM and Chrysler to come up with a restructuring plan before they would receive any bailout money. In the U.S., GM reached an agreement with the United Auto Workers union on a new contract which reduced its costs, but that put pressure on the Canadian Auto Workers union to also reach a new agreement. If they didn't, GM Canada might cease to exist because the government of Canada wouldn't give GM the bailout money it needed to survive. The Canadian government said it had no choice but to get involved in a bailout once the U.S. government decided to give money to GM and Chrysler. The U.S. government essentially told Canada that if its government didn't help out, GM and Chrysler would leave Canada and all those auto jobs would be lost.

Back in 2008, the federal Ministry of Industry said that the government of Canada would not provide bailouts to auto companies. But in the end, the Canadian government agreed to give GM about $10 billion (the U.S. gave GM about $50 billion). Both governments then took an ownership percentage of GM (the U.S.

will own 72 percent of the company and Canada will own 13 percent). As part of the deal, debt holders will trade $27 billion in debt in return for a 15 percent stake in GM. In return for the bailout money from the Canadian government, GM promised to maintain 16 percent of its North American production in Canada (that's down from 22 percent before bankruptcy was declared). GM Canada's workforce will be about 4,400 (it was 20,000 in 2005). The Canadian and U.S. governments also gave bailout money to Chrysler (the U.S. will now own a 20 percent stake in Chrysler and the Canadian government will own 2 percent).

Opponents of bailouts　Critics of the auto bailouts have several objections. The first, and most fundamental, objection is that government should not prop up businesses that are in trouble. If a company is not doing well, it should be allowed to fail. There is an old saying that goes something like this: "Governments are terrible at picking winners, but losers are great at picking governments." The government seems to have forgotten decades of hard lessons that they should not get involved in market-oriented businesses. But now they are involved in the automobile business, and the government is essentially investing money where private citizens would never be willing to put it. Writing in the *National Post* on June 4, 2009, Terence Corcoran said that ". . . along with Chrysler, GM is sliding through a government-backed reorganization and emerging as part of the same old whining, subsidy-seeking, protectionist, union-locked North American auto industry." He also noted that most of the $10 billion bailout is not going to rebuild the company, but to pay off GM's pension commitments to its workers. He says that Canadian taxpayers are paying to cover pensions of auto workers that the union "extorted" from the auto companies. He estimates that over the last 20 years, Canadian car buyers have paid $10 billion in higher auto costs to cover union workers' contracts and pension entitlements. Many Canadians don't have much of a retirement fund, and they make a lot less than auto workers do, but they are being asked to help bail out the pensions of auto workers.

Second, the GM bailout will cost Canadian taxpayers about $1.4 million for each job that is "saved." That is a very high price to pay for each job. There is also concern that GM will need more bailout money in the future, and the company is therefore a poor choice for a bailout. What's worse, bailouts won't save jobs overall. Rather, they will simply destroy jobs at companies like Toyota and Ford, who didn't get bailouts. Ford will now be saddled with more debt than GM or Chrysler, but Ford shouldn't be punished for not needing bailout money in the first place. Mark Milke, director of research at the Frontier Centre for Public Policy, says that the bailouts for GM and Chrysler are nothing more than a transfer of wealth to companies that consumers have already rejected.

Third, the bailouts in the auto industry will likely lead companies in other industries to request bailouts. For example, the forestry, fisheries, auto parts, and commercial airline industries are all having financial problems. The federal government has already announced $1 billion in aid for the pulp and paper industry so they can invest in technology that will make them more energy efficient and environmentally friendly.

Fourth, there is skepticism that the bailout money will ever be repaid. In 1987, GM's assembly plant in Quebec received $220 million in interest free government loans. But GM pulled out of the province in 2002 and didn't repay any of the money. If the latest bailout money is not repaid, Canadians will have to bear the burden through higher taxes and/or cuts to public services. Critics are asking why the government is sinking money into two companies that have been steadily losing market share. Peter Coleman, president of the National Citizens Coalition, says that the bailout money will be useless if people don't start buying cars made by Chrysler and GM. . . ."

Supporters of bailouts　Critics of the bailouts have been very vocal, and their ideas have received a lot of publicity, but there are also defenders of the bailouts. The most fundamental argument in support of bailouts is that they are occasionally necessary when the ups and downs in the economy (oscillations) become so severe that chaos looms. Supporters of bailouts argue that during these times government needs to intervene to reduce the oscillations. They compare the current economic gyrations to the physical gyrations that occurred when the Tacoma Narrows Bridge collapsed. High winds caused oscillations that became progressively more severe until the bridge collapsed in spectacular fashion. Supporters of bailouts argue that government must stop the oscillations in the economic system before they cause a disaster.

The defenders of bailouts also argue that they are necessary to protect jobs. The view is that it would be disastrous to lose all those auto workers' jobs because the people who have those jobs spend a lot of money on a wide variety of goods and services. If those expenditures stopped, the economy would suffer greatly. A study by the Centre for Spatial Economics found that the failure of any of the Big Three domestic car makers would throw Ontario into a deep recession, and 157,000 jobs would be lost (auto production workers, auto dealers, auto parts suppliers, and professional services that are tied to the auto industry). In addition, GM spent $14 billion in 2007 buying products and services from other Canadian companies, and those other companies employ thousands of additional workers. All those workers spend a lot of money and boost the economy. They also pay a lot of income tax, and the government does not want to lose that revenue.

*Source: *Business in the News,* Pearson Canada.

Subsidies

Government assistance to business in the form of subsidies has significant implications in the global business context. Subsidies have been identified as either cash payments, low-interest loans or potentially reduced taxes. Specifically, subsidies in the global context are intended to assist domestic industry to compete against foreign businesses, whether in the home country or through exports. One central argument against subsidies, whether in the domestic or global context, is that businesses should be required to manage their costs without external help, or "handouts," from the government. This is part of the requirement of fair competition, according to the critics. In addition, it is argued that consumers essentially pay for these subsidies. The government collects revenues through income and sales taxes, and it is these funds, collected from the general public, that are used to help some businesses. The question then is, Are subsidies to business an unfair drain on public funds? There is no clear resolution to this ongoing debate.

From the global perspective, there is a second central criticism aimed at companies that receive subsidies from their local government. The criticism asserts that subsidies are not merely harmless forms of assistance to businesses; rather, they constitute a form of trade barrier, just like tariffs, and they create unfair competition. (See Talking Business 7.5.) Why are subsidies viewed as non-tariff trade barriers, and how do they amount to unfair competition? Recently, the WTO has dealt with numerous international cases of allegedly unfair subsidies. The question is: Why should government subsidies to private industry be considered unfair? If the government deems it necessary, why shouldn't a domestic business receive some financial assistance? The answers to these questions have been subject to much debate. In the next section, we consider the issue of subsidies in the global context.

Talking Business 7.5

The Softwood-Lumber Dispute: a Case of Government Subsidies?

One of the highest profile trade disputes between Canada and the United States was the softwood lumber dispute. The origins of the dispute can be traced back to 2001 when Canada exported softwood lumber products to the United States (worth about C$10 billion). The U.S. lumber industry complained to the U.S. government that Canadian lumber producers were competing in an unfair manner since they received a hidden subsidy from their government. In retaliation for this "unfair trade," the United States imposed countervailing duties averaging 27% on Canadian lumber imports. This had a devastating effect on the Canadian lumber industry, particularly in British Columbia, which accounts for about half of the exports. Among the consequences were the closing of Canadian lumber mills, the laying off of thousands of workers and the crashing of profits.

Why was the Canadian lumber industry accused of receiving government subsidies? This claim and indeed the basis of this dispute arose due to the different traditions followed by the two countries. Most U.S. forests are privately owned, and consequently timber prices are set by private contracts or auctions. However, almost all Canadian forests belong to provincial governments. The Canadian government grants companies long-term cutting-rights simply in return for promises about employment numbers and sustainable forestry, while setting the cutting fees according to market conditions. The U.S. lumber industry feels that the Canadian government has given the Canadian lumber industry an unfair advantage and has aided in the competition against U.S. lumber producers. As of 2006, the dispute was essentially resolved.

GOVERNMENT AS GUARDIAN OF BUSINESS IN THE GLOBAL CONTEXT

The pervasiveness of globalization has demanded that governments reconsider the extent to which they feel obligated to maintain a relationship with the private business sector. Thomas Friedman, in his book, *The Lexus and the Olive Tree,* asserts that globalization is, in fact, increasing the importance of government while changing the roles that it plays:

> The ability of an economy to withstand the inevitable ups and downs of the herd depends in large part on the quality of its legal system, financial system and economic management—all matters still under the control of governments and bureaucrats. Chile, Taiwan, Hong Kong and Singapore all survived the economic crises of the 1990s so much better than their neighbours because they had better-quality states running better-quality software and operating systems.[4]

Consequently, while governments may find their role increasingly challenged, and in some ways compromised, by the onslaught of multinationals and globalization, the need for government involvement in certain ways may be increased in this new, global context. The following section, illustrated in Exhibit 7.4, offers reasons for government support for Canadian business. Talking Business 7.6 offers arguments against such support.

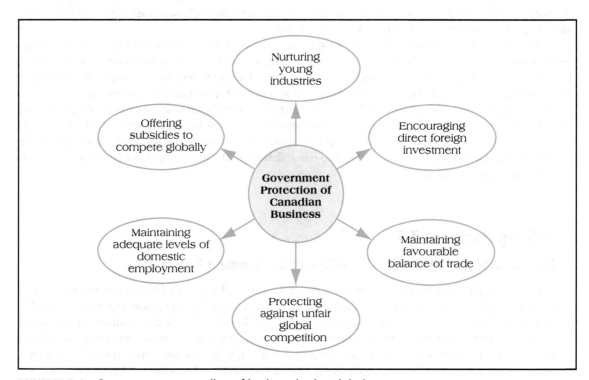

EXHIBIT 7.4 Government as guardian of business in the global context.

Talking Business 7.6

Why Should Government Not Play the Role of Guardian of Business?

Bombardier and its subsidiaries have received $772-million in federal government handouts since 1982, making the company the largest beneficiary of Ottawa's corporate welfare program. This week, the aerospace manufacturer is expected to confirm whether or not it will build a new regional jet.

The project will cost more than $2.5-billion and the company wants governments to pony up a third of the cost. Because Ottawa remains committed to providing business subsidies, Canadian taxpayers should brace themselves for another fleecing as Bombardier returns to the public trough.

Federal ministers will likely describe this giveaway as necessary, important, and a winner for Canada. They might even tell taxpayers the contributions will be repaid one day. But a quick review of Ottawa's collection record will put the lie to such propaganda—since 1996 less than 5 per cent of the tax money "invested" in business projects has been recouped. So in advance of the Bombardier subsidy announcement it is worth restating the case against corporate welfare:*

i) Market decisions should be made by investors, not by politicians and bureaucrats. The proper function of the private capital market is to direct investment to projects, industries or firms that offer investors the best and/or most secure rate of return. The difference between a sound and poor investment for an individual can have profound implications yet there is no similar discipline for government officials when using other people's money.

ii) Corporate welfare is not driven by market imperatives. Investment decisions should be based on financial reward versus risk. Government investment decisions are driven by political imperatives. The top concern when offering subsidies is a preoccupation with the number of jobs created with little concern for profitability or sustainability.

iii) Picking market winners and losers is not a job suited for government officials. Corporate welfare decisions are most often made by individuals with little experience in private investing; moreover, decisions are often made in a politically charged environment. As a result, ensuring that taxpayer-financed projects meet geographical, industrial equity, and politically saleable criteria often become an end in itself. Governments have an abysmal record of picking winners, whereas corporate losers like Bombardier—have a stellar record of finding government handout programs.

iv) Corporate welfare is unfair. Business subsidies create an uneven playing field as money is diverted away from successful companies to less successful, but politically connected ones. Worse still is those firms and their workers which do not receive government grants end up subsidizing their government-supported competitors through their taxes.

v) Corporate welfare undermines public confidence in our decision-makers. Despite assurances from politicians that subsidies serve an overall industrial policy, there is a growing sense among Canadians that government aid to business is about divvying up pork to favoured and politically connected constituencies.

vi) Corporate welfare runs contrary to free and open markets. Business owners lose sight of their competencies, namely to provide customers with a good or service and earn a profit. They become better lobbyists than businesspeople and morph from entrepreneurs into grantrepreneurs.

vii) Corporate welfare creates a culture of dependency. Business owners become so reliant on government assistance they build expectations of handouts into financial plans. This has the perverse effect of directing resources to less productive investment projects, which slows economic growth rather than enhancing it.

viii) Corporate welfare is not a public good. Tax money ought to be spent on projects that provide the largest societal benefits or on social programs that are a priority to citizens. For example, infrastructure such as roads and water treatment; services such as national defence, policing, border control and immigration; and social services like health care, assistance for the disabled and pensions. Business subsidies do not fit these criteria and most taxpayers realize subsidies routinely fail to achieve their public policy objectives.

ix) Corporate welfare leads to higher taxes. All taxpayers end up footing the bill for Canada's $4-billion business subsidy programs.

Taxpayers deserve better than to subsidize well-connected corporations and their shareholders. Ottawa should end corporate [subsidies] and create a business climate that rewards success, not sycophants.

*The nine points were adapted from the CTF report A Taxpayers Audit of Technology Partnerships Canada (Feb. 2002).

Source: Reproduced from John Williamson, The Canadian Taxpayers Association (March 14, 2005) <http://www.taxpayer.com/main/news.php?news_id=1954> with permission of the Canadian Taxpayer Federation.

1. Nurturing Young Industries

The notion that government must play a role in nurturing domestic industry was raised earlier in this chapter. The infant-industry argument asserts that the government should help a young industry to grow and develop by ensuring that the industry maintains a dominant share of the domestic market until it is mature enough to compete against foreign competition. Consequently, this philosophy is still applied, particularly among developing countries. The rationale is that the infant industry may be less competitive, particularly because of initially high output costs; however, with maturity, the production will become more efficient, and protection will no longer be necessary.

At least two risks have been associated with this form of government influence:

- Such protection can discourage domestic industry from increasing competitiveness and engaging in innovation. This is an argument that has been levelled at Canadian business.
- There is a question as to whether consumers are better or worse off from such practices. Not all Canadian parties want the Canadian steel industry to receive this type of protection from foreign rivals (see below). In fact, Canadian purchasers of any good or service arguably would want the lowest-cost supplier to be accessible and, consequently, may not appreciate the protection of infant industry if it comes at the expense of blocking access to cheaper foreign goods or services.

2. Encouraging Direct Foreign Investment

The action of reducing foreign imports may result in the foreign business directly investing in the target country instead. That is, a foreign company can decide to set up business in the target country if it wishes to gain access to that country's consumer market and it is unable to achieve that with imports. Of course, from the domestic country's viewpoint, this foreign investment may be desirable if it increases job opportunities, contributes to the growth of industry and adds to the amount of capital.

3. Maintaining Favourable Balance of Trade

Government may seek to influence the relative status of exports and imports to avoid running a trade deficit. **Trade surpluses** come about when a country's exports exceed its imports and, consequently, more money is entering the country (from foreign consumers buying these exports) than is leaving the country (from domestic consumers buying foreign imports). A **trade deficit** is the reverse—when a country imports more than it exports. Traditionally, governments intervened to ensure a trade surplus by imposing tariffs or quotas or by banning outright some foreign-imported commodities. Typically, the governments would also subsidize domestic industries in order to encourage growth in their exports. (See Talking Business 7.7: When Government Doesn't Stand Guard.)

4. Protecting Domestic Business from Unfair Competition

There is a concern among some businesses that foreign competitors will offer their products at extremely low prices as a means of monopolizing their share of the target country's market. The ultimate consequence would be that domestic producers could potentially be driven out of business and be replaced by the foreign imports. A foreign competitor who manages to export the products at such low prices may be accused of **dumping**—which is pricing the product below cost or below the cost of the target country's product. In other words, a foreign supplier who sells the product at a loss or for less than the price of the seller's domestic market would be considered guilty of dumping.

Traditionally, steel companies have been among the most avid users of anti-dumping legislation in Canada and the United States. Hamilton-based Dofasco Inc. lodged a dumping complaint against steel mills in Asia and South America. The aim was to seek government assistance, which in this case resulted in a decision by the Canadian federal government to place anti-dumping tariffs on low-cost imported steel from these foreign suppliers. In total, these anti-dumping tariffs were aimed at blocking the dumping of steel shipments from nine countries. This echoes similar action taken in the United States. Steel producers in both the United States and Canada have blamed the increasing foreign imports of steel for reducing demand for their product domestically and, consequently, reducing product prices and revenue. It is interesting to note that while Canadian steel producers welcome such government intervention, other domestic players are not happy with the implementation of anti-dumping tariffs, which effectively raise the price of these cheaper goods.

Talking Business 7.7

When Government Doesn't Stand Guard: The Case of Jamaica

A documentary entitled *Life and Debt* produced by Stephanie Black vividly illustrates the devastating effects that globalization has had on Jamaica. The documentary examines the effect of the International Monetary Fund's (IMF) policies on developing countries through Jamaica's experience with the organization. After having gained its autonomy from Britain in 1962, Jamaica was struggling economically. It appeared that salvation would come in the form of financial assistance, a loan, from the International Monetary Fund (the IMF). However, there were several stipulations, including the requirement to devalue the Jamaican currency and reduce trade barriers by withdrawing local import restrictions. Jamaica would thus enter the world market—it was going global. The result was devastating. The local economy became flooded with foreign imports (cheaper than Jamaican goods), and consequently huge losses in jobs and economic self-reliance followed.

This kind of liberalization of policies meant huge benefits to the larger lender (developed countries such as the United States and Britain) but meant real hardship for Jamaica. In his article, "Who Is Aiding Whom," David Sogge speaks of the problems of the international trade liberalization in ways that raise questions in one's mind as to who benefits most—and is referred to as the "dual mandate of western aid." For example, the lender countries do not allow exports from the recipient (borrower) country to be bought and sold in the recipient country, and instead the opposite is done—the lender countries "dump" their exports on the developing (borrower) country. Other issues involved in these agreements include repayment of the debts, which are extremely strenuous and the interest rates are often inordinately high. Other problems include the brain drain in the developing countries where most of the trained professionals of these countries go to take up residence in the developed nations in search of a "better life"—a better standard of living.

With these kinds of imbalances in trade agreements and international relations, developing countries like Jamaica, other Caribbean countries and Latin American countries are at a disadvantage, and the playing field is not level.

Jamaica has been identified as the third most dangerous country in terms of crime and violence in the world today along with other countries including South Africa and Colombia.

According to an article published in the online *Observer*—"Crime, joblessness remain dominant concerns" (December 1, 2005). This article reports that unemployment and high economic price increases have led to the breakdown of community leadership and involvement, and have been replaced with crime.

Source: Stephanie Black, Dir. *Life and Debt in Jamaica.* Film. A Tuff Gong Pictures Production, 2001. (www. newyorkerfilms.com); Holger Henke, "Jamaica Decision to Pursue a Neo-liberal Development Strategy: Realignments in the State-Business-Class Triangle," *Latin American Perspectives* 26(5): 7–33; Hilary Nicholson, Dir. "Together Against Violence," *City Life* series. Videorecording. Oley, PA: Bullfrog Films Inc., 2001; David Sogge, *Give and Take: What's The Matter With Foreign Aid,* pp. 24–39. Halifax, NS; Fernwood Publishing, 2002.

Specifically, western Canadian manufacturers have claimed that the protectionist measures will reduce their ability to compete with Ontario steel manufacturers. Many western steel businesses argued that they will lose access to these cheaper foreign sources and now be forced to rely on costlier steel sources in Ontario. These businesses argue that they should have access to the lowest-cost sources of steel, whether these sources are from Canada or from foreign producers. In this regard, they are opposed to the government's protectionist policy of imposing anti-dumping tariffs.

5. Maintaining Adequate Levels of Domestic Employment

A government knows that society holds it responsible for ensuring the unemployment rates are not high. Imports that come to dominate an industry bring the threat of causing domestic industries to go bankrupt. Consequently, where businesses claim they are under threat of bankruptcy due to foreign competition, the government is forced to consider what action it can take to combat this threat. In the past, the government protected Canadian business and employment from the risk of foreign competition via the implementation of tariffs, as discussed in the previous chapter. Clearly, such an option is complicated by the fact that reducing imports is not necessarily feasible, for reasons also described earlier. Protectionist policies are not compatible with the sentiments of free trade, and thus governments are sometimes placed in the unenviable position of balancing the needs of the domestic economy with the need to honour the rules governing global business. A case in point is the issue of government subsidies.

6. Offering Subsidies to Compete Globally

Whether it is for the purpose of maintaining employment levels or of assisting businesses in the global marketplace, the issue of government subsidies to business has become much more controversial in the context of globalization. Whether it is cash payments, low-interest loans or tax breaks, such financial assistance is referred to as a subsidy. And in the case of the global context, such subsidies are intended to help domestic industry deal with the global competition. In recent years, the WTO (World Trade Organization) has been involved in many international disputes regarding whether a local government has given its domestic industry an unfair advantage through some form of subsidy. The risks of such subsidies, in addition to the potential conflicts they create with regard to facilitating free trade, include the notion that competitive industries should be able to absorb such costs themselves rather than relying on the government for these handouts. The lumber dispute highlighted in Talking Business 7.5 earlier in this chapter is an example of the difficulty in establishing the degree to which government should aid business in the global context. Other examples abound with regard to government aid to business in the global context.

SHOULD GOVERNMENT "MIND ITS OWN BUSINESS"?

Government intervention in the economy has traditionally been greater in Canada than in the United States. For example, government expenditures as a percentage of GOP are typically higher in Canada than in the United States, and public sector employment in Canada has been as much as 30% greater than in the United States. However, Canada has been following the trend of reducing government's involvement in the business sector. Why are we witnessing this reduction in government involvement, and what are the implications of this trend? These questions are addressed in the following sections. (See Exhibit 7.5.)

Deregulation

Earlier, we discussed the issue of government regulation. And, as we mentioned, government regulates the operation of businesses through commissions, tribunals, agencies and boards. Whatever the form, government directly regulates about one-third of the economy through more than 600 organizations. However, what we have witnessed since the 1980s is a trend toward **deregulation**. Deregulation, as the name suggests, involves a reduction in the number of laws or regulations affecting business activity. It also suggests a reduction of the powers of government enforcement agencies and other forms of government control or influence.

In recent years, the process of deregulation in the Canadian economy seems to have accelerated, particularly in industry sectors, such as transportation, telecommunications, financial services and energy services. While the telecommunications sector maintains varying degrees of regulations in different areas, it has created an increased level of competition through deregulation in areas such as overseas calling, domestic long distance, local, wireless and other services. In the Canadian electricity sector, deregulation has recently been applied, particularly in Alberta and Ontario.

Why has the government deregulated certain industries?

Why has the government engaged in privatization?

What areas of business has the government chosen to deregulate or privatize?

What are the benefits of deregulation?

What are the benefits of privatization?

What are the risks of deregulation?

What are the risks of privatization?

EXHIBIT 7.5   Questions to be addressed regarding government intervention.

In fact, in a number of countries, we have witnessed economic deregulation among many industries, including airlines, trucking, railroads, financial markets, energy and telecommunications. At the same time, there has been an increase in regulations that are intended to govern such areas as health and safety and the environment. In order to understand the implications of economic deregulation, it is useful to briefly reconsider why, in fact, there is a need to regulate any industry at all.

As explained earlier in this chapter, regulation is aimed at correcting market failures and inequities that may arise for a variety of reasons, including insufficient competition. However, just as the market can fail, so, too, the government policy of deregulation may not always achieve the goals for which it was intended. While it may be an oversimplification, the significant consequences of deregulation fall into two categories: potential benefit and potential risk.

What's the potential benefit?

- The benefit to consumers of increased competition arising from the reduction of regulations that have formerly restricted the entry of new competitors.

What's the potential risk?

- The risk to consumers of exploitation—e.g., reduction in quality of product or service, increases in consumer fees or price increases as a result of the reduction in laws governing their operation.

The question is—Will deregulation accomplish the central objective of sufficiently loosening constraints in order to encourage the entry of more competitors? Or, will deregulation fail to encourage adequate competition, and will this loosening of constraints instead permit current competitors to abuse the system and exploit consumers in some way? (See Talking Business 7.8.)

Talking Business 7.8
Deregulation of Utilities

Deregulating the Electrical Energy Industry

In order to understand deregulation, it is necessary to briefly explore the history of ownership and regulation of the electric industry in Canada and the United States:

Originally, groups of private investors controlled the ownership and production of electrical energy in both the United States and Canada.

- Over time, electrical energy came to be considered as a natural monopoly, where economies of scale and the importance of electrical energy led to public ownership of most generation facilities.
- In most cases public ownership was at the state or provincial level.
- The end result was vertical integration, where one utility generated, transmitted, and distributed electricity within a certain area.
- The utility had a monopoly over electrical production and distribution in a given area. Customers were unable to choose between different energy providers.

Why Deregulate?

In general, proponents of electrical deregulation hope to gain some or all of the following benefits:

- Cheaper electricity rates for customers through competition, particularly industry and larger businesses who purchase wholesale electricity
- Improved service for some customers through competition
- Greater freedom for customers choosing between different types of energy, including environmentally friendly technologies such as solar energy and wind turbines
- Prevention of companies that gain market power by lowering the price of generation and making up for it by raising the cost of transmission and distribution, which can happen when the three systems are bundled together

Source: Excerpts from Mapleleafweb.com, Department of Political Science, University of Lethbridge, http://www.mapleleafweb.com/features/economy/deregulation/energy/industry.html.

Research evidence from U.S.-based studies has offered strong support for the benefits of deregulation among a variety of sectors, including railway, trucking, airline, telecommunications and financial industries. Comparisons have been made of the U.S. and Canadian railway industries between 1956 and 1974, when the U.S. railway industry was more heavily regulated than the Canadian. While both industries had access to the same technology, productivity growth was much greater in the Canadian (3.3%) than in the U.S. railroads (0.5%). Studies have indicated that unit costs in the U.S. trucking industry decreased significantly in the period following deregulation in 1983. Similarly, the airline industry managed to reduce costs by 25% in the period following deregulation.

The U.S. telecommunications industry has also benefited from deregulation, according to recent studies. For example, by 1996 long-distance telephone rates in the United States had dropped by over 70%. A number of studies have also suggested that deregulation encouraged much more innovation, as reflected in the emergence of such profitable services as cellular telephony and voice messaging. It is interesting to note that the concept of cellular phones was discussed as early as the 1950s, and the technology had become available by the early 1970s, yet the Federal Communications Commission did not issue licences until 1983—an illustration of the inhibiting effect of regulations on innovation.

Deregulation in the financial industries, including securities, investment and banking sectors, has also yielded some positive support from U.S.-based studies with regard to its consequences. For example, it has been estimated that partial deregulation of the banking and savings and loan industry contributed to a 300% increase in productivity, while deregulated brokerage fees resulted in a 25% decrease in rates.

Comparative studies have supported the benefits of deregulation. For example, by 1999, in industries such as the airline industry, the United States was clearly maintaining a significantly higher level of deregulation than many European countries. Advocates of deregulation have asserted that the benefits of deregulation were reflected in the fact that European airline fares were about twice as costly as U.S. airfares, while European companies were neither as efficient nor as profitable as the U.S. carriers. Consequently, supporters of deregulation claim that eliminating price and entry restrictions would increase competition and, ultimately, benefit consumers through lower airfares and better service. Comparisons of the relative differences in levels of regulation between Europe and the United States by the late 1990s drew similar conclusions. It was estimated that many European companies were paying about 50% more for their electricity than their U.S. counterparts. For example, the high level of regulation in Germany's electricity market, including the requirement to purchase electricity from regional producers rather than less expensive alternative sources, was viewed as inhibiting efficiency and productivity. In contrast, the U.K. greatly benefited from energy deregulation with regard to productivity gains, estimated at 70% subsequent to deregulation.

While the findings above certainly point to the potential benefits of deregulation, there is no doubt that support for deregulation is far from universal. While advocates claim that the beneficial impact on consumers and businesses outweighs any costs, opponents suggest the reverse—that the risks of deregulation are too high to enter into this venture. There is likely no area more mixed with regard to the reaction to deregulation than in its impact on developing countries. Nonetheless, there is, again, evidence that is very supportive of the policy of deregulation. For example, deregulation in the telecommunications industry among some Latin American countries has greatly encouraged private sector involvement and led to increased efficiency in services. By the late 1990s, telephone user rates were reduced by about 50% following the deregulation of entry requirements in the long-distance telephone market in Chile. At the same time, studies have pointed out the negative consequences of maintaining regulation in various sectors within developing countries. For example, in the late 1990s Brazil and Argentina's transportation regulations forced businesses to ship largely by road, even though the costs were significantly higher than rail charges.[5]

Example #1: Deregulation in the Transportation Industry

As mentioned, the main objective of government regulation is to protect the public interest. The railroad industry was among the very first to have regulations applied, with the deal made in 1895 between Prime Minister Wilfrid Laurier and the CPR. Essentially, the government promised the CPR the financing it needed to complete a transcontinental line if the CPR would carry wheat produced by western farmers for shipping on a regular basis at a negotiated rate. Many years later, the National Transportation Act created the Canadian Transport Commission (in 1970), whose job it was to regulate and control the various means of transportation in Canada, including motor, air, water transport and railways, among other things. However, on January 1, 1988, the new National Transportation Act came into effect, and brought with it a new era of deregulation. What did this new legislation contain, and how did it bring about deregulation in the transportation industry? Well, just consider its impact on the trucking industry.

This act brought with it the passage of the new Motor Vehicle Transport Act. Prior to that time, anyone wanting to enter the trucking business was required to appear before the provincial licensing board and prove there was a public need for their service in order to get a licence to operate a truck. However, under the new act the prospective trucker must simply present proof that they are insurable and can pass some minimal safety criteria. So what is the result of all this? One of the major benefits of the reduction in requirements for new entrants was increased competition: more truckers entered the industry. Shippers gained from a wider choice of trucking services and more competitive rates. Following the passage of this Act, shippers could negotiate the level of service and price of any domestic movement with any carrier. Consequently, consumers benefited in terms of reduced costs arising from increased competition in highway carriers. In fact, a central aim of this deregulation was to encourage greater efficiency in Canada's over \$2 billion transportation market. In a more recent report of the trucking industry in Canada, the following observation was made:

> What has emerged is a new breed of Canadian trucker—one that is more efficient, value-priced, eager to customize to shippers' needs and adept at filling specialized niches in a North American market dominated by huge and efficient American carriers.[6]

In the related railway shipping industry, recent reports have indicated that shipper rates dropped by 35% since deregulation, and were considered the lowest in the world—60% below the international average.[7] However, there has been a downside for some. With increased competition, some trucking companies have been unable to compete effectively and have gone bankrupt, resulting in the loss of hundreds of jobs. In fact, in 1990 about 130 trucking companies declared bankruptcy—over twice as many as those in the previous year. A major threat has come from U.S. trucking companies, which have lower labour, equipment and tax costs and, consequently, lower operating costs. So there are winners and losers in the trend toward deregulation, and the issue of competition lies at the heart of this. Reducing regulations welcomes more entrants and creates more pressure on existing Canadian companies. During the years following deregulation, the Canadian carriers admitted that they were slow to adapt to new technologies such as electronic data interchange, bar coding and satellite tracking of trailers. For example, by 1997 almost all U.S. truckload tractors were equipped for satellite tracking, while only 50% of Canadian tractors were equipped.[8]

Example #2: Deregulation in the Electricity Industry

The past 10 years or so have seen a great interest in deregulation in the energy sector: specifically energy supply, with Britain and Scandinavia largely initiating this practice in the early 1990s. Traditionally, electricity costs have been higher in Europe than in North America. After a number of European governments privatized their public utilities, the cost of electricity dropped in those regions. Deregulation also welcomed much more competition, which forced the power companies to become more efficient and improve customer service.

The Canadian government, seemingly drawing on the European experience, decided to initiate privatization and deregulation in the energy sector in Canada, beginning with Alberta in 1995. Unfortunately, the reaction to this transition has been mixed, with some observers criticizing the deregulation process in Alberta's electricity industry, and others adding that the purchase of electricity has become more complicated with the advent of deregulation.

Ontario has followed Alberta's lead in electricity deregulation, although it has proceeded somewhat more slowly, and, according to some, more cautiously. While advocates of deregulation feel that, ultimately, the benefits of increased competition will prevail, those opposed to deregulation believe that public ownership should continue to exist for essential services in order to ensure that all members of society will be guaranteed access to the same service at a reasonable price:

> Deregulation was fingered by presenters as the culprit during hearings by the U.S.-Canadian Power System Outage Task Force on the August 14, 2003 electricity blackout. They pointed out that the electricity system is run down because . . . [t]here wasn't enough concern about controlling all these new deregulated companies. . . . Prior to restructuring and deregulation, the goal of utilities was reliable service at minimum long-term cost. In contrast, the goal of newly restructured organizations in a deregulated environment is short-term profit with little concern for the overall system.[9]

The dangers of deregulation are further addressed in Talking Business 7.9.

Talking Business 7.9
The Dangers of Deregulation

In Canada, regulations adopted by every level of government have historically helped to make this one of the safest, most desirable places to raise a family. But many Canadians take for granted that our governments are doing all they can to keep us safe.

Butcher shops, restaurants, water filtration plants, freeways, elevators, rides at the fair, food labels, prescription and natural drug approvals, air travel, toys, baby gear—we trust they're regulated and constantly monitored for problems. We assume our government is behind the scenes, protecting us at work and at play.

What we don't know can hurt us. Over the past generation there has been a slow, steady, and quiet erosion of regulations by governments intent on 'reducing red tape', making Canada 'more competitive' and making governments more 'cost efficient'.

Much of this government activity has gone unnoticed, partly because the changes are promoted as 'smart regulation' when they are actually a reflection of influence peddling. Governments at every level in Canada are under constant pressure by corporations, small businesses, developers and professional lobby groups to cut regulations that are there to keep us safe from harm.

The trend towards deregulation—the weakening or elimination of government regulations—began in earnest after Canada entered into its first free trade agreement with the United States in 1988. Subsequent trade agreements, combined with pressure from powerful corporate lobbyists intent on reducing the size of government and giving markets a freer hand, have led to a serious watering down of Canadian regulations.

New guidelines now require federal departments to ratchet down regulations so they're in line with international trade agreements—a dangerous trend. For instance, instead of taking environmental leadership to clean up the Alberta oil sands, the Canadian government is going in the opposite direction, claiming it wants to 'harmonize' regulations with countries like the U.S.

There are many times when following the international pack is, quite simply, a bad idea. Take financial regulation, for instance. Canada's economy was sheltered from the worst of the 2008 global economic meltdown because our bank regulations are tougher than they are in competing jurisdictions like the U.S. Following our own high standards paid off, and protected Canadians from the economic devastation that brought entire nations such as Iceland and the U.S. to the brink of ruin.

From the Walkerton crisis we learned the provincial government was not enforcing the water quality regulations that were on the books. What was supposed to be a 'cost saving' came at too great a cost for far too many Walkerton residents.

In the case of Maple Leaf Foods, the company assumed full responsibility for the problem but the union representing federal food inspectors warned they did not have enough government inspectors to properly monitor the meat plant.

Source: CCPA—Canadian Centre for Policy Alternatives.

Privatization

What does *privatization* mean? In broad terms, **privatization** refers to the divesting of government involvement in the operation, management and ownership of activities. Typically, privatization involves the transfer of activities or functions from the government to the private sector. Privatization might involve selling off a Crown corporation to the private sector. For example, Air Canada, formerly a Crown corporation, was sold to the private sector in 1988–1989. Also in 1988, the government sold Teleglobe Canada Inc., a handler of overseas satellite calls for the telephone and telecommunications companies, to private business.

Privatization might also involve contracting government jobs to private companies. For example, in some provinces private businesses contract to manage hospitals and other health care institutions previously managed by government employees. Other services that can be contracted out are things like garbage collection and road construction. In addition, public institutions have also contracted out services such as data processing and food and janitorial services to private sector corporations. The closing of some postal stations and the franchising of postal services in retail businesses is yet another example.

In recent years there has been a significant transformation of the organizational landscape across the world, as numerous state-owned monopolies, agencies and other public organizations have privatized. Government ownership in areas from airlines to electricity has been sold to either domestic or foreign investors. In fact, over 15,000 enterprises were privatized during the period from 1980 to 1992. By 1997, worldwide privatization proceeds reached $153 billion.[10]

Privatization has been implemented not only in advanced countries, such as the United States, Canada, the U.K., Australia, France, Germany and Japan, but also in transitional countries such as Poland, Chile, Brazil, Mexico and Argentina. In addition, developing countries have been implementing privatization—including Nigeria, Tunisia and Zimbabwe. It is also expected that privatization will continue to progress around the world and in most economic sectors over the coming decade.

Global privatization accelerated in the 1990s, particularly in Western Europe, with developing countries accounting for about one-third of the annual funds raised by privatization. In the economies of Eastern Europe, the transition to private ownership has reflected a particularly significant political transition, as recently observed:

> The development of a large-scale privatization program is also a highly political act. Almost by definition, privatization represents an ideological and symbolic break with a history of state control over a country's productive assets. Nowhere is this symbolism more apparent than in the economies of Eastern Europe and the former Soviet Union, where privatization of state-owned enterprises has come to signal a nation's transition from communism to democratic capitalism. In Russia, the privatization of enormous petroleum (Lukoil) , natural gas (Gazprom) and telecommunications (Syazinevest) companies represented a fundamental break from socialist state ownership.[11]

Why Do Governments Privatize?

Why have we observed the increased divestiture of government in business activities, including the sale of Crown corporations? What are the reasons for reducing the level of government ownership in business enterprises? Let's consider some of the popular arguments for privatization.

Reasons for Privatization

Belief in the power of competition as a control mechanism   Privatization is considered to be an expected outgrowth of the free enterprise system. That is, private enterprise should be allowed to expand into areas that were once monopolized by the government. Moreover, privatization programs are typically guided by the view that the force of market competition is best suited to fostering efficiency and innovation in an industry. Specifically, the view is that privatization of a state-owned monopoly will open an industry to competition and, consequently, encourage innovation, growth and efficiency. Moreover, where privatization opens an industry to foreign competition, this permits consumers to have access to goods or services developed in other parts of the world, and will stimulate innovation among domestic firms operating in the industry. In addition, opening an industry to foreign investors may also provide access to needed financial and technological resources, and create growth in the industry.

Belief that private business can operate more efficiently   A second, common view, is that transferring the management of organizations to the private sector will result in increased productivity. Studies conducted in a variety of countries have found evidence that the private production of goods and services is typically more efficient than public production. Why should this be considered true? Well, think back to our discussion of why Crown corporations were established: not for profit, but for a social policy consideration—i.e., serving public interests. Consequently, many observers feel that it is difficult for government-owned enterprises to reconcile the social goals of the enterprise with the economic-efficiency goals that must be of concern to any business. Moreover, efficient operation may be difficult given that there are political interests to be considered. Removing the political element of an enterprise allows it to focus on efficiency and avoid potential conflicts of interest. The Ontario government announced that its main goal for privatization was to improve economic efficiency of the underlying organization, as reflected in reduced prices and improved customer service. (See Talking Business 7.10)

Talking Business 7.10
Canada Post is a Prime Candidate for Privatization

The Gazette

Some day, postal service might be irrelevant to our lives as our communications switch to email or something even better. But for now, we still depend on Canada Post to bring us everything from magazines to greeting cards and bills.

Indeed, as more and more of us shop online, physical delivery of the stuff we buy is becoming an increasingly important part of our lives. Sadly for us as owners of the postal service, it isn't much used for this kind of thing, having struggled to compete with outfits like FedEx and UPS.

This might change in a big way, however, if Canada Post were to be run more like a business and less like a department of government. And what could fit better with a Harper government's free-market philosophy?

After all, Canadian National Railways and Air Canada were hardly models of efficiency when they were privatized many years ago. Now both are among North America's most competitive enterprises in their fields.

Edward Iacobucci, a law professor at the University of Toronto, notes that postal services in many other countries have been radically liberalized—some even sold to the private sector—and the results have been quite positive.

Iacobucci, together with a couple colleagues, Michael Trebilcock at the U of T and Tracey Epps from New Zealand's University of Otago, have set out the case for reform at Canada Post in a new study sponsored by the C.D. Howe Institute. They make a persuasive case.

They point out that the problem with commercial organizations operated within the public service has to do with the perverse incentives involved in operating a monopoly that's insulated from market incentives.

The personnel certainly aren't the problem, because in an earlier era, we observed a career civil servant, Paul Tellier, transform Canadian National from a troubled national railway into a formidable North American competitor.

Privatization—or at least major reform—of Canada Post could bring about a similar transformation if it were done properly.

In countries like Germany, the Netherlands, New Zealand and Sweden, where postal services were exposed to more competition, service generally improved and prices remained reasonable, says Iacobucci.

The theory that Canada Post must have a monopoly on letter delivery to ensure that others won't "cream off" delivery profits in big cities and leave remote areas unserved is silly. When you factor in the waste and inefficiency created by the monopoly, it's much cheaper to permit competition and simply pay someone a subsidy to serve unprofitable routes, which is exactly what several other countries do.

The worry about prices rising in a competitive market is also misplaced. New Zealand has permitted competition in postal service, but its reformed postal service manages to keep rates frozen while still providing excellent service.

In New Zealand, the equivalent of first-class mail costs 45 New Zealand cents (the equivalent of 36 cents Canadian). It arrives the next day within the same town and within three days elsewhere in New Zealand.

In Canada, an equivalent letter costs 52 cents and promises two-day delivery in town and four-day delivery within Canada.

Heck, we don't even do well by the standard of the U.S., another postal service that observers say could use liberalization. In the U.S., delivery isn't much faster than in Canada, but home delivery is six days a week and mailmen not only deliver, but pick up from homes (including free pick-up of big packages on request).

And then there's the question of reliability. Our household has been a little wary of Canada Post ever since one member sent half a dozen grad-school applications to universities across the U.S, using an extra-cost premium service that promises speedy, reliable delivery and tracking right to the destination. Two were lost. Canada Post's tracking service couldn't say where.

One application, sent to the San Francisco area, just disappeared without a trace. Another, sent to Boston, showed up in Great Britain, where the surprised recipient was kind enough to telephone our home, get the proper address, and ship it there. The next batch of applications went out by FedEx.

No longer need public involvement in some sectors   Air Canada was established as a Crown corporation at a time when no private company had the resources to develop a transnational airline. In more recent times, there are both domestic and international airlines more than capable of conducting such business and, consequently, there is little need for government ownership in such sectors. Where the enterprise is no longer required by the government to achieve its initial public policy goals, then ownership can be handed over to the private sector. If private industry is willing to offer the same product or service in a reliable and cost-effective manner, why not allow it to do so? As we discussed, in Canada's earlier days, the creation of Crown corporations was deemed necessary, in part, by the "natural monopoly argument" in industries such as public utilities or communications, given that low unit costs of production could be attained only if output were sufficiently high. Consequently, a large government monopoly or a regulated, privately owned monopoly was acceptable and, perhaps, necessary. This argument has weakened in more recent times, when globalization has introduced large, worldwide competitors who may be bigger and more efficient than federal or provincial Crown corporations. (See Talking Business 7.11.)

Talking Business 7.11

Good Time to Sell Government Assets? Depends on the Asset

Bryne Purchase

Governments everywhere are confronted with huge deficits. Economists believe that, in many cases, these are structural deficits—that even in economic recovery, they are unlikely to be eliminated by corresponding revenue growth and the end of recession-related spending.

In this tough fiscal environment, some are urging asset sales. In Toronto, for example, some have suggested the sale of Toronto Hydro. Ontario may be considering the sale of all or parts of Hydro One, Ontario Power Generation, the Ontario Liquor Control Board and the Ontario Lottery and Gaming Corp. New Brunswick has negotiated a potential deal to sell NB Power. The federal government is also reviewing asset sales, such as the power division of Atomic Energy of Canada Ltd.

How should the public evaluate potential government asset sales? Will they help to resolve structural deficits? Will economic performance improve? The answer depends on the nature of the asset.

Take, for example, Toronto Hydro and Hydro One. Technology makes them natural monopolies. It makes no economic sense to have 10 or 20 competing electric wires running through the streets or countryside. Profits are formally regulated by an independent tribunal to ensure that they approximate what would happen in a competitive marketplace.

If a government sells this kind of asset to a private firm, very little changes. There is no evidence that a rate-regulated private monopoly performs better or worse than a rate-regulated publicly owned monopoly. Nor does such a sale address a structural deficit. One-time revenues do nothing to change the underlying and ongoing fiscal problem of too little tax revenue or too much program spending.

In short, such sales would not appear to be in the public interest. They solve no problems but come with transaction costs.

There are, of course, interests that are served by this type of asset sale. They allow the day's political leaders to put off the unpleasant tasks of cutting program spending or raising taxes. Other beneficiaries include the host of financial, legal and political consultants who will personally benefit from serving as advisers to the transaction.

Government businesses, such as Ontario's LCBO and OLGC, are in another category. They are not natural monopolies. They are government-created monopolies, and they have no independent regulatory oversight limiting their profitability. But if they were sold as monopolies to private enterprise, then some new formal regulatory framework would have to be created to protect the public from exploitation by the new private owners.

(Continued)

In short, their monopoly value is likely maximized if left in government hands. Structural deficits could be made worse if they are sold. Moreover, many believe that monopoly pricing by government, by reducing consumption, is socially desirable for alcohol and gambling.

Ontario's OPG and the federal AECL are in yet another category. It is possible that a sale of these assets could help to reduce structural deficits and improve economic performance. Both companies could operate in a competitive marketplace but are currently used by governments to achieve other public purposes.

AECL's power reactor business already operates in a competitive international marketplace. It is an ideal candidate for sale, not because it would yield much one-time cash value but because it would cease to be a drain on future government finances in subsidies to domestic nuclear power technology.

Ontario has used OPG's assets to subsidize the price of electricity. Ending this practice would raise revenue. The government could also sell the assets and move to create a competitive market for electricity generators. These actions would improve economic performance on many fronts.

In short, there is no single answer to whether asset sales are in the public interest. But these are very significant and largely irrevocable decisions. And one thing is certain: Neither ideology nor the short-term interests of current governments or consultants should be allowed to dominate.

To guard against this, we should adopt a convention that all major government asset sales be subject to a truly independent review, with the results of such review made public before any final decision is made.

Source: The Globe and Mail.
http://www.theglobeandmail.com/news/opinions/good-time-to-sell-government-assets-depends-on-the-asset/article1441292/. January 22, 2010.

Financial benefits from selling government-owned assets   Another reason for selling off government-owned enterprises is that the money can be used on other, more needed, areas. Certainly money received from sales of Crown corporations or partial disposition of Crown-owned assets has been applied to government deficit reductions. In addition, opening an industry to private investors may attract, for example, an influx of foreign capital. Maintaining a Crown corporation can be an increasingly costly venture, particularly when high subsidies are made to inefficient state-owned enterprises. Privatization can remove this unnecessary financial burden from government and taxpayers. For example, in the U.K. over US$16.8 billion was raised between 1990 and 1995 through the privatization of two power generating companies, the 12 regional electricity companies and the National Grid. Similarly, Argentina raised over US$4 billion through the partial disposition of government-owned electricity assets and cut its level of debt. Here in Canada, the financial incentive for privatizing Ontario Hydro was based on estimates of a corresponding provincial debt reduction of at least Cdn$8 billion. As well, the initial public offering of shares in CNR in 1995 was Canada's largest stock market flotation at that time. However, during the 1980s and 1990s, privatizations in Canada were most likely to have been conducted through sales to private businesses rather than public share offerings. Revenues from sales of Canada's 10 largest federal corporations amounted to $7.2 billion in the period between 1986 and 1996. Proceeds to the federal government were over $3.8 billion from the sale of shares in CN and Petro-Canada alone.

Challenges to "Going Private"

Stakeholders and objectives   Governments in Canada began to privatize their corporate holdings in the mid-1980s for many of the reasons already cited, including efficiency objectives, financial concerns and the capability of the private sector to fulfill public policy objectives.

It is useful to point out that while these may be objectives of privatization, they are not held equally by all parties affected by a privatization. The objectives of various stakeholders in the privatization of a Crown corporation may be different and potentially conflicting. Consider, for example, the stakeholders affected by the privatization of public utilities, which may include, among others, government owners, other government parties (i.e., other levels of government), creditors, future shareholders of the organization, the unionized and non-unionized employees of the corporation, the regulators, the taxpayers, the consumers and other existing or potential competitors in the industry.

Employees' objectives In effect, the objectives of privatization could all be considered as objectives of the government owners, but some may conflict with elements of the enterprise itself. For example, after initiation of the privatization plan for Ontario Hydro, Hydro's senior management was also agreeable to the province's plan for privatization. In fact, their view was that rapid privatization was necessary in order to face the increasing competition from the United States and from other provincial utilities in the Ontario electricity market, since deregulation began to open up the market for competition. However, within Hydro there has been much disagreement—culminating in a number of strikes by employees opposed to the government's plans.

A possible cost of privatization is massive layoffs of public employees, particularly in developing and transition countries. For example, the privatization of Argentina's national rail company in 1991 involved laying off almost 80% of the company's total workforce as part of the restructuring. However, numerous studies suggest that aggregate employment remains largely unchanged subsequent to privatization efforts.

The public's objectives Another possible conflict is between the objectives cited and the public's concern for their "protection." For example, in the case of Ontario Hydro, some citizens are concerned that private competitors may be less likely to serve the public's interests than a government-owned enterprise. Consequently, some fear that privatization will bring higher rates and safety concerns. Other issues may relate to foreign ownership. For example, there were no foreign ownership restrictions placed on the privatization of Canadian National Railways (which involved a public offering of a majority of shares), and, consequently, 40% of the $2.3 billion share issue was sold outside Canada, largely to U.S. organizations. For some critics, this sale left too much power out of Canadian hands, and there was some question whether the newly controlled enterprise would keep Canadian interests high on their agenda. On the other hand, the government did not restrict foreign ownership, given the view that the Canadian market was not large enough to allow for complete privatization in one attempt. There were, however, other restrictions: no investor could own more than 15% of the shares, and CN must remain headquartered in Montreal.

While privatization has been viewed as a means to generate higher levels of entrepreneurship and efficiency in an industry, simply transferring ownership to the private sector does not guarantee efficiency gains. At least one important qualification is the level of competition that exists subsequent to the privatization. For example, critics suggest that although Air Canada was privatized in the late 1980s, clear efficiency gains and benefits to the user did not readily materialize, because Air Canada continued to operate in an environment that lacked sufficient competition and, consequently, the airline maintained its monopoly status.

Ironically, the technical responsibilities of the government may increase after privatization, because governments are shifting from owning and managing individual companies to potentially regulating an entire sector or industry. Critics have asserted that if the government fails to implement effective regulation over the new private sector owners, then many of the benefits associated with privatization will not materialize. (See Talking Business 7.12.) This risk may be most apparent in the case of government transfer of ownership of natural monopolies, such as electricity or gas utilities, to a single private owner who takes over the monopoly. This was a criticism levelled at the British government when a number of utilities were privatized, yet monopolistic industries were not consistently restructured to facilitate competition. Consequently, some privatized utility companies continued to operate under monopolistic conditions.

Talking Business 7.12

Privatization and Regulation

The government is facilitating the transition from private or public monopolies in certain industries to ones that will ideally foster competition through deregulation. This has naturally changed the mandate of the Competition Bureau from being solely a watchdog of business. The following basic roles for the Competition Bureau and industry regulators have been emphasized as the atmosphere of deregulation and privatization spreads:

(Continued)

1. Ensure Regulators Promote Competition

The Competition Bureau encourages specific regulators to play a clear role in promoting competition. The benefit of providing regulators with a role to promote competition is illustrated in the telecommunications industry. The Telecommunications Act is ultimately aimed at nurturing increased reliance on market forces. Consequently, the Act encourages the industry regulator, the CRTC, to open new areas of the telecommunications industry to competition, such as local telephone service and pay phones in recent years.

2. Implement Regulatory Control over Excessive Pricing from Monopolies

Even in deregulated markets the Bureau recognizes the need for regulators to monitor industries in transition and, potentially, regulate excessive pricing due to the market power held by a competitor. For example, during the initial stage of deregulation in the telecommunications industry, the CRTC continued to regulate long distance rates of telephone companies until the establishment of sufficient competition in the market. Similarly, the Bureau has continued to support regulatory control over Ontario Hydro Generation Company's electricity prices until such time as the Ontario generation market becomes sufficiently competitive.

3. Support Regulatory Control Concerning Essential Facilities

The Bureau advocates regulatory control over essential facilities in an industry—that is, any facilities that businesses require in order to compete in a market, and for which there is no effective competition. Examples of such essential facilities include: transmission and distribution systems in electricity and natural gas, and interconnection to the public switched telephone network by competitive long distance and local exchange carriers. An industry regulator is present in such cases in order to prohibit excessive pricing of essential facilities due to any monopoly power.

4. Establish a Framework for Deregulation

It is recognized that where regulation is not productive for the industry, the aim becomes one that is geared toward creating mechanisms to remove that regulation. Such would be the case where an industry is clearly approaching the perfect competition ideal; that is, when the level of competition is sufficient to prevent any market participant from establishing or sustaining a significant and permanent price increase. On the other hand, even where a lower level of competition exists, deregulation may also be a goal if the costs of maintaining regulation outweigh the benefits.

Source: Based on A. Lafond, Deputy Commissioner of Competition, Civil Matters Branch, Competition Bureau, "The roles and responsibilities of the industry regulator versus the Competition Bureau as regulated industries become competitive," Address to the Conference Board Regulatory Reform Program Meeting, February 19, 1999.

CHAPTER SUMMARY

We have noted the shift toward reduced government involvement in the business sector, reflected in the trends toward deregulation and privatization. Observers suggest that what we are witnessing is a marked decrease in government involvement as public preferences shift toward a more purely private market system. It seems that many observers view the decrease in the level of government influence in business as a positive change. However, some believe that there is good reason for advocating a continued and, perhaps, increased role for government in business. What kind of role should government play in the business sector?

The question of government involvement in business has been debated for years. Certainly, the trend toward reduced government in terms of deregulation, privatization and elimination of tariff barriers seems to reflect the ideology that "less government is better." For some, the answer lies in the government's ability to work with industry in order to develop a long-term industrial strategy to lead the country out of its current problems and ensure a more secure future for working Canadians. Consequently, rather than simply taking a "hands-off" approach, it may be argued that what is required is a clear rethinking of the different types of roles that government can play, or how it may play its current roles in a different manner.

SHOULD GOVERNMENT SUPPORT PRATT & WHITNEY?

Adrian MacNair

The Conservative government has announced it is loaning aerospace giant Pratt & Whitney Canada $300 million for a $1 billion research project to develop the next generation of aircraft engines.

Industry Minister Tony Clement made the announcement on Monday saying it will create 700 high-skilled jobs in the GTA and more than 2,000 over the 15-year lifespan of the project. He also claimed the firm is in the process of hiring 200 engineers. "The project will create and maintain Canadian research jobs and keep Canada at the forefront of the international aerospace industry," Clement said to workers and media at the Pratt & Whitney plant in Mississauga.

'Create and maintain Canadian jobs' has been the Conservative mantra during their recent shift to Keynesian economics and massive long-term deficits for the next half decade. The same political party that once decried government largesse and corporate subsidies (also known as corporate welfare) is now a major player in the 'too big to fail' macroeconomics game.

Tony Clement was on the defensive on Monday, explaining that the investment was a loan and a guarantor of jobs in the important Canadian aerospace industry. But as reported by the CBC, this is the same company that got $350 million in loans just four years ago, and that debt is as outstanding as Stephen Harper's deflection rate during Question Period. . . .

. . . At last glance, Pratt & Whitney owes taxpayers at least $1.2 billion dating back more than 13 years. David Lewis, who coined the term "corporate welfare bums" almost 40 years ago, must be turning over in his grave.

Even if we assume that 200 Canadian workers are hired immediately, those workers would have to pay $100,000 a year in taxes over 15 years for the immediate investment to repay itself. For the investment to really make sense we have to assume that the government's estimates of 2,000 new hires, already qualified as being over the 15-year period, would have to happen sooner than 15 years to make mathematical sense. But the Conservatives have an answer for that one, too. According to Clement's press secretary, "hypothetically, without the project, the workforce would have shrunk." That's the catch-all for the whole stimulus spinning wheel now isn't it? If the economy gets better it's because of stimulus dollars or government subsidies. If it stays the same or gets worse then the government says the situation would have been even worse without the investment.

The company doesn't have to pay any of the loan during the research and development period, expected to take five years. It then has 15 years to repay the money, which means that by the time we (theoretically) get to see a return for the investment, the players who made the decision will have changed ministries, jobs, or governments. And what will it matter by then? The corporation hasn't taken any risk. The taxpayers have. The loan is entirely interest-free because it's being offered under an official government program.

The recession had an effect on the company, which sold almost 20 per cent fewer engines in 2009 than a year earlier. To mitigate the effect, the company began a series of cost-control measures in the past two years, including a hiring freeze, a temporary summer plant shutdown, and layoffs of about 15 per cent of its workforce. This, despite the fact the company has been propped up in Canada with taxpayer funds for at least 13 years. The question might not be how many jobs has the government saved by dumping over $1 billion into Pratt & Whitney over the past decade. It's how many jobs have been stolen from competing companies and industries who haven't had the good fortune to be publicly subsidized? And won't the money merely restore the 15 per cent (1,000 new hires would account for it) of the workforce lost during the recession?

Where the members of the Conservative caucus learned about the invisible hand of economics 101 is anybody's guess. Based on the performance of this government I suspect they skipped it entirely.

National Post

(Continued)

Pratt & Whitney Responds:

Since 1982, Pratt & Whitney Canada has invested $8 billion in research and develop-ment (R&D). The Canadian government has invested $1.5 billion under the Technology Partnerships Canada and Defence Industries Productivity programs. These programs provide repayable R&D assistance to Canadian Aerospace companies. Pratt & Whitney Canada has repaid $371 million in royalties and the total amount repaid is expected to approximately double in the next five years alone.

The reference to an "interest free" loan as described in the editorial is mislead-ing. This agreement is a partnership between the Government of Canada and P&WC, where the Government will receive repayments which, on the contrary, are expected to lead to a positive rate of return for the Government.

Government programs recognize that R&D projects in the aerospace industry require huge investments and very long development periods. It also takes a very long time for R&D initiatives to generate actual revenues. In fact, product lifecycles can be more than 50 years. These factors, along with the support other countries provide to their own industry, make it critical to support policy choices that invest in industry.

Pratt & Whitney Canada's R&D-based strategy has resulted in significant ben-efits to the Canadian economy. We contribute more than $2 billion annually to Canada's GDP and generate hundreds of millions of dollars in taxes to federal and provincial governments. We invest more than $12 million a year in projects carried out with universities and work in close collaboration with 1,500 Canadian suppliers. We provide high-quality jobs for 6,200 people across Canada, including 1,300 highly specialized jobs in our research and development centres in Quebec and Ontario.

Pratt & Whitney Canada is in the process of hiring an additional 200 engineers to support R&D programs for the next generation of aircraft engines. These posi-tions are being filled immediately, not over the next five years as wrongly stated in your article. In total, this investment will create and maintain 700 jobs to support these R&D initiatives. Our total R&D investment allows us to develop the technolo-gies that will be incorporated into our next generation of products. As these new engines enter into production, we will be able to create and maintain the jobs required to build, service and support these engines for the future. Without con-tinued investment in R&D and a solid pipeline of new engine programs, we would be unable to maintain our current workforce nor grow in the future. The discussion of required taxes verses number of employees hired in your article is not appropri-ate. Mr. MacNair has only taken into account that the investment will result in the initial 200 engineers we are hiring right now and not the total number of engineers working on the project, nor the total jobs created and maintained over decades of production and service.

Despite the current difficult economic climate, P&WC remains the No. 1 R&D investor in Canada's aerospace sector, with sustained annual investments of about $400 million a year. This announcement is an example of our commitment to invest in Canada. Earlier this year, we announced the launch of the first phase of our brand new Aerospace Centre in Mirabel, Quebec. The 300,000-square-foot facility will employ approximately 300 people by 2015. In October, P&WC inaugurated an advanced cold weather testing facility in Thompson, Manitoba. These two new facilities are a testament to our commitment to Canada and the continued growth we bring to *the Canadian economy. There is wide recognition that the aerospace sector is an industry of today and tomorrow. In these challenging economic times, we believe that Canadians understand the value of investing in key industries so that we can maintain our leadership position.*

Sincerely,
John Di Bert
Vice President, Finance

Questions:

1. What support is given for the government's subsidy to Pratt & Whitney?
2. What arguments are given to refute the value of the government's role here?
3. Should the government continue to subsidize companies like Pratt & Whitney? Why? Why not?
4. Discuss the role of "government as guardian of business in the global context" and how those issues might be reflected in this case.

The Societal Context

What societal roles and responsibilities must business address in order to be successful? Managing the societal forces requires attention to stakeholder needs. This chapter defines and discusses the notion of stakeholders of business. We will look at the issue of corporate social responsibility, and analyze the debate regarding what role business should play in this area. The latter part of this chapter addresses the challenge of societal issues in global business. The purpose of this chapter is to draw attention to the ethical context of business, and to encourage a more critical understanding of the ethical issues that organizations must confront.

LEARNING OBJECTIVES

By the end of the chapter, you should be able to:

1. Define stakeholders and corporate social responsibility.
2. Analyze the debate for and against the relevance of corporate social responsibility.
3. Understand the challenges of global business in terms of CSR.
4. Identify the controversies caused by free trade.
5. Explain the debate over government responsibility in the global context.

THE BUSINESS WORLD

Gulf of Mexico oil spill (2010)

An explosion on April 20, 2010, aboard the Deepwater Horizon, a drilling rig working on a well for the oil company BP one mile below the surface of the Gulf of Mexico, led to the largest accidental oil spill in history.

The continuing tragedy is the ill and declining health of the Gulf of Mexico, including the enormous dead zone off the mouth of the Mississippi and the alarmingly rapid disappearance of Louisiana's coastal wetlands, roughly 2,000 square miles smaller than they were 80 years ago.

Eclipsed by the spill's uncertain environmental impact is the other fallout: the vast sums in penalties and fines BP will have to pay to the federal government. In addition to criminal fines and restitution, BP is facing civil liabilities that fall roughly into two categories: Clean Water Act penalties and claims from the Natural Resource Damage Assessment process, whereby state and federal agencies tally the damage caused by the spill and put a price tag on it. This could add up to billions, perhaps tens of billions, of dollars.

On April 22, 2011, the Justice Department announced that an agreement had been announced between BP and the trustees who are part of the natural resources damage assessment for BP to provide a $1 billion down payment for early restoration projects, the largest of its kind ever reached.

**The Business Ethics Blog

Chris MacDonald

BP and Corporate Social Responsibility

So, what makes the oil spill a matter of *social* responsibility? Precisely the fact that the risks (and eventual negative impacts) of BP's deep-water drilling operations are borne by society at large. The spill has resulted in enormous negative externalities—negative effects on people who weren't involved economically with BP, and who didn't consent (at least not directly) to bear the risk of the company's operations.

Now, all (yes all) production processes involve externalities. All businesses emit some pollution (directly or indirectly via the things they consume) and impose some risks on non-consenting third parties. So the *question* of CSR has to do with the *extent to which* a company is responsible for those effects, and (maybe) the extent to which companies have an obligation not just to avoid social harms (or risks) but to contribute socially (beyond making a product people value). From a CSR point of view, then, the question with regard to BP is whether the risks taken were reasonable. Most of us would say "no." But then most of us still want plentiful cheap gas.

Thus the BP oil spill provides an excellent way to illustrate the way we *should* understand the scope of the term "corporate social responsibility," and how to keep that term narrow enough for it to retain some real meaning.

p.s., Did you know that, in 2005, BP made it onto the Global 100 list of the "Most Sustainable Companies in the World", a feat the company repeated in 2006. (And yes, that's a reason to be skeptical about such rankings!)

---

*Source: The New York Times.

**Source: The Business Ethics Blog, Chris MacDonald.

BUSINESS AND SOCIETY

"The Business World" story underscores the issue of corporate social responsibility. What constitutes socially responsible business behaviour? In addition, should businesses be required to look beyond their profit objectives in order to help society? Unethical behaviour may be directed against the organization itself, or it may be consistent with the organization's goals but inconsistent with commonly accepted ethical principles. Whether unethical behaviour comes in the form of subtle discrimination against other employees, "padding" expense accounts, paying or accepting bribes, questionable advertising or other forms of fraudulent activity, there is little doubt that the costs of such behaviour eventually accumulate.

The media has increasingly reported a concern over the erosion of business responsibility, and unethical activities in organizations are estimated to cost industry billions of dollars a year.[1] It seems that much of what has been written in the popular press and reported in the news has tended to reflect poorly on the ethics of business. The recent phenomenon of corporate downsizings and massive layoffs has certainly contributed to the public's dim view of business. Other recurring issues that raise questions about the ethics of business include things such as misuse of natural resources, too close a relationship with government, not treating employees properly and corporations being too big and too powerful. All these perceptions, whether accurate or inaccurate, reflect a commonly held view that business and ethics do not go together.

Some scholars have suggested that there is a crisis of confidence in a variety of corporate activities.[2] Perhaps most of the blame for the current distrust of business can be traced to the recent flood of scandals that has permeated the news media reports. If anything has shaken the business-society relationship, it has been the countless, major headline-grabbing scandals, particularly within the past several years. For many observers, the rapidly expanding list of corporate wrongdoers has all but caused a breach in society's trust for business leaders.

Numerous companies worldwide have undermined public confidence in the integrity of business through their scandalous activities. The list of ethics violations is long and has been attributed to such companies as Enron, WorldCom, Tyco International, Conseco, Adelphia Cable and Global Crossing, Xerox and HealthSouth. Elsewhere, recent allegations of fraudulent activities have been leveled at the Dutch food distributor and retailer Royal Ahold, France's Vivendi, Britain's Marconi, SK Corporation in South Korea and Tokyo Electric Power Company in Japan.

Anyone who has attended to news reports understands that Canadian business is no less immune to corporate scandal and wrongdoing than any other business sector in the world. Consider the following Canadian "Hall of Shame" candidates:

- Canada earned the distinction of being home to a company that became the first multinational corporation to be fined ($2.2 million) for bribing a government official involved in a World Bank-funded dam project designed to provide water to South Africa. Acres International, an Ontario-based engineering firm, was found guilty of paying a bribe of $266,000 to the former chief executive of the Lesotho Highlands Water Project in Africa as a means to obtain a $21.5-million technical assistance contract for a multi-dam construction program.
- The Montreal family-entertainment company, Cinar, paid a total of $25 million in lawsuits stemming from fraudulent business ventures.
- The Canadian government, together with a number of Canadian businesses, faced charges of corruption stemming from a government advertising and corporate sponsorship program managed by the federal Public Works Department. The federal auditor general's report indicated that $100 million was paid to a number of communications agencies in the form of fees and commissions, and the program was essentially designed to generate commissions for these companies rather than to produce any benefit for Canadians.
- The Canadian Imperial Bank of Commerce agreed to pay a penalty of US$80 million to settle charges of aiding and abetting the Enron Corporation's accounting fraud.

Whether the business community will be able to adequately respond to society's expectations of greater accountability is largely dependent on the level of attention that business affords this issue. And, given the growing attention directed at corporate behaviour, the onus appears to be on business to develop a much better understanding of the status of societal expectations. (See Talking Business 8.1.)

Managing the Forces of Business and the Stakeholders of Business

Life in business organizations was once simpler. . . . The business organization today, especially in the modern corporation, is the institutional centrepiece of a complex society. Our society today consists of many people with a multitude of interests, expectations, and demands as to what major organizations ought to provide to accommodate people's lifestyles. . . . In a society conscious of an always-improving lifestyle, with more groups every day laying claims to their pieces of the good life, business organizations today need to be responsive to individuals and groups they once viewed as powerless and unable to make such claims on them. We call these individuals and groups stakeholders.[3]

In their text *Business and Society*, Karakowsky, Carroll and Buchholtz (2005) emphasize the notion of managing the stakeholders of business. They suggest that in order to more fully understand the ethical dimension of business, it is critical to appreciate the concept of *stakeholders*. In fact, the stakeholder concept has become a central idea in understanding the business and society relationship. **Stakeholders** are individuals or groups with whom business interacts and who have a "stake," or vested interest, in the business. A stake can range from simply an interest in management's actions to a legal or moral right to be treated a certain way to a legal claim of ownership at the other extreme.[4]

Traditionally, we observe two broad groups of stakeholders—external and internal stakeholders. External stakeholders are composed of such parties as government, consumers and community members. Internal stakeholders can include business owners and employees among the principal groups. The notion here is that stakeholders have legitimate claims on the organization. Consequently, a fundamental responsibility of management is to address and manage the needs of differing stakeholder groups—in addition to the needs of the most obvious stakeholders, the owners/investors or shareholders of the business. Keep in mind that, just as stakeholders can be affected by the actions or decisions of the business firm, these stakeholders also

Talking Business 8.1

Apple Inc Admits Fault in Scandal

Qian Yanfeng

While Apple is enjoying hot worldwide sales of its fashion electronics, its health and environmental responsibilities have come under fire in China.

Poisoned workers at one of Apple's supplier factories on the Chinese mainland have demanded a formal written apology from the Mac maker despite its recent acknowledgment of violations in its supply base. The workers also said that some of them have been asked to leave their jobs.

The California-based maker of iPods, iPhones and iPads acknowledged for the first time in the Apple Supplier Responsibility 2011 Progress Report on Tuesday that 137 workers at the Suzhou facility of Wintek, one of Apple's touch screen suppliers, had suffered adverse health effects following exposure to n-hexane, a chemical in cleaning agents used in some manufacturing processes.

It said the company considered this series of incidents to be "a core violation for worker endangerment" and required the factory to stop using the chemical while it improved its ventilation system.

"Since these changes, no new workers have suffered difficulties from chemical exposure," it said.

The company also said it required Wintek to work with a consultant to improve its environmental health and safety processes and management systems, and it is monitoring the implementation of these corrective actions and preventive measures. A complete reaudit of the facility will be conducted in 2011, it said.

The report said that all 137 affected workers had been treated successfully at Wintek's expense, and that most of them had returned to work at the same factory.

But Jia Jingchuan, a 27-year-old victim at the Suzhou factory, said the Apple acknowledgment meant nothing to victims like him and that their rights continued to be under threat.

"I got a call last week from the company asking me to leave. They promised to give me 140,000 yuan ($21,253) in compensation for my departure, but only on condition that I sign an exemption agreement, which means the company would not take any responsibility if my health worsened in the future," he said.

He added that as far as he knew at least eight victims had already left.

"I don't want to leave the factory . . . What if my health worsened? How can I then afford future medical treatment on my own?" said a worried Jia.

"A leading global company like Apple should see to the conduct of its suppliers and ensure that supplier workers receive fair and respectful treatment," Jia said.

"But what happened here is obviously a violation of its supplier code. Apple should give us a written apology for this."

can influence the organization's actions and decisions. Therefore, the management of stakeholder interests is critical to business success.

In addition to the owners/investors/shareholders, other obvious stakeholders include employees and customers, as well as competitors, suppliers, the community, special-interest groups, the media and society in general. Some observers would also view our environment and our future generations as important stakeholders in the activities of business. The importance of managing diverse stakeholder needs is evident in the following assertion by David Wheeler and Maria Sillanpää:

> In the future, development of loyal relationships with customers, employees, shareholders, and other stakeholders will become one of the most important determinants of commercial viability and business success. Increasing shareholder value will be best served if your company cultivates the support of all who may influence its importance.[5]

Managing the Challenges of the Societal Force

So what does it take to successfully manage the challenges of the societal force? An organization that adequately addresses the societal force will, by definition, fulfill its responsibilities to the variety of stakeholders. What is the connection between the societal force and fulfilling the responsibilities to various stakeholder groups? To answer that question we need to understand the concept of **corporate social responsibility** (CSR).

CORPORATE SOCIAL RESPONSIBILITY

The historical "ethical yardstick" for business has been profit—the "bottom line." Scholars such as economist Milton Friedman argued that the workings of the free and competitive marketplace will "moralize" corporate behaviour.[6] Therefore, business need only be concerned with the profit motive, since the "invisible hand" of the free market will produce a "systematic morality." Similarly, John Kenneth Galbraith argued that corporate responsibilities should be purely rational and economic.[7] However, according to Galbraith, it is the regulatory hands of the law and the political process, rather than the invisible hand of the marketplace, that turns these objectives to the "common good." Both views reject the exercise of independent moral judgment by corporations as actors in society. On the other hand, most scholars concerned with the study of business ethics[8] implicitly reject these views and instead argue that it is the responsibility of business organizations to develop a "moral conscience" and exercise ethical judgment or social responsibility.

The term *social responsibility* refers to those obligations or responsibilities of an organization that involve going beyond

- the production of goods/services at a profit
- the requirements of competition, legal regulations or custom.

Social responsibility involves an obligation to create policies, make decisions and engage in actions that are desirable in terms of society's values and objectives. (See Talking Business 8.2)

Talking Business 8.2

Being Socially Responsible

At its worst, a corporation can poison the water we drink, prop up brutal dictatorships, assassinate inconvenient indigenous leaders, kill 3,800 people with chemicals (Union Carbide in Bhopal, India, 1984), swindle billions from shareholders and governments through tax and accounting evasion, or bring proud men or women to tears by shattering their job security.

... At its best, however, the modern corporation can be an incubator for human progress and wealth creation. A well-run corporation can help sustain the communities that sustain it by contributing to public programs through the payment of its full taxes and even picking up the slack or innovating public goods in space where the government cannot or will not.

... A well-run corporation can be a place where its workers—some of whom spend more waking hours at work than home—not only make a living wage, but a place where they build their self-worth and satisfy the most primordial of human needs: to be part of something bigger than one's self. ... A well-run corporation can transfer know-how, capital, and culture to Third-world nations; a fusion that aids the impoverished and teaches us new perspectives that are essential to our long-term survival. ... A well-run corporation not only strives to minimize environmental harm, but can help to wipe out the long trail of environmental degradation by developing new ways of doing things that are environmentally sound, such as fuel cells, wind power, water filtration without chemicals, and organic crop techniques ... A well-run corporation can make life less worrisome by providing products that meet only the highest safety and quality standards, even if it costs a little more in the short-term. ... A well-run corporation allows all its shareholders—no matter how small—to propose resolutions by providing transparency on the Triple-Bottom Line (financial, social, and environmental), and by compensating people based on the value they bring to the enterprise rather than their proximity to the firm's power brokers.

Source: Reproduced with permission from "Canada's Best 50 Corporate Citizens: An Introduction," *Corporate Knights.ca* <http://www.corporateknights.ca/content/page.asp?name=2002intro>.

We can elaborate upon this definition by referring to one of the most commonly cited definitions of CSR. Archie Carroll's four-part definition asserts that the social responsibility of business encompasses the economic, legal ethical, and discretionary (philanthropic) expectations that society has of organizations at a given point in time.[9] See Exhibit 8.1.

Carroll's definition indicates that there are issues above economic and legal ones that a business must confront. Obviously, a business must address economic responsibilities—it must generate goods or services that society wants. And further, a business must abide by the laws in order to fulfill its legal responsibilities. However, this definition suggests that just fulfilling these two areas of concern is insufficient. Ethical responsibilities include the standards or expectations that reflect what the societal stakeholders regard as fair. Finally, business has somewhat voluntary or philanthropic responsibilities that, while voluntary, do reflect part of the implicit agreement between business and society and can include such activities as corporate donations, volunteerism and any other kind of voluntary involvement of the business with the community or other stakeholders.[10]

Consider such acts of CSR as those demonstrated by Levi Strauss & Co., which has tried very hard to maintain strict work standards to protect employees in operations in different parts of the world. In addition, the company is consistently lauded for its efforts in the social sphere, an effort summarized recently in an article:

> Besides patching together jeans, Levi Strauss has a long history of funding projects that help patch together groups of people. Project Change, an independent nonprofit originally funded by the Levi Strauss Foundation (and still closely associated with it), combats racism in communities where the company has manufacturing operations. There are now sites in Albuquerque, El Paso, Knoxville, and Valdosta, Ga. In Albuquerque . . . , research showed that people of colour were twice as likely as whites to be denied home loans, regardless of their income. Project Change established a Fair Lending Center to help customers comparison-shop among local banks and to encourage banks to lend in poor New Mexico neighbourhoods. In Valdosta, the project talked nine banks into funding mortgages for low-income first-time home buyers.[11]

This is certainly admirable corporate behaviour, but is it necessary? That is, does Levi Strauss & Co. have an ethical obligation as a business to do this? While we applaud the efforts of companies like Canadian Tire, Levi Strauss Co., Magna, Southwest Airlines, should we demand such behaviour from all organizations? And more generally, does business have a moral responsibility to us—whether we are employees, customers, creditors or society in general?

The CSR Debate

There is much diverse opinion regarding the degree to which business should practise social responsibility. Some argue that, at best, business should have very limited social responsibilities, while others argue that the social responsibilities of business should be extensive. What are the arguments for believing that business

EXHIBIT 8.1 The four components of CSR.

CSR Responsibilities	Societal Expectation	Examples
Economic responsibilities	Society *requires* business to fulfill these responsibilities.	Generate rational business strategy, make profits, minimize costs. . . .
Legal responsibilities	Society *requires* business to fulfill these responsibilities.	Honour all relevant laws and regulations governing business activities. . . .
Ethical responsibilities	Society *expects* business to fulfill these responsibilities.	Engage in business practices that are in line with what society considers acceptable, fair, just. . . .
Philanthropic responsibilities	Society *desires* business to fulfill these responsibilities.	Engage in activities that help the betterment of society—e.g., volunteerism, charity. . . .

Source: Karakowsky, Carroll & Buchholtz, 2005

EXHIBIT 8.2 The CSR debate.

Against Social Responsibility	For Social Responsibility
1. Business is business.	1. Business should conform to societal expectations.
2. Business plays by its own rules.	2. CSR is a practical strategy.
3. Business should not dictate morality.	3. Must acknowledge network of stakeholders.
4. Organizations cannot be held accountable for their actions.	4. Long-term benefits.

should take on extensive social responsibilities, and what is the rationale used by those who believe business should not be required to take on the mantle of social responsibility? Let's consider the cases first against, and then for, social responsibility. (See Exhibit 8.2.)

The Case Against CSR

1. Business Is Business Probably one of the best-known arguments against social responsibility for business comes from the work of economist Milton Friedman, who argued, quite simply, that profit maximization is the primary purpose of business, and to have any other purpose is not socially responsible! Friedman points out that in a free enterprise, private property system, a manager is an employee of the owners of the business and, consequently, is directly responsible to them. In other words, Friedman and others argue that a business's primary responsibility is to the owners or shareholders. Clearly, owners and shareholders want to maximize profit, and so this should be the business's highest priority.

Some have argued that a regard for ethical values in market decisions might lead businesspeople to confuse their economic goals with altruistic goals so that they fail to fulfill the basic business function of operating efficiently. While most scholars in the field advocate one form or another of corporate responsibility, they also acknowledge the difficulty of adopting an ethical corporate objective. Albert Carr argued that no company can be expected to serve the social interest unless its self-interest is also served, either by the expectation of profit or the avoidance of punishment.[12]

Consider the case of Bata. Here was a company, Bata Ltd., a Canadian-based national company, known for its socially responsible behaviour—including establishing a plant where no community formerly existed. Yet, recently, it chose to shut down its Ontario plant and move operations overseas. (See Talking Business 8.3.)

Is it socially responsible for a company to take away the jobs that it initially created? On the other hand, given the significant drop in annual profits, if the company did not move production overseas, where costs were much cheaper, the company would be in dire straits. Consequently, jobs were shifted from Canadian workers to those in China, where labour was much cheaper. Is this socially responsible? If you consider Bata's responsibility to its owners and its creditors, they would argue that it would have been irresponsible *not* to move production abroad.

2. Business Plays by Its Own Rules This sentiment suggests that business cannot be judged by the same set of rules or standards of moral conduct that we apply outside of business. Carr, in a famous article written for the *Harvard Business Review*, raised the question of whether, indeed, we should expect that business managers apply the same ethical standards we might apply in our personal lives. Carr suggested that "bluffing" (i.e., lying), which may be viewed as an unethical practice in social relations, can be viewed as legitimate behaviour within the boundaries of business activity. Carr compared corporate activity to a poker game, whereby ethical standards within the boundaries of the "game" may differ from societal standards.[13] The "players" (business executives), therefore, may engage in activity that is acceptable within the "rules" of business, even though this activity may be viewed as unethical by the public (those outside the "game" of business). Therefore, individuals may employ ethical standards in business that differ from those generally employed in their non-working lives. That is, where "business bluffing" has been accepted as a form of business conduct, members come to believe in this behaviour as an accepted way of doing business. For example, union and management negotiations are subject to negotiator tendencies to demand more than what might otherwise be equitable, as a means of bargaining. Similarly, a company may convince customers

Talking Business 8.3

Should These Corporate Behaviours be Mandated?

CN	Established the CN Safe Community Fund, which offers an annual $25,000 incentive award to encourage communities across the country to incorporate rail safety initiatives and campaigns with local school participation.
Sears	Sears works together with the Boys and Girls Clubs of Canada to offer support and funding for youth-focused programs such as *I Can Swim* and the *Sears Ontario Drama Festival. Sears Young Futures* initiative has contributed over $3 million to youth groups across Canada.
TELUS	Working in co-operation with the Alberta School Boards, TELUS provides a portion of the funding, office space and the technology to help teachers and educators develop the necessary skills to effectively use the Internet as a teaching tool and to develop online educational materials.
Petro-Canada	Provides financial support, and assists the Canadian Association of Food Banks with business planning and marketing communications directed at providing food to those in need and raising public awareness about hunger in Canada.
Home Depot Canada	Provides funding and materials to community-based organizations for the development and building of safe community playgrounds across Canada.

that its product is worth significantly more than the cost of producing it, as a means to accrue a high profit. Members of organizations will engage in behaviour compatible with accepted beliefs, although these behaviours might otherwise be viewed as unacceptable.

Given this, why should we expect businesses to be good citizens in the same way as individuals? We might expect that a business will try to advertise its product in a manner that suggests it may be of much higher quality than it really is. That's part of the rules of business—which are largely focused on profit maximization and not necessarily on seeking the truth in advertising, for example.

Is business a game?   Do you accept the notion that business is like a game and should be played by its own rules? Is it acceptable to leave our moral standards at the door, so to speak, when we enter the workplace? Recall the scenario earlier of the CEO and the gift in order to achieve the $22-million contract. Would you give the gift? Why, or why not? If this is considered a bribe and therefore unethical, why would you give the gift? The common response is because it is part of the "rules of the game." This is the expectation that, in business, this is a legitimate, commonly accepted practice. However, there is a danger in de-coupling behaviour—in avoiding scrutiny of business behaviour. First, it makes an assumption about what is and what is not acceptable in business. In this case, for example, businesses are increasingly frowning upon giving gifts to clients or customers. Consequently, what is acceptable for business and society is not necessarily a stable factor. In addition, for some individuals, it is unacceptable to trade off one's ethics in the "line of duty." The question becomes, What is acceptable for you?

3. Business Should Not Dictate Morality   Given that business enterprises are fundamentally responsible to the owners or shareholders, their mandate is to maximize profit, and that is their area of expertise. They are economic institutions, and they should leave the issue of social policy to the jurisdiction of government. Managers are simply not skilled in the area of social policy, and consequently should not be held responsible to carry out duties of social responsibility. If businesses enter the area of social policy, they are, in effect, expanding their power. How? Well, a corporation that is engaging in extensive social programs is essentially performing a political function in addition to its economic purpose. Some critics suggest that allowing business to have both economic and political power in its hands is potentially dangerous. As an article in *The Economist* argued:

> It is no advance for democracy when public policy is "privatized," and corporate boards take it upon themselves to weigh competing social, economic and environmental goals. That is a job for governments, which remain competent to do it if they choose. And when it comes to business ethics, it is worth remembering that managers do not, as a rule, own the companies they are directing. Their first duty is to serve the people who are paying their salaries, so long as they stay within the law and the canons of ordinary decency. In the political arena, the chief executive of the biggest multinational has just one vote—and that is how it should be.[14]

Consequently, those opposed to businesses venturing into the social sphere, for this reason, argue that government can simply enforce regulations to ensure that business is socially responsible rather than allowing business to take it upon itself to judge matters of social responsibility.

4. Organizations Cannot Be Held Accountable   While society may judge somewhat cynically the ethics of "big business," who exactly is to be held accountable for the actions taken by individuals on behalf of their company? It is not always easy to place blame when the entity responsible for an action is not an individual but, rather, a corporation. Many scholars have asserted that rather than observing organizations, it is the corporation's leaders and their constituents whose behaviour must be studied. Following this line of reasoning, Carroll argued that unethical business behaviour is the result of two ethical standards—personal and business. Carroll's research suggested that individuals under pressure compromise their personal standards in order to achieve the goals of the organization.[15] Similarly, Carr argued that "the ethic of corporate advantage invariably silences and drives out the ethic of individual restraint."[16]

Can we hold organizations responsible for their crimes? Should IBM be somehow held accountable for its alleged involvement in the Holocaust, as reported in Talking Business 8.4? What responsibility do organizations have to ensure their products are not misused? Do businesses have a responsibility not to associate with countries that are violating human rights? Or, on the other hand, should business strategy be guided purely by profits?

Talking Business 8.4

IBM and the Holocaust

A book written by Edwin Black, entitled *IBM and the Holocaust*, offers compelling evidence that IBM played an important role in some of the most horrific events of the 1930s and 1940s in Europe. Specifically, IBM's production of hundreds of Hollerith machines, the precursor to the computer, played a central role in the first racial censuses conducted by the Nazis. Beginning in 1933, the Hollerith machine was used by the German government to identify its intended targets. As Black comments in his book:

> Nearly every Nazi concentration camp operated a Hollerith Department . . . in some camps . . . as many as two dozen IBM sorters, tabulators and printers were installed . . . [I]t did not matter whether IBM did or did not know exactly which machine was used at which death camp. All that mattered was that the money would be waiting—once the smoke cleared.

The author suggests that IBM's involvement with Nazi Germany helps explain one mystery of the Holocaust—how so many people were killed in so little time. With the knowledge of top IBM management in the United States, IBM's European subsidiaries actually perfected the means for the Nazis to quickly collect census data for its murderous plans. Hitler awarded IBM chairman Thomas Watson a medal for his company's work.

Source: Based on Edwin Black, *IBM and the Holocaust: The Strategic Alliance between Nazi Germany and America's Most Powerful Corporation* (New York: Crown Publishers, 2001), p. 375.

The Case for CSR

Now that we have looked at some of the more common sources of support for ignoring social responsibility, let's consider the counterargument. Why should business be concerned with the issue of social responsibility? Why might business be obliged to take on social responsibility? Why should business go beyond its legal requirements or industry standards?

1. Conform to Societal Expectations   Scholars in the field of business ethics have argued that business and society need not be seen as distinct entities but, rather, that business plays a role within society: fundamentally, businesses are created to serve public needs. It is for this same pragmatic reason that a business will not act in any way that will reduce its legitimacy in the eyes of the public. Given that the very existence of business enterprise is largely dependent on acceptance by society, there is an obligation not to violate societal beliefs regarding socially responsible behaviour—particularly if such violations would undermine the credibility of an enterprise's role in society. Scholars have suggested that the doctrine of corporate social responsibility can also be understood as part of an effort to reconcile the intentions and results of capitalism. Advocates of corporate social responsibility understand the importance of the profit motive: however, they view this as only part of the social responsibility of business.

Shareholders of major corporations have shown increased expectations that businesses behave responsibly. Shareholder proposals permit investors to present issues of concern to corporate management, and to other shareholders who can then vote in order to support or reject the proposals. Proposals were submitted to Hudson's Bay Co. and Sears Canada on the issue of sweatshop labour. Both Sears and the Bay have faced allegations that they purchase apparel from sweatshop factories in Lesotho, where child labour, unsafe conditions and sexual harassment have been reported. A 2002 shareholder initiative calling on Hudson's Bay Company to put in place a process to end alleged sweatshop abuses in its supply chain was supported by more than 36% of the shareholders voting at the annual shareholders' meeting. The resolution put forward at the meeting urged the board of directors to adhere to the International Labor Organization's Declaration on Fundamental Principles and Rights at Work and report to shareholders annually on compliance.

2. Adopt CSR as a Practical Business Strategy   A second, even more pragmatic, reason for businesses to be socially responsible is to avoid public criticism or scrutiny that might inadvertently encourage more government involvement or regulation. For example, we have recently witnessed a number of organizations accused of unfair business practices and attempting to create a monopoly. Other organizations, like Nike, have been heavily criticized for shutting down operations in America in favour of setting up business where labour is cheap, and in some cases where sweatshop-like conditions exist among the factories of the foreign contractors. A lack of concern for social responsibility may invite public scrutiny.

The practical side of being socially responsible can be seen in the realm of business-consumer relationships. The notion of exploiting the consumer for profits would be both socially irresponsible and unwise for any business. There are many cases of consumer lawsuits aimed at businesses who lacked responsibility for their treatment of consumers. For example, an individual from British Columbia filed a class action lawsuit against Shell Canada. The suit alleged that Shell didn't do enough to notify consumers about a problem with its gasoline. Shell subsequently admitted that an additive in its gas was responsible for causing damage to fuel gauges or pumps in certain cars. The lawsuit also claimed that Shell continued to sell the product even though it was aware of the problem. A Shell representative issued a news release that offered a "sincere apology for any inconvenience this problem may have caused." Shell also had discreetly compensated consumers for months by offering Air Miles or free gas. In response to Shell's behaviour, a representative of the Automobile Protection Association, a consumer advocacy group, commented that "It's a longstanding principle that when you put out something that's defective, you put the word out. It would appear the company sort of ducked when they had a decision to make."[17] In a different case, the Competition Bureau ruled that Sears Canada practised "deceptive marketing" by advertising false sale prices on five lines of automobile tires. The Bureau's commissioner said Sears intentionally deceived consumers by pretending to offer them special prices on major lines of all-season tires, while having little intention of selling substantial quantities of the tires at the regular prices.[18] These types of practices bring "unwelcome" public attention and scrutiny to the guilty businesses.

3. Acknowledge Membership in a Broader Network of Stakeholders   As described earlier, stakeholders refer to any individuals or groups who bear some type of risk as a result of the corporation's actions. Stakeholders might have financial, physical or human stakes or interests in the corporation. Who are the potential stakeholders in business activity? Among the list of stakeholders and the corporation's responsibilities to them, we can include those identified in Exhibit 8.3.

Among some of the other potential stakeholders in a business are **suppliers**, the **government** and **society** in general—each of whom may also be affected in some way by corporate activity and, consequently, must be considered in conducting business. In any actions a business takes, then, the business should consider the impact on any party that has a stake in its operations: i.e., that is affected by its behaviour. Aside from ethical considerations, there are practical reasons to attend to all the stakeholders' interests, even when they conflict: if management focuses on only the concerns of a minority of stakeholders, such as the owners, other stakeholders may withdraw their participation with and support for the enterprise and, consequently, harm the business. Thus, to suggest that business need not be socially responsible is to ignore the fact that business enterprises regularly interact with, and affect, numerous stakeholders. (See Talking Business 8.5.)

There are many examples of corporations making a difference in communities through volunteer activities. CIBC, Canadian National, Hewlett-Packard (Canada) Ltd., Suncor Energy Inc., and TransCanada PipeLines Ltd. joined together with the National Aboriginal Achievement Foundation in 2002 to establish a project called Taking Pulse. This private-sector effort is aimed at increasing the participation of Aboriginal people in the Canadian workforce. In the words of Rick George, the president of Suncor Energy Inc., "This is an excellent opportunity for involvement in creating a long-term strategy that will benefit Aboriginal people and indeed the great economy. . . . We are committed to corporate social responsibility and strongly believe our workforce should be reflective of the communities in which we work." Microsoft Canada engaged in a partnership with the non-profit organization Boys and Girls Club of Canada to increase computer accessibility for children who lacked the opportunity. Microsoft Canada received high accolades from Imagine Canada

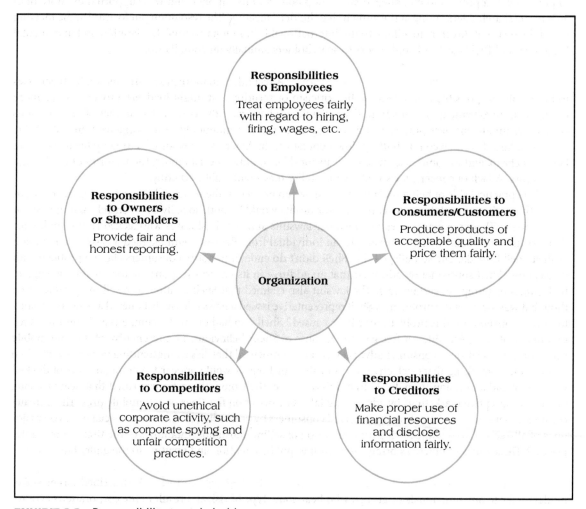

EXHIBIT 8.3 Responsibility to stakeholders.

Talking Business 8.5

Mining for Social Responsibility

Historically, decisions to permit mining industries in less developed countries (LDCs) have been made by the central government of the local region in the less developed country. Often, this development is undertaken with the support and encouragement of international development agencies, who are seeking to encourage private investment in order to generate such benefits for the underdeveloped host country. Jobs are created, technology can be introduced and poverty can be alleviated in many cases. Unfortunately, there are also negative consequences at times.

One of the most significant and problematic consequences can be the impact on the physical, economic, cultural and social environment. A case that illustrates this issue is the story of two groups of people, the Teberebe and Bogoso, who live in the Wassa West District of Ghana, West Africa.

For generations, the Teberebe and Bogoso were land owners who farmed the land that surrounded them. Now, their entire community has been displaced and resettled in an unfamiliar environment. The decision that brought about this harsh change was made by a local chieftain, who, on behalf his people, placed a thumb print in lieu of a signature on a document, not knowing the implications it would have on his people. This document has changed not only a culture, but also a way of life and has greatly impacted the region.

The mining companies have not made any real efforts to provide the people with adequate resettlement training to adjust to their new environment. Instead of providing the citizens with an adequate transition into the now industrialized environment via education and training, the citizens have been left to fend for themselves, on land that was once their own. The mining companies view this as purely a business transaction. The mining companies have not broken any laws. They have legally acquired the land and they have created jobs where no jobs existed in prior years, which can help reduce poverty. In addition, the mining companies feel they have no obligation beyond paying for this purchase.

Supporters of the mining companies suggest that this situation is consistent with any intelligent business practice—does any business consider its social impact? Does Wal-Mart avoid setting up business where it might interfere with local competitors? No. Consequently, how can these mining companies be expected to consider the social plight of the region? That, according to the mining companies, would simply be unfair and costly to the company.

There is increasing pressure from many human rights groups to make the mining industry more socially responsible. To achieve this, there will need to be an expanded understanding and awareness of the human impact of the mining industry; a willingness to include in the decision-making processes the interests and concerns of those who lack political power and who are without economic resources; and a commitment to considering new and alternative approaches to mining industry.

for its contributions to the community, including its financial donations in the millions of dollars, software, resources, online support and training by employee volunteers.

4. Gain Long-term Benefits of CSR   Advocates of corporate social responsibility suggest that even if an action does not result in immediate benefits for the enterprise, engaging in socially responsible behaviour is wise from a longer-term strategic perspective. This, perhaps, connects to the first point made—regarding the relationship of business with society. A business that fosters this relationship will more likely continue to receive acceptance from, and be considered legitimate by, the public. The notion of building and maintaining goodwill with the public and a positive image are certainly influenced by social responsiveness (see Talking Business 8.6). For example, Johnson & Johnson, the maker of Tylenol, was faced with major disaster in the 1980s after a number of tragic deaths were found to be the result of poisoned Tylenol capsules. While the cause was later found to be tampering at the retail location, not at the manufacturers' site, Johnson & Johnson took complete, extensive responsibility in withdrawing all their Tylenol capsules from the market (retail value of over $100 million) and running television commercials and establishing telephone hotlines urging the public not to use them. And this also prompted Johnson & Johnson to reintroduce the product in tamper-proof packages. While the company's social responsibility was costly, the company made up for that loss by restoring public confidence in its reputation.

Talking Business 8.6

CSR at Canadian Tire

Ninety per cent of Canadians live within 15 minutes of one of 1,100 Canadian Tire retail outlets. This corporate giant is attempting to use its enormous capacity to reach the public to raise social awareness and affect change, according to the president of the Canadian Tire Foundation for Families.

Gordon Cressy spoke at the Rotman School of Management conference March 19 on Corporations in the Community: A Canadian View of Corporate Social Responsibility.

Corporate social responsibility is not just public relations but a new way of operating to rebuild trust between corporations and consumers in a post-Enron world . . . At Canadian Tire, there are 450 independent retail dealers and the success of the company is due to their community involvement, he says. "Corporate social responsibility is about grassroots involvement." At the grassroots level, the company has a policy of double-matching local contributions to local projects and has aided more than 300 charitable projects across the country, Cressy says. In addition, the foundation plan calls for input at a time of crisis and provides disaster relief in such instances as floods and the fires in the Kelowna and Kamloops area. "We have the clothing, propane tanks and other things needed and we can supply them quickly," he says.

The Canadian Tire Foundation for Families has also developed a national program to encourage young people to become involved in sports and recreation. The foundation is partners with others including government and not-for-profit organizations to advocate for increased recreational opportunities for youth at a time when health issues and lack of exercise for young people are raising national concerns.

"This national signature program unleashes the power of the corporation behind a cause," Cressy says. "We have enormous capacity to reach the Canadian public and, working with partners, can leverage that power to affect social awareness and make changes."

Source: Reproduced with permission from John Driscoll, "Canadian Tire Foundation pushes company's CSR agenda," *Axiom News* (March 26, 2004). Web site: <http://www.axiomnews.ca/index.htm>.

IS CORPORATE SOCIAL RESPONSIBILITY ON THE RISE?

The central arguments that support the case against business enterprises taking a more active role in the area of social responsibility were outlined above. One remaining question is, Where are we now? That is, how have the views of corporate social responsibility changed over the years? What philosophy are more and more businesses adopting currently with regard to social or moral obligations? According to some observers, we are undergoing a gradual transformation that increasingly involves shaping organizations to reflect higher levels of social responsiveness. There is an increasing push for organizations to balance the profit objective with goals of social responsibility. In other words, business enterprises have begun to make greater efforts to recognize and balance the needs of different stakeholders.

How corporations govern and oversee their own behaviour has been a central issue. The long list of corporate scandals has drawn attention to this notion of "who safeguards" the interests of owners/shareholders of large corporations. Recent legislation has attempted to hold organizations more accountable for their behaviour and to offer greater disclosure of their activities to the public. One such major piece of legislation originated in the United States and is called the Sarbanes-Oxley Act.

The aftermath of the scandals in the early 21st century were the biggest impetus for change, which led to the enactment of such legislation as the 2002 Sarbanes-Oxley Act in the United States and the initiation of similar legislation in Canada. The Sarbanes-Oxley Act was introduced in the United States following the flood of accounting scandals at companies such as Enron and WorldCom. The Act was aimed at re-establishing corporate accountability and investor confidence. The Act's central purpose was to make public companies more accountable by increasing transparency or disclosure in their financial reporting. This required additional regulations governing public company accounting, corporate responsibility and investor protection. In order to accomplish this, increased requirements were also placed on CEOs (chief executive officers), CFOs (chief financial officers), and the functions that they oversee.

The significant impact of the Sarbanes-Oxley Act is evident to many observers, such as Megan Barnett, who made the following comments:

> More than just a buzzword born in the depths of the corporate scandals, good governance has turned into a new way of life for some company gatekeepers. . . . Under the new rule regime, boards find themselves under intense scrutiny. They have fired members who have conflicts of interest, possess thin credentials, or are past their prime. They have hired new directors they believe are beyond reproach, with no skeletons and talents more suited to the job. They have more meetings, more conference calls, and more questions to ask of senior management. They face the challenge of simultaneously beefing up controls to meet new regulatory requirements while remaining active in shaping the company's strategy. They consult more with their lawyers. . . . Boards must now comprise mostly independent directors, which means the individuals must not have any material ties (à la Enron) to the company or its management.[19]

While the Sarbanes-Oxley Act itself is not directed at Canadian jurisdictions, it does affect Canadian companies that trade on U.S. stock exchanges, and it has served as an impetus for similar Canadian legislation. In 2004, the OSC (Ontario Securities and Exchange Commission) presented 18 new corporate governance standards for boards of publicly traded companies. These evolving standards are intended to make corporations more accountable for their behaviour and financial reporting methods.

Of course, how business responds to different stakeholders may be represented on a continuum from a purely pragmatic, self-interest approach to a socially responsible approach. The traditional pragmatic approach has been one that focuses on strategies that consider only the objectives of the owners or shareholders. It places emphasis on the needs of one group of stakeholders—the owners or shareholders. This reflects the notion that the primary orientation of business is to fulfill economic, as opposed to social, interests. On the other hand, there is a drive to adopt a more socially responsible approach. This approach does not ignore the responsibility of business to owners or to shareholders to maximize profits; however, this should not be accomplished at the expense of other stakeholders. Managers are challenged to use ethical principles to guide managerial actions when faced with competing interests among different stakeholders. (See Talking Business 8.7.)

Talking Business 8.7
Coca-Cola and Corporate Social Responsibility

In 1993 Coca-Cola entered the Indian market when the Indian government began to open up its borders to foreign direct investment and quickly gained a lead in the Indian beverage market. Over the past 12 years, Coca-Cola invested more than US$1 billion in India, making it one of the country's top international investors. The company directly employs approximately 6,000 local people in 76 bottling plants throughout India and indirectly creates employment for more than 125,000 people in related industries through an extensive supply and distribution structure.

While bringing many benefits to the local economy, Coca-Cola also presented significant problems. On April 22, 2002, more than 2,000 angry protestors assembled at the gates of the Coca-Cola factory in Plachimada, Kerala, claiming that the plant was destroying their livelihoods and taking away their right to clean water. The Coca-Cola factory in Kerala extracts up to 1.5 million litres of water daily from local wells in the region, creating hardship for local farmers due to reduced availability of water for irrigation purposes. These farmers, who depend heavily on groundwater for their livelihoods, discovered that their crop yield dropped dramatically as a result of Coca-Cola's actions.

According to observers, the indiscriminate mining of groundwater by Coca-Cola dried up many wells and contaminated the remainder, yielded undrinkable water, which devastated local communities. According to local estimates, Coca-Cola's water mining parched the lands of more than 2,000 people residing within 1.2 miles of the factory. On the other hand, company officials defended their behaviour and instead blamed the problems on area drought conditions. The local citizens were infuriated once again in August 2003 when tests on Coke beverages carried out by various accredited government and

(Continued)

non-government laboratories found high concentrations of pesticides and insecticides in several beverage samples, making them unfit for consumption. Again, Coca-Cola denied much of the accusations and argued that the company adhered to both local and national laws for food processing and labelling. However, in June of 2005, the U.S. Food and Drug Administration (USFDA) rejected shipments of Coke beverages from India because they were deemed unsafe based on U.S. laws.

Sources: http://www.coca-colaindia.com/about_us/abo_coca_cola_india_int.html; Nityanand Jayaraman, "Coca Cola Parches Agricultural Lands in India," *CorpWatch India* (May 28, 2002); http://www.indiatogether.org/environment/water/drinkcoke.htm; Steve Stecklow, "How a Global Web of Activists Gives Coke Problems in India," *Wall Street Journal* (June 07, 2005); "Coke, Pepsi contain cocktail of pesticide residues, claims CSE" *Our Corporate Bureau* (August 6, 2003); http://www.coca-colaindia.com/quality/quality_technical.html.

†GLOBALIZATION AND ITS DISCONTENTS: IS FREE TRADE THE PROBLEM?

Business in the Global Society

Some social activists, human rights organizations, and anti-market groups worry about what they see as the harmful consequences of international trade. At a student demonstration against free trade, one passionate activist asked the crowd,

> "Who made your T-shirt? . . . Was it a child in Vietnam? Or a young girl from India earning 18 cents per hour? . . . Did you know that she lives 12 to a room? . . . That she is forced to work 90 hours each week, without overtime pay? . . . That she lives not only in poverty, but also in filth and sickness, all in the name of Nike's profits?"

Anti-globalization critics view uncontrolled international trade as the cause of many undesirable problems in developing countries: low wages, poverty, poor working conditions, farmers who can no longer make a living, high-priced drugs from Western pharmaceutical companies, environmental damage, and local governments undermined by bureaucrats from international organizations. These critics view the competition from expanded international trade as a "race to the bottom" that will result in low wages, low standards for working conditions, greater pollution, and lower taxes (especially on corporations) in every country, both developing and developed.

Many anti-globalization protestors target two international organizations—the World Bank and the International Monetary Fund (IMF).

The World Bank and International Monetary Fund

At the end of World War II, the same 1947 international conference that created GATT also created the World Bank and the IMF. These international organizations—currently with 186 member nations—were created as the world struggled to recover from the devastation of war. Their mission was to support countries' economic growth and development through trade.

The World Bank is not a traditional bank. Its name is an abbreviation for two related institutions—the International Bank for Reconstruction and Development (IBRD) and the International Development Agency (IDA). Currently, the World Bank describes its mission as "inclusive and sustainable globalization." The IRBD focuses on reducing poverty in middle-income countries, while the IDA focuses on the world's poorest countries. The World Bank does act like a bank in loaning money at low interest or no interest to countries for economic development projects.

The IMF describes its mission as fostering global monetary cooperation, securing financial stability, facilitating international trade, promoting high employment and sustainable economic growth, and reducing poverty.

You are probably wondering why anti-globalization protestors target these organizations, whose missions do not seem to match the criticisms. The story behind the protests comes from the policies that the World Bank and IMF use to achieve their missions.

---

†Unless otherwise credited, content from here to the end of this chapter is taken from *Economics for Life: Smart Choices for All?*, by Avi J. Cohen and Ian Howe.

Hands-Off Policies for Developing Countries

Economists and policymakers at the World Bank and the IMF believe that free trade policies based on comparative advantage are best for helping developing countries achieve rising standards of living. Specialization, trade, competition, and connected international markets will, they argue, create a tide of wealth that will eventually lift all countries up. These free trade policies come directly from the "Yes" camp's answer to the fundamental macroeconomic question:

> If left alone by government, do the price mechanisms of market economies adjust quickly to maintain steady growth in living standards, full employment and stable prices?

Using this hands-off view of the role of government, policymakers at the World Bank and IMF set "free market" conditions on loans and assistance to developing countries, especially during the 1990s. Those conditions required governments to enforce contracts and property rights—cracking down on pirated software, DVDs, and low-cost copies of expensive pharmaceutical drugs. Other hands-off conditions included removing regulations from labour markets, eliminating protectionist tariffs and quotas to allow imports from developed countries, lowering taxes on businesses to encourage private investment, and privatizing state-run industries—returning those industries to private businesses.

Economists usually support freer trade and a prominent role for markets. But these hands-off views were especially strong during the 1990s. That decade saw the collapse of state communism in East Germany and the USSR, and the failure of their notoriously inefficient state-run industries. There was also rampant corruption among many governments of developing countries. Hands-on policies could not succeed if governments could not be trusted to spend loan money on the projects and people who needed it most. There was much evidence supporting a hands-off position. Government failure seemed a bigger problem than market failure.

Joseph Stiglitz Changes the Debate

Economists often dismiss protestors opposing free trade and free markets as misguided do-gooders who simply do not understand the concept of comparative advantage. But the globalization debate changed when a prominent economist added his voice to those of the protesters.

Joseph Stiglitz, a professor at Columbia University, served on the Council of Economic Advisors under U.S. President Bill Clinton. In 1997, Stiglitz became chief economist at the World Bank. He left the World Bank after three years, and was awarded the Nobel Prize in Economics in 2001. As an insider at the World Bank, and winner of the most prestigious prize an economist can get, Stiglitz's criticisms counted. He published an influential, bestselling book in 2002 which provides the title of this section—*Globalization and Its Discontents* (see Talking Business 8.8).

Talking Business 8.8

Joseph Stiglitz, a Nobel Prize–winning economist, was the chief economist at the World Bank from 1997 to 2000. His arguments against a strictly hands-off position for world monetary institutions gave stronger support for the anti-globalization critics.

Stiglitz's criticisms of the strongly hands-off policies of the World Bank and the IMF, and the responses from other pro-trade economists (see Talking Business 8.9) helped to reconcile the apparent contradiction between pro-trade arguments that gains for trade are the key to rising living standards, and the anti-globalization accusations that global trade causes harm in so many ways.

In order to understand the debate triggered by World Bank and IMF policies, protestors, and Stiglitz's book, it is helpful to first establish some facts about globalization.

What Is Globalization?

Controversy swirls around the consequences of globalization—is globalization a force for good or for evil? Does globalization bring rising living standards or a descent into poverty?

Voluntary trade is motivated by self-interest, profits from innovation, and mutually beneficial gains. Connections to bigger ponds in international markets provide new opportunities for gains, but also new competitors and new threats of creative destruction. There are winners and losers from globalization, just as there are winners and losers from trade within a country.

Self-interest is always present as a motive for expanded trade. The pace of globalization is speeding up due to falling costs for both transportation and communications technologies. It is quickly becoming cheaper and easier to connect markets among countries, in the same way that the railroad reduced the cost of connecting markets across Canada.

Globalization is also speeding up from the elimination of government barriers to trade. Free trade agreements between countries, decreasing tariffs, quotas, and domestic subsidies combined with efforts of the WTO, World Bank, and IMF to reduce protectionist policies impeding trade speed globalization.

Globalization itself—the integration of economic activities, across borders, through markets—is neither good nor bad. But the consequences of globalization for different groups can be good or bad.

Sweatshops versus Farms

The new markets and opportunities that arise from globalization may not look good to us, even though the participants see them as a vast improvement in their lives. When we hear of the low pay and working conditions in some sweatshops, our first thoughts—like those of the activist quoted at the start—may be that these workers are being exploited in the interest of corporate profits (see Talking Business 8.10).

Talking Business 8.9

Globalization and its Discontents

Controversy over globalization and the roles of the World Trade Organization (WTO), World Bank, and International Monetary Fund (IMF) made a dramatic public appearance with raging street battles and huge demonstrations at the 1999 meeting of the WTO in Seattle, Washington. Conflict erupted at most major meetings of these organizations over the next few years.

The Economist magazine published an important "Survey on Globalization" in September 2001, in anticipation of the scheduled joint annual meeting of the World Bank and IMF. That meeting was cancelled in the wake of the September 11 attacks in the United States.

Stiglitz's book appeared in 2002 with much publicity, and prompted many responses. Two of the more notable responses were *In Defense of Globalization* (2004), by Jagdish Bhagwati, another Columbia University professor and columnist for *The New York Times* and *The Wall Street Journal* and *Why Globalization Works* (2004) by Martin Wolf, a former senior economist at the World Bank and associate editor of the *Financial Times* in London.

Naomi Klein, a Canadian activist and columnist for *The Nation* and the *Guardian* published *The Shock Doctrine: The Rise of Disaster Capitalism* in 2007, continuing the controversy. Klein argues that America's "free market" policies have come to dominate the world through the exploitation of disaster-shocked people and countries.

Talking Business 8.10

People in the West may regard low-paying jobs at Nike as exploitation, but for many people in the developing world, working in a factory is a far better option than staying down on the farm and growing rice.

—Joseph Stiglitz, 2001 Nobel Prize in Economics

www.amazon.ca/Globalization-Its-Discontents-Joseph-Stiglitz/dp/039334397

But that does not explain why millions of young Chinese women voluntarily choose low-wage factory jobs over life on the farm in rural China. One woman, Liang Ying, who fled to the Shenzhen factory zone in southern China, felt almost anything was better than life on the family rubber farm:

> "Every morning, from 4 a.m. to 7 a.m. you have to cut through the bark of 400 rubber trees in total darkness. It has to be done before daybreak, otherwise the sunshine will evaporate the rubber juice. If you were me, what would you prefer, the factory or the farm?"

In evaluating sweatshop jobs always ask a key question about opportunity cost. Are workers lives better, or worse, compared to a situation without globalization, trade, and the factory jobs that follow? Are they better off with specialization and trade, or better off being self-sufficient? Behind the law of supply is the basic idea that to hire labour (or any other input), businesses must pay at least the value of the best alternative use of the worker's time.

When workers voluntarily choose the sweatshop over the farm, it is because, from their perspective, factory jobs make them better off. What looks like poverty to us, and is poverty by Western standards, is a rising standard of living for the workers by their standards.

Sweatshops Throughout History

The story of workers migrating from farms to factory jobs is not new. In the original English cotton factories of the late 1700s, people with few opportunities moved from farms to the original sweatshops in cities (see Talking Business 8.11). While the working conditions and pay were abysmal, they were better than the alternative.

The same pattern repeated in the U.S. cotton industry in New Hampshire and Massachusetts in the 1800s, where many French Canadians worked. The pattern continued in the Japanese textile industry in the 1920s and in Korea and Taiwan in the 1970s and 1980s. In all of these countries, standards of living and working conditions improved over time. Some of those improvements came from governments playing a hands-on role, and some happened when the government took a hands-off position.

As globalization connected the original British textile industry to new markets and new competitors, less competitive textile industries in older countries declined. Creative destruction created winners and losers. But since overall standards of living have continued to rise in the countries whose textile industries ultimately lost out to new competitors—first England, then the United States, Japan, South Korea, and Taiwan—new and better-paying jobs were created in other export industries where the countries held a comparative advantage.

Talking Business 8.11

The term *sweatshop* comes from England in the 1800s where the middleman who directed others in garment-making was called a *sweater*. Merchants purchased garments from the middleman, who subcontracted the work to women and children who were paid by the piece for clothing they produced. The workplaces created for this sweating system were called sweatshops. Sweatshops now refer to any factory or workshop where manual workers are employed at low wages for long hours and under poor conditions.

Winners and Losers From Globalization

Globalization continues this pattern today. While specialization and trade can bring mutually beneficial gains to countries, there are individual groups within a country who win and who lose.

Jamaica, for example, reduced trade barriers to milk imports in 1992. Local dairy farmers were losers, having to compete with cheaper imports of milk powder. Jamaican milk production dropped significantly. But poor children, who could get imported milk more cheaply, were winners.

HANDS-OFF OR HANDS-ON AGAIN? GOVERNMENTS AND GLOBAL MARKETS

Hands-On for Stiglitz

One of Stiglitz's valuable contributions to the globalization debate is to make explicit the importance of the hands-off versus hands-on question.

Although a great believer in markets, Stiglitz's own position is hands-on, favouring an "important, if limited, role for government to play." He contrasts his hands-on position with the free-market, free-trade policies supported by the World Bank and the IMF in the 1990s—the hands-off position criticized by anti-globalization protestors.

"The IMF's policies . . . based on the . . . presumption that markets, by themselves, lead to efficient outcomes, failed to allow for desirable government interventions in the market, measures which can guide economic growth and make everyone better off. What was at issue . . . is . . . conceptions of the role of the government . . ."‡

Social Safety Nets

The hands-on position believes government has a responsibility to maintain a social safety net to support the economic welfare of citizens left behind by trade and markets—especially labour markets which determine incomes. Specialization, trade, and creative destruction—whether within a country or between countries—inevitably create winners and losers. In Canada, there are many government programs to assist those who lose from expanded trade. There are Employment Insurance benefits for the unemployed, job retraining programs, social assistance payments, and health care benefits that do not depend upon a person having a job.

Most poor, developing countries lack a social safety net, so the competitive forces of creative destruction can lead to poverty and misery as jobs disappear in import-competing industries. Social safety net programs cost money that governments in poor countries may not have. But even if those governments wanted to create such programs, the strong hands-off policies prescribed by the World Bank and the IMF in the 1990s restricted their ability to operate or finance—through higher taxes—such safety net programs. The strong hands-off policies for labour markets also discouraged government regulation of working conditions. Bureaucrats and policymakers at the World Bank and IMF, rather than local governments, influenced decisions about local social programs.

Opening the Door to Trouble

Stiglitz's book appeared to validate many concerns of anti-globalization critics. But his hands-on policy choice, like any choice, has an opportunity cost. And the opportunity cost of allowing the government to act hands-on brings us to the arguments presented by the hands-off position.

Hands-Off for *The Economist Magazine*

Once governments take a hands-on role in helping people and industries who lose from the creative destruction of market competition, the door is open for special interest groups to ask for government help in protecting them from such competition in the first place.

Buried in Wool

The protectionism that exists today in global trade is not new. In England in the 1600s—before the rise of the cotton textile industry—virtually all clothes were made of wool from domestic sheep. The British East India Company connected to new markets in India, and began importing hand-spun calico cotton into England.

---

‡www.amazon.ca/Globalization-Its-Discontents-Joseph-Stiglitz/dp/0393324397

The new fabric was cheap, light, washable, colourful, and was an instant hit with consumers. Of course, local wool sales suffered, and the wool industry persuaded parliament to pass protectionist measures. All students and professors at the universities were required by law to wear only wool garments, and corpses could only be buried wrapped in wool.

A law was passed in 1701 banning all imports of calico cotton entirely (a quota of zero!). The wool industry thought it had won, but the innovative profit-seeking forces of creative destruction led English entrepreneurs to set up industrial cotton factories in England that eventually crushed the sales and political influence of the wool industry.

In hindsight, such protectionist measures look ridiculous. But the motivation for protectionism is exactly the same today as it was then.

Whose Side Are They On?

The Economist magazine has been reporting from England on global economic stories, including stories on the cotton industry, since 1843. *The Economist* supports free markets and globalization, and generally opposes government "interference" in economic or social activity.

As part of the debate over globalization, *The Economist* published the following editorial. What is striking is the support it seems to give to the anti-globalization critics.

> Rich countries' trade rules, especially in farming and textiles, still discriminate powerfully against poor countries. Rich countries' subsidies encourage wasteful use of energy and natural resources, and harm the environment. . . . rich countries' protection of intellectual property discriminates unfairly against the developing world. And without a doubt, rich countries' approach to financial regulation offers implicit subsidies to their banks and encourages reckless lending; it results, time and again, in financial crises in rich and poor countries alike.
>
> All these policies owe much to the fact that corporate interests exercise undue influence over government policy. [Critics] are right to deplore this. But undue influence is hardly new in democratic politics; it has not been created by globalisation forcing governments to bow down. . . . If allowed to, all governments are happy to seek political advantage by granting preferences.

The Economist's argument is that the harm that poor countries suffer is caused not by market forces but by government action.

Here is one example. Some of the poorest countries in the world are in Africa. The cotton-growing industry in West Africa, where the climate is ideal for growing cotton, is destitute. The problem, which is connected to global trade, is that the U.S government pays Texas farmers a domestic subsidy for growing cotton of up to 19 cents on a 59 cent pound of cotton. If Texas farmers had to produce without that subsidy, West African cotton would be competitive on world markets. But with the subsidy to U.S. farmers, the world price of cotton is less than what it takes for the West African farmers to make a living.

Practice What You Preach

Some of the opposition to the free trade policies of the World Bank, IMF, and WTO stem from what from anti-globalization critics and governments of poor countries perceive as the hypocrisy of Western trade proposals. In recent WTO negotiations, richer Western countries pushed for reduced tariffs, quotas, and subsidies on products they exported, but continued to protect their own industries—especially agriculture and textiles—where import competition from poorer developing countries might threaten their domestic industries. This was noted by *The Economist* in the editorial above.

To be fair, poorer developing countries did the same during the negotiations. They pushed for expanded access to Western markets for products they export, while still trying to protect their domestic industries from Western import competition.

Terms of Trade

This is a power struggle between governments of rich and poor countries, which explains the impasse of the current WTO negotiations. The terms of trade—quantity of exports required to pay for one unit of imports—are largely determined by prices in international markets. The power struggle over tariffs and subsidies, though, strongly influences the terms of trade.

Stiglitz argues that an earlier, 1995 round of WTO negotiations yielded an agreement that *lowered* the prices some of the poorest countries in the world received for their exports relative to what they paid for their imports. The result was that some of the poorest countries were actually made *worse off* as a result of this agreement.

Shake Hands?

Specialization and trade—whether within a country or across the globe—inevitably create winners and losers. The competitive forces of creative destruction will generally cause rising standards of living, but can also cause poverty and misery as jobs disappear in import-competing industries. Both the hands-on and hands-off positions recognize these unfortunate outcomes as the side effects of specialization, trade, and economic growth.

Limited Role for Government?

Stiglitz's hands-on position sees an important, but limited, role for government. Government should, he argues, maintain a social safety net to support the economic welfare of citizens left behind by trade and markets—especially labour markets that determine incomes.

The hands-off position sees many of the unfortunate outcomes resulting not from trade, but from government interference in markets. Tariffs, quotas, and domestic subsidies—responses to political pressure from industries and workers harmed by competing imports—can distort the terms of trade and put industries and workers in the poorest countries at a disadvantage.

Markets Failure or Government Failure?

As a citizen of Canada and the world, you must decide which policies you will support around globalization and trade. There are no right or easy choices, only trade-offs.

If you think it is important for government to help those who lose from expanded trade in import-competing industries—in Canada or abroad—you run the risk that the government will also succumb to political pressure and implement protectionist policies that slow both the expansion of trade and economic growth. If you support this hands-on position, you are betting that market failure is worse than government failure. The failure of markets to produce rising standards of living, full employment, and stable prices is more likely and costly than government failing by succumbing to political pressure from special interests for market protection.

If you think the markets are best left alone to produce economic growth that will eventually benefit all, you run the risk that those who lose from expanded trade in import-competing industries will end up in poverty and misery. If you support this hands-off position, you are betting that government failure is worse than market failure. The failure of government, that comes from implementing protectionist policies that are not in society's best interests, is more likely and costly than markets failing in the form of falling living standards for those in import-competing industries.

Exhibit 8.4 summarizes the trade-offs for the hands-off and hands-on positions on government's role in trade policy.

EXHIBIT 8.4 Government and global markets: Hands-off or hands-on?

	Camp	
	Yes—Left Alone, Markets Quickly Self-Adjust: Hands-Off	**No—Left Alone, Markets Fail to Adjust: Hands-On**
Role of government	None	Limited to maintaining social safety net supporting those left behind by trade and markets
Risk of chosen role for government	Losers in import-competing businesses get no assistance in adjusting	Government succumbs to political pressure for protectionism
Which failure is worse?	Believe government failure is worse than market failure	Believe market failure is worse than government failure

Travels of a T-Shirt

Pietra Rivoli, a business school professor at Georgetown University, witnessed a student demonstration against free trade reported on page 188. In response, she decided to travel the world, following the globally integrated production path of a T-shirt. She bought the T-shirt in Florida. It was made from Texas cotton and manufactured in China. She was trying to determine whether the accusations of the student activist about the harmful effects of globalization were justified (see Talking Business 8.12).

In the conclusion of the book that she wrote about her travels (see below) she asked what she should say to the student activist demonstrating against free trade who was

> "so concerned about the evils of the race to the bottom, so concerned about where and how her T-shirt was produced? I would tell her to appreciate what markets and trade had accomplished for all of the sisters in time who have been liberated by life in a sweatshop, and that she should be careful about dooming anyone to life on the farm. I would tell her that the poor suffer more from exclusion from politics than from the perils of the market, and that if she has activist energy left over it should be focused on including people in politics rather than shielding them from markets."

Rivoli's travels led her to the conclusion that the harmful outcomes we witness from globalized trade have less to do with market forces, and more to do with governments protecting domestic industries and workers. Those tariffs, quotas, and domestic subsidies, she argues, force prices below subsistence levels for producers in poorer countries. The resulting adverse terms of trade and poverty, she maintains, are due to government protectionist policies.

Her advice, to anyone who agrees with her argument, is to become politically involved to protect the interests of foreign workers, but not by opposing free trade. Instead, she suggests opposing protectionist policies while supporting safety net policies. It is a combination of hands-off and hands-on.

Talking Business 8.12

Travels of a T-Shirt in the Global Economy

Many of the stories about textiles in this chapter can be found in the easy-to-read and fascinating book by Pietra Rivoli, *The Travels of a T-Shirt in the Global Economy: An Economist Examines the Markets, Power, and Politics of World Trade* (2009).

Your Hand at the Ballot Box

The globalization debate includes many points of view. You have read arguments by the World Bank and IMF, *The Economist*, and Professors Stiglitz and Rivoli. It is possible that the suggestion of Professor Rivoli combining hands-off and hands-on policies is achievable—if government failure is less likely than market failure. It is also possible that her suggestion will make things worse—if the government failure she fears is more likely than market failure.

Governments respond to political pressure. If you care about globalization, you will have to decide on your own stand when voting for elected politicians—the people who set policy.

CHAPTER SUMMARY

This chapter attempted to underscore the social contexts of organizations. There is a diverse range of challenges for business in addressing stakeholder needs. Globalization has generated much more challenges from a CSR perspective. An understanding of the social responsibility of business organizations and their constituents may help create a more productive and trusting relationship between business and society.

TALISMAN IN THE SOCIETAL CONTEXT

In 2002, Talisman Energy sold the twenty-five per cent share it bought in a massive oil project in southern Sudan.

When Talisman moved into the East-African country, it became implicated in a long and bloody civil war between the Islamic dictatorship in the North and non-Muslims in the South—a conflict that has dragged on for nearly twenty years, killed more than two million people and displaced millions more. And those are conservative numbers.

Talisman's business partner in this endeavour was the country's government. (Sudan has been described by Washington as a "rogue" and terrorist state.) Dozens of religious and human rights groups accused the Canadian company of fuelling the civil conflict and helping to tip the scales in favour of the country's military.

That's because oil royalties earned by the government help to pay for things like gunships, bombers and "death squads"—the paramilitary goons who nailed spikes in the temples of people suspected of helping rebel troops.

It's also alleged by many human rights groups, including Amnesty International, that the Sudanese military has used a Talisman airstrip to launch aircraft for attacks on innocent civilians.

The company has insisted it was an instrument for positive change in Sudan, pointing to infrastructure improvements for which it is responsible, such as a health clinic and water wells.

But critics have blasted the Canadian company for providing "moral cover" for a corrupt and ruthless regime in Khartoum, saying that the Sudanese government was murdering and displacing innocent people so that more oil exploration could be done, more profits could be made and shareholders could get a healthy return.

The allegations cast a large shadow. Many people—and, indeed, many municipalities, the City of Edmonton being one of them—profited from investments in Talisman Energy.

One of Talisman's harshest critics is Eric Reeves, an English professor at Smith College in Massachusetts. The prof pulls no punches: "The sale by Talisman Energy of its twenty-five per cent stake in Sudan's Greater Nile oil project marks the end of a deeply disgraceful chapter in Canadian history. Canada's reputation as a stalwart defender of human rights and human security has been permanently stained by the complicity of a Canadian corporation in the ongoing oil-driven destruction of Sudan."

Reeves goes on to point fingers at both Canadian politicians and the Canadian media, saying they share some of the responsibility for allowing the company to "exacerbate massive human suffering and destruction." But, he says, final responsibility for this "moral catastrophe" must be borne by the CEO of Talisman Energy and the company's Board of Directors, as it was they who "failed to respond to the devastating indictment of Talisman's operations in Sudan, rendered by every single credible human rights report on oil development in this torn country."

But, of course, Talisman *was* forced to respond. The company's operations in Sudan had become a huge public relations nightmare, not only for the company but for those who invested in it. When all was said and done, it was the need to preserve profits and returns for shareholders that seems to have forced Talisman's hand.

Talisman CEO Jim Buckee put it this way, "Although I believe our presence in Sudan has been a force for good, we are ultimately in the business of creating value for our shareholders."

So Talisman is leaving Sudan, but its Sudanese headache will follow them. Skirmishes will continue in at least one courtroom.

Talisman and the Government of Sudan are defendants in a civil-suit launched in New York City this year by the Presbyterian Church of Sudan and a coalition of Sudanese refugee groups.

The suit, filed in February, alleges Talisman and its business partner collaborated "in a joint strategy to use military forces in a brutal ethnic cleansing campaign against a civilian population."

The company vigorously denies the charges and is fighting to have the case thrown out.

Two Alberta-based groups, Freedom Quest International and the Federation of Sudanese Canadian Associations, are thinking about launching their own lawsuits in Canada.

Mel Middleton of Freedom Quest says they're waiting to see what comes out of the suit in New York. He thinks it might be possible to hold the Calgary company accountable under Ottawa's new "anti-terror" legislation. Middleton says he will continue to press for accountability and for reparations to be paid to the victims of Sudan's "oil-fuelled genocide."

Natalina and Morris Yoll of the Federation of Sudanese Canadian Associations say, "Talisman's past complicity is neither forgotten nor forgiven."

Source: Reproduced with permission from Byron Christopher, "No Graceful Exit," *RabbleNews* (November 5, 2002) <http://www.rabble.ca/news_full_story.shtml?x=16719>.

Questions:

1. How is CSR an issue in this case?
2. Why should Talisman be expected to act in accordance with societal expectations?
3. Could you argue that Talisman was just "doing its job"?

Responding to the Environment: Developing Business Strategy

The ability to respond effectively to the environment of business is the fundamental challenge of strategic management. How does a business create and sustain its competitive advantage? One of the fundamental internal forces that organizations must address is the issue of strategy. This chapter examines the nature and role of strategic management and the challenges it presents. We will explore the importance of understanding the nature of an organization's specific industry.

LEARNING OBJECTIVES

By the end of the chapter, you should be able to:

1. Describe the nature of strategic management.
2. Identify key forces in determining an industry structure.
3. Describe the roles of organization resources and capabilities in firm performance.
4. Describe three generic strategies.
5. Explain the nature of corporate strategy.

THE BUSINESS WORLD

The rise of Walmart's small box

Joe Castaldo

Walmart is synonymous with all things big. It is America's biggest corporation by revenue, after all. Its workforce is sprawling, its profits huge, and its stores bewilderingly large.

But in its home market, Walmart may be growing too big. There are roughly 3,800 stores in the U.S., most of them just shy of 200,000 square feet, and some analysts are concerned the

---

I am grateful to Professor You-Ta Chuang, York University, who served as author of this chapter, and Ania Czyznielewski, who contributed the section entitled "Strategy in Action: The Case of McDonald's" to this chapter.

company has limited opportunity to expand without hurting sales at existing locations. The way to continue growing, therefore, might just be to shrink.

At the University of Arkansas last month, the company quietly opened a 3,500-square-foot outlet dubbed Walmart on Campus that is essentially a convenience store and pharmacy. Walmart insists it has no immediate plans to open more, but analysts say the new format could play an important role in the company's future. "This is definitely an area where there is huge potential for expansion," says Raphael Moreau, a retailing analyst with Euromonitor International.

The Walmart on Campus format could address some of the company's challenges. For starters, U.S. locations have been suffering from declines in same-store sales for a number of quarters. Part of the problem is of Walmart's own making. The chain removed many popular brands from its shelves and—in an effort to tidy up locations—axed certain in-store displays that were actually generating big sales. (Walmart is now reversing these moves.) The chain also faces threats from more sophisticated dollar stores that grew during the recession. "Walmart, in theory, should have been absolutely rocking," says Doug Stephens, president of Retail Prophet Consulting in Toronto. "And they're not."

The big-box model that worked well in the past may be showing signs of strain, too. The format thrived when baby boomers flocked to the suburbs and easy credit fuelled consumption. These trends are now slowing or reversing, with people scaling back and moving closer to urban centres. After the housing crash, there are also fewer new developments in the U.S. able to support a giant Walmart.

The chain is well aware of these issues. Bill Simon, CEO of the U.S. division, said in October that up to 40 new stores built this year will be small or mid-sized, but disclosed little else. Walmart has experimented with smaller formats in the past, namely its grocery-centric Neighborhood Market and Marketside concepts, but the fact that it has not rolled either one out in a big way indicates the results have not been as successful as hoped.

Analysts say the convenience format is intriguing, however, because it could allow Walmart to enter urban centres. Unions and city councils have thwarted attempts to open metropolitan locations in the past, such as in New York City, but smaller stores could have an easier time winning approval. In this way, Walmart can target more customers with less risk of cannibalizing sales. Starting out on a university campus is also a clever strategy, Stephens says. One of the chain's weaknesses is that its appeal to younger consumers is not as strong as with baby boomers. "What better time to build a connection to the future consumer than when they are about to graduate?" he says. (Canadians hoping to see a convenience-store-sized Walmart may not want to hold their breath; the country is not nearly as overbuilt with retail as the U.S.)

The strategy is not risk-free. Smaller stores add more complexity to the supply chain—goods need to be delivered more frequently, for example, which increases fuel costs—and the company has to find the correct mix of products to sustain healthy profit margins. Prime real estate is limited in cities, and rents are higher. "You have to drive huge traffic and huge volume in these places because of the high rent," says Matt Arnold, a consumer analyst with Edward Jones in St. Louis.

Walmart isn't the only big-box retailer looking at smaller formats. Target and Tesco have experimented as well, mostly unsuccessfully. "The urgency for Walmart mainly comes from whether another competitor gets it right first," Arnold says.

That's not to say Walmart won't figure it out. "I wouldn't put anything past Walmart," Stephens says. "It's a voracious organization."

Source: *Canadian Business Magazine.*

WHAT IS STRATEGIC MANAGEMENT?

Strategic management consists of the analysis, decisions, implementations and evaluations a firm undertakes in order to create and sustain its competitive advantages. As such, strategic management can be an ongoing process where managers of a firm constantly analyze their external and internal environments, make decisions about what kinds of strategies they should pursue, implement the strategies and evaluate the outcomes of the implementations to make any change if necessary. The ongoing process of strategic management is critical to firm performance and survival in that an effective process of strategic management can allow a firm to sustain its competitive advantage, which in turn enhances it performance and survival chances. As shown in "The Business World," Walmart is revisiting which markets it should compete in and how it should compete with other retailers. Talking Business 9.1 further illustrates the importance of strategic management.

But what is strategy? Most can agree that much of the success of Walmart, Canadian Tire, or even highly profitable corporations can be attributed to, in part, the strategies these firms have pursued. However, there is no consensus on how to actually define the concept of a firm's strategy. Some definitions are long and complex; others are deceptively simple. Throughout this chapter, strategy is defined as the plans made or the actions taken, in an effort to help an organization/firm obtain its intended purposes. Such a definition corresponds to our prior discussion on the process of strategic management, where managers assess their

Talking Business 9.1

Brazil at Heart of Google's Latin America Strategy

Alejandro Lifschitz and Helen Popper

Brazil is on the way to becoming Google Inc's (GOOG-Q527.06-3.40-0.64%) sixth-largest global market, Chief Executive Eric Schmidt said Friday as the company opens new offices in the fast-growing Latin American region.

The world's No. 1 Internet search company saw its revenue in the region surge last year on the back of brisk economic growth, with countries showing growth of 50 per cent to 100 per cent last year.

"That means you're almost doubling (revenue) every year," Schmidt told Reuters in the company's offices in Buenos Aires. "That's a lot due to the effect of the economic recovery from a global recession, but also to the development of broadband and the development of the electronic commerce."

Schmidt will be replaced as CEO in April by Google co-founder Larry Page, a move to make the company more nimble at a time when competition heats up with fast-growing rivals like Facebook.

Latin America accounts for 2 per cent to 3 per cent of the California-based company's revenue, which totaled $29.3-billion last year, mostly from its business in the United States and Europe.

But Schmidt said the region's relatively modest share should grow fast.

"It will become a much larger percentage very quickly. Brazil is, for example, already on its way to becoming our sixth-largest country in revenue," he said.

Google has about 500 employees in Latin America, where it has opened new premises in Chile, Colombia and Peru.

"Latin America is our fastest-growing region in the world. You can see it everywhere," Schmidt said, highlighting the company's Orkut social network—one of Brazil's most-visited websites.

"I disagree that the only thing Google can do in social networking would be buying Twitter simply by the observation we have a very successful social network in Brazil, Orkut, which is growing and expanding," Schmidt said when asked if Google had held takeover talks with the microblogging site.

While Google has dominated Internet search for a decade, it has struggled to find its footing in social networking, with a new crop of Web companies including Facebook and Twitter stealing Web traffic and engineering talent.

Meanwhile, Schmidt said Google was not too anxious to see YouTube showing a profit, defending the scale of investments in its online video site.

"Profitability is not that important for us. For YouTube, what's really important is to build the great business for the partners," he said, adding that YouTube remained "almost profitable."

external and internal environments to plan and take actions to pursue organizational goals, either short term or long term. Putting both strategy and strategic management together, a firm can be viewed as a goal-directed entity. By and large, the goals of most publicly traded firms are normally to maximize shareholders' returns through various means.

Although strategy is goal-directed and -intended, it sometimes can unintentionally evolve with either the internal or external environment. Henry Mintzberg argues that, due to the unpredictability of environments, managers in organizations cannot thoroughly plan out any strategy that would achieve the long-term goals of their firms. As such, some strategies would never be carried out, and managers would pursue strategies that they had not planned at the beginning of the strategic management process. For example, a number of years ago, the SARS crisis in Canada led firms in the hospitality industry to pursue many different strategies in attempt to win back tourists, including cutting prices and seeking financial and non-financial supports from provincial governments. The unexpected crisis forced managers in these firms to change their strategies in response to a decline in their performance. Another example, Microsoft's entry to the Internet browser market (i.e., Internet Explorer) was not intended by its top management team. It was an idea forwarded by one of its software engineers.

In the next two sections, we will survey different approaches to strategy analysis, which is often the first stage of strategic management. Throughout the chapter, we will discuss different types of strategies and how to implement the strategies that are identified in the early stages of strategic management processes.

ANALYZING THE EXTERNAL ENVIRONMENT

By external environment, we will be focusing on five major groups associated with an industry. Before we look at each group in depth, we first need to define *industry*. *Industry* has been defined in many different ways. The definition used throughout this chapter is a group of organizations/firms that share similar resource requirements. The resource requirements range from raw materials, to labour, to technology, to customers. For example, Air Canada, Westjet, Jetgo, and Harmony Airways operate in the airline industry, where the four airline carriers share similar technology (e.g., aircrafts), labour (e.g., flight attendants) and customers (e.g., people who prefer air transportation). FedEx and UPS, however, are not in the airline industry because the customers those two companies serve are different from those of Air Canada, Westjet, Jetgo and Harmony Airways, although all of them share similar technology (e.g., aircrafts).

The Five-Forces Model

How can we systematically analyze the industry environment? Michael Porter drew upon research from industrial organization economics to propose a powerful, prescriptive model—**the five-forces model**, which allows us to systematically assess the industry environment. The thrust of the model is that the relationships between these five forces and the incumbent firms determine the attractiveness of the industry environment, which in turn helps us make strategic decisions in terms of how to achieve organizational goals or to find a position in the industry where we can best defend ourselves against competition. The five forces include threats of new entrants, bargaining power of suppliers, bargaining power of customers, threats of substitute products or services, and rivalry among existing firms (see Exhibit 9.1). These forces can either independently or jointly affect the attractiveness of the industry. Let's examine each force in more detail.

1. Threats of New Entrants

New entrants can take two basic forms, such as new startups and diversification of existing firms in other industries. Regardless, the entrants bring new capacity, desire to gain market share and substantial resources and capabilities. Prices can be bid down or incumbents' costs inflated as a result, reducing profitability. As such, the new entrants may impose significant threats to incumbents. Thus, incumbents need to consider how to create entry barriers to deter potential new entrants. There are five major sources of entry barriers from the potential new entrants' point of view.

Economies of Scale **Economies of scale** refer to spreading the costs of production over the number of units produced. The cost of a product per unit declines as the number of units per period increases. From the new entrants' point of view, the entry barrier is increased (the threat of new entrants is reduced) when incumbents enjoy the benefits of economies of scale. Economies of scale can provide the incumbents cost advantages to compete with new entrants on the price, if necessary.

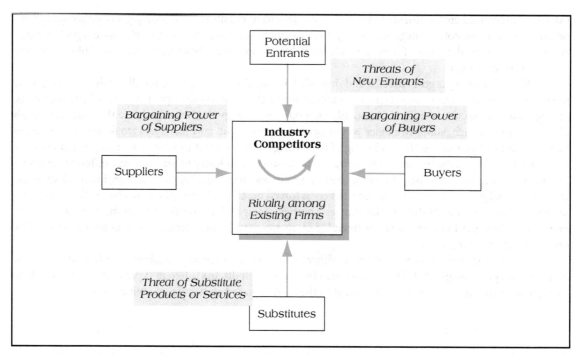

EXHIBIT 9.1 Forces driving competition within an industry.

Source: Reproduced with the permission of The Free Press, a Division of Simon & Schuster Adult Publishing Group, from *Competitive Strategy: Techniques for Analyzing* by Michael E. Porter. © 1980, 1998 by The Free Press. All rights reserved.

Capital Requirements   For some industries, such as airline and mining industries, the required capital to establish a new firm is significantly high. Accordingly, the level of required capital for entering the industries creates the barriers to potential new entrants. Thus, the threat of new entrants is reduced as the level of required capital increases.

Switching Costs   **Switching costs** refers to the costs (monetary or psychological) associated with changing from one supplier to another from the buyer perspective. When the switching costs are minimal, customers can easily switch buying products from one firm to another. This creates an opportunity for potential new entrants in that the new entrants can easily acquire customers from incumbents. Thus, the threat of new entrants (the barrier of new entrants) increases (decreases) as the switching costs decreases.

Access to Distribution Channels   Accessibility to distribution channels can be an entry barrier for potential new entrants. In the situation where incumbents control most of the distribution channels, potential entrants would find it difficult to distribute their products or services, which in turn defers new entry. Accordingly, the threat of new entrants (the barrier of new entrants) decreases (increases) as accessibility to distribution channels decreases.

Cost Disadvantages Independent of Scale   The prior four sources are primarily associated economic advantages. However, sometimes, some advantages incumbents hold over potential entrants are independent of economic factors. Such advantages include governmental policies, legal protection (e.g., patents and trademarks) and proprietary products. These advantages create the barriers for potential new entrants, which defer their entries.

2. Bargaining Power of Suppliers

When considering supplier power, our focus is on the firms, organizations, and individuals that provide raw materials, technologies, or skills to incumbents in an industry. Suppliers can exert bargaining power over incumbents in an industry by demanding better prices or threatening to reduce quality of purchased goods or services. Therefore, the power suppliers hold direct impact on the industry profitability as well as the incumbents' performance. There are two major factors contributing to suppliers' power in relation to incumbents in an industry.

The first one is the criticality of resources the suppliers hold to the incumbents. Quite often, when the raw materials suppliers provide are critical to incumbents in an industry, the suppliers are in a good position to demand better prices. The second factor is the number of suppliers available relative to the number of incumbents in an industry. Specifically, when the number of suppliers relative to the number of incumbents is low, the incumbents compete against each other for the relative small number of suppliers. As such, this gives suppliers power in that suppliers would have opportunities to negotiate better prices between incumbents. These two factors can independently contribute to supplier powers. And suppliers will have the highest power when these factors couple together.

Looking at the personal computer manufacturing industry, for example, there are many incumbents, like Dell, Hewlett-Packard, IBM and others. However, there are only two major firms, Intel and AMD, that supply the processor chips. Thus, the suppliers hold significant bargaining power over computer manufacturers because the processor chips are critical components of personal computers, and there are only two firms that supply this key component.

3. Bargaining Power of Buyers

When we consider buyer power, our attention focuses on the power held by individuals or organizations that purchase incumbents' products or services. Buyers can affect industry performance by demanding lower prices, better quality or services, or playing incumbents against one another. These actions can erode industry profitability as well as firm performance. There are many factors contributing to buyer power in relation to incumbents in an industry.

Switching Costs   Similar to the role of switching costs in threats of new entrants, the bargaining power of buyers increases as switching costs decrease. Specifically, when buyers can easily switch incumbents with little cost in terms of products or services, the incumbents would have little power over the buyers to enhance their performance.

Undifferentiated Products   Relatedly, when incumbents provide similar products or services to buyers, they would not be in a good position to negotiate with the buyers. Undifferentiated products allow buyers to find alternatives from other incumbents. They can also provide an opportunity to buyers to play against incumbents to get a better price, quality or service. Then, the bargaining power of buyers is enhanced.

Importance of Incumbents' Products to Buyers   Similar to our discussion on bargaining power of suppliers, when products or services that incumbents offer are important or critical to buyers, the power of buyers would be diminished.

The Number of Incumbents Relative to the Number of Buyers   The bargaining power of buyers could be diminished when there are relatively few incumbents offering products or services the buyers need, since the buyers do not have many alternatives to choose from.

Looking at grocery retailers in Canada, for instance, Loblaws, Dominion, Sam's Club, Sobey's and others are the key players in the industry. They are the buyers in relation to the grocery producers. The grocery producers do not hold significant bargaining power over these retailers because the number of producers is relatively high compared to the number of retailers, the switching costs for retailers are minimal, and the degree of differentiation among producers is relatively low. As such, the retailers enjoy significant bargaining power over the grocery producers.

4. Threats of Substitutes

All firms in an industry often compete with other firms in different industries, where the firms provide substitute products or services with similar purposes. For example, the traditional form of newspapers faces the substitutes, including the Internet, radio stations, television stations and so on. Such substitutes would gain newspaper subscribers and advertising revenues that might have belonged to the newspaper industry. As such, they threaten the profitability of the newspaper industry as a whole.

5. Rivalry among Existing Firms

The final force that affects industry structure is rivalry. The rivalry among incumbents in an industry can take many different forms. For example, Canadian insurance providers compete against each other by using different strategic actions, including cutting prices, providing new insurance products, improving operational efficiency, advertising, and through mergers and acquisitions. More broadly, rivalry can be intensified by several interacting factors.

Lack of Differentiation or Switching Costs   When products are significantly differentiated or switching costs of customers are minimal, customer choices are often based on price and service. Under this situation, incumbents may experience pressure to launch more strategic action in an attempt to attract more customers or keep existing customers by enhancing their short-term performance. Accordingly, the rivalry among incumbents is intensified.

Numerous or Equally Balanced Competitors   When there are many incumbents in an industry, the likelihood of mavericks is great. Some firms may believe that they can initiate strategic action without being noticed. As such, their strategic action intensifies the rivalry among incumbents. In addition, the rivalry between firms tends to be highest when the firms are similar in size and resources. The firms similar in size and resources often target similar market niches and share similar resources requirements. These lead them to compete hand to hand.

High Exit Barriers   Exit barriers refer to economic, strategic and emotional factors that keep firms competing even though they may be earning low or negative returns on their investments. Examples of exit barriers include visible fixed costs, specialized assets, escalating commitment of management and government and social pressures.

Overall, the five-forces model provides managers with an assessment of the industry structure to help get some sense of industry attractiveness. Specifically, from the potential entrant point of view, the five-forces model helps the potential entrants understand the potential competitive environment of the industry and to make the entry decision. From the incumbent point of view, the model helps managers to assess their position in the industry relative to their rivals'. Sometimes, it also provides an overall picture of industry attractiveness to allow managers to make any exit decisions.

Each model has its limitations, however. Although the five-forces model offers a powerful tool for managers to examine an industry's attractiveness, it exhibits some shortcomings. First, the model does not explicitly take roles of technological change and governmental regulations into consideration. Specifically, it does not address how technological change and governmental regulations affect the power relationships between forces. Second, the focus of this model is primarily on the power relationships between each force at a given point in time. As such, it may have limited implications for future strategic decision making. Finally, the model assumes that all incumbents experience the same power relationship with each force. However, incumbents differ in terms of their resources and firm size, which can give them more or less power in influencing their suppliers or customers. (See Talking Business 9.2.)

Given the above limitations, in order to have a precise assessment, managers need to use the model with great caution. Specifically, they need to anticipate the effects of technological change, governmental regulations and industry trends on industry structure and their firm positions in the industry.

Talking Business 9.2
The Profits and Perils of Supplying to Wal-Mart

Emily Schmitt

When Taunya Painter worked as a senior corporate counsel for Wal-Mart (WMT), she noticed that many of the small suppliers that wanted contracts with the world's biggest retailer, known for pressuring suppliers to cut prices, hadn't done all their homework. Few fully understood what they would be signing and few took advantage of Wal-Mart's supplier development team, a free resource designed to help less-experienced suppliers forge enduring relationships with managers and buyers. (Other large retailers, including Home Depot (HD), Best Buy (BBY), and Ace Hardware have in-house teams meant to serve similar purposes.) Painter, who worked for the mega-retailer from 2002 to 2007, says more of the entrepreneurs she dealt with might have managed to secure and renew contracts if they had familiarized themselves with these two pieces of the supplier-retailer puzzle.

While there are more pieces to the puzzle, by taking the time at first to understand what the contract entails, a potential supplier can determine whether or not it even makes sense to try to become one of Wal-Mart's 57,000 U.S. suppliers. The contract, commonly known as the vendor agreement, outlines the mechanics of how the supplier and retailer will work together. The agreement generally addresses sales and delivery timeframe, arbitration, and termination rights, and liability. As a rule, Wal-Mart uses a non-negotiable boilerplate. Charley Moore, CEO and founder of legal service RocketLawyer.com, says this means potential suppliers can study similar contracts online before meeting with the buyer.

Wal-Mart generally starts out smaller suppliers in a local market, delivering goods to up to 50 stores, as a test run. If the supplier provides a high-selling product and proves reliable, it might be considered for national distribution. Bruce Zutler, CEO and co-founder of MCI Products Group, a New York-based company that specializes in new product development and overseas sourcing, recommends small suppliers think of the test-run as the time to prove they are capable. "If you have a good product and you strengthen their sales, then the buyer will stay with you," says Zutler.

Broad Customer Base a Must

But suppliers should know that Wal-Mart will only work with suppliers that can prove three-quarters of their business comes from entities other than Wal-Mart, per Wal-Mart policy. After proving that, the key to impressing a buyer is to show understanding of the potential market, says Theresa Barrera, vice-president of supplier diversity for Wal-Mart. "What sets some of these smaller suppliers apart is being innovative and knowing what sells in their regions."

It is also up to suppliers to understand the impact of national trends on Wal-Mart and be prepared to adapt, says Excell La Fayette, director of supplier development. He, too, urges suppliers to do their research before they call. "A lot of people think Wal-Mart is kind of a free-for-all; that if they come in we'll buy anything."

Fair Oaks Farms cooks, packages, and ships the meat for Wal-Mart's Great Value brand breakfast sausage to more than 50 stores in different regions across the country. Michael Thompson, president and CEO of the Pleasant Prairie (Wis.)-based company, says the key to landing a deal and getting the contract renewed over the companies' ongoing five-year relationship was conveying an understanding of growth opportunities and explaining what his 300-person company could do to meet Wal-Mart's needs. Beyond that, he says it is important for hopeful suppliers to remain persistent, be patient, and bring their "A-game" to the meeting with the buyer.

Liable for Chargebacks

Of course, even if a supplier does manage to convince Wal-Mart to sign a supplier agreement, it almost never obligates the retailer to buy anything. "I tell people not to pop the cork when the contract is signed, but pop it when the purchase order comes in," says Painter, who now runs her own law firm in Texas, specializing in domestic and international business litigation. Wal-Mart says its payment cycles vary by category, but that most suppliers are paid within 30 to 45 days.

And suppliers looking to sign should also know that even if everything is done right, the state of the economy could derail chances that the relationship is profitable, at least in the short term. Nina Kaufman, a business attorney in New York who posts frequently on her blog, AskTheBusinessLawyer.com, says suppliers should be aware of how large retailers like Wal-Mart manage low sales that result in surplus inventory. Those designated "guaranteed suppliers" guarantee that their product will sell. If they don't, a provision in the contract makes them liable for chargebacks.

Ultimately, understanding all aspects of the supply chain is key to landing—and renewing—a deal with Wal-Mart. Painter says getting an experienced supplier to serve as a mentor can also be invaluable. "I always suggest tapping into resources the retailer has other than the buyer," says Painter "It's important to know who are your allies in the organization."

Source: *Business Week.*

ANALYZING THE INTERNAL ENVIRONMENT

After discussing how to analyze the industry environment, let's look at strategy analysis from another viewpoint—the internal environment. Indeed, research shows that the effects of the industry environment on firm performance are smaller than those of a firm's internal environment. Furthermore, if we look at all firms in an industry, we will see some firms are doing much better than others. This implies that how managers organize firm resources and capabilities plays a critical role in firm performance and survival. In order for managers to effectively organize firm resources and capabilities to enhance firm performance and survival, they need to know what kinds of resources and capabilities the firm has in the first place. Jay Barney provides a prescriptive VRIO (value, rareness, imitability, organization) model that can help managers examine the resources and capabilities in a systematic way. Before we discuss the model, we will first talk about what resources and capabilities are.

A firm's resources and capabilities include all of the financial, physical, human and organizational assets used by the firm to develop, manufacture and deliver products or services to its customers. Financial resources include debt, equity, retained earnings and so forth. Physical resources include the machines, production facilities, plants and buildings firms use in their operations. Human resources include all the experience, knowledge, judgment, risk-taking propensity and wisdom of individuals associated with a firm. (See Talking Business 9.3.) Organizational resources include the history, relationships, trust and organizational culture that are groups of individuals associated with a firm, along with a firm's formal reporting structure, management control systems and compensation policies.

The VRIO Model

Barney suggests that managers need to look inside their firms for competitive advantage. In order for a firm to achieve high performance, managers need to look at their resources and capabilities and ask four important questions: (1) the question of value (V), (2) the question of rareness (R), (3) the question of imitability (I), and (4) the question of organization (O).

The Question of Value

Managers need to ask if their firm's resources and capabilities add any value to capture market share or enhance profitability, either through exploiting emerging opportunities or neutralizing threats. Some firms do have such resources and capabilities. For example, NeoSet, a Canadian furniture maker, specializes in customized designs of home and office furniture. Its capability in customization of high-quality furniture allows the firm to obtain profitability from a small market, where other large furniture retailers, like IKEA, The Brick, and Leon's, do not compete.

The Question of Rareness

Although valuable resources and capabilities help firms to survive, those resources and capabilities need to be rare. In other words, they will have to be controlled by only a small number of firms in order for the firms to obtain competitive advantage. Thus, managers need to assess if their valuable resources and capabilities are unique among their competitors. For example, for many years, Wal-Mart's skills in developing and using point-of-purchase data collection to control inventory gave it a competitive advantage over its competitors, like K-Mart, a firm that has not had access to this timely information technology. Thus, during those years, Wal-Mart's capability to control inventory gave the company its competitive edge over its major competitor, K-Mart.

The Question of Imitability

Valuable and rare resources and capabilities can provide firms with competitive advantage; however, how long the advantage lasts depends on how *quickly* imitation could occur. When imitation occurs, it diminishes the degree of rareness, which may further erode the value of the resources and capabilities. Thus, managers need to ask themselves if their resources and capabilities are difficult to be imitated by other firms and then determine how to create the barriers for imitation.

The Question of Organization

The last question managers have to consider is whether their firms can be organized in effective and efficient ways to exploit their valuable, rare and difficult-to-imitate resources and capabilities to maximize their potentials. Organization of a firm is critical for firm success. Quite often, firms with valuable resources and

Talking Business 9.3

Lazy Worker or Flawed Work Culture?

Chris Atchison

Managing lackadaisical workers can be a major challenge. Simply put, helping them improve skills to meet standards demanded of a position can be easier than fundamentally transforming their work ethic and attitude.

One senior vice-president of human resources at a major Canadian not-for-profit—who requested anonymity because of the sensitive nature of her position—has seen lazy employees not only cause headaches for management, but affect entire departments with their unproductive behaviour.

She recalls an example of one employee who had come up the ladder watching superiors ahead of him sit in corner offices with teams of assistants, finally crack the executive ranks. Trouble was, times had changed and the days of having secretaries and large staffs to which to delegate work had disappeared.

Too bad the employee hadn't been keeping up with the times.

"When he got to management, he had to do a lot of the work himself," she recalls. "After 15 years of a lack of discipline, he could literally do the work in a skill-based way, but couldn't get over his resentment and continually missed deadlines, over-delegated to his juniors and, in some cases, tried to delegate upwards."

The worker was terminated.

But what, exactly, is a lazy employee?

As Lynn Brown, managing director of Toronto-based human resources consultancy Brown Consulting points out, lazy is a broad term that can refer to workers who don't meet performance expectations or fail to go above and beyond the call of duty.

However, she stresses, perceived laziness can sometimes be the result of personal issues, from health issues to coping with a sick child at home. It can also be a symptom of disengagement, which is typically a result of a broken workplace culture.

A great deal of the time, Ms. Brown says, lazy employees aren't hired but, rather, created by a company that's run off the rails.

"Companies need to take a holistic step back and ask, 'Is this an isolated incident with this person, or do we see the disengagement across the organization?'" she advises. "Is this showing up in higher turnover rates or is it in pockets? Then you can focus on the individual employee to determine what the causes are, or work to fix the cultural issues."

Cultural challenges can be difficult to overcome and could include an imbalance on the increasingly important work-life balance front, a lack of communication on the part of management or a lack of recognition of employee achievements.

Workplace shortcomings also typically result when employers fail to set proper expectations, says Tiffany Goodlet, a partner at human resources consulting firm Verity International Ltd.

"Employers need to define what the deal is between them and their employees," she says. "What's in it for them if they uphold their end of the bargain, or don't? What does success look like for them, and how are they going to rate the employee on success?"

From there, she explains, employers need to manage expectations, measure performance and reward or correct behaviour.

Providing feedback, Ms. Goodlet stresses, is an area where many managers or business owners fall short as they struggle to identify areas for improvement and then present it in a constructive way without alienating the employee.

Many dread this necessary duty so much they either hand it off to a more junior—and even less experienced—manager, or skip it altogether.

Her advice: Structure the feedback around what the employee should start doing, what they should stop doing, what they should do more of and, if necessary, what they should do less of.

Tim Rutledge, a Toronto-based workplace retention and engagement consultant and author of *Getting Engaged: The New Workplace Loyalty,* adds that companies need to act fast to change an underperforming employee's behaviour, lest it infect the rest of the company.

One way to tackle the problem: Focus on the big picture.

(Continued)

"It can be very helpful to help the employee connect what they do to something bigger," Mr. Rutledge says. "Help them understand what gets better as a result of what they do every day. Employees who can make that link are much more likely to be engaged with their work than people who can't, and it's a supervisor's job to make that connection on a daily basis if necessary."

What if all constructive methods of employee development and progressive discipline—such as warning letters or suspensions—have failed? Mr. Rutledge says the final option is dismissal, but only as a last resort.

To avoid hiring lazy employees or creating a culture that invites or harbours them, he recommends working harder at the hiring stage to ensure a prospective staffer's attitude gels with the company's existing culture, and involve existing employees in the hiring process so that everyone has a stake in a new employee's success.

As the senior vice-president at a not-for-profit recalls, working with these seemingly lazy employees to improve performance and attitude can work.

In one case, she saw an employee restore his reputation after management began asking deeper questions about his interests.

It turns out the highly qualified worker was doing a job that thoroughly bored him.

"Once he got into the right role," she says, "there was no sign of laziness."

Source: Special to *The Globe and Mail*.

capabilities experience a decline in performance because they do not have appropriate organizational structure and design, compensation policies, and organizational culture to exploit their resources and capabilities.

These four questions provide managers with important guidelines to assess their competitive advantage relative to their competitors. If the answers to these questions are all in their firm's favour, then the firms will have sustainable competitive advantage over competitors (see Exhibit 9.2). If any of the answers to these questions are not in their firm's favour, then the firm would only have temporal advantage over competitors. In this situation, the firm's performance may be threatened by the competitors at any time in the near future. Managers will have to act quickly to develop or acquire new resources or capabilities that help them to create sustainable competitive advantage.

EXHIBIT 9.2 VRIO model.

	Question of Value	Question of Rareness	Question of Imitability	Question of Organization	Competitive Advantage
A particular set of resources and capabilities	In favour of the firm	In favour of the firm	In favour of the firm	In favour of the firm	Sustainable competitive advantage
A particular set of resources and capabilities	In favour of the firm	In favour of the firm	Not in favour of the firm	In favour of the firm	Temporal competitive advantage
A particular set of resources and capabilities	In favour of the firm	Not in favour of the firm	In favour of the firm	In favour of the firm	Temporal competitive advantage

SWOT Analysis

At this point, we have discussed two basic and important models that managers can apply to assess their firm's position in the competitive environment. To some extent, these two models complement and supplement each other to tell us about where opportunities and threats are situated in the external environment and how good or how bad we are in terms of the resources and capabilities we have. In other words, the conclusions of analyses from these two models can be summarized by **SWOT analysis** (strengths, weaknesses, opportunities and threats). The strategic logic be hind SWOT analysis (see Exhibit 9.3) is that firms that strategically use their internal strengths in exploiting environmental opportunities and neutralizing environmental threats while avoiding internal weaknesses, are more likely to increase market share, sales or profitability than other firms.

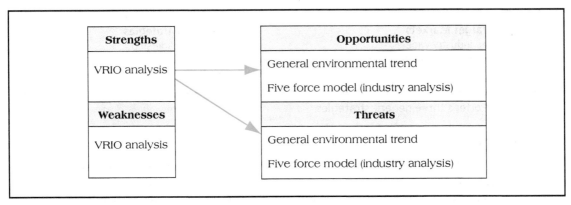

EXHIBIT 9.3 SWOT analysis.

Specifically, managers could use the VRIO analysis to identify what kinds of resources and capabilities their firm has that provide sustainable competitive advantage and what kinds of resources and capabilities present the firm's weaknesses. Managers could also examine the trends of general environments and analyze industry structure (i.e., five force model) to assess opportunities and threats in the external environment. As such, the conclusion from the SWOT analysis can provide insights for managers into strategy formulation for the future.

For example, Starbucks, a specialty coffee retailer, realized that high quality of coffee beans are sensitive to environmental conditions (e.g., weather) and that the coffee-beans suppliers have great power over specialty coffee retailers because the coffee beans are critical inputs for the retailers. Starbucks used their capability in effective supply-chain management to neutralize the threats imposed by specialty coffee-beans suppliers through diversifying their suppliers and through precise inventory control. At one point, the number of Starbucks' suppliers reached over 1,500 worldwide. In addition, Starbucks understood that its brand reputation and image are valuable, rare and costly to imitate in the industry. It quickly harvested its brand reputation and image through entering the international markets and selling its Starbucks coffee in grocery stores. As such, Starbucks enjoyed enormous success for quite a long period of time.

The recent Google mania is another example. Google used its strengths in search engine and operation-system design capabilities to compete in the highly competitive computer industry. It identified the opportunities situated in the Internet search-engine market and the personal computer operation systems market by analyzing the weaknesses of incumbents' products. Google then used its capabilities in product design to capture the opportunities, which in turn gave it great success and challenged Microsoft's market positions in these two markets.

Both Starbucks and Google clearly understood how to use their sustainable competitive advantage (e.g., strengths) to capture opportunities in the marketplace (e.g., opportunities) or to neutralize the threats embedded in the industry environment. As such, both firms captured a significant portion of market share in their particular industry.

DIFFERENT LEVELS OF STRATEGIES

To this point, we have discussed how managers can perform strategic analysis to identify opportunities and threats situated in their industry environment and strengths and weaknesses embedded within their firms. In addition, managers need to know whether or not their strengths are sustainable for long-term performance. In this section, we will discuss what kinds of strategies managers can pursue given the opportunities, threats, strengths and weaknesses they have identified.

Conceptually, we can categorize strategies into two levels—business and corporate levels. Business-level strategy is the strategy a firm chooses to compete in a given market. As such, which market a firm intends to operate in is a given. Corporate-level strategy is about how a firm allocates its resources in different markets to create synergy in order to achieve its organizational goals.

Business-level Strategy

There are three business strategies that have been widely discussed in the literature and have sometimes been called generic business strategies. They are cost leadership, product differentiation and focus (see Exhibit 9.4).

Target Markets
- Industry wide
- Particular market segment/buyer group

Generic Strategies
- Cost leadership
- Differentiation
- Focus

EXHIBIT 9.4 Porter's three generic strategies.

Cost Leadership

The purpose of cost leadership is to gain competitive advantages by reducing economic cost below that of all competitors. It often requires aggressive construction of efficient-scale facilities, vigorous pursuit of cost reductions from experience, tight cost and overhead control, avoidance of marginal customer accounts, and cost minimization in areas like R&D, service, sales force, marketing and adverting, general administration and so on. Accordingly, a great deal of managerial attention to cost control is necessary to achieve these aims. There are three sources of cost leadership: (1) economies of scale, where firms can increase their production volume to reduce marginal costs; (2) learning curve economies, where firms can reduce marginal costs by experience, such as learning-by-doing, and decreasing defects of productions or services; (3) low-cost access to factors of productions, referring to access to low costs of raw materials, labour, location and so on. Although each of these sources could be relatively easily imitated by competitors, a combination of these three can make imitation difficult, which in turn gives firms competitive advantages.

There are two major advantages associated with cost leadership. First, being a cost leader gives a firm the highest profit margins in the industry, which allows the firm to obtain abnormal returns, at least for the short term. The second advantage is that it gives firms flexibility in response to pressures coming from five forces in the industry environment. This is particularly critical in the situation where an industry becomes less attractive to competitors. More specifically, when competition among firms moves toward price competition, like what happens in mature industries, a firm with a cost leadership strategy would be likely to survive the competition because the firm can reduce its price and still obtain positive profit margins. Such a firm can also ensure increases in cost of raw materials when suppliers charge higher prices; its competitors might not be able to absorb the higher prices from the suppliers; as a result, they may have to transfer the costs to customers. As such, the firm would be able to win its competitors' customers over by charging lower prices. Furthermore, in a situation where buyers demand lower prices, the firm, compared to its competitors, could more flexibly respond to customers' demand by reducing its price to maintain or even expand its customer base. Finally, the threat of new entrants would be lower for the firm, compared to other incumbent firms. Since the firm has advantages of economies of scale, learning curve economies and low access to production factors, the new entrants are unlikely to able to charge the same price as the firm does. Accordingly, the new entrants are not likely to impose immediate threat to the firm in terms of its short-term performance.

Numerous firms have pursued cost-leadership strategies. For example, Wal-Mart, a retailer giant, is famous for its lowest prices in the marketplace. If you look at Wal-Mart closely, you will find it not only has the lowest prices in the marketplace, but is also the cost leader in the retailer industry. Wal-Mart obtains its economies of scale by high volume of purchasing and services. It also locates its stores in areas where the rents are not expensive. Furthermore, Wal-Mart uses state-of-the-art information technology to monitor its inventory in order to reduce inventory costs. Although these are small activities, the cumulative cost savings can be huge. Most important, the organization of these small activities makes it difficult for competitors to imitate Wal-Mart's operation. The managerial attention to cost reduction from various activities gives Wal-Mart a competitive edge in the highly competitive retailing industry.

Product Differentiation

Product differentiation is about firm's attempts to gain competitive advantages by increasing the perceived value of their products or services relative to that of other firms' products or services. The other firms can be either competitors in the same industry or firms from other industries. For example, Starbucks provides high-quality flavoured and specialty coffees as well as high-quality store design to differentiate itself from Tim Horton's and Country Style. As such, Starbucks is able to charge high-price premiums to customers given the value created.

Firms can create value for their products or services to differentiate themselves from other firms in many ways, including product features, linkages between functions, location, product mix, links with other firms, and service (see Exhibit 9.5 for examples). However, managers need to keep in mind that the existence of product differentiation, in the end, is always a matter of customer perception. Sometimes, products sold

EXHIBIT 9.5 Examples of product differentiation.

Ways to Create Value	Examples
Product features	Apple's Mac vs. PC
Linking between functions	Traditional televisions vs. Televisions with DVD players
Location	Pusatari's, a high-end grocery chain, locates its stores in expensive neighbourhoods
Product mix	McDonald's combo, including burger, soft drink and fries
Link with other firms	American Express credit card links with Air Miles
Service	Staples' next-business-day delivery service

by two different firms may be very similar, but if customers believe the first is more valuable than the second, then the first product has a differentiation advantage. Therefore, the firm with that product may be able to charge a higher price than the other firm.

For firms that obtain competitive advantages by pursuing product differentiation, they are often in good positions to defend the pressures from the five forces. More specifically, the threats of new entrants and substitutes for the firms would be lower than for others since the firms have imposed switching costs for their customers. In a situation where the suppliers pressure to increase the prices of raw materials, the firms could transfer the increased costs to the customers as long as the new prices do not exceed the value the firms created. When rivalry among firms becomes fierce, the firms would be unlikely to trap into price competition since the value they provided could protect them from the price wars.

That being said, managers who intend to pursue product differentiation need to consider if the value they are going to create is sustainable, at least for a certain period of time. As we discussed in the previous session, in order to achieve abnormal returns, firms need to obtain sustainable competitive advantages. Therefore, managers need to think about how to create value that is rare and difficult to imitate or substitute. For example, Apple successfully created an MP3 player, iPod, which it then sold nearly 2 million of in a relatively short period of time. Although Apple's success invited imitation from Creative, Sony, iRiver, Samsung and others, Apple has built up its brand loyalty through its product differentiation (e.g., unique product designs). Even though these competitors offered MP3 players with different functions and lower prices, the differences in price and functionality did not significantly attract customers' attention. As a result, Apple could continue to harvest its iPod's success.

Focus

While cost leadership and product differentiation are oriented to broad markets, focus strategy targets a particular buyer group, a segment of the product line or a geographic market. Specifically, the focus strategy rests on the premise that a firm is able to compete efficiently or effectively by targeting a particular narrow market. The firm thus can achieve either differentiation by better meeting the needs of a particular buyer group or lower costs in serving this group, or both. Accordingly, the firm may potentially earn above-normal returns by adopting either focused low-cost strategy or focused differentiation strategy.

For example, before 2003, Westjet's strategy was an example of focused low-cost strategy. Westjet primarily served the markets in western regions of Canada, such as British Columbia and Alberta. The company also focused on achieving cost advantages in which it emphasized reducing costs through all value chain activities. IKEA is another example of a focused low-cost strategy adopter, where it targets the buyers, including young families and frequent movers, and it is able to sell knockdown furniture with low pricing through its efficient value-chain management. Companies like Godiva chocolates, Haagen-Dazs, and Hugo Boss employ differentiation-based focused strategies targeted at upscale buyers wanting products and services with world-class attributes. These firms focus on the high-income buyers and differentiate their products from other firms in terms of quality. As such, they are able to achieve high performance.

Corporate-level Strategy

In contrast to the business-level strategy that concerns how to compete in a given market, corporate-level strategy addresses two related challenges: (1) what businesses or markets a firm should compete in, and (2) how these businesses or markets can be managed so they create synergy. (See Talking Business 9.4.) In other words, the issues managers deal with concern determining which markets their firms should diversify into, in an attempt to create maximum synergies for the firm and then to achieve high performance. These are

Talking Business 9.4

BCE-CTV Deal Remakes Media Landscape

Iain Marlow

BCE Inc. has agreed to acquire full ownership of CTV Inc. in a $1.3-billion deal that dramatically reshapes the landscape of Canadian media and telecommunications, and changes the ownership structure of The Globe and Mail.

The merger of Canada's largest telecom carrier and the country's No. 1 broadcaster is the latest in a series of deals heralding a new era of convergence between media companies and the cable and phone giants that distribute their content.

"This is truly an historic day for Bell," said George Cope, BCE's president and CEO, on a call with analysts on Friday morning. "We are purchasing 100 per cent of Canada's No. 1 media company."

"I think he got CTV cheap," said Ivan Fecan, CTV's chief executive officer, referring to Mr. Cope. "We have emerged from the recession and the market is picking up, and given our very strong leading positions in speciality and conventional and radio, we're incredibly well positioned to benefit from the market picking up."

Later in the day, Mr. Fecan told CTV staff in a memo that he planned to retire once the regulatory process for the deal was complete.

With the deal, which has yet to be cleared by federal regulators, Bell Canada Enterprises acquires all of CTV's television assets, including the CTV network and specialty cable channels such as TSN, Bravo and the Business News Network.

The transaction also breaks apart CTVglobemedia Inc., created a decade ago when CTV merged with The Globe and Mail. Woodbridge Co. Ltd., the holding company of the Toronto-based Thomson family, will regain majority ownership of the Globe with an 85-per-cent stake. BCE will retain its current 15-per-cent share of Canada's largest circulation national newspaper and its related websites.

"The pleasure for me is immense today," David Thomson, chairman of Woodbridge, said. "We are blessed with an extraordinary business in Thomson Reuters. The Globe really matters to the family. We are now ready to put teams together to innovate and implement. We are the premiere content provider in this country, and we only seek to become better."

Phillip Crawley, publisher of The Globe and Mail said: "We suddenly just don't separate from CTV. We've got all kinds of relationships with CTV. They'll carry on for the time being."

BCE's move into broadcasting has obvious echoes of then-CEO Jean Monty's bid in 2000 to form a converged media and communications empire, first by spending $2.3-billion to acquire CTV, then by combining it with the Globe to create Bell Globemedia, in which it had a controlling stake of about 70 per cent.

That experiment was eventually rejected by the market, and in 2005, Mr. Monty's successor, Michael Sabia, sold off the bulk of BCE's stake to Woodbridge, The Ontario Teachers' Pension Plan and Torstar Corp. The company was then renamed CTVglobemedia to reflect Bell's diminished influence.

This latest move marks the departure of Teachers and Torstar, which held 25 and 20 per cent, respectively, of CTVglobemedia. BCE put the total transaction value at $3.2-billion, including debt.

For CTV, being part of BCE gives the media company an assured spot in the 130-year-old telecom company's national communication lines, which consist of TV, Internet and wireless networks. It also guarantees CTV that as other distribution companies sew up exclusive content arrangements and strike deals, the media company won't be left behind.

Also, as television audiences increasingly migrate to watching video online, CTV's relationship with Bell, which has millions of Internet customers, might allow the broadcaster to more effectively hang on to its audience and wring profit from ratings.

critical issues for managers because continuing to grow in a single market has become very difficult in today's business world, and the globalization trend also presents new market opportunities. Successfully managing diversification can give a firm enormous profitability and competitive advantage. In this section, we will discuss motives of diversification, types of diversification and the means to diversify.

But first, we need to define *diversification*. Diversification refers to a situation where a firm operates in more than one market simultaneously. The market can take many different forms. For example, Rogers operates in three major markets: cable provider, cellular phone service provider and Internet service provider markets. Canadian Imperial Bank of Commerce, Bank of Nova Scotia, Bank of Montreal and TD Canada Trust have all diversified into international markets. Most large Canadian insurance companies are highly diversified in terms of their insurance products and where they sell their products. In fact, if we look at the top 300 corporations in the *Financial Post* 1000, we will find the majority of the 300 corporations are highly diversified.

Motives for Diversification

Why are the majority of the top Canadian corporations highly diversified? More generally, why do firms pursue diversification? There are many motives driving managers to pursue diversification. We can group these motives into two major categories: intra-firm and inter-firm dynamics.

The motives derived from intra-firm dynamics include means to growth and managerial self-interests. Firms operating in single markets, up to a point, will face some difficulties to continue growth in the markets even if they have sustainable competitive advantage. The difficulties may come from market saturation and intense competition within the markets they operate in. Accordingly, diversifying to new markets provides them with opportunities to sustain growth and increase revenue. By diversifying into new markets, firms have opportunities to share related activities, which in turn achieve economies of scope and then increase profitability and revenue. **Economies of scope** here refers to the situation where the total costs for serving two markets or producing the products for two markets are less than the costs for serving them or producing them alone. Such cost savings may derive from sharing production facilities, personnel or marketing activities. In addition to benefits from economies of scope through sharing activities, diversification allows firms to leverage their core resources and capabilities to explore growth opportunities in new markets.

For example, Bell Canada, competing in cellular phones and Internet service provider markets, provides retailing service through its retail stores, where customers can purchase both cellular phone products and Internet bundles. Through single store services, Bell Canada saves the costs associated with physical facilities and duplicated personnel. Second Cup diversified into different markets in the specialty coffee industry by using its core capability—producing high-quality flavoured coffee. It sells its coffee through its coffee houses and other distribution channels (e.g., Harvey's and Swiss Chalet).

The motive of growth rests on the assumption that CEOs and top executives are rational human beings—that is, they act in the best interests of shareholders to maximize long-term shareholder value. In the real business world, however, that assumption is tenuous. Quite often, CEOs and top executives act in their own self-interest. Specifically, there are huge incentives for executives to increase the size of their firm, and many of these are hardly consistent with increasing shareholder wealth. In particular, when executives' compensations are based on their firm's short-term performance, they are likely to pursue diversification in an attempt to boost their compensation at the cost of putting their firms in vulnerable positions in the long term.

The motives driven from inter-firm dynamics include market power enhancement, response to competition and imitation. When a firm pursues diversification and related diversification (see the definition of related diversification following), the firm can increase its market power within the industry it operates in. In this case, market power can come from increases in market share or revenue. As such, the firm can be in a better position to negotiate better prices or higher quality with its suppliers due to higher volume of purchases. The firm can therefore have more leverage to compete against its competitors. Similarly, diversifying into different markets can be due to the intense competition a firm experiences. When competition within an industry intensifies, a firm can either diversify into related markets or pursue vertical integration (see the definition of vertical integration following). Diversifying into related markets allows the firm to sustain growth or enhance revenue. Pursuing vertical integration provides a means for the firm to secure and control their raw materials or distribution channels. Finally, diversification can be driven by inter-firm imitation that can be independent of economic motives (e.g., growth, profitability, securing supply). Research has shown that firms are likely to adopt the diversification strategy when highly successful firms, large firms, or their comparable firms have adopted the strategy; even other firms pursuing diversification have experienced poor performance. Such imitation can lead to firms in dangerous positions in that diversification may not be consistent with either their short-term or long-term objectives. Eventually, it could fail the firms in the marketplace.

Types of Diversification

There are three major types of diversification—related, unrelated and vertical integration. Related diversification refers to the situation where a firm expands its core businesses or markets into related businesses or markets. Such an expansion usually involves horizontal integration across different business or market domains. It enables a firm to benefit from economies of scope and enjoy greater revenues if these businesses attain higher levels of sales growth combined than either firm could attain independently. By diversifying into related markets, a firm can create synergies through sharing activities (e.g., production facilities, distribution channels, sale representatives) and leverage its resources and capabilities. Related diversification also potentially gives a firm greater market power to compete against its competitors and greater bargaining power over its suppliers and customers.

The recent announcement of Lowe's entry to Canada is an example of related diversification. Lowe is a home renovation components retailer. It is a market leader in the U.S. home renovation market and has a reputation of excellent service and product quality. By entering Canadian markets, Lowe creates synergies for its own firm through leveraging its resources and capabilities. Its bargaining power over suppliers is also enhanced in that its potential high volume of purchases would enable Lowe to demand lower prices or higher quality of its suppliers. Similarly, one of the core capabilities embedded in Procter & Gamble is marketing competence. Many times, Procter & Gamble has successfully used its marketing competence to promote different but related products to increase customer loyalty and then increase customers' psychological switching costs, which in turn give Procter & Gamble more bargaining power with customers and help increase its revenues.

The second type of diversification is unrelated diversification, where a firm diversifies into a new market that is not similar to its current market domains. This kind of unrelated diversification tends to provide little synergies for a firm, given that there are few opportunities for sharing activities or leveraging resources and capabilities. An extreme example of such diversification is holding companies. Onex Corporation, one of the biggest holding companies in Canada, is involved in different industries, ranging from electronic manufacturing, health-care insurance, consumer care products, to transportation and logistics. Then, why do firms pursue unrelated diversification? A firm pursuing unrelated diversification tends to have (or believe) the synergies created (or to be created) through corporate office's management skills. Specifically, management skills in restructuring and financial controls allow a corporation to potentially maximize financial returns of each business unit and the corporation as a whole. When a particular business unit no longer provides financial returns to the corporation, it would be divested by the corporation in order to ensure the corporation's overall profitability.

The final type of diversification is vertical integration. Vertical integration refers to an extension or expansion of firm value chain activities by integrating preceding or successive productive processes (see Exhibit 9.6). That is, the firm incorporates more processes toward the source of raw materials (backward integration) or toward the ultimate customers (forward integration). For example, M&M Meat Shop, instead of selling its products through grocery stores, has its own retail stores to serve its customers. Ben & Jerry sells its ice cream products both through its own retail stores and Loblaws, Sobey's, and other supermarkets.

Clearly, vertical integration can be a viable strategy for many firms. It provides firms with benefits including securing raw materials or distribution channels, protecting and controlling over valuable assets, and reducing dependence on suppliers or distributors. By absorbing preceding or successive processes into a firm, the firm has better control over the prices and quality. Sometimes, it can increase the profit margins, especially when suppliers' or distributors' markets are highly profitable. Most important, the firm would have strategic control in terms of its overall strategic direction. As shown in Talking Business 9.5, Apple intends to offer Apple's experience to its customers through its own retail stores. This is consistent with the overall strategy Apple has been pursuing. Relying upon other means of distribution fails to deliver a complete Apple experience to its customers, which in turn may erode Apple's market performance. That said, there are risks associated with vertical integration. One of the major risks is increasing administrative costs associated with managing a more complex set of activities. As a firm absorbing new activities into its internal structure, the complexity of administration further increases. The increases in complexity can come from additional physical facilities; coordination between units, departments, or divisions; monitoring employees; and so on. Accordingly, carefully managing vertical integration is needed.

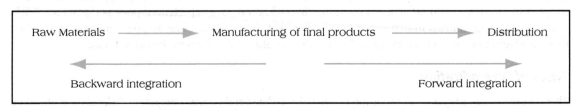

EXHIBIT 9.6 Two types of vertical integration.

Talking Business 9.5

Apple Retail Stores

On May 20, 2005, Apple Computer opened its first retail store in Canada at Yorkdale Mall, Toronto, Ontario. Although opening its own store triggered significant reaction from Apple's retailers in Ontario, Apple has not been completely satisfied with customer services provided by its retailers. Most important, Apple's intention is to provide a complete Apple experience. As stated in its press release, part of Apple's philosophy in founding the stores is that it wants customers to touch its products, feel them, experience the products before they buy them. In its more than 100 retail store locations over the world, Apple provides various classes that allow customers to get as educated as they choose to be in any given area. Such a forward integration enables Apple to have better control over its customer service and to secure and enhance its market position in the highly competitive personal computer market.

Means to Diversify

There are many ways to achieve diversification, either related or unrelated. Each way has its own advantages and disadvantages. The first is diversification through internal development. For example, Microsoft entered the video game market through its internal development of Xbox, while Sony and Apple opened their own retail stores to compete in the retailing sectors. Through internal development, firms have full control of the process of diversification and solely capture the potential revenue and profitability. That said, internal development has two major disadvantages. First, quite often, diversifying into new markets requires significant resource commitment. If firms do not have slack resources, then they might find it difficult to pursue internal development for diversification. Furthermore, internal development also requires time to develop the capability unique to the new markets. When the time window for the new market opportunity is narrow, firms might miss the opportunity, after developing the capability, to compete in the new market. The second disadvantage is the risk associated with diversification. While internal development allows firms to solely absorb the potential returns, it also implies that the firms have to bear alone the risk associated with diversification.

The second way to achieve diversification is through mergers and acquisitions. In general, mergers refer to two firms merging together to create a new firm with a new identity. Acquisitions refer to a firm's acquiring the majority of shares of another firm. In some cases, the acquired firm will become a division of the acquiring firm. In other cases, the acquired firms still operate independently or retain their brand or firm identity. For example, Johnson & Johnson, one of the leading pharmaceutical and consumer care companies, has pursued many acquisitions in the past decade (including ALZA Corporation, Tibotec-Virco N.V., 3-Dimensional Pharmaceuticals, Egea Biosciences, Inc.). One of its acquisitions was Neutrogena, which retained its brand identity. In fact, acquisition has been viewed as one of Johnson & Johnson's capabilities. Through its acquisition experience, Johnson & Johnson has developed specific capabilities to handle issues associated with acquisitions. Merger and acquisition has been one of the popular ways to diversify into new markets or to enhance market power. The number of mergers and acquisitions in Canada has typically been over 1,000 in each year since 2000. Mergers and acquisitions certainly provide firms with quick access to new resources and capabilities to compete in the new markets. They also allow the firms to increase market power or market share in a relatively short period of time. However, mergers and acquisitions share the same disadvantages as internal development—risk in the new market. Moreover, mergers and acquisitions have their own unique disadvantages or challenges. Quite often, managers face significant challenges in massaging two firms into one in terms of administrative issues and organizational culture. Failure in managing the processes of mergers and acquisitions can create significant employee turnover and can erode firm performance.

Mergers not only provide means for firms to increase market power and acquire new capabilities, they can also help two merged firms save enormous costs, which in turn increases their profit margins, like what Cineplex Galaxy expected in its merger with Famous Players Inc.:

> Cineplex Galaxy LP expects to save as much as $20-million a year in operating costs once its proposed merger with rival Famous Players Inc. is complete, chief executive officer Ellis Jacob said yesterday. Speaking to analysts on a conference call, Mr. Jacob said the merged movie exhibitor will save money by combining its purchasing clout, cutting workers and renegotiating contracts

with suppliers, after the deal closes some time in the third quarter of this year. . . . "Our goal is to choose the best of the best from the people in both companies," he said. The company will also save money by trimming what it pays in professional fees. For example, "we'll only need one audit, not two," Mr. Jacob told the analysts. There might also be opportunities to renegotiate theatre leases when they come up for renewal, he said.

In 2004, the two companies collectively spent $42-million on administrative and management costs—$15-million at Cineplex Galaxy and $27-million at Famous Players. After the merger process is complete, in six to 12 months, Cineplex Galaxy hopes to benefit from a boost in revenue, as well as cost cutting. For instance, the new entity should be able to increase advertising revenue by installing, in many Famous Players theatres, the digital projectors that are now used for "preshow" advertising in Cineplex Galaxy theatres, Mr. Jacob said. . . . Cineplex Galaxy also officially launched its selloff of 35 theatres in the combined group, a process required by the federal Competition Bureau when it granted permission for the merger. Even after the sale of those theatres, the combined company will be by far the biggest movie exhibitor in Canada, with 132 theatres and about 1,300 screens, in six provinces from Quebec to British Columbia.[1]

The third way to achieve diversification is through strategic alliances. **Strategic alliances** refer to two or more firms or organizations working together to achieve certain common goals. Strategic alliances can take various forms and serve various purposes. There are three major forms of strategic alliances: non-equity alliances, equity alliances and joint ventures. Non-equity alliances refer to the participating firms working together based on contractual agreements. Equity alliances refer to one firm having partial ownership in the other firm and the two firms working together to pursue common goals. Finally, **joint ventures** refer to two or more firms contributing to certain resources to form an independent entity. The purposes of strategic alliances can range from marketing activities, to manufacturing production, to distribution arrangements, to research and development.

Generally, strategic alliances provide firms with quick access to new resources and capabilities contributed by alliance partners. (See Talking Business 9.6.) As such, strategic alliances can be less costly and less of a resource commitment. Firms also share risks associated with diversification with alliance partners. On the

Talking Business 9.6
Using Alliances to Obtain New Resources and Capabilities: Evidence from Biovail Corporation

Biovail Corporation, one of the leading biotech and pharmaceutical firms in Canada, has recently initiated many strategic alliances in an attempt to quickly diversify into different market segments. The following are three of its alliance initiatives. Through strategic alliances, Biovail is able to access resources and capabilities of its alliance partners in expanding its market reach.

In April 2002, Ethypharm announced that Biovail had made an equity investment to acquire a minority stake in Ethypharm. This strategic investment will help finance Ethypharm's growth strategies, and further enhance the commercialization of its product portfolio, while giving Biovail access to complementary drug delivery technologies. Biovail has invested approximately € 74 million (US$65 million) to acquire 15% of the issued and outstanding shares of Ethypharm.

In December 2002, Biovail Corporation announced that it had entered into an agreement with Glaxo Group Limited of England (Glaxo) to acquire the Canadian rights to Wellbutrin® SR and Zyban®. Through this agreement and upon marketing approval from Canadian authorities, Biovail has the option to market Wellbutrin® XL, a once-daily bupropion product for the treatment of depression. Wellbutrin® SR is usually prescribed twice daily for the treatment of depression and Zyban® is administered for the treatment of nicotine addiction as an aid to smoking cessation. Both products are formulations of bupropion hydrochloride.

In July 2002, DepoMed entered into a development and license agreement with Biovail that granted to Biovail an exclusive license in the United States (including Puerto Rico) and Canada to manufacture and market DepoMed's Metformin GR(TM). Under the terms of the agreement, DepoMed will be responsible for completing the clinical development program in support of Metformin GR.

other hand, firms will have to share potential revenue or profits with alliance partners. Furthermore, there are some specific risks associated with strategic alliances, with the partner selection in particular. Since alliance partners play a key role in success of strategic alliances, firms need to carefully select the partners in order to achieve their purposes in pursuit of diversification. Quite often, firms choose wrong partners due to the following: (1) the firms misperceive the partners' resources and capabilities; (2) the partners mispresent their resources and capabilities; and (3) the partners behave solely based on their own interests. Altogether, these could significantly impair strategic alliance operations, which ultimately fail to achieve the common purposes.

STRATEGY IN ACTION: THE CASE OF MCDONALD'S

McDonald's Corporation is the largest restaurant company in the world.[2] Formed in 1954, it now operates more than 30,000 restaurants worldwide and has had a tremendous impact on culture and society. It is estimated that McDonald's is responsible for 90% of new jobs in the United States; it hires about one million people annually; it is the largest purchaser of beef, pork and potatoes, and the second largest purchaser of chicken in North America. It is also the largest owner of retail property in the world, while its logo, the "Golden Arches," is more widely recognized than the Christian cross.[3]

Throughout most of its corporate life, McDonald's has been unrivalled in the fast-food industry. However, when stock prices hit a seven-year low in 2002 and the organization posted its first-ever quarterly loss in 2003,[4] it became apparent that the fast-food giant's long run as a growth company had ended, and that it needed to change or risk organizational death. The pressures from drastic changes in market demand have forced McDonald's to transform its leadership, business strategies and corporate culture in an effort to revive the mature brand so that it can continue to effectively compete in today's global economy.

McDonald's big wake-up call for change came in March of 2002. The company was on the brink of disaster. Shares were trading at $13—well below the 52-week high of $30.72; and restaurants were being closed as franchisees saw their profit margins dip from 15% to 4%. At its lowest point, an estimated 20 franchisees left McDonald's every month.[5] In addition to its financial troubles, the company was also struggling with quality issues and poor performance in customer satisfaction. For nine consecutive years, the company ranked dead last in the American Customer Satisfaction Index,[6] and was feeling the consequences of lost market share to its competitors.

McDonald's long-time rivals were turning up the heat and were posting increased earnings and profits during the same period that McDonald's market share was eroding. For example, Wendy's saw its stock soar 57%, and Tricon Global, owners of KFC, Pizza Hut and Taco Bell, enjoyed 65% increases in 2002, whereas shares in McDonald's only rose 4% since April 2001.[7] In addition, new competitors like Quizno's were entering the marketplace, making "fast-casual" the largest growing segment in the restaurant industry.[8]

In an attempt to revive the organization and remain competitive in the industry, the board of directors at McDonald's staged a management shakeup. On December 5, 2002, they ousted chief executive officer Jack M. Greenberg and brought veteran executive Jim Cantalupo out of retirement to turn the company around.[9] Despite shareholders' general preference for an outsider, Cantalupo was the only candidate the board seriously considered, because members felt they needed someone who knew the company well and who could move quickly to respond to the challenges of expanding a mature company in what was a fast-changing consumer landscape.

Cantalupo was a fearless leader who was quick to recognize that "[t]he world has changed. We have to change too."[10] He echoed analysts who argued the organization lacked direction and focus, and that "the McDonald's way" failed to adapt quickly enough to match changing taste patterns.[11] Joined by a younger team of executives, Cantalupo quickly set about to re-energize the mature organization and presented a revitalization plan to decrease capital expenditures, scale back global expansion, raise dividends and lower growth targets.[12]

Under Cantalupo's vision and leadership, the turnaround at McDonald's was to begin by removing company initiatives that didn't successfully focus on the organization's restaurants or customers. This included a movement away from the "Made For You" food preparation system, originally launched in 1998 to improve product quality, but that resulted in doubled waiting times in restaurants.[13] His main focus was to get back to "speed at the drive-through, friendly service, marketing leadership, and product innovation."[14]

To achieve these goals, Cantalupo introduced a revitalization strategy, called "Plan to Win,"[15] which called for sweeping operational changes at the restaurant level. The plan included several initiatives: cutting more than 80 menu options; adjusting prices so that each ended in a zero or a five, for ease of computation on the customer's part; switching to an automated beverage-dispensing system to cut seven hours of labour per week; retrofitting fryers with a device that automatically cleans and changes oil, for a savings of 14 crew hours per week; packaging burgers in boxes instead of wrapping them, to cut serving time; and adding more premium menu options such as a new grilled-chicken sandwich on a whole-wheat bun and the McGriddle breakfast sandwich.[16] Many of these changes were aimed at achieving "restaurant optimization" and also focused heavily on reducing serving times at the restaurants. In the fast-food industry, promptness of service is a critical component that has a direct impact on the bottom line. According to former CEO Greenberg, saving six seconds at a drive-through increases sales 1%.[17]

The operational changes from Cantalupo's optimization program resulted in dramatic improvements to McDonald's service speeds. Wait times at the drive-through were reduced from 130 seconds to 99 seconds, while walk up customers got their orders in 30 seconds.[18] Although these operational improvements were a step in the right direction, Cantalupo realized that a successful transformation could not be achieved without changing McDonald's corporate culture.

According to Cantalupo, first and foremost, McDonald's has had to change the way that it viewed growth:

> For the past 49 years, the company lived by building new restaurants and changing that into a culture and perspective of bringing more customers into your existing restaurants—it's a whole culture change and then accepting the fact you might not be a 15% growth company and setting more realistic growth targets.[19]

To facilitate this change in growth perception, at a meeting between analysts, investors and journalists, McDonald's admitted that it was all grown up rather than trying to convince investors that it could maintain its history of powerful growth. In April 2003, the company announced that store openings would be pared to 360 from a high of 2,585 in 1996.[20] Its sales growth estimates were slashed from 15% to only 2%, and only 250 new outlets were planned for the United States—40% fewer than in 2002.[21]

The logic behind these unprecedented moves was to bring more customers into restaurants that were already up and running instead of spending billions each year to open new ones[22]—the latter of which reduces both market share and profits from existing locations. According to Cantalupo, "We have to rebuild the foundation. It's fruitless to add growth if the foundation is weak."[23] For that reason, McDonald's management is pouring money back into *existing* stores, cleaning up their appearance, extending hours and speeding up service.[24] All of these improvements are expected to attract "more customers, more often" while encouraging them to be more brand loyal.[25]

Another piece of this optimization strategy has been to reinstate a tough grading system that will kick out underperforming franchisees. The decline in McDonald's service and quality can be traced to its rapid expansion in the 1990s when headquarters stopped grading franchises for cleanliness, speed and service, and to when training declined as a result of a tight labour market.[26] As a result, McDonald's is now enforcing a program that uses mystery shoppers and unannounced inspections to assess restaurants on these key areas. Owners that fail the rating and inspection system will be given a chance to clean up their act, but, if they don't improve, they will lose their franchises.

The final and perhaps most critical component of McDonald's revitalization strategy has been to instill a customer perspective that focuses on and responds to changing customer demands. This is a very common strategy often used by mature organizations that are trying to achieve renewal. Cantalupo best expressed McDonald's commitment to focusing on customer needs, when he stated the following:

> We are a mass marketer. When you are that, or decide to be that, you have to broaden your appeal . . . Our focus is going to continue to be on our customers and what they're looking for. We're going to listen to them. We're going to give them choice and variety and try the best we can to satisfy as many of their needs as we can because that's what's going to build our business.[27]

The most significant change in consumer demands that has affected McDonald's resulted from the dramatic change of societal attitudes toward the fast food industry in recent years. For example, fat has become a major concern not only in North America but globally as well. In 2001, the Surgeon General declared a public health crisis and announced that 61% of the American population was overweight, causing 300,000 deaths a year.[28] In Europe, obesity was reported as the single biggest health challenge of the 21st century by the International Obesity Taskforce, which recommended that restrictions be placed on the targeting of young children to consume inappropriate food and drink.[29] At the request of national governments needing to reduce the burden on their health services, the World Health Organization also published a wide-ranging report on obesity and nutrition. Among its recommendations were reducing the demand for high-sugar and high-fat foods; increasing the use of recommended daily amounts of nutrients on packaging; and more controversially, the idea that governments consider levying taxes to control the sale of foods deemed unhealthy.[30]

Negative media reports have also compounded this situation. McDonald's has been forced to deal with the fallout of events such as the "Government's War on Obesity,"[31] the 2002 class action lawsuit brought against McDonald's by a group of overweight children seeking compensation for obesity-related problems,[32] and most recently, the release of the documentary, *Super Size Me,* which details the dangers of what can happen if someone were to eat nothing but fast food for an entire month.[33]

The overall results of these events have led to the restaurant industry changing its ways due to fears that it could become the next foodservice version of "Big Tobacco," with hefty lawsuits to match.[34] McDonald's has specifically responded to the changing consumer demands with a host of healthy initiatives, including the introduction of a line of premium salads,[35] developing more "wholesome food choices," such as substituting apple slices for fries in Happy Meals,[36] and producing ads on children's TV that star Willie Munchright to advise kids on balanced eating and exercise.[37]

The organization has also decided to shrink its menu as part of a broader initiative to streamline choices and provide customers with healthier alternatives. This includes phasing out 2% milk, 1.25-litre soft drinks and the 400-gram fruit-and-yogurt parfait.[38] Other recent efforts include eliminating the "super size" option from menus, using white chicken meat in McNuggets, and introducing a "Go Active! Adult Happy Meal" featuring a salad, a bottle of Dasani water and a "stepometer" to track the daily steps to measure physical activity.[39] The company is also using a new oil that reduces trans-fatty acids by 48% and saturated fats by 16%.[40]

McDonald's healthy lifestyle plan also includes partnerships with nutrition and fitness experts to fulfill a commitment to help consumers lead healthier, active lives. For example, in April 2004 the company launched an exercise and diet marketing campaign with Bob Greene, Oprah Winfrey's personal trainer.[41] Other global marketing initiatives have included a new tagline, "I'm lovin' it," with MTV-style commercials that are targeted at women, and regional advertising, ranging from billboards to ads in magazines like *O* and *Marie Claire* that recommend McDonald's salads, milk and juices to women who are concerned with nutrition.[42] These new menu choices are McDonald's attempts to change its image of offering only junk food, and are a way of appealing to women, who are considered to drive change with regard to eating patterns.[43]

Furthermore, in response to increasing pressures from politicians and lobbyists, McDonald's responded to the changing environment by retooling its corporate Web site to provide consumers with fat and calorie profiles of whole meals rather than individual items. Consumers can now select up to five menu items and place them in a virtual bag where a nutritional profile is calculated. McDonald's is also considering adding nutritional information to all its wrappings and is thinking about integrating healthy-eating messages into its ads as part of a plan to tackle the obesity allegations leveled against it.[44]

To date, the outcome of McDonald's multi-pronged turnaround strategy has been very positive. The company posted a fourth-quarter profit in 2004, one year after its first-ever quarterly loss[45] and sales at stores that have been open for more than a year rose 7.4%, while same-store sales rose 2.4% compared with a decline of 2.1% in 2002.[46] It is reported that McDonald's sold more than 150 million orders from its new salad menu,[47] accounting for up to 6% of the company's increased sales.[48] According to Mary Vega Nichols, a McDonald's franchisee, "[McDonald's] is seeing a big sales increase from the additions to the menu. Frequency has increased because [customers] can come and eat every day. They have a choice now."[49]

Although McDonald's turnaround strategy appears to have resulted in a successful rebound of the fast-food giant, the company still needs to prove to its customers that it has transformed. For example, while McDonald's customer ratings are up overall, its outlets still trail competitors in critical areas such as line waits, order accuracy and store cleanliness.[50] Food quality also continues to be a problem and still comes in last for taste and quality of ingredients.[51]

In addition, the company has recently experienced hardship concerning its leadership team, which has stakeholders wondering whether McDonald's can keep the turnaround on track. Only 16 months into his leadership term, Cantalupo died unexpectedly of a heart attack in late April 2004. Two weeks later, the company was forced to disclose that its new CEO and president, Charles H. Bell, Cantalupo's right-hand man and successor, had colorectal cancer.[52] The revelations have shaken investor and franchisee confidence in the organization's ability to continue the revitalization process and have resulted in flat share prices since the announcements.

However, even in the face of this adversity, McDonald's is continuing to press forward with its efforts to revitalize the organization. For 2004, fast, accurate and friendly service remained a key issue for CEO Charles Bell. He is planning to remodel as many as 1,800 of 13,600 U.S. restaurants to create a more welcoming and contemporary ambience, and keep them open 24 hours.[53] He is also introducing a new payment system that will allow customers to make purchases by credit card at more than 8,000 restaurants by year-end. These initiatives are intended to boost sales and speed service.

The company is also continuing to follow the three key strategies outlined in Cantalupo's revitalization plan: to right the ship by returning McDonald's to the operational excellence and leadership marketing for which it was once famous; to align the system around the company's "Plan to Win" program, as a way to revitalize the brand and make it more relevant to a broader group of people by consistently delivering exceptional customer experiences; and to manage for financial strength by reducing capital spending and using the money remaining to pay down debt and return cash to shareholders.[54]

It is clear that there is a firm commitment at McDonald's to re-energize the mature organization and transform it into one that will grow and sustain itself well into the 21st century. The company has taken many positive steps toward changing its leadership, business strategies and corporate culture in order to achieve its objectives of attracting new customers, encouraging repeat sales, building brand loyalty and creating enduring profitable growth. Only time will tell in terms of whether McDonald's can continue to adapt itself successfully to a changing environment.

CHAPTER SUMMARY

How to develop strategy is a critical task that managers face. Managers need to constantly assess both the internal and external environments to formulate appropriate strategy in order to sustain their firm performance and survival. In this chapter, we discussed two models that help managers to effectively assess the environment—Michael Porter's five-forces model and Jay Barney's VRIO model. In using these models, managers can identify opportunities and threats in the external environment as well as strengths and weaknesses embedded within their firms. Business-level strategy focuses on how to compete in a given market, including cost leadership, product differentiation and focus. Corporate-level strategy emphasizes creating synergies through diversification, such as related and unrelated diversifications and vertical integration.

CONCEPT APPLICATION

STARBUCKS TARGETS QUEBEC'S 'CAFÉ CULTURE'

S. John Tilak

Colin Moore, Starbucks' Americas president, said the world's largest coffee chain is targeting Quebec and the Atlantic provinces, which together he sees as a huge untapped market.

Starbucks Corp. opened its first Canadian store in Vancouver—a three-hour drive from its Seattle headquarters—in 1987, and most of the 1,070 stores the company now operates in Canada are in Ontario and the Western provinces.

It has fewer than 50 stores in Quebec, a market that has traditionally been a tough one to crack for non-francophone businesses.

"We have aggressive growth plans for Quebec and the Atlantic provinces," Moore told Reuters in an interview.

He said the push could see Starbucks bring its Quebec store count to more than 200, but did not say when expansion to that number would be complete.

Quebec has "a good espresso consumer café culture" and would be "a great fit for Starbucks," he added.

Moore, 55, oversees Starbucks' operations in Canada and Latin America and is based in Toronto. Starbucks opened its first Toronto store in 1996 and expanded rapidly. It has 340 stores in Ontario.

The growth has resulted in market share improvement.

"We're making gains in the total share of stomach," said Moore, a Canadian who says his favourite drink is a vanilla latte.

"We're far and away the largest player in the specialty category."

The company's main rivals in Canada are Second Cup Ltd. and Tim Hortons Inc. Second Cup has about 350 stores. Tim Hortons, an iconic name in the country, has more than 3,000 restaurants in Canada.

Starbucks' expansion plans come as the price of coffee beans soars and coffee chains raise prices globally. Starbucks is the only major coffee chain in Canada that has not announced plans to pass on the higher cost of the commodity to its customers.

"We're trying to hold the line on pricing," Moore said, adding the company has enough inventory globally to take it through to September.

Moore said Starbucks was also pursuing more growth in Latin America, where many of the countries are coffee producers.

Brazil, a coffee-producing country, is likely the company's most underserved market.

"Brazil is a huge opportunity—coffee drinking, coffee producing, very strong economy, strong currency. We have a very embryonic presence in the country," Moore said. Starbucks has only 25 stores there.

"It is destiny that Brazil would be a larger market for Starbucks than Canada over time," said Moore, who is looking at a five- to 10-year horizon for that to play out.

TIM HORTONS TIPTOES INTO STARBUCKS TERRITORY

Coffeehouse Tim Hortons is making a cautious foray into the Starbucks zone, doing a test market run selling espressos, cappucinos and lattes in what could lead to the "Walmartization" of specialty coffees.

At a handful of stores in the Toronto area, the biggest coffee chain in Canada has launched its own version of the specialty Italian beverages at prices significantly below that of its specialty coffee chain competitors.

The move highlights the growing popularity of espresso drinks, whose sales have increased more than 20% in the last year, according to market researcher NPD Group Canada. "There is continued strong growth in the specialty coffee market," said Jane Graham, general manager of food service at NPD.

If Tim Hortons, with more than 2,500 outlets in Canada, decides to do a countrywide rollout of the drinks, it could affect Starbucks' continued penetration into smaller urban markets, retail experts say. The quick-serve restaurant chain is the top seller of brewed coffee in Canada, and derives close to half of its sales from the hot liquid.

Starbucks Corp. has about 600 outlets in Canada.

"This could pre-empt a move by Starbucks into smaller markets to a certain extent," said Richard Talbot, president of Unionville, Ont.-based Talbot Consultants.

"People's tastes have changed and they are more educated about European coffee. If you are selling coffee now and not offering, [espresso drinks] you are a bit out of step with the rest of the industry across Canada. But the key here will be the quality—people will try a latte from Tim's but if it's not up to par they won't go back."

Mr. Talbot said in a typical retail life cycle, a product—for example, roller blades, will enter the market through specialty retailers and remain there for years before it achieves widespread

(Continued)

demand and is adopted by mass retailers, such as Canadian Tire and Wal-Mart, which offer the item at lower prices.

Tim's is selling lattes and cappucinos for $1.99 (medium), $2.39 (large) and $2.69 (extra large) before tax. By comparison, similarly sized drinks at Starbucks cost $2.90, $3.65 and $4.05 respectively.

At Tim's, the espresso and milk are doled out automatically by a machine that grinds up the fresh beans before it pours a shot. Starbucks also dispenses espresso shots from an auto-mated machine (in more traditional cafés, ground espresso is poured into a hand-held filter and compressed into a puck shape before it is inserted into an espresso machine). Starbucks and competitor Second Cup offer myriad drink permutations from there, including an option for decaffeinated and choices on everything from the fat or lactose content of milk to the amount of foam and the heat level of the drink.

Tim's options are basic: caffeinated espresso drinks made with 2% milk in a variety of sizes.

Ken Wong, a marketing professor at Queen's University in Kingston, Ont., doubts many Starbucks aficionados will switch to Tim's if the chain begins to widely offer its low-priced espressos.

"Starbucks had always marketed the experience as much as the beverage. It has been about sitting in the cafe and enjoying the ambience while sipping on your latte. Tim Hortons is more about convenience and saving time. I don't think this would have a sizable impact in terms of increasing [Tim's] customer base."

Tim Hortons will gauge consumer reaction to the market test for several months before it makes a decision about whether to add espresso drinks to its menu, said spokesman Greg Skinner.

In the meantime, investors are eagerly awaiting the initial public offering of Tim Hortons shares, set for March on the Toronto and New York stock exchanges. The issue has yet to be priced.

Questions:

1. Making any assumptions required, discuss the coffee industry with regard to Porter's Five Forces Model.
2. Conduct a VRIO analysis of Starbucks using any assumptions required.
3. Discuss which of the three kinds of business strategy you think Starbucks and Tim Horton's employ.

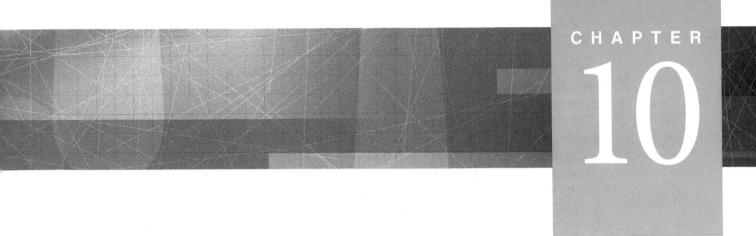

Confronting Changing Contexts*

To succeed in today's business environment requires the ability to quickly adapt to changing market conditions. Consequently, it is fitting that we devote specific attention to a discussion of the nature of change. What does change entail? What are the forces for change? We will examine the methods adopted to facilitate change. Within this discussion, the concept of the "learning organization" will be explored. In addition, we will consider how organizations may facilitate or impede change. The chapter ends with a discussion of the issue of change in the context of organizational mergers.

LEARNING OBJECTIVES

By the end of the chapter, you should be able to:

1. Consider the forces encouraging change in organizations.
2. Understand the value of Theory E and Theory change.
3. Examine the process of transformational change.
4. Explain the relationship of learning with organizational change.
5. Identify the role of "the tipping point" and its impact on change.

THE BUSINESS WORLD

This revolution is changing companies

Michael Slaby

The social media revolution—the phenomenon that has my mother friend-ing me on Facebook and asking me what "following on Twitter" means—is more about society than it is about media. In a similar way, the differences in the ways small businesses and big enterprises engage social media are more about social structure and organizational dynamics than they are about media tactics.

Social media is fundamentally a shift in the culture and the expectations of how people consume and, more importantly, participate in media. In a world where communications must contend with an audience that expects an opportunity to engage, expects that an organization will listen

(Continued)

---

*I am grateful to Professor Igor Kotlyar, University of Ontario, who served as co-author for this chapter.

and converse, and expect people's voices to be amplified as loud or louder than those of media outlets, how we communicate is fundamentally different from the broadcast-driven, one-way silos we grew to accept over the latter part of the 20th century.

Social media forces organizations to reconsider not just where, when, and how they communicate, but why. We tend to get caught up in discussions about platforms and tactics. We argue over questions like "should I be on Twitter?" or "does my CEO need to be writing a blog?" or "how should we be using Facebook?" But we need to ask "why" first.

This will drive us to question who we are as an organization and what our purpose is.

The business school definition of corporations—entities that exist to maximize shareholder value—is no longer a sufficient framework for driving organizational strategy and it is definitely not an effective communications strategy. If we believe that social behaviours in media have altered the expectations of the people with whom we want and need to communicate, are we willing to participate with them, and do we genuinely believe in the value and power of that engagement?

If the answer to those questions is yes, and we have spent time thinking about the values and missions of our organizations and the role of communities in driving our goals, we can start asking how leveraging social media platforms and programs can help us engage the communities—internal and external, big and small—that are essential to our success.

As companies of all sizes pose these questions, the biggest differences in the answers they find lay in the social structure at play in the organizations. In order to engage in social spaces, businesses must be prepared to engage in more open dialogue about themselves, their products, and sometimes their competition than they are typically used to. They will absolutely be forced to collaborate more efficiently internally than most of them have ever even attempted.

A person asking a question of your organization on your Facebook wall doesn't care about your org chart. My mom isn't going to hunt through your sitemap to track down the right expert on her problem—if I'm lucky she'll try to ask you instead of calling me. She doesn't care that the marketing department manages the Facebook presence, or that there is an entirely separate process she is supposed to follow to solve her problem. She has a question, she's asked you, and it's up to you to find ways to collaborate within your organization to connect the marketing departments and customer service group to answer her—if you want to keep her as a customer.

In this way, big enterprises often find social media engagement more internally disruptive than more agile smaller organizations—especially as they take their first steps.

The second reality of social media engagement is that for organizations used to the 20th century media landscape of silos and one-way communications, they more than likely lack some of the subject-area expertise and tactical understanding required to execute digital communications and social media effectively. In small organizations where employees often wear multiple hats and function in multiple roles, expanding into an entirely new area of expertise on top of existing tasks can be daunting at best and impossible at worst.

Big enterprises that have and can expand specialized employees more readily may be able to extend their internal capabilities more quickly. Additionally, they can often lean outside agencies for expertise and strategic guidance, training, and consulting to ease the internal evolution required to align with the new realities of social media engagement.

Social media can help any organization create more meaningful relationships with the communities around them—employees, customers and partners. Fundamentally it isn't about size of audience or opportunity, it's really about what social media does to a company and what the organization is capable of that defines the different challenges. Engagement is always about a willingness to listen, telling compelling and authentic stores, and a genuine desire to participate.

In the end the essential understanding is that participating in social spaces is about being more engaged, not appearing more engaged.

Source: Special to The Globe and Mail

CHANGE AND THE ENVIRONMENT OF BUSINESS

"The Business World" article underscores the significant challenges organizations face in confronting a changing environment. What are the sources of change directed at organizations? How do these changes affect the nature of organizations and work? In every chapter in this book, from management thought to business ethics, we have, often, recognized that just about every important area of business is undergoing some kind of change. How is the organizational environment changing? Consider a number of issues addressed in this book, including issues like globalization, free trade, deregulation, privatization, the changing emphasis on corporate social responsibility. Much of what we have addressed involves issues that are undergoing dramatic change.

Regardless of the target for the change, it is critical to understand what factors in the organization's environment dictate the need for change.

Forces for Change

As discussed in Chapter 1, organizations are open systems that are in continual interaction with their external environment. Success and survival require organizations to continually develop a "fit" with their dynamic and evolving environment. Consequently, the ability to change, is central to the success of any organization. On the other hand, there is a paradox at play—while change is ultimately required in order to adapt to a changing environment, the success of any organization depends on the capability to maintain stable and reproducible organizational processes and outcomes. See Exhibit 10.1 for an illustration of the forces for change, which we discuss next.

1. Economic Changes

Is the economy healthy or weak? Clearly, organizations must adapt to changing economic conditions. Downsizings are more likely to occur in lean times than in rich. Organizational expansion cannot occur in an economic vacuum, as the following indicates:

> We have watched what the new workplace rules mean in periods of economic expansion. The decade long boom of the 1990s occurred just as downsizing became de rigueur at American companies. The greater efficiency with which companies allocated their human resources spurred enormous gains in economic growth and productivity. Companies hired contract consultants who could deliver specific expertise on a project, and they hired temporaries to handle the surge periods of the business day.[1]

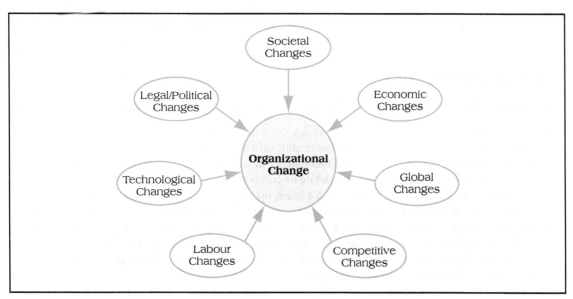

EXHIBIT 10.1 Forces for change.

This quote alludes to a few of the changes that resulted from changing economic circumstances. Certainly, such changes have also facilitated changes to the nature of the employer-employee relationship. Lifetime employment appears to be a thing of the past. Consider the 1950s or the 1970s: these were actually times where employment meant security. The dominant model was long-term employment—stability. However, a change to this implicit employment contract occurred sometime in the 1980s. And, as we identified in an earlier chapter, the age of downsizing began—with large, secure organizations beginning to lay off employees. Part-time and temporary work arrangements have become much more common than in the past:

> Organizations are typically responding to this challenging new organization world by becoming preoccupied with improving performance and bottom line results while losing sight of the importance of a people/performance balance in achieving lasting success. In these organizations, slashing costs, continuous restructuring, downsizing, trying endless quick fix programs and solutions, announcing new visions, values, and goals that everyone is expected to embrace, and lots of well intended talk about the importance of people and values is becoming common place. It is a push, cut, slash, slice, talk, quick fix management mentality and strategy that places a high emphasis on performance and a low emphasis on people and often creates an illusion of doing well while the organization is regressing and in some cases unraveling! It appear to employees to be a "built to sell or built to fail" strategy that assumes that you can manage or shrink your way to success.[2]

We have also witnessed a change with regard to the pattern of career movement within an organization. Traditionally, employees attempted to move up the corporate hierarchy throughout their career. However, the flattening of many organizational hierarchies has tended to substitute horizontal or lateral career movement for the former vertical movement, so that you might move around an organization into different areas rather than directly up the hierarchy. The following quote reflects the new era of the "free agent":

> Employees and workers must view their careers in terms of what skills they can offer. As individual identity has become uncoupled from a particular company, people have focused on functional career areas, such as law, human resources, financial, sales and marketing, and manufacturing. In the 1990s, professional associations and functional groupings have seen explosive membership gains. More and more people have sought community and networking opportunities in the company of like-minded career professionals.[3]

Companies that don't address economic change effectively, are unlikely to survive (see Talking Business 10.1).

2. Competitive Changes

Chapter 4 underscored the importance of identifying how industries change or evolve over time. Competitive processes do evolve, and understanding what to expect and what drives evolution along the lifecycle of an industry

Talking Business 10.1

Economic Change: A&P (Great Atlantic & Pacific Tea Co.) Supermarket

A&P, like many grocers, struggled with the weak economy, reduced spending by consumers and more and more lower priced competition from nontraditional food retailers like warehouse clubs, discount chains such as Wal-Mart Stores Inc., and dollar stores. It was a giant in its time, but somehow didn't change with the changing economic times, while its competition did change.

In 2011, the U.S.'s oldest grocer filed for bankruptcy protection after years of struggling with enormous debt, falling sales and rising competition from low-priced peers. A&P operated almost 400 supermarkets under names including Waldbaum's, Food Emporium and Pathmark. The tougher economy meant that buyers looked elsewhere for better prices, including megaretailers like Wal-Mart and Target, wholesale clubs and drugstores. A shift in consumer spending to wholesale clubs, drugstores and supercenters hurt sales badly in recent years.

Sources: http://www.businesspundit.com/ap-bankruptcy-was-a-long-time-coming/; http://www.bloomberg.com/news/2010-12-12/a-p-grocery-store-owner-files-for-bankruptcy-as-competition-heightens.html.

is critical for surviving turbulent times. As we identified in Chapter 4, there are major phases and milestones that mark an industry's evolutionary path from emergence and shakeout to maturity and decline. At each stage of the industry lifecycle, the organizational skills and capabilities needed to survive and grow change in significant ways.

Organizations must adapt to change as competition evolves in markets from fragmented and fast-growing to concentrated and declining. In addition, competition, both domestic and foreign, certainly has demanded an acceleration in innovation among firms in many industries. Organizations, to compete effectively, must continually create new and better methods of serving customers. For example, while globalization has opened up larger markets for businesses, it has also facilitated much higher levels of competition. Globalization, as discussed elsewhere in this book, opened the floodgates for competitors. Clearly, the number of competitors and the nature of competition will dictate changes in organizational strategy (see Talking Business 10.2).

3. Technological Changes

Technology is both a continuously changing variable and one that permits and demands organizational change. One scholar observed the following:

> In recent years, there has been considerable discussion of whether the development and application of information and communications technology have changed the . . . economy in a fundamental way, promising a golden future of rapid growth, low unemployment and inflation, perpetual economic expansion, and a booming stock market. The change is sometimes called the "Information Revolution"; more commonly, it is called the "New Economy." . . . As the economy absorbs any new technology, what typically happens first is that existing economic activities are performed at lower cost. E-commerce is no exception . . . Only a few firms have gone through the deep organizational changes needed to become web-based organizations, but those that have done so have achieved remarkable results, like cutting administrative costs by 75 percent.[4]

Talking Business 10.2

Competitive Change: Facebook Knocks Out MySpace

- MySpace has fallen from great heights and the once dominant social network looks set to be sold by parent company NewsCorp, meaning it could possibly become obsolete altogether as consumer interest in the site wanes. The site was slow to innovate, had no real understanding about itself as a brand, held minimal financial control and seemed unable to keep up with its ever-ageing audience. For example, MySpace was also slow to adopt technologies such as Ajax, which allows users to send messages without the need to open a new browser window; programs to import e-mail address books into friends lists; and instant messaging. Facebook trumped it on all three.

  (EXCERPTED FROM: http://www.marketingweek.co.uk/sectors/media/four-reasons-why-myspace-failed-to-retain-the-social-network-crown/3022208.article (this article speaks to the lack of innovation))

- In 2004, like everyone else, MySpace wasn't sure what would make a social network click. So it let its members figure it out, offering them to design their own pages with widgets, songs, videos, and whatever design they pleased. The result was a wasteland of cluttered and annoying pages that were as garish as the self-designed home pages on MySpace's 1.0 predecessor, Geocities. Facebook, meanwhile, opted for a cleaner, Google-like interface that resonated with a broader audience. The design was predominantly blue and white, and the company rolled out features piecemeal: email, instant messaging and then live feeds of their activities. The platform was unadorned, intuitive, structured to reflect how people were already communicating online—and in contrast to MySpace's anything-goes approach, it was soothingly Spartan. So while MySpace appealed to the early adopters of social networking sites, Facebook resonated more with a more mainstream audience. At its peak in 2006, MySpace had more than 100 million unique users per month in 2006, a number that has declined to 70 million in 2010, according to News Corp.'s SEC filings (NWS).

  (EXCERPTED FROM: http://tech.fortune.cnn.com/2010/11/19/how-facebook-learned-from-myspaces-mistakes/)

Technology has been a double-edged sword for business—bringing both benefits and threats. It can create new industries and destroy old ones (see Talking Business 10.3). Benefits from technology have also included the ability to gain more flexibility in work arrangements such as the practice of telework:

> The idea of telecommuting isn't new, but companies still have a long way to go to fully exploit the benefits of a networked economy. Indianapolis pharmaceutical company Eli Lilly and Co. lets all its knowledge workers work from home occasionally, and a formal telework program lets a smaller number of employees keep their primary offices at home. Such telecommuting generally had been considered a concession to work-life balance, but these days, the company is also thinking about it as a means to drive productivity, say Candi Lange, director of workforce partnering. "We bring in such smart people who are responsible for so much important work in the company," she says. "Why not let them control their own schedules as well?"[5]

Part-time work has increased dramatically in recent years, and we also continue to see the increasing use of compressed workweeks and flex-time—all in all, this means that the nine-to-five job is certainly no longer a fixed rule.

4. Labour Force Changes

Business must understand and respond to changing demographics in the working population. Immigrants who came to Canada in the 1990s have accounted for approximately 70 percent of the total growth of the

Talking Business 10.3
Technological Change: Polaroid

- It was a wonder in its time: A camera that spat out photos that developed themselves in a few minutes as you watched. You got to see them where and when you took them, not a week later when the prints came back from the drugstore. But in a day when nearly every cellphone has a digital camera in it, "instant" photography long ago stopped being instant enough for most people. So today, the inevitable end of an era came: Polaroid is getting out of the Polaroid business.

  (EXCERPTED FROM: http://thelede.blogs.nytimes.com/2008/02/08polaroid-abandons-instant-photography/?hp)

- Polaroid was the leader of an amazing niche technology—instant film photography—but went bankrupt in 2008 because it misread the impact of digital imaging on their highly profitable instant film business. Polaroid misread the shift in people's preferences and the impact of digital imaging on their highly profitable instant film business.

  (EXCERPTED FROM http://www.spruancegroup.com/blog/bid/32860/Polavision-Polaroid-s-disruptive-innovation-failure)

- Polaroid missed the boat on the digital camera evolution. Around the late 90's when digital cameras were really becoming popular, and companies were making their forays into that area, Polaroid decided to stick with its proprietary technology, instant photography. . . (Knox). Polaroid eventually did develop digital imaging technology, but introduced it into the market late, which caused more of a loss than a profit for the company. Additionally, Polaroid failed to improve its base technology.

  (EXCERPTED FROM (http://www.planetpapers.com/Assets/4467.php))

- Polaroid continued to see digital as an "outer ring" relative to the company's core business of instant photography. Management believed that instant imaging would continue to be their main competitive weapon. Resource allocation, effort and energy were still centered on chemical film imaging. Digital was supported as a secondary product offering (Pruyne and Rosenbloom, 1997). Subsequently, digital products and technology exploded on the market and eclipsed film and instant imaging. Polaroid was ill equipped to compete in this market, as its attention to digital had been an afterthought, overshadowed by the company's dedication to chemical film. The core competencies of the firm, chemical R & D, were ineffective in the new market structure, and the firm's capabilities relative to digital were weak, relative to many rivals.

  (EXCERPTED FROM: http://etd.ohiolink.edu/send-pdf.cgi/Weisenbach%20Keller%20Eileen%20Dolores.pdf?kent1133196965 (p. 2–3)) labour force in recent years. Women also comprise a significant component of the Canadian labour force and account for about half of both the employed work force and all union members. Visible minorities and people with disabilities, together with women, make up over 60 percent of Canada's labour force. Diversity in our work force is also reflected in the growing presence of older workers. All these issues need to be considered in designing effective corporate policy. (See Talking Business 10.4.)

Talking Business 10.4

More Women in the Workplace is Good For Business

Deborah Gillis

The heads of many of Canada's largest corporations are concerned about a significant business issue: the underrepresentation of women at senior levels.

Last week, Catalyst Canada played host to more than 500 prominent business leaders at an event celebrating three champions of women in business. These senior leaders convened to discuss the importance of advancing talented women—not because they have quotas to fill but because they recognize that the underrepresentation of women in leadership roles is a serious issue.

Given that women make up almost half of the work force and are now earning more than half of the university degrees, senior leaders are beginning to recognize that they represent a critical talent pool. Yet, two persistent misconceptions have clouded the discussion: the mistaken assumption that women have made it and the playing field has levelled, and the equally mistaken view that promoting women is a concession to political correctness or a response to imposed quotas.

When we look to the people holding the most senior positions in Canada, it's clear women haven't "made it." Women hold only 17.7 per cent of corporate officer positions in FP500 companies and 24.7 per cent of seats in the House of Commons. An astounding 44.9 per cent of public companies on the FP500 don't have a single woman on their boards of directors.

As Bill Downe, president and CEO of BMO Financial Group, said as chair of the Catalyst Canada honours dinner, "The business environment today is borderless and hyper-competitive. This reality compels companies to foster business cultures that are barrier-free and where talent and ability are what defines success."

It's all about talent. And the goal is to identify and remove workplace barriers so that talented employees can rise to the top, regardless of gender, race, ethnicity or other characteristics. Catalyst research tells us that the barriers to women's advancement are, sadly, still very real—gender-based stereotypes, a lack of access to informal networks, few role models, not enough senior-level mentors or sponsors.

A focus on gender diversity doesn't mean hiring or promoting less qualified women merely to meet targets. Rather, it's the recognition that barriers must be tackled to ensure all employees have equal opportunity to succeed and contribute their talents. As Ed Clark, president and CEO of TD Bank Financial Group, said on accepting one of this year's Catalyst Canada honours, "This is not about favouring one group over another. It's about removing explicit and implicit barriers, levelling the playing field so that everybody gets to play and they get to play at their best."

Business leaders have seen the numbers. Catalyst research shows that companies with more women in corporate officer positions and on boards of directors, on average, financially outperform those with fewer women. Companies with more women corporate officers had a 35-per-cent higher return on equity and a 34-per-cent higher total return to shareholders. And companies with more women board directors had a 53-per-cent higher return on equity, a 42-per-cent higher return on sales and a 66-per-cent higher return on invested capital.

Moreover, having different perspectives around the table makes good business sense—diverse teams support innovation and can help companies mirror and serve a diverse marketplace. Clearly, to be competitive in our increasingly complex global economy, companies can't afford to leave 50 per cent of our talent on the table and underutilize the tremendous potential that talented women offer.

Change doesn't just happen. Everyone has a role to play in levelling the field for women and advancing top talent. When our economy can reap the benefits of our nation's diverse talent, everyone wins—men, women and business.

In addition, organizations need to understand how relationships with the labour pool can change over time. In the context of labour relations, many businesses need to consider how labour or union demands can impact corporate policy and decision making. Unions have changed over time and their purpose has also expanded. Some industries need to cope with conflicts in industrial relations, while others need to address new demands that are triggered by other environmental changes. (See Talking Business 10.5.)

Talking Business 10.5

Union Warns of Air Canada Maintenance Outsourcing

Brent Jang

Union leaders are warning that Air Canada AC.B-T is on a course to divert aircraft maintenance work to lower-cost plants in the United States and El Salvador.

The International Association of Machinists and Aerospace Workers says hundreds of Canadian jobs are at risk of being transferred to foreign aircraft repair companies over a 10-year period, if Air Canada's heavy maintenance contract is allowed to expire in mid-2013.

The union cautions that jobs in Canada at Aveos Fleet Performance Inc., formerly named Air Canada Technical Services, are at risk of being shifted to lower-wage jurisdictions at competing repair shops in places such as Nashville, Plattsburgh, N.Y., and Rome, N.Y.

Lenders have majority ownership of Montreal-based Aveos while Air Canada's stake is estimated by the union to be 17 per cent.

Marcel St-Jean, president of IAMAW Local 1751 in Montreal, said he's especially concerned about Aveos' expansion plans for its Aeroman division in San Salvador, the capital of El Salvador.

"We are very scared that jobs will go to El Salvador," Mr. St-Jean said. "After mid-2013, there isn't any obligation on Air Canada's part to do heavy maintenance on the planes in Canada."

In 2009, Canadian employees at Aveos earned between $1,700 and $5,500 a month, depending on their skills and experience, compared with $350 to $1,200 a month at Aeroman.

Aveos spokesman Michael Kuhn said management has repeatedly told union leaders that their fears are unfounded. "We don't have plans to move Air Canada work to the locations indicated," he said.

Air Canada spokesman Peter Fitzpatrick added in a statement that "contrary to false rumours that have been circulated, Air Canada has no plans to send any airframe maintenance work to Aeroman."

Despite such assurances, the lack of job security remains the big topic among IAMAW members, said Lorne Hammerberg, the Winnipeg-based president of Local 714 of the union.

Mr. Hammerberg said most of the 540 unionized mechanic and technician jobs in Winnipeg could be eventually wiped out because Aeroman does work on narrow-body Airbus and Embraer jets—the same type of aircraft handled in the Manitoba capital.

Union officials also warn that roughly half of the 2,000 workers at Aveos's Montreal plant could see their jobs vanish if Air Canada doesn't extend its heavy maintenance contract. Many of the 580 Vancouver and 100 Mississauga, Ont., positions are also at risk, the officials say.

Dave Ritchie, IAMAW general vice-president, said on Tuesday that the union is counting on Ottawa to review the Air Canada Public Participation Act. Under the act, the Montreal, Winnipeg and Mississauga bases must remain open and active, he said.

Air Canada said in a statement that it "complies with and will remain compliant with the Air Canada Public Participation Act."

The union is sounding the alarm as the work force at Aveos undergoes a transition to being represented by an Aveos bargaining unit that will be separate from Air Canada. "This process will allow eligible employees to bid, on the basis of seniority, for positions at Air Canada and Aveos. The transition process also provides those employees with seven different options when choosing which employer they prefer and deals with pension matters for employees transitioning to Aveos," Air Canada said.

While Air Canada accounts for most of the work at Aveos in Canada, the maintenance, repair and overhaul company also has other contracts, including one for Yellowknife-based Canadian North's Boeing 737s. Aveos subcontracts certain heavy maintenance, called "C checks," to Costa Rica, said Canadian North president Tracy Medve.

5. Global Changes

As we observed in Chapter 6, globalization has been among the most pervasive forces affecting not only business in Canada but in almost every corner of the world. We also noted the tremendous growth of "borderless" corporations. The increasing ability of multinational corporations to move freely across borders and set up business just about anywhere reflects the title "borderless corporation." The term *multinational* is a bit inaccurate, however, given that many of these companies do not claim any specific nationality but, in fact, gear their planning and decision making to global markets. For example, goods could be designed in one country, raw material obtained from a second country, manufactured in a third country and shipped to consumers in another country.

In a broader sense, globalization has also influenced profound changes in the relationship of business to its external stakeholders (see Talking Business 10.6).

As one observer noted, globalization has changed the nature of business and communities:

> Employees and communities were once critical factors in companies' long-term strategic decisions. Moving factories and jobs to another area of the country was unthinkable because of the damage it would do to the local community. In recent years, thousands of companies—including UPS, J.C. Penney, and Boeing—have moved their headquarters or operations from cities where they had deep roots. The old business structure—with a dominant CEO, a largely ceremonial board of directors, and employees willing to put the goals of the company first—is nearly extinct. . . . Several primary forces created systemic change in the American economy in the 1980s and 1990s, leaving the former system in shambles. One such factor was globalization, which forced the United States out of isolation. Companies began to look for new markets overseas. Coca-Cola and McDonald's spread throughout the world. NAFTA, GATT, and free trade brought down barriers that had prevented the flow of goods and services and human resources around the world. The law of unintended consequences worked its way into the American economy. Protected industries such as auto manufacturing faced serious competition from overseas for the first time, with devastating consequences.[6]

6. Legal/Political Changes

Deregulation and privatization, discussed in an earlier chapter, are clear examples of the importance of considering governmental changes on business strategy. Are legal regulations facilitating, or restricting, certain strategies? The legal environment of business can dictate changes in how business competes, as well as what services it offers and how they can be offered.

> The deregulation of protected industries in the 1980s and 1990s created competition for companies where none had previously existed. The telecom, banking, energy, and aerospace industries were ruled by the change. As the dominant companies in these sectors were forced to compete in an open market, they started letting sizable numbers of people go. The breakup of the Bell System into AT&T, Lucent, and the seven Baby Bells unleashed a surge of technology inventiveness. It was not surprising that telecom, financial services, and aerospace dominated the list of industries experiencing the heaviest downsizing in the early to mid-1990s.[7]

In the workplace, we have witnessed an increasing emphasis on organizational justice—i.e., how employees are treated. This has translated into more laws governing fairness in the workplace. One such area that has been dramatically affected is compensation. Pay equity has been among numerous issues involved in redressing inconsistencies in pay treatment among men and women, for example. We have also witnessed an increasing emphasis on merit-based pay, and pay-for-performance, which all attempt to more closely link actual effort to performance (versus seniority-based pay, which bases pay on the number of years you have been with the organization).

7. Societal Changes

Business must respond to society: consumer tastes change, for example, and business must adapt to such changes. Similarly, the types of organizations that service societal demands can change. The aging population (see also Talking Business 10.7) suggests greater emphasis needs to be placed on such industries as the health care sector:

> The growing number of people with advanced educational degrees is another force hurtling knowledge forward at a higher rate. As more people become educated, knowledge expansion increases

geometrically simply because there are more people to move the cutting edge of knowledge ahead. Geniuses emerge who could not have appeared in past eras because they did not have access to the then-current state of knowledge necessary to push the thought boundaries. Unprecedented numbers of people today are working at the cutting edge of research in a variety of fields. And the glass ceiling is breaking apart because young women are achieving the advanced degrees necessary for economic and social advancement.[8]

The increasing education level of the workforce has also generated changes to the nature of work. As we discussed in an earlier chapter, there has been, for some time, a movement away from high job specialization, where jobs are broken down into simple, distinct packages. The trend has been to generate jobs that demand employees be multi-skilled in order to handle more challenging and enriched work. Consequently, employees are also tending to work more in teams, and are responsible for a larger piece of the work, so to speak. Knowledge work demands a more highly educated workforce.

Talking Business 10.6

Fair Trade Pays Off

Jodi Lai

In the corporate world, maximizing profit sometimes entails cutthroat practices and ample exploitation, whether it be of workers or the environment, but two Canadian fair-trade companies have proven they can be responsible global citizens and make money.

"I think it's a great time for people to be tuning up their ethical antennas," says Stacey Toews, co-founder of Level Ground Trading Ltd., a fair-trade coffee company. "But we're not going out there trying to save the world. We're just trying to run an ethical business."

Being fair trade isn't just about singing campfire songs and preaching world peace. Companies with a focus on ethics face challenges typical companies don't; mainly the delicate balance of profit and growth versus philosophy and sustainability.

"Most tension arises in our company because we were founded on some very strict and lofty ideals," says Mr. Toews, whose company is based in Victoria. And those ideals, he says, cannot be compromised.

Shannon Passero, co-founder of St. Catharines, Ont.-based Pure Handknit, a fair-trade women's clothing company, shares that view. "Profit is not really the be all, end all of what our company is," she says. "Our company could probably be double the size it is now if we took all the orders people wanted to give us. So we've had to decline a lot of business to ensure fair trade mantra."

Both companies employ workers all over the world and are focused on long-term relationships with those communities, the key, they say, to being fair trade and producing quality products. Pure Handknit employs more than 4,500 knitters in Thailand, some of whom have been with the company since its inception in 1998. "Our workers are more like family to me," Ms. Passero says. "I've gone to their weddings and funerals and seen them raise kids." She says this long-term connection is part of the reward because happy workers make the best products. Pure Handknit clothing is sold in 2,500 boutiques across Canada and the United States.

Besides paying a salary that "should allow everybody to live a comfortable life," Ms. Passero says the company provides two full-time English teachers at the eco-friendly Chiang Mai factory, a health care plan, free meals, transportation and staff housing. Four of the staff have also completed MBAs funded by Pure Handknit. The company also donates 1% of all sales to various women's organizations in Thailand.

Level Ground, which pays small-scale farming communities in Colombia, Bolivia, Peru, Tanzania and Ethiopia fair-trade rates, grants scholarships to many farmers and their children, has a zero-landfill facility on Vancouver Island, and says because of their solid trade relationships, people in communities can have access to health care and education. "I think a lot of people would presume we're a development organization," Mr. Toews says.

"We believe superior quality is the No. 1 product of long-term relationships with farmers," he says. "We're getting the best coffee out of those communities, so that's the best payoff." Quality is important in keeping a fair-trade company profitable, he says. "We don't even try to lead on ethics. We lead on quality because people will buy an ethical product the first time based on the marketing message, but they won't buy it a second time unless its quality substantiates it." He said if consumers enjoy the product, "they stop to ask more questions about who we are and what we're doing."

One of the most difficult things for Level Ground, Mr. Toews says, is educating consumers. "How to define, clarify and communicate what being a fair-trade business [means] is a lot of what we do," he says, adding that a lot of time and money has been spent enlightening consumers on the difference between companies that sell fair-trade products versus companies that practice fair-trade philosophies. Twenty years ago, multi-national companies were seen as the problem because they exploited foreign workers and their land, and fair trade was seen as a solution, he says. "Now, these companies are typically moving the highest volume of fair-trade products, but they are not fair-trade companies. They were founded on un-fair-trade practices," Mr. Toews says.

"Fair trade was meant to quantifiably impact producer communities in a positive way, but typical shoppers are going into stores thinking, 'I hope I feel less guilty by buying fair-trade products.'"

On this Ms. Passero disagrees. She says consumers are beginning to take a less shallow approach to understanding fair trade. "I think there is a lot more consumerism where people are asking the next question. They want to know the impact of the product on the person who made it."

With the prices of cotton and coffee rising, both companies say there has been a greater strain on profits. Rather than pass the costs down to the workers or farmers, Pure Handknit absorbed the increases, while Level Ground implemented a price bump for consumers.

"It is about time to get out of our little Canadian bubble. Global citizenship is something we have to take into consideration," Ms. Passero says. "Everyone should ask themselves how a product impacts each person who touches it. Educating yourself has to be at the forefront of fair trade."

Source: Financial Post

Talking Business 10.7

Aging Population a Challenge for Auto Industry

CBC News

Demographic trends are working against the auto industry, the Bank of Nova Scotia says.

While predicting a rebound in Canadian sales this year, bank economist Carlos Gomes said the aging population will cut into future sales, starting as soon as 2013.

"Growth in the vehicle buying population is set to moderate to the slowest pace in more than 50 years," he said in a report Friday.

By 2013, the number of North Americans over 60—when people often retire and start to drive less—will overtake the important age group that boosts vehicle sales, the 16-to-29 year olds.

"The auto industry is relying on generation Y to partly offset the retirement of the baby boomers, but the sharp fall-off in driving by retirees will have an enormous negative impact on new vehicle demand," he said. Generation Y includes people born between 1978 and 1994.

That will become more evident in 2013, when the number of people over 60 in North America overtakes the number of generation Y people.

Gomes said the baby boomers, born between 1945 and 1963, pushed annual new vehicle sales to a peak of 17.4 million in 2000 from about 10 million a year in the 1960s. But the boomers are starting to retire, and retirees drive much less than people still working.

Moreover fewer members of generation Y are getting their driver's license than young people did a generation ago, he said.

In the short term however, there is one positive factor that stands to help the auto industry. Many cars on the road are old and will soon have to be replaced.

Source: CBC News

TYPES OF CHANGE

According to Dean Anderson and Linda Ackerman Anderson, organizations may confront three fundamentally different types of change: developmental, transitional and transformational.[9] Any organization must comprehend the nature of the change that it is attempting to undergo—this is a precursor to successfully managing any type of change.

1. **Developmental change.** This type of change attempts to improve upon what the business is currently doing, rather than creating something completely new. This may include the improvement of existing skills, processes, methods, performance standards or conditions. For example, increasing sales or quality of goods, interpersonal communication training, simple work process improvements, team development and problem-solving efforts may all be considered forms of developmental change.

2. **Transitional change.** This type of change actually replaces what already exists with something completely new and requires the organization to depart from old methods of operating while the new state is being established. Examples of transitional change include reorganizations, simple mergers or acquisitions, creation of new products or services that replace old ones, and information technology implementations that do not require a significant shift in culture or behaviour.

   There are two factors that largely distinguish transitional from transformational change:

   • It is possible to determine the final destination or state in detail before the transitional change is implemented. This permits the change to be managed.
   • Transitional change largely impacts employees only at the levels of skills and actions, but not at the more personal levels of mindset, behaviour and culture.

3. **Transformational change.** This type of change is far more challenging to manage compared to the other types of change for at least two reasons. First, the future state or destination caused by the change is unknown when the transformation begins. Rather, the final state is determined through trial and error as new information is gathered. Consequently, transformational change cannot be managed with predetermined, time-bound or "linear" plans. While an overarching change strategy can be created, the actual change process only really emerges, somewhat unpredictably, as the change is implemented. This means that managers and employees must operate in the "unknown"—where future outcomes are quite uncertain. Second, the future state is so dramatically different from the current operating state that employees and their culture must change in order to successfully implement this type of change. New mindsets and behaviours are required to adapt to this transformed state.

Methods of Change: Theory E and Theory O Change

Whether it is the presence of new competitors, new technologies or changes to any of the other forces facing business, organizations often respond to the challenges of change with a variety of programs that might include the following:

• Structural change: e.g., mergers, acquisitions, etc.
• Cost cutting: e.g., eliminating nonessential activities
• Process change: e.g., re-engineering
• Cultural change: e.g., change approach to doing business or change the relationship between management and employees.

In broader terms, Beer and Nohria discuss two fundamentally different approaches to change. Each of these methods of change are based on different assumptions regarding what successful change tools must be employed in order to achieve a desirable final outcome for the organizations. These two different approaches are referred to as Theory E change and Theory O change:

Two dramatically different approaches to organizational change are being employed in the world today, according to our observations, research, and experience. We call these Theory E and Theory O of change. Like all managerial action, these approaches are guided by very different assumptions by corporate leaders about the purpose of and means for change. In effect these two approaches to organizational change represent theories in use by senior executives and the consultants and academics who advise them. By "theory in use" we mean an implicit theory that one can deduce from examining the strategies for change employed.[10]

"Theory E has as its purpose the creation of economic value, often expressed as share-holder value. Its focus is on formal structure and systems."[11]

The central goal of this approach to change is based on the notion of maximizing shareholder value. The methods used to achieve this goal are changes to organizational structure and systems. The planning for this type of change tends to emanate from the highest levels of the organization, making it a "top-driven," programmatic approach to change. Among the specific mechanisms employed to achieve such change are performance bonuses, personnel reduction, asset sales, strategic restructuring of business units.

An example of Theory E change can be seen in the changes implemented by Scott Paper, operating largely in the consumer package paper business. About a decade ago, Al Dunlap, CEO of Scott Paper, embarked on a series of changes. His main objective was to increase shareholder value by 200%. Among the changes were the following:

- 11,000 terminations were conducted throughout Scott Paper.
- Certain business units within Scott Paper were sold off.
- The location of the head office was moved.
- Financial incentives were given to executives that met new performance criteria.

The changes at Scott Paper were consistent with the spirit of Theory E change. While the short-term goal was achieved, the company did not achieve long-term viability and eventually was sold to Kimberly-Clark. There had been no lasting change achieved within the organization or its workforce.

"Theory O has as its purpose the development of the organization's human capability to implement strategy and to learn from actions taken about the effectiveness of changes made."[12]

The central goal of Theory O change is to develop organizational capabilities. The focus is on developing an organizational culture that supports learning and a high-performance employee population. The planning for this type of change is essentially emergent and participative rather than programmatic and top-driven. The mechanisms employed to facilitate such change include the following: flatter structure (to increase involvement of employees); increased bonds between organization and employee; employee commitment to the change.

An example of Theory O change involves the case of Champion International, operating in the same industry as Scott Paper. In response to poor performance, CEO Andrew Sigler of Champion International initiated an organizational change effort aimed at altering the culture and behaviour of management, unions and workers. Sigler developed a vision of the new Champion, called the Champion Way, which reflected such values as involvement of all employees in improving the company, fair treatment of workers, support for the community around its plants and openness in the company. In the years that followed, Champion's management implemented one of the most effective organization development efforts witnessed in several decades. Champion used a high-involvement method called sociotechnical redesign to change its approach to organizing and managing people in all of its plants.

To support these changes, Champion improved its relations with its unions, and compensation systems were aligned with culture change objectives. A skill-based pay system was installed to encourage employees to learn multiple skills. A corporation-wide gains-sharing plan was introduced to help unify union workers and management with a common goal. Throughout this change effort, occurring over a decade, there were no layoffs. Ironically, this Theory O change did not actually result in any improvement in shareholder value.

The advice from the experts is clear—Theory E and Theory O must be combined in order to achieve successful, long-term change. As Beer and Nohria assert:

> Where the objective is to enable an institution to adapt, survive, and prosper in the long run, Theory E change must be combined with Theory O. In effect we are arguing for the and/also, for the management of a paradox. It is the way to get rapid improvements in economic value while also building sustainable advantage inherent in building organizational capability.[13]

THE PROCESS OF TRANSFORMATIONAL CHALLENGE: AN ILLUSTRATION

The story of transformational change at IBM is clearly told in the book, *"Who Says Elephants Can't Dance?"* Specifically, it documents IBM's transformation from the period 1993 to 2002 under the leadership of Louis V. Gerstner, Jr. (also the author of the book). In the book's foreword, Gerstner writes that his reason for writing *"Who Says Elephants Can't Dance?"* is to "tell [the] story of the revival of IBM" in order to answer the questions posed by those who wanted to know how IBM was saved. Gerstner modestly acknowledges that he did not transform IBM alone, and maintains that "without the heroes among [his] IBM colleagues" and the "thousand of IBMers who answered the call," IBM would not have been restored to its former glory.[14]

1. Understanding the Forces for Change

At a time when the external marketplace was changing rapidly, IBM had not realized that its customers, technology and competitors had changed; nor had it adapted to meet those changes. Gerstner writes that "IBM's dominant position had created a self-contained, self-sustaining world for the company"; however, by the early 1990s, it woke up to find itself perilously close to bankruptcy.

Gerstner accepted the job at IBM after being told that the company needed and wanted a "broad-based leader and change agent" who was "skilled at generating and managing change." IBM's management team, led by Gerstner, had to quickly assess and react to the rapidly changing external environment.

As part of Gerstner's orientation into the company, he went out into the field to learn about IBM, the IT industry and the external business environment. He quickly learned that IBM had lost touch with the outside world and the external forces that were changing as IBM stood still, lost in time. One distinct advantage Gerstner held over IBM's previous leaders was that he was from the outside and had been one of IBM's former customers; therefore, he had first-hand knowledge of IBM's lack of customer focus.

According to Beatty and Ulrich, mature organizations "establish a relatively fixed mindset."[15] This creates a huge resistance to change. Gerstner, essentially, had to attempt to implement *transformational change* within IBM. Among the fundamental changes that Gerstner initiated are the elements highlighted below.

2. The Change Vision and Implementation

Gerstner had to develop and implement a program that would be accepted and adopted by the stakeholders (employees, customers and shareholders). Gerstner writes that restructuring the organization, implementing a new compensation program and consolidating its marketing plans was relatively easy compared to having to change the corporate culture and establishing strategies for the new business environment. Gerstner writes, "Fixing IBM was all about execution."

While management scholar, Todd Jick, warns that "change lists" and guidelines don't guarantee success, he nonetheless offers ten "rules" that can be used as a tool to assist in the implementation process.[16] It appears that Gerstner did in fact follow most of these rules in one sense or another:

- Analyze the organization and its need for change—Gerstner, as well as the business community knew that IBM needed to change just to survive.
- Create a shared vision and common direction—a common corporate focus was created—customer focus—which instilled a common direction.
- Separate from the past—At his first meeting, Gerstner told IBM executives that "there was no time to focus on who created [IBM's] problems."
- Create a sense of urgency—IBM's precarious cash flow problems made urgency a high priority.
- Support a strong leader role—Based on his previous leadership record, Gerstner was selected by IBM's search committee as the one who could lead the organization.
- Line up political sponsorship—Gerstner involved IBM senior management team from the beginning, even including them in Operation Bear Hug.
- Craft an implementation plan—"Win, Execute, and Team" became what Gerstner felt was what "all IBMers needed to apply in their goals."
- Develop enabling structures—Gerstner restructured the organizations and reset the compensation system to create a sense of ownership.
- Communicate, involve people, and be honest—Just six days after his arrival, Gerstner wrote a note to his employees. From there he continued with a strong, open, honest employee communication strategy.

- Reinforce and institutionalize change—Gerstner writes that "execution is all about translating strategies into action programs and measuring their results" and that "proper execution involves building measurable targets and holding people accountable for them."

3. The Need for Cultural Change

"Big Blue," an "institution" in its own right, had culture, behaviour and beliefs uniquely its own. Traditions ran deep at IBM and Gerstner candidly admits, "the company has been known as much for its culture as for what it made and sold."

Historically, IBM has been a paternalistic, family-oriented company, providing its employees with generous compensation and benefits packages, lifelong employment and plenty of opportunities for advancement; as a matter of fact, IBM was not the standard—IBM set the standards. According to Denise Rousseau, there are two ways to change the *psychological contract*—that is, the set of implicit assumptions that underlie the expectations of employees with regard to their employment status:

- Accommodation, which means to modify or alter the terms "within the context of the existing contract so that people feel the old deal continues despite the changes" or
- Transformation, which means a radical change that replaces the old mindset with new ones.[17]

By all accounts, the psychological contract had been "transformed" by Gerstner's predecessor, who had made significant alterations to the company's commitment to lifelong employment by laying off tens of thousands of employees and capping future medical benefits. Gerstner further transformed the psychological contract by implementing a new compensation program, which was based on *pay for performance* rather than on corporate loyalty, long service or entitlement.

By implementing a pay-for-performance compensation program, Gerstner followed the opinion of Bob Knowling, who says that "changing a culture from one of entitlement into a culture of accountability"[18] is a starting point for making a successful change.

According to Rousseau, "a core issue in the management of contract change involves how change is framed"; this means that the "reasons for the change" must be validated and communicated.[19] Gerstner knew and understood that it was "essential to open up a clear and continuous line of communications with IBM employees" and that the end result of a "successful corporate transformation" was to publicly acknowledge the "existence of a crisis." He felt that if the IBM employees didn't believe that there was a real threat, they wouldn't make or accept the need for the urgently needed changes.

Just in the manner in which Gerstner acknowledges the hard work and determination of the "thousands of IBMers who answered the call, put their shoulder to the wheel, and performed magnificently" and how he dedicates this book to acknowledge their efforts, it's evident that the IBMers responded to his plea for change. No stranger to change, Gerstner knew that "management doesn't change culture. Management invites the workforce itself to change the culture."

4. Leading Change Through Communication

Instrumental to the change was Gerstner's acceptance that he needed to assume the role of chief communicator, which he did willingly and in an outstanding fashion. Gerstner's outstanding communication and leadership skills were the most influential contributing factors in IBM's transformation. By becoming the change agent and the communicator Gerstner was able to express his passion about leading the company into a new era, visibly demonstrate that he was committed to the change, and ready to face the challenges along with the rest of his leadership team. Rosabeth Moss Kanter writes in her article "The Enduring Skills of Change Leaders" that leaders should be "offering a dream, stretching their horizons, and encouraging people to do the same" rather than just "announce a plan, launch a task force, and then simply hope that people find the answers."[20]

Gerstner also championed many of the other skills recommended by Kanter, such as "transferring ownership to a working team." Gerstner's belief is that "Great institutions are not managed; they are led," meaning that managers should set goals and objectives, and allow their teams to determine the most appropriate manner in which to attain these goals and objectives. Kanter also recommends perseverance; Gerstner admits that it takes time to implement large changes and that it took him "more than five years of daily attention" to transform IBM.

According to Mary Young and James E. Post, the most effective organizations are those that communicate openly, honestly, consistently and continuously. They also developed a list of factors that determine the effectiveness of employee communications.[21] It is evident that IBM's successful transformation was facilitated through Gerstner's adherence to these principles:

- The chief executive as the communications champion—Gerstner appointed himself to the position of chief communicator, realizing that this task could not be delegated to anyone else and that he had to personally set the example for others to follow.
- Matching the words to the actions—Gerstner led IBM by demonstrating his passion, his anger, his directness, which in his own words was "very un-IBM. Very un-CEO-like." Gerstner even went so far as to tell his team that he was "looking for people who make things happen, not who watch and debate things happening." Commitment to two-way communications—Gerstner went out into the field to listen to and solicit input from the field employees; he held customer focus sessions, used the internal messaging system to "talk to employees" as well as listen to their concerns, comments and advice.
- Emphasis on face to face communications—Gerstner met regularly with executives and senior members of management; however, he omits to mention how often employees had opportunities to speak with him "live, face-to-face." Face-to-face communication is important; however, with 90,000 employees in 44 countries, *what* is communicated is certainly more important than the medium in which it is communicated.
- The bad/good news ratio—Gerstner felt it was imperative that employees knew and understood that IBM was in crisis, otherwise they would continue to operate in the same manner; while he felt it was important to communicate the "crisis, its magnitude, its severity, and its impact," he also felt it was necessary to communicate "the new strategy, the new company model, the new culture."
- The employee communication strategy—Young and Post stress that communication is a process, not a product; communication should include the whys and hows, not only the whats; it should be timely, continuous, help employees understand their roles and should allow employees to formulate their own feelings and opinions. Based on his actions, Gerstner followed this advice and developed an effective communication strategy that helped in IBM's transformation.

5. Reinforcing the Change

After assessing and reacting to the external environment, creating a new corporate strategy and vision, implementing the change program, convincing sceptical and resistant stakeholders of the need to change, Gerstner's last challenge was to instill a culture that may not necessarily embrace change, but at the very least would not shun and avoid change at any cost.

Gerstner believes that "great companies lay out strategies that are believable and executable" but also writes that "these plans are then reviewed regularly and becomes in a sense, the driving force behind everything the company does." He also points out that "execution is all about translating strategies into action programs and measuring their results" and "holding people accountable for them."

Peggy Holman explains that "Change is a process, not an event" and that while "events can be helpful in focusing people's attention, they are only part of the change equation" and explains that "organizations and communities also need to focus on actively supporting the plans and improvements achieved during the event" otherwise "without such ongoing support, conditions may return to what they were before the event occurred."[22]

Unfortunately, making people accountable and measuring results makes them feel as if they are being tested or evaluated; however, when it comes to objectively evaluating a change program there is no other objective manner in which to assess the program other than to use quantifiable measures. It is a vital part of the change process and can help determine what further changes are needed, because there is always room for continuous improvement.

CREATING THE LEARNING ORGANIZATION

A view among many management scholars is that organizations that effectively change or adapt to changes in their environment are ones that have first "learned"—they have learned how to recognize the need for change, and they have learned what actions are necessary to adapt. This notion of the central role of change is reflected in one of the many definitions of a learning organization: "an organization that facilitates the learning of all its members and consciously transforms itself and its context."[23] Learning, in this sense, involves three aspects of learning:

- adapting to their environment
- learning from their people
- contributing to the learning of the wider community or context of which they are a part

Organizations, like individuals, need to develop and grow—not necessarily in size, but in their capacity to function effectively. Clearly, this demands organizational change. Organizational development has been defined as the following:

> a process of planned system change that attempts to make organizations (viewed as social-technical systems) better able to attain their short- and long-term objectives. This is achieved by teaching the organization members to manage their organization processes, structures, and culture more effectively.[24]

Chris Argyris and Donald Schon made a tremendous contribution to the management literature and to the topic of organizational change through their examination of the issue of **organizational learning**.[25] How do organizations learn? Do organizations learn from their mistakes? This seems to be an abstract notion, and yet it is a very real topic. Argyris and Schon suggested that organizational learning represents the collective experience of individuals within the organization and comes about when organizational procedures change as a result of what has been learned. In this sense, organizational learning has been defined as the detection and correction of error.[26] Organizations can learn through individuals acting as agents in an effort to critically examine the methods and functioning of their organization. Argyris and Schon make a distinction between two types of learning: single-loop learning and double-loop learning. It is the latter that constitutes genuine organizational learning, and that leads to significant organizational change. (See Exhibit 10.2.)

Single-loop learning involves the correction of errors that employees may find in organizational methods of performance in order to keep the system working. This approach assumes that the organization has the right systems established but simply needs to fine-tune the present system. For example, an organization may find that downsizing permits it to be more flexible with lower costs. However, does reducing the workforce achieve flexibility? Individuals engaging in single-loop learning or adaptive behaviour are essentially functioning within the boundaries or constraints of the presented problem. Single-loop behaviour typically results in making *incremental* improvements and improving efficiency. Such behaviour involves, at best, the modification of strategies or assumptions underlying the strategies in ways that maintain the existing organizational approaches to problems. That is, single-loop learning results in the organization continuing its present policies or achieving its current objectives.

Double-loop learning requires that individuals assess whether an error or problem exists in an organization because the systems themselves need to be changed. Changing organizational systems or assumptions requires a deeper level of examination, and typically is a precursor to significant organizational change. For example, if an organization wants to achieve "flexibility," is this achieved simply through a reduction in the workforce? Perhaps the objective itself of "flexibility" needs to be re-evaluated.

Double-loop learning leads to the organizations modifying its underlying policies or goals. The double-loop learning process requires innovation and involves challenging the status quo within an organization. Individuals engaged in double-loop learning are not bound by the constraints of the presented problem. Rather, double-loop learning involves an examination of the assumptions and values underlying an organization's functioning. This critical examination culminates in fundamental changes to the present system and in

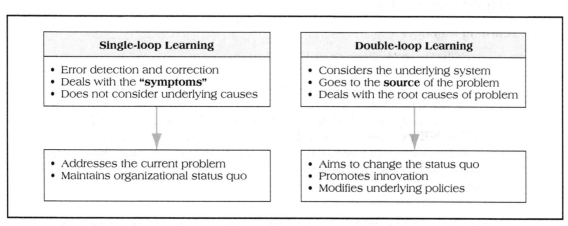

EXHIBIT 10.2 Organizational learning.

recognition of new problems to be solved. These new problems and new solutions will ultimately transform current strategies and assumptions.

Single-loop learning results from addressing the *symptoms* of a problem, while double-loop learning results when individuals attempt to uncover the *root causes* of the problem—questioning why the problem arose in the first place.

What type of learning is dominant in most organizations? Many scholars have suggested that most organizations, at best, encourage single-loop, but not double-loop, learning. Moreover, it has been suggested that organizations typically create systems that, in fact, inhibit double-loop learning. For example, the bureaucratic nature of most organizations encourages employees to be methodical and disciplined and, consequently, less likely to question the basic assumptions of most organizational practices.

How do organizations change? According to Argyris and Schon, change is accomplished through double-loop learning. This demands that individuals increase their awareness of the nature of the status quo and of those elements that deserve and require change. What is the ultimate goal? As one scholar commented:

> [The] ultimate goal [is] to help individuals unfreeze and alter their theories of action so that they, acting as agents of the organization, will be able to unfreeze the organizational learning systems that also inhibit double-loop learning.[27]

Argyris and Schon assert that people tend to adopt a single-loop learning approach in organizations rather than developing double-loop learning skills.[28] Argyris stated that "We strive to organize our individual and organizational lives by decomposing them into single-loop problems because they are easier to solve and to monitor."[29]

Is the job of management one that demands learning? This is an interesting question. Some critics suggest that management, with its emphasis on concrete results (typically measured in profits, dollars, costs, etc.) has traditionally de-emphasized the importance of learning as a necessity of proper management. (See Talking Business 10.8.)

Double-Loop Learning and Shifting Paradigms

It would seem that radical organizational change can only come about when the members of an organization are encouraged to engage in double-loop learning—the concept we discussed above. It is akin to making a dramatic departure from the present way of doing things. This has also been referred to in the notion of *shifting paradigms*. Joel Barker, a management consultant and author, in his popular book *Paradigms* (1993), talks about the failure of many organizations to adapt to change. Consider the case of the Swiss watchmakers. Way back in 1968, who dominated the watch industry? Yes—the Swiss, with about 65% of the unit sales in the world. And in fact, back then, if anyone was asked to predict who would remain the leader even 20 or 30 years later, they would probably say the Swiss. However, by 1980, who came to dominate the world watch market? You may have correctly guessed Seiko of Japan. By that year, the Swiss share had fallen to

Talking Business 10.8

The Learning Manager

Management scholar Steven Henderson noted the following:

> Why is it that managerial work is not generally as scientific, or learning-oriented, as it could be? In many ways, the process of scientific thinking would appear to be significantly different to that of management thinking, since managers rarely set knowledge as the prime target of their activity. Indeed, the so-called learning curve or learning effect is seen as a consequence of carrying out managerial activity (typically production) rather than prerequisite. Organizations structured along the lines of a "learning laboratory" remain isolated exceptions.

Source: Steven Henderson, "Black swans don't fly double loops: the limits of the learning organization?" *The Learning Organization* (1997) 4(3): 99. (Note omitted.)

10% of the market, while Japan (who had held about 1% of the market in 1968) was the dominant force, with Seiko owning about 33% of the world market. From 1979 to 1981 about 50,000 of the 62,000 Swiss watchmakers lost their jobs—a huge disaster for Switzerland. What happened? Well, Japan had focused on electronic technology—the electronic quartz was a natural outcome. Where did this technology come from that allowed Japan to demolish the Swiss's domination of the watch market? The technology came from the Swiss themselves—a research institute in Switzerland.

This story has a particularly ironic twist, because it suggests that the Swiss could have easily maintained their market leadership. However, when the Swiss researchers presented their new idea to Swiss manufacturers back in 1967, the manufacturers rejected it! They considered it inferior—who would want to buy a watch that didn't have a mainspring, didn't need bearings, nor, almost, any gears, and was electronic with battery power? So the manufacturers rejected it, but let their researchers display what they thought was useless technology at the world Watch Congress that year. Seiko, upon observing this invention, had a completely different view— and the result was a dramatic turnaround for Japan and a dramatic failure for the Swiss. What happened here, according to Joel Barker, was a failure to make a **paradigm** shift.

In Barker's view, change is all about adopting new paradigms. What is this strange concept called a paradigm, and how did it cause the downfall of the Swiss watch industry at that time?

The term *paradigm* can be considered as referring to our set of beliefs or mental framework for understanding how the world operates. We see the world through our paradigms. You might also think of a paradigm as our theories, our assumptions, our beliefs or customs. As Joel Barker writes: "A paradigm in a sense tells you that there is a game, what the game is and how to play the game according to the rules." Barker argues that overcoming resistance to change is all about being able to do two things:

1. Recognize the current paradigms that govern our behaviour.
2. Shift to a new paradigm.

So, how does this apply to our example of the Swiss watch industry?

You might consider the Swiss manufacturers as being prisoners of their old paradigm—they could not conceive of the watch industry as ever changing, so it was the old, traditional Swiss watches that would always dominate the market. However, the industry did, in fact, experience a paradigm shift, brought about by Seiko, which did adapt its thinking to recognize new consumer tastes: the paradigm governing the rules of the watch industry game changed, but the Swiss still thought they could play the game by the old rules, based on the old paradigm. Consequently, they were victims of failing to adapt to changing conditions, failing to shift away from their old paradigm. The ability to critically examine our paradigms, how we see the world, is very much a part of our ability to accept change, both at the individual and at the organizational level.

Why don't organizations encourage double-loop learning and, consequently, innovation? Clearly, innovation is a desirable objective, yet organizations tend to manifest rules and regulations that facilitate consistency and stability—qualities needed to function effectively on a day-to-day basis. Ironically, it is innovation and the ability to change that are the skills necessary for long-term survival. Unfortunately, organizations do not tend to encourage double-loop learning. If organizations are guilty of inhibiting genuine learning (double-loop learning) and, consequently, failing to generate real change, what are the sources of this dysfunction? We will consider those sources next.

Do Organizations Encourage or Discourage Learning and Change?

Peter Senge, in many ways, popularized the concept of the learning organization as one that encourages all employees to engage in the learning process through dialogue, experimentation and learning from each other.[30] It has been acknowledged that "learning organizations" cannot exist without "learning employees."[31] That is, organizational learning and development are facilitated through individual learning and development. The ability of organizations to adapt to, and change with, a changing environment is dependent on the ability of their members to change and adapt.

Individual change is really about learning—learning new skills, learning or developing new perspectives and new ways of dealing with everyday challenges. Do organizations facilitate individual learning and development? Can organizations provide a learning environment for their employees whereby employees can grow and develop throughout their careers? Given that the traditional bureaucratic organizational structures are rapidly being replaced with more organic structures, it would seem critical to similarly shift greater attention to a more adaptive, innovative type of employee, better suited to the changing needs of the new organization, and capable of changing and developing along with the organization.

Can Employees Learn?

Workplace experiences comprise a significant portion of people's lives and, consequently, it is understandable that the manner in which individuals experience their workplaces will have a considerable impact on their growth and development.[32] Adults continue to learn throughout their lifetimes, and their past experience can help or hinder this learning.[33] A number of developmental theorists have emphasized the presence of challenge and stimulation in the environment as a means to encourage learning and development. Environments or experiences that challenge individuals will help bring about development.[34] The workplace is an important element in adult development, with the power to foster or impede development of its members. For example, organizations that encourage self-exploration, and information-seeking, will facilitate individual growth and development.[35] The workplace's influence on individual development results from its ability to promote individual challenge and critical reflection through the introduction of new tasks and responsibilities.[36]

What is adult learning development? There is not one all-encompassing definition of adult learning or development. Among the streams of thought in adult learning and development theory is the notion that development grows out of the interaction of both internal/psychological events and external/social events.[37] Adult development is based on change rather than stability, and this change or growth occurs at a predictable rate and sequence.[38] Individuals can learn from their experience if they can effectively see what changes are involved and how they can be accomplished.[39]

Based on the views cited above, learning from experience essentially involves changing both what one does and how one sees things. As we identified earlier, according to Argyris and Schon, learning in organizations involves the process of detecting and correcting "error."[40] When individuals begin to question or confront the underlying organizational norms and goals that relate to this process of error detection and correction, this constitutes double-loop learning. The questions of interest in this regard are, Do organizations contain elements that encourage or impede challenge, confrontation and enquiry as a means to facilitate double-loop learning or paradigm shifting in organizations among individuals? A consideration of the "institutional" nature of organizations offers some insights in this regard.

Bureaucracies and Roles

To understand the ability of organizations to influence individuals in the manner described above, it is useful to consider a theory of organizational behaviour that considers the institutional nature of organizations: **institutionalization theory**.[41] In order to determine what institutionalization theory has to offer in terms of understanding the influence of organizations on adult learning and development, it is necessary to understand what this theory says about the nature of organizations and their influence on individual behaviour.

Institutionalization involves the processes by which shared beliefs take on a rule-like status. *Institutionalization* has been defined as a social process through which individuals create a shared definition of what is appropriate or meaningful behaviour.[42] Meyer and Rowan suggested that organizations that incorporate societally legitimated elements in their formal structures maximize their legitimacy and increase their resources and survival capabilities.[43] Essentially, this perspective acknowledges that organizations often generate "accepted practices" that tend to govern how things are done. These practices may continue even when they are no longer functional, simply because they have become an "ingrained" part of the organization.

Single-loop learning would seem to be a natural consequence of adherence to institutionalized structures. Single-loop learning is emphasized in organizations governed by institutionalized structures—following organizational policy without critically examining behaviour or the policy that dictates behaviour. This is reflected in the image of the "mindless bureaucrat" who follows rules and regulations without considering the necessity of such rules. On the other hand, when individuals are not forced to conform with myriad rules and regulations, they are more likely to engage in thoughtful consideration of the utility of workplace policy in order to determine whether such policies are effective or ineffective. Consequently, organizations where institutionalized structures are deeply entrenched are less likely to provide an environment conducive to adult learning and development.

Cognitive Scripts

Organizational policy can discourage employees from thinking "outside the box," so to speak. This is also reflected in the notion of **cognitive scripts**. What are cognitive scripts? They are scripts we all carry with us in the performance of our jobs. Though they are not concrete or tangible, they are very real. That is, any organization possesses shared meaning regarding how its members should conduct themselves in the performance of their duties.[44] Cognitive scripts or schema have been described as mental pictures (most often unconscious) that serve to organize knowledge in some systematic fashion. Essentially, organizational members can function efficiently in organizations through the use of scripts or schema, to reduce the mass of information to be processed as a means to guide their performance. That is, cognitive scripts may guide thought and behaviour and are based on beliefs about people, situations, or behaviours. A script is a type of schema that serves to help understand and enact dynamic patterns of behaviour. A script provides knowledge about expected sequences of events, and guides behaviour for a given situation.

What are the implications of organizational scripts for learning and development in the workplace? Cognitive learning is one learning domain that assumes that people have characteristic ways of making sense of the world by organizing that world into abstract categories.[45] These categories change with age and, ideally, should be in the direction of growth. How do organizations impact cognitive learning? Individuals, within social settings, form and use categories in such processes as perception, decision making and conceptualization. As explained earlier, this categorization is intended to reduce the cognitive complexity of the environment. In other words, individuals within organizations often rely on pre-programmed methods of conduct (scripts) and cognitive pictures of their environment. In effect, scripts internalize a routinized approach to performance on the job. Similarly, the use of scripts to guide behaviour in the workplace can potentially discourage individuals from critically examining events and situations each time performance is required.

The reliance on cognitive scripts and schema in the workplace reduces the need to continually question and confront environmental cues. Rather, a pre-programmed approach to dealing with others in the workplace seems to be developed. To the extent that reliance is placed on these scripts and schemas, confrontation and change will be discouraged, and, consequently, learning and development will be impeded.

Employees can differ in the degree to which they rely on scripts or pre-programmed performance guidelines to govern their work conduct. Work behaviour that is largely scripted discourages employees from engaging in critical evaluation of how their work is conducted. Through their need to maintain reliability and consistency in employee performance, cognitive scripts that we use to function in our jobs can actually generate obstacles to individual-level change and learning. Organizations that encourage a critical evaluation of these scripts are more likely to motivate learning and development among members than are organizations that discourage the critique of established methods of work.

IMPLEMENTING CHANGE THROUGH TIPPING POINT LEADERSHIP

> What must underlie successful epidemics, in the end, is a bedrock belief that change is possible, that people can radically transform their behaviour or beliefs in the face of the right kind of impetus.[46]

What Is the Tipping Point?

Malcolm Gladwell's 2002 book, *The Tipping Point*, offers a unique and thought-provoking framework for understanding change and serves to explain some of the reasons for change when it happens in rather unexplained ways. Through the use of terminology borrowed from epidemiology, Gladwell describes change as seeing a virus when it reaches critical mass, or, as he references, "the boiling point." He develops this term to lend itself to an examination of what he refers to as "social epidemics." While the book speaks to many social phenomena dating back to the American Revolution, it also has great relevance to organizational change.

One of the ideas that he discusses is the phenomena of *word of mouth* and its ability to bring about change. As well, the book addresses the notion of change occurring as an epidemic within an organization, beginning at the periphery and moving to the core. Finally, contrary to the idea of slow and steady change, the premise of Gladwell's book is to understand change that happens quickly and successfully.

Three Rules of the Tipping Point

Gladwell has developed three rules of epidemics: (i) The Law of the Few—that is, there are exceptional people who possess social connections, personality, energy and enthusiasm to be able to spread "the word" (i.e., idea or product) in epidemic proportions; (ii) The Stickiness Factor—that is, there are specific ways to make a message memorable in terms of presenting and structuring information to influence the impact it will make; (iii) The Power of Context—discussed in two parts, essentially that "... human beings are a lot more sensitive to their environment than they may think."[47]

The Law of the Few

The Law of the Few divides these "exceptional" people who essentially control the power of word-of-mouth epidemics into three categories. They are, as Gladwell has named them, Connectors, Mavens and Salesmen. **Connectors,** most simply put, know a lot of people. They are critical to the instigation of a word-of-mouth epidemic. Gladwell repeatedly uses the example of Paul Revere, who sparked the American Revolution by riding miles during the night to warn of Britain's impending attack. Gladwell contrasts the success of this word-of-mouth campaign with William Dawes, who, in collaboration with Revere, embarked on the same ride but with a lower success rate: fewer people were called into action by Dawes than by Revere. This, Gladwell explains, attests to the fact that Revere was a Connector, someone who had a great social network. Connectors, Gladwell describes, are so well connected because "... they manage to occupy many different worlds and subcultures and niches."[48] Hence, the ability to be able to diffuse an idea is greatly increased. Finally, he states, "... that the closer an idea or product comes to a Connector, the more power and opportunity it has."[49] Therefore, based on this explanation, had Dawes been a Connector his success rate would have been greater.

The second category of people in the Law of the Few are **Mavens,** from the Yiddish, meaning "... one who accumulates knowledge."[50] This term, also employed as a marketing concept, is important to economists analyzing Mavens's effect on the marketplace. Mavens are people who have information "on a lot of different products or prices or places."[51] Gladwell introduces a Maven by the name of Mark Alpert, whom he describes as pathologically helpful, even so far as writing to *Consumer Reports* to offer corrections. Mavens, he describes, are important in starting word-of-mouth epidemics because "... they know things the rest of us don't."[52] Mavens have the ability to start word-of-mouth epidemics not only because of their knowledge and social skills, but also because their motivation is pure, based on a desire to "help out" and therefore appeared to be unbiased, people accept their message or information more willingly.

The final category, **Salesmen,** have the skills to persuade those who are not convinced by the data provided by the Mavens or the message spread by the Connectors. Salesmen possess natural exuberance and are finely tuned (albeit often subconsciously) to non-verbal communication. Moreover, it is the subtle, hidden and unspoken communication that often hinges the Salesmen's success. While Salesmen are known for their persuasiveness, it is not through overt tactics that they are able to persuade. It is a genuine interest that makes them mesmerizing and, in turn, persuasive.

The Stickiness Factor

The second rule of epidemics is called the *Stickiness Factor*—that is, the quality of a message to ensure that it "sticks"; it is the method of presenting information in a memorable way. The tangible descriptor Gladwell uses is the television program *Sesame Street* and how it was created to cause an epidemic of literacy in children. The creators of the television program endeavored to create a program that would increase literacy in children through a medium that was not known to elicit such a reward. Gladwell describes a process of testing and reworking the program to arrive at a "sticky" version that accomplished its intended goal. The importance of "Stickiness" is that the idea needs to resonate with people so that it becomes memorable. Gladwell poses a question as he considers the notion of Stickiness in comparison to the importance of the messenger: "Is it so memorable, in fact, that it can create change, that it can spur someone to action?"[53] Although the Law of the Few states that it is the exceptional people who start the epidemics and all that is required is you find them, Stickiness has the same applicability—there is a simple way to present information to make it irresistible, and the only requirement is you find the right way. To sum: while the messenger is critical to spreading the message, the content of the message is equally important.

The Power of Context

The third rule of epidemics is called the *Power of Context,* which is described in two parts. The first part pertains to the environment: "epidemics are sensitive to the conditions and circumstances of the times and place in which they occur."[54] Gladwell illustrates this using the "Broken Windows" theory, borrowed from criminologists James Q. Wilson and George Kelling. The theory states that if a window is broken and left unrepaired, people will draw the conclusion that there is no place for authority and order, and in turn more windows will be broken, inviting a graduation in the severity of crimes committed.[55] He posits that the Broken Window theory and Power of Context are one and the same in that the smallest changes in the environment can lead to an epidemic that can be tipped or reversed. He states that behaviour is a ". . . function of social context" and that in this situation ". . . what really matters is little things."[56]

The second part of the Power of Context is the critical role that groups play in social epidemics. Gladwell introduces the notion of groups and their importance in initiating and sustaining change by creating a community to practice and support the change. Borrowing from cognitive psychology and research by anthropologist Robin Dunbar, Gladwell describes the Rule of 150, which asserts that human beings are most capable of having genuine social interaction with a maximum of one hundred and fifty individuals.[57] He describes an organization that uses this model and has had tremendous success. The strength behind this notion is that ". . . in order to create one contagious movement, you often have to create many small movements first."[58]

Applying the Tipping Point to Organizational Change

As mentioned previously, human interaction is of great importance in how we receive information, specifically information pertaining to change. Therefore, the concept of the Law of the Few has strong relevance to the organizational context.

"Word-of-mouth" change may seem like an unorganized and unconventional approach to implementing change within an organization. For an organization to draw upon hidden resources such as the Connectors, Mavens and Salesmen already within the ranks, there exists the potential to bring about a change epidemic.

Wanda Orlikowski and J. Debra Hofman discuss the need for change to be flexible and not based on a fixed beginning, middle and end point. To accomplish this they suggest being more open to the opportunities that arise during change.[59] A word-of-mouth change "epidemic" in an organization requires at least some prior commitment by the "few" key organizational members.

A second approach to change based on Gladwell's framework is implementing change from the periphery (i.e., small groups) in an organization and then moving to the corporate core, as is suggested by Beer, Eisenstat and Spector.[60] What the authors suggest is change that is mandated from the most senior levels within the organization and delivered in a "top-driven" fashion will not lead to success, as opposed to change that begins far from corporate headquarters and initiated by line managers and employees. The underlying rationale is that at the "grassroots" level there is a greater understanding of the individual roles and responsibilities and the changes that are required to bring about change. Instead, senior management should create a culture for change and support initiatives at the grassroots level, or the periphery, and allow it to move to the corporate core, as opposed to mandating change in the opposite direction.

Again, if we look at the Law of the Few and assume that an organization has a culture that encourages change, then it is possible that change can be initiated or "tipped" by either a Connector, Maven or Salesmen. This outside/in-driven philosophy could remedy the failures that organizations encounter when attempting top-driven change. Of course, this philosophy does require participation and awareness from the senior levels, primarily in understanding and seeking out, perhaps from the human resources function, these Connectors, Mavens and Salesmen and engaging them in an idea, or further allowing them to engage the organization with their ideas.

The concept of identifying and allowing the role of a change agent to move from a senior leadership function to an employee line-driven process for a change initiative to take hold and "tip" within an organization is a powerful notion. As suggested by Beer et al., the potential for change could be significantly increased if initiated by employees and if the process of engagement is also employee driven. If employees see the value in the change and it is initiated by a respected peer (i.e., a Salesman or Connector), employee support for the change would increase significantly as opposed to a mandated or programmatic change that does not have employee "buy-in" or support.

The *Power of Context* also has relevance here as Gladwell states that groups also play a critical role in initiating and sustaining change. Further, as stated earlier, in order to have one contagious movement you often have to have many small movements first. Again, speaking to the power of change occurring at the *periphery* and moving inward, if there are many small movements started locally the power of these movements to grow into one large movement and eventually "tip" into large-scale change is a strong possibility and presents a compelling and lasting model for change.

If organizations are willing to accept some risk, to take some of the control away from senior management and place it in the hands of the Connectors, Mavens and Salesmen and place more emphasis on the impact that employees can have on one another, the potential for any change to "tip" (i.e., spread) within an organization is great. We must embrace the idea that change is possible, that people can change behaviour and that it can happen quickly. All we need to do is consider the right "triggers" to make it all happen.

CHAPTER SUMMARY

Every organization must contend with a changing environment. These changes may stem from economic, labour, global, competitive, legal/political, technological or societal sources. This chapter emphasized the importance of understanding how organizations facilitate or resist change. We considered the notion of double-loop and single-loop learning, and how organizations might effect these types of learning among their employees. We discussed the tipping point for change as a theory of how to spread change in an organization. Sources of resistance to change were specifically identified, as well as organizational responses to resistance.

CONCEPT APPLICATION

NETFLIX AND BLOCKBUSTER

How Netflix (and Blockbuster) Killed Blockbuster

Rick Newman

When Blockbuster, the huge video-rental chain, set up a mail-delivery service in the summer of 2004, rival Netflix watched its stock price tumble. Netflix had invented the business in the late '90s, and already survived one competitive scare after Wal-Mart began dabbling in DVD rentals. By 2004, Wal-Mart was backing out, having decided that video rentals weren't part of its core business. But Blockbuster, the nation's largest video-rental chain, was a much bigger threat. Video rentals were its entire business. Its very survival depended on conquering Netflix. . . .

. . . Six years later, Blockbuster is in tatters, leaving Netflix as the undisputed winner in the DVD-by-mail business. Blockbuster's long-anticipated bankruptcy filing is clear proof that the company clung far too long to an outdated strategy and failed to understand changes that others eagerly exploited. The chain's downfall reflects the huge risk any firm faces today by just standing still. "Legacy investments create a legacy mindset," say Vijay Govindarajan, a professor at Dartmouth's Tuck School of Business and co-author of *The Other Side of Innovation*. "Blockbuster got stuck in the box. They never changed their business model."

Blockbuster was an upstart itself when it was formed in 1985 as a small, flashy video-rental chain in Florida. Businessman Wayne Huizenga bought the company in 1987 and began a series of acquisitions that eventually made Blockbuster the world's biggest video-rental company. While swelling in size, however, Blockbuster began to alienate customers with strict late fees and unimaginative, warehouse-style stores. It also overlooked e-commerce while sticking to its long-held retail strategy, even looking into buying the defunct Circuit City in 2009. Blockbuster's cardinal sin, says Govindarajan, was maintaining its commitment to a vast retail network, even when that was no longer the way movie renters wanted to shop.

Netflix was founded in 1997 as a more convenient way to rent movies—and to take advantage of lightweight DVDs that would be much cheaper to mail than bulky videocassettes. But the new firm's first idea flopped. Netflix originally charged a set fee for each movie rented, just like Blockbuster, which didn't catch on. Then CEO Reed Hastings decided to change the business to a subscription model that allowed customers to pay a flat monthly fee and rent as many movies as they wanted—with no late fees. That got traction.

As Netflix became successful, competitors emerged because its business model seemed simple: Simply keep DVDs in a warehouse and mail them out when orders came in. But Netflix's business is anything but simple, and that's why the competition has faltered. Quick delivery, for example, depends on having regional distribution centers in just the right places, and in its early days Netflix suffered from many complaints about slow delivery. It took several years for Netflix to get its distribution layout right. Managing a huge inventory of movies is another challenge. Ensuring quick delivery means stocking thousands of titles and having plenty of copies of the most popular films. That can get expensive. But a slim inventory that leaves customers waiting for movies would drive business away.

Then there is Netflix's secret sauce: Algorithms that allow users to rate movies and then receive recommendations for other films they might like, including some they may never have heard of. This kind of technology is common today, as sites like Pandora and Amazon make it a routine part of their users' experience. But Netflix was an early innovator, and Hastings seems to have understood that enhancing customers' experience would build brand loyalty that's crucial in such a cutthroat industry. "Most people think you should be riveted on the competition," says Andy Rachleff, a Stanford Business School professor and Silicon Valley venture capitalist who has known Hastings for years. "Absolutely not. Be riveted on delighting your customer. If you do that all they can do is follow you. That's why Netflix is so far ahead of Blockbuster. They're focused on delighting the customer."

Netflix, of course, hasn't been Blockbuster's only competition. In 2004, Redbox began offering video rentals for $1 a night through vending machines at fast-food restaurants, grocery stores, and other retail outlets, stealing Blockbuster customers with practically none of the overhead that comes from running actual stores. Redbox now has 24,000 kiosks nationwide, eight times as many locations as Blockbuster. Apple is now in the movie-rental business, offering movie downloads for many popular devices. Cable and phone companies have also started offering video-on-demand straight to their customers' TVs, a service that suffers from a limited supply of movies but obviously offers the ultimate convenience. Netflix, for one, saw this coming, and has been aggressively developing its own on-demand offerings for subscribers, including converters that allow streaming straight to the TV.

Blockbuster has copied moves like these, but it has also been consistently late to the game with no real innovations of its own. Meanwhile, it has been burning cash over the last few years, stuck between a costly commitment to retail real estate and fast-moving competitors with no such baggage. That left Blockbuster struggling to get more revenue from fees without alienating consumers. The recession sealed the deal, as business declined and Blockbuster was finally unable to make its debt payments, resulting in bankruptcy. . . .

Source: "How Netflix (and Blockbuster) killed Blockbuser," Rick Newman, *US News & World Report.*

Questions:

1. What forces changed in Blockbuster's environment?
2. What were the sources of resistance to change in Blockbuster?
3. In what way is Netflix a learning organization and a paradigm shifter?

ENDNOTES

Chapter 1

1. Gareth Morgan, *Images of Organization* (Sage: Newbury Park, 1986).
2. J. Pfeffer and G.R. Salancik, *The External Control of Organizations* (New York: Harper & Row, 1978).
3. K. Weick, "Educational organizations as loosely coupled systems" *Administrative Science Quarterly* 21: 1–19.
4. E. Goffman, *Interaction Ritual* (Garden City, NY: Doubleday, 1967).
5. L. Pondy et al. (Eds.), *Organizational Symbolism* (Greenwich, CT: JAI Press, 1983).
6. J.D. Thompson, *Organizations in Action* (New York: McGraw-Hill, 1967); D. Katz and R.L. Kahn, *The Social Psychology of Organization* (New York: Wiley, 1978).
7. The Conference Board of Canada, "Executive Summary," *Canadian Outlook Long-Term Economic Forecast: 2005* (January 2005) at http://www.conferenceboard.ca/documents.asp?rnext=1153.
8. Mel Hurtig, "Canadian Democratic Movement, Foreign Investment? No. Foreign Ownership and Control? Yes!" (October 19, 2005) from Canadian Democratic Movement Web site: http://www.canadiandemocraticmovement.ca/ index.php?name=News&file=article&sid=757.
9. "Scandals pile up in world of Canadian business," By Derek Abma, Postmedia News July 2, 2011 ; http:// www.ottawacitizen.com/business/Scandals%2Bpile%2Bworld%2BCanadian%2Bbusiness/5038421/story. html#ixzz1TPz3KzaP.

Chapter 2

1. "Canada's 500 Largest Corporations," *The Financial Post*, June 2009, 42–43.
2. Richard Blackwell, "Canada Ranks High in Low Business Costs," *The Globe and Mail*, March 31, 2010, B5.
3. Robert A. Collinge and Ronald M. Ayers, *Economics by Design: Principles and Issues*, 2nd ed. (Upper Saddle River, NJ: Prentice Hall, 2000), 41–42; Michael J. Mandel, "The New Economy," *BusinessWeek*, January 31, 2000, 73–77.
4. Richard I. Kirkland Jr., "The Death of Socialism," *Fortune*, January 4, 1988, 64–72.
5. Andres Oppenheimer, "Latin America Is Skeptical," *The Orlando Sentinel*, February 20, 2006, A19.
6. James Kynge, "Private Firms' Growth in China Striking: Report," *National Post*, May 11, 2000, C14.
7. See Karl E. Case and Ray C. Fair, *Principles of Economics*, 5th ed. (Upper Saddle River, NJ: Prentice Hall, 1999), 69–74; Robert A. Collinge and Ronald M. Ayers, *Economics by Design: Principles and Issues*, 2nd ed. (Upper Saddle River, NJ: Prentice Hall, 2000), 51–52.
8. Andres Oppenheimer, "While Latin America Nationalizes, India Opens Up," *Orlando Sentinel*, January 22, 2007, A11.
9. Barry Critchley, "Canada Post Should Be Privatized: OECD; Productivity Issue," *National Post*, March 11, 2010, FP2.
10. "Canada's Maple Syrup Output Rises in '09," *National Post*, March 11, 2010, FP6.
11. For a detailed analysis of the rise in food prices, see Sinclair Stewart and Paul Waldie, "The Byzantine World of Food Pricing: How Big Money Is Wreaking Havoc," *The Globe and Mail*, May 31, 2008, B4–B7.
12. See Paul Heyne, Peter J. Boettke, and David L. Prychitko, *The Economic Way of Thinking*, 10th ed. (Upper Saddle River, NJ: Prentice Hall, 2003), 190, 358–359.
13. Karl E. Case and Ray C. Fair, *Principles of Economics*, 6th ed., updated (Upper Saddle River, NJ: Prentice Hall, 2003), 300–309.
14. *Hoover's Handbook of World Business 2002* (Austin: Hoover's Business Press, 2002), 74–75.
15. Timothy Aeppel, "Show Stopper: How Plastic Popped the Cork Monopoly," *The Wall Street Journal*, May 1, 2010, A1.
16. "Royal Mail's Reign Comes to an End," *The Globe and Mail*, January 2, 2006, B7.
17. Eric Bellman, "As Economy Zooms, India's Postmen Struggle to Adapt," *The Wall Street Journal*, October 3, 2006, A1, A12.
18. See Jay B. Barney and William G. Ouchi, eds., *Organizational Economics* (San Francisco: Jossey-Bass, 1986), for a detailed analysis of linkages between economics and organizations.
19. Karl E. Case and Ray C. Fair, *Principles of Economics*, 6th ed., updated (Upper Saddle River, NJ: Prentice Hall, 2003), 432–433.
20. Karl E. Case and Ray C. Fair, *Principles of Economics*, 6th ed., updated (Upper Saddle River, NJ: Prentice Hall, 2003), 15.
21. Karl E. Case and Ray C. Fair, *Principles of Economics*, 6th ed., updated (Upper Saddle River, NJ: Prentice Hall, 2003), 15.
22. Richard Blackwell, "The 'R' Word," *The Globe and Mail*, October 16, 2008, B5.
23. Bank of Canada Banking and Financial Statistics, Table H1 (May 2010): S96.
24. Matthew McLearn, "Our Dangerous Addiction to GDP," *Canadian Business*, October 12, 2009, 23.
25. Green Economics website, www.greeneconomics.ca/gpi, accessed June 9, 2010; Barry Marquardson, "GDP Fails as a Measurement," *The Globe and Mail*, July 16, 1998, B2.

26. Conference Board of Canada website, www.conferenceboard.ca/hcp/details/economy/income-per-capita.aspx, accessed June 7, 2010.

27. Olivier Blanchard, *Macroeconomics*, 3rd ed. (Upper Saddle River, NJ: Prentice Hall, 2003), 24–26.

28. OECD website, http://stats.oecd.org/Index.aspx?DatasetCode=LEVEL, accessed June 9, 2010; Kevin Lynch, "Canada's Productivity Trap," *The Globe and Mail*, January 29, 2010, B1.

29. Jay Heizer and Barry Render, *Operations Management*, 6th ed. (Upper Saddle River, NJ: Prentice Hall, 2001), 15–16.

30. Statistics Canada website, www40.statcan.gc.ca/l01/cst01/gblec02a-eng.htm, accessed June 9, 2010.

31. Greg Hitt and Murray Hiebert, "U.S. Trade Deficit Ballooned to a Record in 2005," *The Wall Street Journal*, February 11–12, 2006, A1, A10.

32. Neil Reynolds, "Stimulating Our Way into a Crisis," *The Globe and Mail*, February 18, 2009, B2.

33. Paul Viera, "Federal Deficit for 2009 Smaller than Expected, Finance Department Says," *The Financial Post*, May 29, 2010.

34. Canadian Federal Budget website, www.budget.gc.ca/2010/pdf/budget-planbudgetaire-eng.pdf, accessed June 9, 2010.

35. Neil Reynolds, "U.S. Debt: Don't Worry, Be Happy (till 2017)," *The Globe and Mail*, April 3, 2009, B2.

36. Celia Dugger, "Life in Zimbabwe: Wait for Useless Money, Then Scour for Food," *The New York Times*, October 2, 2008, A1, A14.

37. Geoffrey York, "How Zimbabwe Slew the Dragon of Hyperinflation," *The Globe and Mail*, March 23, 2009, B1.

38. Tavia Grant, "A Snapshot of How We Spend," *The Globe and Mail*, April 20, 2010, B2; Tavia Grant, "Lard in 1913, Plasma TV Now: CPI Tracks Changes," *The Globe and Mail*, April 21, 2005, B1, B15.

39. Bruce Little, "There's Been a Huge Shift in How Consumers Spend," *The Globe and Mail*, July 5, 2004, B4. Figure 2.3 shows how inflation has varied over the last 20 years in Canada.

40. Statistics Canada website, www.statcan.gc.ca/subjects-sujets/labour-travail/lfs-epa/t100604a1-eng.htm, accessed June 10, 2010.

41. Jeremy Torobin and Tavia Grant, "Slow Jobs Growth, Growing Debt Fears: U.S., European Recoveries Show Signs of Strain," *The Globe and Mail*, June 5, 2010, B1, B5.

Chapter 3

1. Marc C. Suchman, "Managing Legitimacy: Strategic and Institutional Approaches," *Academy of Management Review*, 20(3) (1995): 571–610 at 574.

2. Howard Aldrich, *Organizations Evolving* (California: Sage Publications, 1999); Michael T. Hannan and R. Carroll Glenn, *Dynamics of Organizational Populations: Density, legitimation and competition* (New York: Oxford University Press, 1992).

3. Phillip A. Anderson and Michael Tushman, "Technological discontinuities and dominant designs: A cyclical model of technological change," *Administrative Science Quarterly* 35 (1990): 604–33.

4. Kim Cameron, "Strategies for successful organizational downsizing" *Human Resource Management* 33 (Summer): 189–211 at 192.

5. Ibid., 189–211.

6. Dan Worrell, Wallace Davidson and Varinder Sharma, "Layoff announcements and shareholder wealth" *Academy of Management Journal* 34 (September): 662–78.

7. Peggy Lee, "A comparative analysis of layoff announcements and stock price reactions in the United States and Japan" *Strategic Management Journal* 18 (December): 879–94.

8. Wayne Cascio, "Downsizing? What do we know? What have we learned?" *Academy of Management Executive* 7 (February): 95–100.

9. Terry H. Wagar, "Exploring the consequences of workforce reduction" *Canadian Journal of Administrative Sciences* (December 1998) 15(4): 300–309.

10. Mark Mone, "Relationships between self-concepts, aspirations, emotional responses, and intent to leave a downsizing organization" *Human Resources Management* 33 (Summer): 281–98; Lisa Ryan and Keith Macky, "Downsizing organizations: Uses, outcomes and strategies" *Asia Pacific Journal of Human Resources* 36 (Winter): 29–45.

11. Jeffery A. Tomasko, *Downsizing: Reshaping the Corporation of the Future* (New York: AMACON, 1990); Wayne Cascio, "Downsizing? What do we know? What have we learned? *Academy of Management Executive* 7 (February): 100; J. Brockner, "The effects of work layoff on survivors: Research, theory, and practice" *Research in Organizational Behaviour* 10(1): 213–56; Brockner et al., "Interactive effects of procedural justice and outcome negativity on victims and survivors of job loss" *Academy of Management Journal* 37 (June): 397–409; Sutton & D'Aunno, 1989; and K. McLellan and B. Marcolin, "Information technology outsourcing" *Business Quarterly* 59 (Autumn): 95–104.

12. Wayne Cascio, "Downsizing? What do we know? What have we learned? *Academy of Management Executive* 7 (February): 100; Kim Cameron, "Strategies for successful organizational downsizing" *Human Resource Management* 33 (Summer): 189–211.

13. Connie Wanberg, Larry Bunce and Mark Gavin, "Perceived fairness of layoffs among individuals who have been laid off: A longitudinal study" *Personnel Psychology* 52 (Spring): 59–84.

14. Marjorie Armstrong-Stassen, "Downsizing the federal government: A longitudinal study of managers' reactions" *Canadian Journal of Administrative Sciences* 15 (December): 310–21.

15. Stephen Havlovic, France Bouthillette and Rena van der Wal. "Coping with downsizing and job loss: Lessons from the Shaughnessy Hospital closure" *Canadian Journal of Administrative Sciences* 15 (December): 322–32.

16. Wayne E. Baker, "Bloodletting and Downsizing Executive Excellence" *Provo* (May 1996) 13(5): 20.

17. P. DiMaggio and W. Powell, "The iron cage revisited: Institutional isomorphism and collective rationality in organizational fields" *American Sociological Review* 48(1): 147–60; J. Meyer and B. Rowan, "Institutional organizations: Formal structure as myth and ceremony" *American Journal of Sociology* 83: 440–63.

18. P. DiMaggio and W. Powell, ibid.

19. John W. Meyer and B. Rowan, "Institutional organizations: Formal structure as myth and ceremony" *American Journal of Sociology* 83: 440–63.

20. P. DiMaggio and W. Powell, "The iron cage revisited: Institutional isomorphism and collective rationality in organizational fields" *American Sociological Review* 48(1): 147–60; W. McKinley, C. Sanchez and A. Schick, "Organizational downsizing: Constraining, cloning, learning" *Academy of Management Executive* 9(3): 32–41.

21. W. McKinley, C. Sanchez and A. Schick, "Organizational downsizing: Constraining, cloning, learning" *Academy of Management Executive* 9(3): 32–41.

22. Martin G. Evans, Hugh P. Gunz and R. Michael Jalland, "Implications of organizational downsizing for managerial careers" *Canadian Journal of Administrative Sciences* 14: 359–71.

23. W. McKinley, C. Sanchez and A. Schick, "Organizational downsizing: Constraining, cloning, learning" *Academy of Management Executive* 9(3): 32–41.

Chapter 4

1. William J. Abernathy and James M. Utterback, "Patterns of Industrial Innovation," *Technology Review* 80(7) (1978): 40–47; James M. Utterback, *Mastering the Dynamics of Innovation* (Boston: Harvard Business School Press, 1994).

2. Phillip A. Anderson and Michael Tushman, "Technological discontinuities and dominant designs: A cyclical model of technological change," *Administrative Science Quarterly* 35 (1990): 604–33.

3. R. Foster, "The S-Curve: A New Forecasting Tool," *Innovation, The Attacker's Advantage* (New York, N.Y.: Summit Books, Simon and Schuster, 1986), pp. 88–111.

4. Michael Hammer and James Champy, *Reengineering the Corporation* (New York, NY: HarperBusiness, 1993).

5. Varun Grover, William J. Kettinger and James T.C. Teng, "Business process change in the 21st century" *Business and Economic Review* (Jan.–Mar. 2000) 46(2): 14–18. Reproduced with permission of the authors.

6. Ibid.

7. David Brown, "CIBC HR department halved as non-strategic roles outsourced" *Canadian HR Reporter* (June 4, 2001) 14(11): 1.

Chapter 5

1. "Diversity as Strategy, by *David A. Thomas, Harvard Business Review."*

2. Trafford, Abigail (2005) *The Age of Discrimination,* The Washington Post Company, February 8, 2005, p. HE01.

3. Krenn, Manfred et al (2001) *Integration of the Ageing Workforce: Thematic Paper presented to DG Employment & Social Affairs, Thematic Paper No 3* The European Work Organization Network (EWON).

4. Bradley, Dana Burr (2007) *Encyclopedia of Ageism: Mirror, Mirror on the Wall,* Vol 47, No 1, Haworth Press, Binghamton, NY.

5. In Canada, union density is normally defined as the percentage of paid non-agricultural workers belonging to unions. A rationale for excluding agricultural workers from the union density "denominator" is that such workers have often been excluded from unionization and in any case seldom join. However, as Murray (1995:162) points out, this rationale is not entirely consistent since members of other groups excluded from unionization rights, such as managers and confidential IR personnel, are counted as part of that denominator.

6. Aggregate union membership rates used in this book are generally higher than the disaggregated rates drawn from Akyeampong's Labour Force survey data. In note 1 of his 1997 article, Akyeampong explains the difference as follows: "CALURA density rates in the construction industry in particular have traditionally been higher than those captured by household surveys like the Labour Force Survey, mainly because CALURA union membership includes both the unemployed and retired, and the household surveys do not."

7. For a more detailed look at legislative provisions and their effect on union growth, see Ng (1992), Martinello (1996), Godard (2003), Johnson (2002b) and Johnson (2004).

8. The four NDP or PQ governments in provinces with above average density levels served for at least 10 years.

Chapter 6

1. Foreign Affairs and International Trade Canada, "Canada's International Policy Statement: A Role of Pride and Influence in the World" http://itcan-cican.gc.ca/IPS/IPS-commerce01-en.asp.
2. Philip Preville, "Exclusive Report: How to fix Canada—On the brink," *Macleans Magazine,* (November 27, 2006) http://www.macleans.ca/topstories/business/article.jsp?content=20061127_137129_137129#.
3. Offshore Outsourcing World Staff, "Spotlight India: Globalization," *Offshore Outsourcing World* (February 26, 2004 at 5:08 am) http://www.enterblog.com/200402260508.php.
4. David Ticoll, "'Offshoring' will soon be making waves" *The Globe and Mail* (February 19, 2004). Reproduced with permission.
5. *Entrepreneur Magazine,* "Entrepreneur's top global franchises for 2004" http://www.microsoft.com/smallbusiness/resources/startups/franchise/top_global_franchises.mspx
6. Foreign Affairs and International Trade Canada, "Canada's International Policy Statement: A Role of Pride and Influence in the World" http://itcan-cican.gc.ca/IPS/IPS-commerce01-en.asp.
7. Anthony Spaeth, "Get Rich Quick," *Time Magazine* (April 13, 1998) http://www.time.com/time/magazine/article/0,9171,988175,00.html.
8. Harry Sterling, "Is free trade a realistic option for East Asia?" *National Post* (March 13, 2001).
9. David Crane, "Canada in a shifting world," *Foreign Affairs Canada,* 2005 http://www.dfait-maeci.gc.ca/canada-magazine/01-title-en.asp.
10. Government of Canada http://www.dfait-maeci.gc.ca/can-am/menu-en.asp?act=v&did=2890&mid=46&cat=2132&tp=1.
11. Bruce Campbell, "NAFTA's Broken Promises," The CCPA Monitor (July 1, 2006) http://www.policyalternatives.ca/MonitorIssues/2006/07/MonitorIssue1415/index.cfm?pa=DDC3F905.
12. Ibid.
13. Philip Preville, "Exclusive Report: How to fix Canada—On the brink," *Macleans Magazine,* (November 27, 2006) http://www.macleans.ca/topstories/business/article.jsp?content=20061127_137129_137129#.
14. Ibid.
15. Bruce Campbell, "NAFTA's Broken Promises," The CCPA Monitor (July 1, 2006) http://www.policyalternatives.ca/MonitorIssues/2006/07/MonitorIssue1415/index.cfm?pa=DDC3F905.
16. Ibid.
17. Jeff Faux, "NAFTA at 10," *The Nation* (February 10, 2004) http://www.thenation.com/doc/20040202/faux.

Chapter 7

1. Legislative Assembly of New Brunswick, Legislative Committees, "Looking Back" http://www.gnb.ca/legis/business/committees/previous/reports-e/electricityfuture/look-e.asp.
2. William Echikson with Jack Ewing, "Who'll get stomped in Europe's postal wars?" *Business Week* (May 31, 1999).
3. Economic Council of Canada, *Responsible Regulation: An Interim Report* (Ottawa: Ministry of Supply and Services, 1979).
4. Thomas L. Friedman, *The Lexus and the Olive Tree* (New York, NY: Farrar Strauss Giroux, 1999).
5. J. Luis Gausch and Robert W. Hahn, "The cost and benefits of regulation: implications for developing countries" *The World Bank Research Observer* 14(1): 137–58.
6. Garrett Wasney, "A new road for Canadian truckers" *World Trade* 10(2): 50.
7. Anonymous, "Deregulations' real winner: The consumer" *Railway Age* 202(1): 20.
8. Garrett Wasney, "A new road for Canadian truckers" *World Trade* 10(2): 50.
9. Tom Campbell, Jack Casazza, Marjorie Griffin-Cohen, John Wilson and Carl Wood, "Another Blackout Looming: Gov't inaction could leave millions in the dark again soon" (March 1, 2005). Retrieved September 2, 2006 from BC Citizens for Public Power Web site http://www.citizensforpublicpower.ca/articles/mt/archives/2005/03/another_blackou.html.
10. Shaker A. Zahra and Carol Dianne Hansen, "Privatization, entrepreneurship, and global competitiveness in the 21st Century" *Competition Review* 10(1): 83–103.
11. William Megginson, "Privatization" *Foreign Policy* (Spring, 2000): 14.

Chapter 8

1. D. Jones, 1997. "Doing the wrong thing: 48% of workers admit to unethical or illegal acts" *U.S.A. Today* (Apr. 4–6, 1997).
2. M. Mahar, "Unwelcome legacy: There's still a big unpaid tab for the S and L bailout" *Barron's* 72(48): 16.
3. L. Karakowsky, A. Carroll and A. Buchholtz, *Business and Society* (Toronto: Nelson Thomson, 2005), p. 66.
4. Ibid.

5. David Wheeler and Maria Sillanpää, *The Stakeholder Corporation: A Blueprint for Maximizing Stakeholder Value* (London; Pitman Publishing, 1997).

6. M. Friedman, *Capitalism and Freedom* (Chicago: University of Chicago Press, 1962); M. Friedman, "The social responsibility of business is to increase its profits" *New York Times Magazine* (September 13, 1970).

7. John Kenneth Galbraith, *The Affluent Society* (Boston: Houghton Mifflin Company, 1958).

8. K.E. Goodpaster, and J.B. Matthews, Jr., "Can a corporation have a conscience?" in T.L. Beauchamp and N.E. Bowie (eds.), *Ethical Theory and Business* (Englewood Cliffs, NJ: Prentice Hall, 1983).

9. L. Karakowsky, A. Carroll and A. Buchholtz, *Business and Society* (Toronto; Nelson Thomson, 2005).

10. Ibid.

11. Natasha Tarpley, "Levi's Mends the Social Fabric" *Fortune* (July 10, 2000). © 2001 Time Inc. All rights reserved.

12. A.Z. Carr, "Is business bluffing ethical?" *Harvard Business Review* 46: 127–34.

13. Ibid.

14. *The Economist* (November 17, 2001), p. 70.

15. A.B. Carroll, "Linking business ethics to behaviour in organizations" *SAM Advanced Management Journal* 43: 4–11.

16. A.Z. Carr, "Is business bluffing ethical?" *Harvard Business Review* 46: 127–34.

17. CBC Web site, "Car Owner Sues Shell for Bad Gas" (July 8, 2002): http://www.cbc.ca.

18. Simon Tuck, "Tribunal Hears First Allegations of 'Deceptive Marketing' by Sears," *The Globe and Mail* (October 28, 2003).

19. Megan Barnett, Margaret Mannix, and Tim Smart, "The New Regime; Corporate Reform Measures Are Forcing Boards of Directors to Clean Up Their Act," *U.S. News & World Report* (Vol. 136, No. 6, February 16, 2004), E.2.

Chapter 9

1. Richard Blackwell, Media Reporter, "Movie Marriage Promises Blockbuster Savings," *The Globe and Mail* (June 22, 2005), B3. Reproduced with permission from *The Globe and Mail*.

2. S. Leung, "McDonald's Flips to Profit as Sales Provide the Sizzle," *Wall Street Journal (Eastern edition)* (January 27, 2004), A6.

3. E. Schlosser. *Fast Food Nation*. New York: Houghton Mifflin, 2001.

4. S. Leung, "McDonald's Flips to Profit as Sales Provide the Sizzle," *Wall Street Journal (Eastern edition)* (January 27, 2004), A6.

5. P. Gogoi and M. Arndt, "Hamburger Hell: McDonald's Aims to Save Itself by Going Back to Basics. But the Company Needs More Than a Tastier Burger to Solve Its Problems," *Business Week* (March 3, 2003) 3822: 104–106.

6. A. Zuber, "McD McShakeup? Mgmt., menu eyed," *Nation's Restaurant News* (March 3, 2003) 37(9): 1–3.

7. Anonymous, "Has McDonald's Lost the Plot?" *Strategic Direction* (April 2003) 19(4): 14–17.

8. P. Gogoi and M. Arndt, "Hamburger Hell: McDonald's Aims to Save Itself by Going Back to Basics. But the Company Needs More Than a Tastier Burger to Solve Its Problems," *Business Week* (March 3, 2003) 3822: 104–106.

9. S. Leung, "McDonald's Flips to Profit as Sales Provide the Sizzle," *Wall Street Journal (Eastern edition)* (January 27, 2004), A6.

10. N. Pachetti, "Back in the kitchen," *Money* (July 2003) 32(7): 44–45.

11. Anonymous, "Has McDonald's Lost the Plot?" *Strategic Direction* (April 2003) 19(4): 14–17.

12. N. Pachetti, "Back in the kitchen," *Money* (July 2003) 32(7): 44–45.

13. Anonymous, "Has McDonald's Lost the Plot?" *Strategic Direction* (April 2003) 19(4): 14–17.

14. S. Leung, "McDonald's Makeover; CEO Cantalupo's Focus on Improving Food and Service Sparks Turnaround; Catering to the Low-carb Crowd," *Wall Street Journal (Eastern edition)* (January 28, 2004), B1.

15. A. Garber, "Salad Days? McD Says Turnaround on Menu," *Nation's Restaurant News* (June 2, 2003) 37(22): 4–5.

16. Anonymous, "McD's Plots Supersized Ops, Menu Makeovers," *Restaurant Business* (May 1, 2003) 102(8): 12–14.

17. P. Gogoi and M. Arndt, "Hamburger Hell: McDonald's Aims to Save Itself by Going Back to Basics. But the Company Needs More Than a Tastier Burger to Solve Its Problems," *Business Week* (March 3, 2003) 3822: 104–106.

18. Anonymous, "McD's Plots Supersized Ops, Menu Makeovers," *Restaurant Business* (May 1, 2003) 102(8): 12–14.

19. S. Leung, "McDonald's Makeover; CEO Cantalupo's Focus on Improving Food and Service Sparks Turnaround; Catering to the Low-carb Crowd," *Wall Street Journal (Eastern edition)* (January 28, 2004), B1.

20. N. Pachetti, "Back in the kitchen," *Money* (July 2003) 32(7): 44–45.

21. P. Gogoi and M. Arndt, "Hamburger Hell: McDonald's Aims to Save Itself by Going Back to Basics. But the Company Needs More Than a Tastier Burger to Solve Its Problems," *Business Week* (March 3, 2003) 3822: 104–106.

22. N. Pachetti, "Back in the Kitchen," *Money* (July 2003 32(7): 44–45.

23. P. Gogoi and M. Arndt, "Hamburger Hell: McDonald's Aims to Save Itself by Going Back to Basics. But the Company Needs More Than a Tastier Burger to Solve Its Problems," *Business Week* (March 3, 2003) 3822: 104–106.

24. D. Stires, "McDonald's keeps right on cookin'," *Fortune* (May 17, 2004) 149(10), 174.

25. A. Garber, "Burger Giants Weigh in with More Healthful Menu Ideas," *Nation's Restaurant News* (May 26, 2003) 37(21): 1–2.

26. P. Gogoi and M. Arndt, "Hamburger Hell: McDonald's Aims to Save Itself by Going Back to Basics. But the Company Needs More Than a Tastier Burger to Solve Its Problems," *Business Week* (March 3, 2003) 3822: 104–106.

27. S. Leung, "McDonald's Makeover; CEO Cantalupo's Focus on Improving Food and Service Sparks Turnaround; Catering to the Low-carb Crowd," *Wall Street Journal (Eastern edition)* (January 28, 2004), B1.

28. S. Brooks, "Seeing the Lite," *Restaurant Business* (September 15, 2003) 102(15): 18–24.

29. C. Murphy, "Health Crackdown Hits Food," *Marketing* (February 20, 2003), 24–26.

30. Ibid.

31. "Client file: Salad days," *The Lawyer* (July 5, 2004), p. 11.

32. M.M. Mello, E.B. Rimm, and D.M Studdert, "The McLawsuit: The Fast-food Industry and Legal Accountability for Obesity," *Heath Affairs* (November/December 2003) 22(6): 207–16.

33. J.K. Nestruck, "Super Size Me: Would You Like Fries with Your Film?" *CanWest News* (May 5, 2004), p. 1.

34. S. Brooks, "Seeing the Lite," *Restaurant Business* (September 15, 2003) 102(15): 18–24.

35. Ibid.

36. R. Gibson, "Food: McDonald's to Drop 'Super Sizes' from Its Menu," *Wall Street Journal (Eastern edition),* (March 3, 2004), D3.

37. S. Brooks, "Seeing the Lite," *Restaurant Business* (September 15, 2003) 102(15): 18–24.

38. A. Park, "Would You Like to Un-super Size That?" *Time* (Canadian edition) (March 15, 2004) 163(11): 65.

39. S. Gray, "McDonald's Feels the Heat and Offers Some Healthier Fare; Would You Like Some Apples with Your Happy Meal? Here's Your 'stepometer'," *Wall Street Journal (Eastern edition)* (April 16, 2004), A11.

40. The Corporation, "Fixing the Fat," *Business Week* (September 16, 2002) 3799: 67.

41. R. Gibson, "Food: McDonald's to Drop 'Super Sizes' from Its Menu," *Wall Street Journal (Eastern edition),* (March 3, 2004), D3.

42. S. Gray, "McDonald's Feels the Heat and Offers Some Healthier Fare; Would You Like Some Apples with Your Happy Meal? Here's Your 'stepometer'," *Wall Street Journal (Eastern edition)* (April 16, 2004), A11.

43. S. Brooks, "Seeing the Lite," *Restaurant Business* (September 15, 2003) 102(15): 18–24.

44. C. Murphy, "Health Crackdown Hits Food," *Marketing* (February 20, 2003), 24–26.

45. S. Leung, "McDonald's Flips to Profit as Sales Provide the Sizzle," *Wall Street Journal (Eastern edition)* (January 27, 2004), A6.

46. S. Leung, "McDonald's Flips to Profit as Sales Provide the Sizzle," *Wall Street Journal (Eastern edition)* (January 27, 2004), A6.

47. M. Arndt, "McDonald's: Fries with that salad?" *Business Week* (July 4, 2004) 3890: 82–84.

48. S. Brooks, "Seeing the Lite," *Restaurant Business* (September 15, 2003) 102(15): 18–24.

49. Ibid.

50. M. Arndt, "McDonald's: Fries with that salad?" *Business Week* (July 4, 2004) 3890: 82–84.

51. N. Pachetti, "Back in the kitchen," *Money* (July 2003) 32(7): 44–45.

52. M. Arndt, "McDonald's: Fries with that salad?" *Business Week* (July 4, 2004) 3890: 82–84.

53. Ibid.

54. McDonald's Corporation, *2003 Financial Report* http://www.rmhc.com/corp/invest/pub/annual_rpt_archives/2003Archive.RowPar.0004.ContentPar.0001.ColumnPar.0001.File.tmp/2003%20Financial%20Report.pdf [Date accessed: 2006-11-02].

Chapter 10

1. John A Challenger, "The transformed workplace: How can you survive." Originally published in Nov./Dec. 2001 Issue of *The Futurist*. Used with permission from the World Future Society, 7910 Woodmont Avenue, Suite 450, Bethesda, Maryland 20814. Telephone: 301/656-8274; Fax: 301/951-0394; <http://www.wfs.org>.

2. D.D. Warrick, "The illusion of doing well while the organization in regressing," *Organization Development Journal* 20(1): 56–61.

3. John A Challenger, "The transformed workplace: How can you survive." Originally published in Nov./Dec. 2001 Issue of *The Futurist*. Used with permission from the World Future Society, 7910 Woodmont Avenue, Suite 450, Bethesda, Maryland 20814. Telephone: 301/656-8274; Fax: 301/951-0394; <http://www.wfs.org>.

4. Timothy Taylor, "Thinking about a 'new economy'," *Public Interest* 143: 3–19.

5. Diane Rezendes Khirallah, "The tug of more Informationweek," *Manhasset* 883: 32–40.

6. John A Challenger, "The transformed workplace: How can you survive." Originally published in Nov./Dec. 2001 Issue of *The Futurist*. Used with permission from the World Future Society, 7910 Woodmont Avenue, Suite 450, Bethesda, Maryland 20814. Telephone: 301/656-8274; Fax: 301/951-0394; <http://www.wfs.org>.

7. Ibid

8. Ibid.

9. Dean Anderson and Linda Ackerman Anderson, "What Is Transformation? Why Is It So Hard to Manage?" *Workforce Performance Solutions* (April 2005). <http://www.wpsmag.com/content/templates/wps_section.asp?articleid=124&zoneid=29>.

10. Harvard Business School, Working Knowledge Web site: http://hbswk.hbs.edu/item/2166.html (Access 2006-11-21.)

11. Ibid.

12. Ibid.

13. Ibid.

14. L.V. Gerstner, Jr., *Who Says Elephants Can't Dance* (New York, NY: HaperCollins Publishers Inc., 2002).

15. R.W. Beatty and D.O. Ulrich, "Re-energizing the Mature Organization" *Organizational Dynamics* 20(1): 16–30.

16. T.D. Jick, "Implementing Change" in T.D. Jick and M.A. Peiperl, *Managing Change: Cases and Concepts,* Second Edition (New York, NY: McGraw-Hill/Irwin, 2003), pp. 174–83.

17. D.M. Rousseau, "Changing the Deal While Keeping the People," *Academy of Management Executive* 10 (1996): 50–59.

18. N. Tichy, "Bob Knowling's Change Manual," *FastCompany Magazine* (April 1997): 76–99 <http://www.fastcompany.com/magazine/08/change2.html>.

19. D.M. Rousseau, "Changing the Deal While Keeping the People," *Academy of Management Executive* 10 (1996): 50–59.

20. R.M. Kanter, "The Enduring Skills of Change Leaders," *Leader to Leader,* 13 (Summer 1999). 15–22. Available on-line: <http://leadertoleader.org/leaderbooks/121/summer99/kanter.html>.

21. M. Young and J.E. Post, "Managing to Communicate, Communicating to Manage," *Organizational Dynamics,* 22(1) (Summer 1993): 31–43.

22. Peggy Holman, Draft of "Unlocking the Mystery of Effective Large-Scale Change," *At Work,* 8(3): 7–11. Available on-line: "A Change Agent's Quest," <http://www.opencirclecompany.com/thequest.htm>.

23. J. Pedler, R. Burgoyne, and A. Boydell, *The Learning Company* (Maidenhead, Surrey: McGraw-Hill, 1997), p. 3.

24. W.L. French, C.H. Bell, Jr., and R.A. Zawacki (eds.), *Organization Development and Transformation: Managing Effective Change,* 4th ed. (Burr Ridge, IL: Irwin, 1994), p. 7.

25. C. Argyris and D.A. Schon, *Organizational Learning: A Theory of Action Perspective* (Reading, MA: Addison-Wesley Publishing Company, 1978).

26. Ibid.

27. Ibid., p. 4.

28. Ibid.

29. C. Argyris, *Reasoning, learning and action* (San Francisco: Jossey-Bass, 1982), p. xii.

30. P. Senge, *The Fifth Discipline: The Art and Practice of the Learning Organization* (New York: Doubleday, 1990).

31. M. Dogson, "Organizational learning: A review of some literatures" *Organization Studies* 14: 375–94.

32. J.S. Glaser, "Connecting the workplace and adult development theory: Self directed work teams as a petri dish for adult development." Paper presented at the 7th Annual Meeting of the Society for Research in Adult Development, Toronto, Canada, June 1992.

33. D.H. Brundage and D. Mackeracher, *Adult Learning Principles and Their Application to Program Planning* (Toronto: Ministry of Education, 1980).

34. J. Mezirow, "Perspective transformation" *Adult Education* 28(2): 100–10.

35. R. Kegan, *The Evolving Self: Problem and Process in Human Development* (Cambridge: Harvard University Press, 1982).

36. M. Basseches, *Dialectical Thinking and Adult Development* (Norwood, NJ: Ablex, 1984).

37. E. Erikson, "Identity and the life cycle" *Psychological Issues Monograph* 1(1) (New York: International Universities Press, 1968).

38. Ibid.

39. E. Cell, *Learning to Learn from Experience* (Albany: State University of New York Press, 1945).

40. C. Argyris and D.A. Schon, *Organizational Learning: A Theory of Action Perspective* (Reading, MA: Addison-Wesley Publishing Company, 1978).

41. J. Meyer and B. Rowan, "Institutional organizations: Formal structure as myth and ceremony" *American Journal of Sociology* 83: 440–63; L.G. Zucker, "Institutionalization as a mechanism of cultural persistence" *American Sociological Review* 42(2): 726–42.

42. L.G. Zucker, "Institutionalization as a mechanism of cultural persistence" *American Sociological Review* 42(2): 726–42; Meyer and B. Rowan, "Institutional organizations: Formal structure as myth and ceremony" *American Journal of Sociology* 83: 440–63.

43. J. Meyer and B. Rowan, "Institutional organizations: Formal structure as myth and ceremony" *American Journal of Sociology* 83: 440–63.

44. J.P. Sims, Jr., D.A. Gioia, and Associates, *The Thinking Organization* (San Francisco: Jossey-Bass, 1986).

45. J. Piaget, *The Construction of Reality in the Child* (New York: Basic Books, 1954); L. Kohlberg, "Stage and sequence: The cognitive developmental approach to socialization" in D.A. Goslin (ed.), *Handbook of Socialization Theory and Research* (Chicago: Rand McNally, 1969), pp. 347–480.

46. M. Gladwell, *The Tipping Point: How Little Things Can Make a Big Difference* (New York: Little, Brown and Company, 2002), p. 258.

47. Ibid., p. 29

48. Ibid., p. 48.

49. Ibid., p. 55.

50. Ibid., p. 60.

51. Ibid., p. 62.

52. Ibid., p. 67.

53. Ibid., p. 92.

54. Ibid., p. 139.

55. Ibid., p. 141.

56. Ibid., p. 150.

57. Ibid., p. 179.

58. Ibid., p. 192.

59. W.J. Orlikowski and J.D. Hofman, "An Improvisational Model for Change Management," *Sloan Management Review* (Winter 1997): 11–21. Available on-line: <http://ccs.mit.edu/papers/CCSWP191/ccswp191.html>. [The article is directed at technological change; however, I am applying the model more broadly to beyond that type of change to change initiatives as I think it has great relevance.]

60. M. Beer, R.A. Eisenstat and B. Spector, "Why Change Programs Don't Produce Change" in T.D. Jick and M.A. Peiperl, *Managing Change, Cases and Concepts* (pp. 229–41) (New York: McGraw Hill/Irwin, 1990).

CREDITS

REFERENCES

Abernathy, William J., and James M. Utterback. 1978. "Patterns of Industrial Innovation," *Technology Review* 80(7): 40–47.

Adams, J.S. 1965. "Inequity in social exchanges" in L. Berkowitz (ed.), *Advances in Experimental Social Psychology*, pp. 267–300. New York: Academic Press.

Aldrich, H. 1979. *Organizations and Environments*. Englewood Cliffs, NJ: Prentice Hall.

Aldrich, Howard. 1999. *Organizations Evolving*. California: Sage Publications.

Alpert, M., and H. Raiffa. 1982. "A progress report on the training of probability assessors" in D. Kahneman, P. Slovic, and A. Tversky (eds.), *Judgment under Uncertainty: Heuristics and Biases*, pp. 294–305. New York: Cambridge University Press.

Anderson, Phillip A., and Michael Tushman. 1990. "Technological discontinuities and dominant designs: A cyclical model of technological change," *Administrative Science Quarterly*, 35: 604–33.

Andreasen, A.R. 1996. "Find a corporate partner." *Harvard Business Review* 74: 47–56.

Anonymous. 1999. "The privatization of public services." *The Worklife Report* 11(4): 13–14.

Argyris, C. 1982. *Reasoning, learning, and action*. San Francisco: Jossey-Bass.

Argyris, C., and D.A. Schon. 1989. *Theory in Practice: Increasing Professional Effectiveness*. San Francisco: Jossey-Bass.

Argyris, C., and D.A. Schon. 1978. *Organizational Learning: A Theory of Action Perspective*. Reading, MA: Addison-Wesley Publishing Company.

Armstrong-Stassen, Marjorie. 1998. "Downsizing the federal government: A longitudinal study of managers' reactions." *Canadian Journal of Administrative Sciences* 15 (December): 310–21.

Ashforth, B.E., and F. Mael. 1989. "Social identity theory and the organization." *Academy of Management Review* 14(1): 20–39.

Bandura, A. 1977. "Self-Efficacy: Toward a unifying theory of behavioral change." *Psychological Review* (May): 191–215.

Barker, J. 1993. *Paradigms: The Business of Discovering the Future*. New York: Harper Business.

Barlett, C. A, and S. Ghoshal. 2002. "Building competitive advantage through people," *MIT Sloan Management Review*, 43: 34–41.

Barny, J. B. 1991. "Firm resources and sustained competitive advantage," *Journal of Management*, 17: 99–120.

Barnard, C. 1938. *The Functions of the Executive*. Cambridge, MA: Harvard University Press.

Barnard, C.I. 1976. "Foreword" in H.A Simon, *Administrative Behaviour*, 3d Ed. New York: Free Press. (Original work published 1945.)

Basseches, M. 1986. "Cognitive-structural development on the conditions of employment." *Human Development* 29: 101–223.

Basseches, M. 1984. *Dialectical Thinking and Adult Development*. Norwood, NJ: Ablex.

Bateson, G. 1972. *Steps to an Ecology of Mind*. New York: Ballantine Books.

Baumhart, R.S.J. 1961. "How ethical are businessmen?" *Harvard Business Review* 39: 6–31.

Bazerman, M.H. 1998. *Judgment in Managerial Decision Making*, 4th Ed. New York: John Wiley.

Bazerman, M.H. 1990. *Judgment in Managerial Decision Making*, 2d Ed. New York: John Wiley.

Bazerman, M.H., J.R. Curhan, D.A. Moore, and K.L. Valley. 2000. "Negotiation." *Annual Reviews Psychology* 51: 279–314.

Beauchamp, T.L., and N.E. Bowie. 1983. *Ethical Theory and Business*. Englewood Cliffs, NJ: Prentice Hall.

Becker, G. 1976. *The Economic Approach to Human Behaviour*. Chicago: University of Chicago Press.

Becker, N. 1992. *Shifting Gears: Thriving in the New Economy*. Toronto: HarperCollins.

Beer, Michael, and Nitin Nohria. 2001. *Breaking the Code of Change*. Boston, MA: HBS Press.

Berger, I.E., and M.E. Drumwright. 2000. "The role of marketing in the development and distribution of social capital." Special Topic Session proposed for Marketing and Public Policy Conference 2001, Washington, DC.

Bird, B.J. 1989. *Entrepreneurial Behaviour*. Glenview, IL: Scott, Foresman.

Blau, P.M. 1970. "A formal theory of differentiation in organizations." *American Sociological Review* 35: 201–18.

Brockner, J. 1992. "The escalation of commitment to a failing course of action: Toward theoretical progress." *Academy of Management Review* 17(1): 39–61.

Brockner, J. 1988. "The effects of work layoff on survivors: Research, theory, and practice." *Research in Organizational Behaviour* 10(1): 213–56.

Brockner, J., M. Konovsky, R. Schneider, R. Folger, M. Christopher, and R. Bies. 1994. "Interactive effects of procedural justice and outcome negativity on victims and survivors of job loss." *Academy of Management Journal* 37 (June): 397–409.

Brooks, L.J. 1989. "Corporate codes of ethics." *Journal of Business Ethics* 8: 117–29.

Brown, T.J., and P.A. Dacin. 1997. "The company and the product: Corporate association and consumer product responses." *Journal of Marketing* 61: 68–84.

Brundage, D.M. 1986. *The Maturation Process and Learning.* Proceedings of the Annual Conference of The Canadian Association for Studies on Adult Education, Winnipeg.

Brundage, D.H., and D. Mackeracher. 1980. *Adult Learning Principles and Their Application to Program Planning.* Toronto: Ministry of Education.

Buckley, M.R., D.S. Wiese, and M.G. Harvey. 1998. "An investigation into the dimensions of unethical behaviour." *Journal of Education for Business* 73(5): 284–90.

Bunner, P. 1999. "The next wave of privatization." *Report/Newsmagazine* (Alberta Edition) (December 6) 26(43): 10.

Burak, R. 1997. *Building the Ontario Public Service for the Future: A Framework for Action.* Toronto: O.P.S. Restructuring Secretariat, Government of Ontario.

Burgelman, R.A. 1983. "Corporate entrepreneurship and strategic management: Insights from a process study." *Management Science* 29(12): 1349–64.

Burgelman, R.A. 1985. "Managing the new venture division: Research findings and implications for strategic management." *Strategic Management Journal* 6(1): 39–54.

Burns, T., and G.M. Stalker. 1961. *The Management of Innovation.* London: Tavistock.

Business Week. 1990. "The stateless corporation." (May 14), pp. 98–104.

Busenitz, L.W. 1999. "Entrepreneurial risk and strategic decision making: It's a matter of perspective." *Journal of Applied Behavioral Science* 35(3): 325–40.

Busenitz, L.W., and G.B. Murphy. 1996. "New evidence in the pursuit of locating new businesses." *Journal of Business Venturing* 2: 221–31.

Cameron, K. 1994. "Strategies for successful organizational downsizing." *Human Resource Management* 33 (Summer): 189–211.

Cameron, K., S. Freeman, and A. Mishra. 1991. "Best practices in white-collar downsizing: Managing contradictions." *The Academy of Management Executive* 5(3): 58.

Canada and the World Backgrounder. 2001. "Small is beautiful: Going further than deregulation, a major trend in government has been to sell off publicly owned assets in the hope of raising cash to help offset deficits." *Canada and the World Backgrounder* (March) 66(5): 12–15.

Carr, A.Z. 1968. "Is business bluffing ethical?" *Harvard Business Review* 46: 127–34.

Carroll, A.B. 1978. "Linking business to behaviour in organizations." *SAM Advanced Management Journal* 43: 4–11.

Carter, N. 1975. *Trends in Voluntary Support for Non-Governmental Social Service Agencies.* Ottawa: Canadian Council on Social Development.

Carter, N., W.B. Gartner, and P.O. Reynolds. 1996. "Exploring start-up events sequences." *Journal of Business Venturing* 2: 151–66.

Cascio, W. 1993. "Downsizing? What do we know? What have we learned?" *Academy of Management Executive* 7 (February): 95–104.

Cell, E. 1945. *Learning to Learn from Experience.* Albany: State University of New York Press.

Chandler, A.D. Jr. 1962. *Strategy and Structure: Chapters in the History of the Industrial Enterprise.* Cambridge, MA: M.I.T. Press.

Clark, C. 1996. "Privatization and industrial policy as U.S. competitiveness strategies: Lessons from East Asia." *ACR* 4(1): 101–28.

Clark, P.B., and J.O. Wilson. 1961. "Incentive systems: A theory of organizations." *Administrative Sciences Quarterly* 6: 129–66.

Clegg, S. 1990. *Modern Organizations.* Newbury Park, CA: Sage.

Cooper, A.C., W.C. Dunkelberg, and C.Y. Woo. 1988. "Entrepreneurs' perceived chances for success." *Journal of Business Venturing* 3: 97–108.

Craig, S.C., and J.M. McCann. 1979. "Assessing communications effects on energy conservation." *Journal of Consumer Research* 5: 82–88.

CUPE Report. 1999. "The privatization of public services." *Worklife* 11(4): 13–14.

Cyert, R.M., and J.G. March. 1963. *A Behavioral Theory of the Firm.* Englewood Cliffs, NJ: Prentice Hall.

Daft, R.L. 2001. *Organizational Theory and Design,* 7th Ed. Cincinnati, OH: South-Western College Publishing.

Daniels, J.D.J., and L.H. Radebaugh. 1998. *International Business: Environments and Operations.* Reading, MA: Addison-Wesley.

Deal, T., and A. Kennedy. 1982. *Corporate Cultures: The Rites and Rituals of Corporate Life.* Reading, MA: Addison-Wesley.

De Castro, J.O., and K. Uhlenbruck. 1997. "Characteristics of privatization: Evidence from developed, less developed, and former communist countries." *Journal of International Business Studies* 28(1): 123–43.

Deci, E.L. 1975. *Intrinsic Motivation.* New York: Plenum.

De George, R.T. 1999. *Business Ethics,* 5th Ed. Upper Saddle River, NJ: Prentice Hall.

DiMaggio, P., and W. Powell. 1983. "The iron cage revisited: Institutional isomorphism and collective rationality in organizational fields." *American Sociological Review* 48(1): 147–60.

Dogson, M. 1993. "Organizational learning: A review of some literatures." *Organization Studies* 14: 375–94.

Doherty, N., and J. Horsted. 1995. "Helping survivors to stay on board." *People Management* 1 (January): 26–31.

Dollar, D. 1993. "What do we know about the long-term sources of comparative advantage?" *AEA Papers and Proceedings* (May): 431–35.

Drucker, P.F. 1973. *Management: Tasks, Responsibilities and Practices* (Chapter 7). New York: Harper & Row.

Drucker, P.F. 1967. *The Effective Executive.* New York: Harper & Row.

Drucker, P.F. 1954. *The Practice of Management.* New York: Harper & Row.

Duchesne, D. 1989. *Giving Freely: Volunteers in Canada.* Statistics Canada, Labour Analytic Report, Cat: 71-535 No. 4. Ottawa: Minister of Supply and Services, Canada.

The Economist. 1994. "The global economy" (October 1): 3–46.

Ellen, P., L. Mohr, and D. Web. 1997. "Can retailers benefit from cause marketing?" Working Paper, Georgia State University.

Erikson, E. 1968. "Identity and the life cycle." *Psychological Issues Monograph* 1(1). New York: International Universities Press.

Erikson, E.H. (ed.). 1976. *Adulthood.* New York: W.W. Norton.

Evans, B., and J. Shields. 1998. *Reinventing the State: Public Administration 'Reform' in Canada.* Halifax: Fernwood Publishing.

Evans, M.G., H.P. Gunz, and R.M. Jalland. 1997. "Implications of organizational downsizing for managerial careers." *Canadian Journal of Administrative Sciences* 14: 359–71.

Fayol, H. 1930. *Industrial and General Administration.* New York: Sir Isaac Pitman and Sons.

Ferrell, O.C., and L.G. Gresham. 1985. "A contingency framework for understanding ethical decision making in marketing." *Journal of Marketing* 49: 87–96.

Fiol, C., and M. Lyles. 1985. "Organizational learning." *Academy of Management Review* 10: 803–13.

Fischhoff, B., P. Slovic, and S. Lichtenstein. 1977. "Knowing with certainty: The appropriateness of extreme confidence." *Journal of Experimental Psychology: Human Perception and Performance* 3: 552–64.

Flynn, J.P., and G.E. Web. 1975. "Women's incentives for community participation in policy issues." *Journal of Voluntary Action Research* 4: 137–45.

Follett, M.P. 1942. "Dynamic administration" in H. Metcalf and L.F. Urwick (eds.), *Dynamic Administration: The Collected Papers of Mary Parker Follett.* New York: Harper & Row.

Follett, M.P. 1934. *Creative Experience.* London: Longmans, Green.

Foster, M.K., and A.G. Meinhard. 1996. "Toward transforming social service organizations in Ontario." Presented at Babson Conference on Entrepreneurship, Seattle, WA.

Foster, R. 1986. "The S-curve: A New Forecasting Tool, "*Innovation, The Attacker's Advantage,* pp. 88–111. New York, N.Y.: Summit Books, Simon and Schuster.

Fredrickson, J.W., and A.L. Iaquinto. 1989. "Inertia and creeping rationality in strategic decision processes." *Academy of Management Journal* 32(3): 516–42.

French, W.L., C.H. Bell, Jr., and R.A Zawacki. (eds.). 1994. *Organization development and transformation: Managing effective change,* 4th Ed. Burr Ridge, IL: Irwin.

Friedman, M. 1962. *Capitalism and Freedom.* Chicago: University of Chicago Press.

Friedman, T.L. 1999. *The Lexus and the Olive Tree.* New York, NY: Farrar Strauss Giroux.

Fulford, D. 2000. Personal communication, Director of Business Planning, Management Board Secretariat, Queen's Park, Toronto.

Gagnon, L. 1997. "In praise of state-owned liquor outlets." *The Globe and Mail* (December 27).

Galbraith, J.K. 1958. *The Affluent Society.* Boston: Houghton Mifflin Company.

Galbraith, J.R. 1977. *Organization Design.* Reading, MA: Addison-Wesley.

Galbraith, J.R. 1973. *Designing Complex Organizations.* Reading, MA: Addison-Wesley.

Garten, J.E. 1998. "Cultural imperialism is no joke." *BusinessWeek* (November 30).

Gatewood, E., K. Shaver, and W. Gartner. 1995. "A longitudinal study of cognitive factors influencing start-up behaviors and success at venture creation." *Journal of Business Venturing* 10: 371–91.

Gatewood, R.D., and A.B. Carroll. 1991. "Assessment of the ethical performance of organizational members: A conceptual framework." *Academy of Management Review* 16: 667–90.

Gausch, J.L., and R.W. Hahn. 1999. "The cost and benefits of regulation: implications for developing countries." *The World Bank Research Observer* 14(1): 137–58.

Gersick, C.J.G., and J.R. Hackman. 1990. "Habitual routines in task-performing groups." *Organizational Behaviour and Human Decision Processes* 47: 65–97.

Gidron, B., R.M. Kramer, and L.M. Salamon. 1992. *Government and the Third Sector: Emerging Relationships in Welfare States.* San Francisco: Jossey-Bass.

Gilbreth, F.B. 1911. *Principles of Scientific Management.* New York: Van Nostrand.

Gilmore, T.N., and R.K. Kazanjian. 1989. "Clarifying decision making in high-growth ventures: The use of responsibility charting." *Journal of Business Venturing* 4: 69–83.

Gioia, D.A. 1986. "Symbols, scripts, and sensemaking: Creating meaning in the organizational experience" in H.P. Sims, Jr., D.A. Gioia, and Associates, *The Thinking Organization: Dynamics of Organizational Social Cognition,* pp. 49–74. San Francisco: Jossey-Bass.

Gladwell, M. 2002. *The Tipping Point: How Little Things Call Make a Big Difference.* New York: Little, Brown and Company.

Glaser, J.S. 1992. "Connecting the workplace and adult development theory: Self directed work teams as a petri dish for adult development." Paper presented at the 7th Annual Meeting of the Society for Research in Adult Development, Toronto, Canada (June).

Gluck, R. 1975. "An exchange theory of incentive of urban political party organization." *Journal of Voluntary Action Research* 4: 104–15.

The Globe and Mail. 2001. "Who's minding the Crown corporations?" (March 5).

Goffman, E. 1967. *Interaction Ritual.* Garden City, NY: Doubleday.

Goodpaster, K.E., and J.B. Matthews, Jr. 1983. "Can a corporation have a conscience?" in T.L. Beauchamp and N.E. Bowie (eds.), *Ethical Theory and Business.* Englewood Cliffs, NJ: Prentice Hall.

Goold, M. and K. Luches. 1993. "Why diversify? Four decades of management thinking," *Academy of Management Executive,* 7: 7–25.

Greider, W. 1997. *One World, Ready or Not: The Manic Logic of Global Capitalism.* New York: Simon & Schuster.

Griffin, R.W., and M.W. Pustay. 1998. *International Business: A Management Perspective,* 2d Ed. Reading, MA: Addison-Wesley.

Grover, S.L. 1993. "Why professionals lie: The impact of professional role conflict on reporting accuracy." *Organizational Behaviour and Human Decision Processing* 55: 251–72.

Hall, A.D., and R.E. Fagen. 1956. "Definition of system." *General Systems: The Yearbook of the Society for the Advancement of General Systems Theory* 1: 18–28.

Hall, R.H. 2002. *Organizations: Structures, Processes, and Outcomes.* Upper Saddle River, NJ: Prentice-Hall.

Hambrick, D.C., and L. Crozier. 1985. "Stumblers and stars in the management of rapid growth." *Journal of Business Venturing* 1(1): 31–45.

Hambrick, D.C., and S. M. Schecter. 1983. "Turnaround strategies for mature industrial product business units," *Academy of Management Journal,* 26: 231–48.

Hammer, M., and J. Champy. 1993. *Reengineering the Corporation.* New York, NY: HarperBusiness.

Hannan, Michael T., and R. Carroll Glenn. 1992. *Dynamics of Organizational Populations: Density, legitimation and competition.* New York: Oxford University Press.

Havlovic, S., F. Bouthillette, and R. van der Wal. 1998. "Coping with downsizing and job loss: Lessons from the Shaughnessy Hospital closure." *Canadian Journal of Administrative Sciences* 15 (December): 322–32.

Heath, C., and A. Tversky. 1991. "Preferences and beliefs: Ambiguity and competence in choice under uncertainty." *Journal of Risk and Uncertainty* 4: 5–28.

Hegarty, W.H., and H.P. Sims. 1979. "Organizational philosophy, policies, and objectives related to unethical decision behaviour: A laboratory experiment." *Journal of Applied Psychology* 64(3): 331–38.

Hegarty, W.H., and H.P. Sims. 1978. "Some determinants of unethical decision behaviour: An experiment." *Journal of Applied Psychology* 63(4): 451–57.

Heracleous, L. 1999. "Privatisation: Global trends and implications of the Singapore experience." *The International Journal of Public Sector Management* 12(5): 432–44.

Hertzberg, F., B. Mausner, and B. Snyderman. 1959. *The Motivation to Work.* New York: John Wiley.

Higgins, A., C. Power, and L. Kohlberg. 1984. "The relationship of moral atmosphere to judgments of responsibility" in W.M. Kurtines and J.L. Gewirtz (eds.), *Morality, Moral Behaviour and Moral Development,* pp. 74–106. New York: Wiley.

Hirschhorn, L., and T. Gilmore. 1992. "The new boundaries of the 'boundaryless' company." *Harvard Business Review* (May/June): 104–15.

Hogarth, R.M. 1987. *Judgement and Choice: The Psychology of Decisions.* New York: John Wiley.

Holstrom, B. 1979. "Moral hazard and observability." *Bell Journal of Economics* 10: 74–91.

Huber, V.L., and M.A. Neale. 1987. "Effects of self and competitor's goals on performance in an interdependent bargaining task." *Journal of Applied Psychology* 72: 197–203.

Hunt, S.D., and S. Vitell. 1986. "A general theory of marketing ethics." *Journal of Macromarketing* 6(1): 5–16.

Industry Canada and Statistics Canada. 1998. *Small Business Quarterly Report* (Summer).

Industry Canada. 1991. *Small Business in Canada.*

Jackall, R. 1988. *Moral Mazes: The World of Corporate Managers.* New York: Oxford University Press.

Janger, A.R. 1979. *Matrix Organizations of Complex Businesses.* New York: The Conference Board.

Janis, I.L., and L. Mann. 1977. *Decision Making: A Psychological Analysis of Conflict, Choice, and Commitment.* New York: Free Press.

Jick, T.D. and M.A. Peiperl. 2003. *Managing Change, Cases and Concepts.* New York: McGraw Hill/Irwin.

Jones, T.M. 1991. "Ethical decision making by individuals in organizations: An issue-contingent model." *Academy of Management Review* 16(2): 366–95.

Kahn, R., D. Wolfe, R. Quinn, J. Snoek, and R. Rosenthal. 1964. *Organizational Stress: Studies in Role Conflict and Ambiguity.* New York: John Wiley.

Kahn, W.A. 1992. "To be fully there: Psychological presence." *Human Relations* 45(4).

Kahn, W.A. 1990a. "Toward an agenda for business ethics research." *Academy of Management Review* 15(2): 311–28.

Kahn, W.A. 1990b. "Psychological conditions of personal engagement and disengagement at work." *Academy Management Journal* 33(4): 692–724.

Kahneman, D. 1992. "Reference points, anchors, norms, and mixed feelings." *Organizational Behaviour Human Decision Process* 51: 269–312.

Kahneman, D., and D. Lovallo. 1993. "Timid choices and bold forecasts: A cognitive perspective on risk taking." *Management Science* 39(1): 17–31.

Kahneman, D., P. Slovic, and A. Tversky. (eds.) 1982. *Judgment under Uncertainty: Heuristics and Biases.* New York: Cambridge University Press.

Kahneman, D., and A. Tversky. 1979. "Prospect theory: An analysis of decision under risk." *Econometrica* 47: 263–91.

Kant, I. 1785. *Grounding for the Metaphysics of Morals.* Trans. James W. Ellington [1993]. Indianapolis, IN: Hackett.

Karakowsky, L. 1994. "The Influence of Organizational Context on Ethical Behaviour in the Workplace: Linking Institutionalization Theory to Individual-Level Behaviour." *Proceedings of the Administrative Sciences Association of Canada* 15(12): 21–30.

Karakowsky, L., and A.R. Elangovan. 2001. "Risky decision making in mixed-gender terms: Whose risk tolerance matters?" *Small Group Research* 32(1): 94–111.

Karakowsky, L., A. Carroll, and A. Buchholtz. 2005. *Business and Society.* Toronto: Nelson Thomson.

Katz, J.A. 1992. "A psychosocial cognitive model of employment status choice." *Entrepreneurship Theory and Practice* 17(1): 29–37.

Katz, D., and R.L. Kahn. 1978. *The Social Psychology of Organization,* 2d Ed. New York: Wiley.

Kegan, R. 1982. *The Evolving Self: Problem and Process in Human Development.* Cambridge: Harvard University Press.

Kegan, R. 1979. "The evolving self: A process conception for ego psychology." *The Counselling Psychologist* 8: 5–34.

Kikeri, S., J. Nellis, and M. Shirley. 1994. "Privatization: Lessons from market economies." *World Bank Research Observer,* 241–72.

Kohlberg, L. 1969. "Stage and sequence: The cognitive developmental approach to socialization" in D.A. Goslin (ed.), *Handbook of Socialization Theory and Research,* pp. 347–480. Chicago: Rand McNally.

Kolb, D.A. 1984. *Experiential Learning: Experience as the Source of Learning and Development.* Englewood Cliffs, NJ: Prentice Hall.

Kotler, P., and R.E. Turner. 1995. *Marketing Management,* Canadian 8th Ed. Toronto: Prentice Hall.

Knouse, S.B., and R.A. Giacalone. 1991. "Ethical decision-making in business: Behavioral issues and concerns." *Journal of Business Ethics* 11: 369–77.

Knox, A.B. 1977. *Adult Development and Learning.* San Francisco: Jossey-Bass.

Kram, K. 1985. *Mentoring at Work.* Glenview, IL: Scott Foresman.

Kram, K.E., P.E. Yeager, and G.E. Reed. 1989. "Decisions and dilemmas: The ethical dimension in the corporate context" in J.E. Post (ed.), *Research in Corporate Social Performance and Policy,* Vol. 1, pp. 21–54. Greenwich, CT: JAI Press.

Krueger, N., and P. Dickson. 1994. "How believing in ourselves increases risk taking: Perceived self-efficacy and opportunity recognition." *Decision Sciences* 25: 385–400.

Krugman, P.R., and M. Obstfeld. 1997. *International Economics: Theory and Policy.* Reading, MA: Addison-Wesley.

Kuhnle, S., and P. Selle. 1992. *Government and Voluntary Organizations: A Relational Perspective.* Aldershot: Avebury.

Latham, G.P., and G.A. Yukl. 1975. "A review of research on the application of goal setting in organizations." *Academy of Management Journal* (December): 824–45.

Lawrence, P., and J. Lorsch. 1969. *Developing Organizations: Diagnosis and Action.* Reading, MA: Addison-Wesley.

Lawrence, P.R., and J.W. Lorsch. 1967a. *Organization and Environment.* Boston: Graduate School of Business Administration, Harvard University.

Lawrence, P.R., and J.W. Lorsch. 1967b. "Differentiation and integration in complex organizations." *Administrative Science Quarterly* (June): 1–47.

Lee, P. 1997. "A comparative analysis of layoff announcements and stock price reactions in the United States and Japan." *Strategic Management Journal* 18 (December): 879–94.

Leontief, W. 1954. "Domestic production and foreign trade; The American capital position re-examined." *Economia Internationale* (February): 3–32.

Levac, M., and P. Wooldridge. Financial Markets Department. 1997. "The fiscal impact of privatization in Canada." *Bank of Canada Review* (Summer): 25–40.

Levering, R., M. Moscowitz, and M. Katz. 1985. *The 100 Best Companies to Work for in America.* Scarborough, New York: New American Library.

Levinson, D.J., C.N. Darrow, E.B. Klein, M.H. Levinson, and B. McKee. 1978. *The Seasons of a Man's Life.* New York: Ballatine Books.

Lewin, K. 1951. *Field Theory in Social Science.* New York: Harper & Row.

Lewis, P.V. 1985. "'Defining business ethics': Like nailing jell-o to a wall." *Journal of Business Ethics* 4(5): 377–83.

Lichtenstein, S., B. Fischhoff, and L. Phillips. 1982. "Calibration of probabilities: The state of the art to 1980" in D. Kahneman, P. Slovic, and A. Tversky (eds.), *Judgment under Uncertainty: Heuristics and Biases,* pp. 306–34. New York: Cambridge University Press.

Lipman, J. 1990. "When its commercial time, TV viewers prefer cartoons to celebrities any day." *The Wall Street Journal* (Feb. 16): B1, B4.

Locke, E.A. 1968. "Toward a theory of task motivation and incentives." *Organizational Behaviour and Human Performance* (May): 157–89.

Locke, E.A., L.M. Saari, and G.P. Latham. 1981. "Goal setting and task performance." *Psychological Bulletin* (January): 125–52.

Locke, John. 1690. *Second Treatise on Civil Government.* Cambridge: Cambridge University Press.

Low, M.B., and I.C. MacMillan. 1988. "Entrepreneurship: Past research and future challenges." *Journal of Management* 14(2): 139–61.

Luthans, F. 1973. "The contingency theory of management: A path out of the jungle." *Business Horizons* 16 (June): 62–72.

March, J.G., and H.A. Simon. 1958. *Organizations.* New York: Wiley.

Masi, D.A. 1981. *Organizing for Women: Issues, Strategies, and Services.* Lexington, MA: Lexington Books.

Maslow, A. 1954. *Motivation and Personality.* New York: Harper & Row.

McGregor, D. 1960. *The Human Side of Enterprise,* pp. 33–58. New York: McGraw-Hill.

McKinley, W., C. Sanchez, and A. Schick. 1995. "Organizational downsizing: Constraining, cloning, learning." *Academy of Management Executive* 9(3): 32–41.

McLellan, K., and B. Marcolin. 1994. "Information technology outsourcing." *Business Quarterly* 59 (Autumn): 95–104.

McMillan, C.J., and E.M.V. Jasson. 2001. "Technology and the new economy: A Canadian strategy" in T. Wesson (ed.), *Canada and the New World Economic Order,* 2d Ed. Toronto: Captus Press.

McMurdy, Deirdre. 1995. "Rummage sales." *Maclean's* (July 24) 108(30): 32.

Mertens, B. 1998. "The push for privatization." *Asian Business* 34(6): 42–45.

Merton, R.K. 1957. *Social Theory and Social Structure,* 2d Ed. New York: Free Press.

Meyer, J., and B. Rowan. 1977. "Institutional organizations: Formal structure as myth and ceremony." *American Journal of Sociology* 83: 440–63.

Mezirow, J. 1978. "Perspective transformation." *Adult Education* 28(2): 100–10.

Miles, R.E., and C.C. Snow. 1978. *Organizations: Strategy, Structure and Process.* New York: McGraw-Hill.

Milgram, S. 1974. *Obedience to Authority.* New York: Harper & Row.

Mill, J.S. 1861. *Utilitarianism.* Edited by Oskar Piest. [1948] New York: Liberal Arts Press.

Mill, J.S. 1859. *On Liberty.* Edited by Oskar Piest. [1975] New York: Norton.

Miller, D., and P.H. Friesen. 1984. *Organizations: A Quantum View.* Englewood Cliffs, NJ: Prentice Hall.

Mintzberg, H. 1979. *The Structuring of Organizational Structures.* Englewood Cliffs, NJ: Prentice Hall.

Mintzberg, H. 1974. "The manager's job: Folklore and fact." *Harvard Business Review* (July/August): 49–61.

Mintzberg, H. 1973. *The Nature of Managerial Work.* Englewood Cliffs, NJ: Prentice Hall.

Mitroff, I.I. 1983. *Stakeholders of the Organizational Mind: Toward a New View of Organizational Policy Making.* San Francisco: Jossey-Bass.

Molm, L.D. 1991. "Affect and social exchange: Satisfaction in power-dependence relations." *American Sociological Review* 56(4): 475–93.

Mone, M. 1994. "Relationships between self-concepts, aspirations, emotional responses, and intent to leave a downsizing organization." *Human Resource Management* 33 (Summer): 281–98.

Morgan, G. 1986. *Images of Organization*. Sage: Newbury Park.

Morrison, C. 2000. "Beyond booze." *Summit* 3(4): 21–22.

Murray, V. 1995, "Improving board performance." *The Philanthropist* 13(4).

Neale, M.A, and M.H. Bazerman. 1991. *Cognition and Rationality in Negotiation*. New York: Free Press.

Newell, A., and H. Simon. 1981. "Computer science as empirical inquiry: Symbols and search" in J. Haugeland (ed.), *Mind Design*. Cambridge, MA: MIT Press.

Nicolini, D., and M. Mezner. 1995. "The social construction of organizational learning: Conceptual and practical issues in the field." *Human Relations* 48(7): 727–47.

Northcraft, G., and M. Neale. 1994. *Organization Behaviour: A Management Challenge*. Chicago: Dryden Press.

Northcraft, G., and M. Neale. 1987. "Experts, amateurs, and real estate: An anchoring perspective on property pricing decisions." *Organizational Behaviour and Human Decision Processes* 39(1): 84–87.

Novelli, W.D. 1981. "Social Issues and direct marketing: What's the connection?" Paper presented at the Annual Conference of the Direct Mail/Marketing Association, Los Angeles, California, March 12.

Ogilvy, D., and J. Raphaelson. 1982. "Research on advertising techniques that work and don't work." *Harvard Business Review* 60 (July–August): 14–18.

Ohlin, B. 1933. *Interregional and International Trade*. Cambridge, MA: Harvard University Press.

Olson, M. 1965. *The Logic of Collective Action; Public Goods and the Theory of Groups*. Cambridge: Harvard University Press.

Osborne, D., and T. Gaebler. 1993. *Reinventing Government: How the Entrepreneurial Spirit Is Transforming the Public Sector*. New York: Plume.

Ottesen, O. 1977. "The response function" in M. Berg (ed.), *Current Theories in Scandinavian Mass Communications Research*. Grena, Denmark: GMT.

Pal, L.A. 1997. "Civic re-alignment: NGOs and the contemporary welfare state" in Raymond B. Blake, Penny E. Bryden and J. Frank Strain (eds.), *The Welfare State in Canada: Past, Present and Future*. Concord, Ontario: Irwin Publishing.

Parson, H.M. 1974. "What happened at Hawthorne?" *Science* 183: 922–32.

Pastin, M. 1986. *The Hard Problems of Management: Gaining the Ethics Edge*. San Francisco: Jossey-Bass.

Pava, M.L. 1998. "Religious business ethics and political liberalism: An integrative approach." *Journal of Business Ethics* 17(15): 1633–52.

Payne, S.L., and R.A. Giacalone. 1990. "Social psychological approaches to the perception of ethical dilemmas." *Human Relations* 43: 649–65.

Pedler, J., R. Burgoyne, and A. Boydell. 1997. *The Learning Company*. Maidenhead, Surrey: McGraw-Hill.

Perrow, C. 1979. *Complex Organizations*, 2d Ed. Glenview, IL: Scott, Foresman.

Perry, W.G., Jr. 1970. *Forms of Intellectual and Ethical Development in the College Years*. New York: Holt, Rinehart, and Winston.

Peters, T.J., and R.H. Waterman. 1982. *In Search of Excellence*. New York: Harper & Row.

Pettigrew, A.M. 1979. "On studying organizational cultures." *Administrative Science Quarterly* 24: 570–81.

Pfeffer, J. 1982. *Organizations and Organizational Theory*. Boston: Pitman.

Pfeffer, J., and G.R. Salancik. 1978. *The External Control of Organizations*. New York: Harper & Row.

Piaget, J. 1954. *The Construction of Reality in the Child*. New York: Basic Books.

Pondy, L.R., P. Frost, G. Morgan, and T. Dandridge. (eds.) 1983. *Organizational Symbolism*. Greenwich, CT: JAI Press.

Porter, M.E. 1998. "Clusters and the new economics of competition." *Harvard Business Review* (November/December): 77–90.

Porter, M.E. 1990. *The Competitive Advantage of Nations*. New York: Free Press.

Porter, M.E. 1980. *Competitive Strategy: Techniques for Analyzing Industries and Competitors*. New York: Free Press.

Porter, M.E., and Monitor Company. 1991. A study prepared for the Business Council on National Issues and the government of Canada, October.

Pritchard, R.D., K.M. Campbell, and O.J. Campbell. 1977. "Effects of extrinsic financial rewards on intrinsic motivation." *Journal of Applied Psychology* (February): 9–15.

Rawls, J. 1993. *Political Liberalism*. New York: Columbia University Press.

Rawls, J. 1971. *A Theory of Justice*. Cambridge, MA: Harvard University Press.

Rumelt, R. 1974. *Strategy, Structure, and Economic Performance*. Cambridge, MA: Harvard University Press.

Ray, D.M. 1994. "The role of risk-taking in Singapore." *Journal of Business Venturing* 9(2): 157–77.

Rein, I., P. Kotler, and M. Stoller. 1987. *High Visibility: How Executives, Politicians, Entertainers, Athletes and Other Professionals Create, Market and Achieve Successful Images*. New York: Dodd, Mead.

Rest, J.R. 1986. *Moral Development: Advances in Research and Theory.* New York: Praeger.

Reynolds, P., and B. Miller. 1992. "New firm gestation: Conception, birth, and implications for research." *Journal of Business Venturing* 7: 405–17.

Ricardo, D. 1996. *The Principles of Political Economy and Taxation.* [Originally published London, New York: J.M. Dent & Sons, 1911.] Amherst, NY: Prometheus Books.

Rogers, C.R. 1961. *On Becoming a Person.* Boston: Houghton Mifflin.

Runes, D.D. 1964. *Dictionary of Philosophy.* Littlefields: Adams and Co.

Ryan, L., and K. Macky. 1998. "Downsizing organizations: Uses, outcomes and strategies." *Asia Pacific Journal of Human Resources* 36 (Winter): 29–45.

Salamon, L.M. 1987. "Partners in public service" in W.W. Powell (ed.), *The Nonprofit Sector: A Research Handbook,* pp. 107–17. New Haven: Yale University Press.

Salamon, L., R. List, W. Sokolowski, S. Toepler, and H. Anheier. 1999. *Global Civil Society: Dimensions of the Nonprofit Sector.* Baltimore: John Hopkins University, Centre for Civil Society Studies.

Schein, E.M. 1985. *Organizational Culture and Leadership.* San Francisco: Jossey-Bass.

Schumpeter, J. 1936. *The Theory of Economic Development.* Cambridge: Harvard University Press.

Schwenk, C.R. 1988. "The cognitive perspective on strategic decision making." *Journal of Management Studies* 25(1): 41–55.

Scott, W.R. 1981. *Organizations: Rational, Natural, and Open Systems.* Englewood Cliffs, NJ: Prentice Hall.

Seidle, F.L. 1995. *Rethinking the Delivery of Public Services to Citizens.* Montreal: Institute for Research on Public Policy.

Selznick, P. 1943. "An approach to a theory of bureaucracy." *American Sociological Review* 8: 47–54.

Senge, P. 1990. *The Fifth Discipline: The Art and Practice of the Learning Organization.* New York: Doubleday.

Sethi, S.P. 1982. *Against the Corporate Wall.* Englewood Cliffs, NJ: Prentice Hall.

Shapira, Z. 1995. *Risk Taking: A Managerial Perspective.* New York: Russell Sage Foundation.

Simon, H. 1957. *Models of Man.* New York, NY: Wiley.

Simon, H.A. 1945. *Administrative Behaviour.* New York: Free Press.

Sims, J.P. Jr., D.A. Gioia, and Associates. 1986. *The Thinking Organization.* San Francisco: Jossey-Bass.

Sims, R.R. 1991. "The institutionalization of organizational ethics." *Journal of Business Ethics* 10: 493–511.

Smalhout, James. 1999. "Keep the state out of business." *Euromoney* (March) 359: 36–41.

Smith, A. 1937. *The Wealth of Nations.* Edited by E. Cannan. [First Modern library edition 1937.] New York: Modern Library.

Smith, D.H. 1982. "Altruism, volunteers, and voluntarism" in J. Harmon (ed.), *Volunteerism in the Eighties: Fundamental Issues in Voluntary Action.* Washington DC: University Press of America.

Sonnenfeld, J.A. 1985. "Shedding light on the Hawthorne studies." *Journal of Occupational Behaviour* 6: 111–30.

Spence, A.M. 1981. "The learning curve and competition," *The Bell Journal of Economics,* 12: 49–70.

Starbuck, W.H. 1976. "Organizations and their environments" in M.D. Dunnette (ed.), *Handbook of Industrial Psychology,* pp. 1069–123. Chicago: Rand McNally.

Staw, B.M. 1981. "The escalation of commitment to a course of action." *Academy of Management Review* 6: 577–87.

Staw, B.M., and J. Ross. 1987. "Behaviour in escalation situations: Antecedents, prototypes and solutions" in L.L. Cummings and B.M. Staw (eds.), *Research in Organization Behaviour* 9: 39–78. London: JAI Press.

Steers. R.M., and L.W. Porter. 1979. *Motivation and Work Behaviour,* 2d Ed. New York: McGraw-Hill.

Stene, E.O. 1940. "An approach to a science of administration." *American Political Science Review* 34: 1129ff.

Sternthal, B., R.R. Dholakia, and C. Levitt. 1978. "The persuasive effect of source credibility: Test of cognitive response." *Journal of Consumer Research* 4: 242–50.

Stewart, W. 1996. *The Charity Game: Waste and Fraud in Canada's $86-Billion-a-Year Compassion Industry.* Toronto: Douglas & McIntyre.

Stone, C.D. 1975. "The culture of the corporation" in W.M. Hoffman and J.M. Moore (eds.), *Business Ethics,* 2d Ed. New York: McGraw-Hill.

Stryker, S., and R.T. Serpe. 1982. "Commitment, identity salience, and role behaviour: Theory research example" in W. Ickes and E.S. Knowles (ed.), *Personality, Roles and Social Behaviour,* pp. 199–218. New York: Springer-Verlag.

Suchman, Marc C. 1995. "Managing Legitimacy: Strategic and Institutional Approaches," *Academy of Management Review,* 20(3): 571–610.

Sutherland, E., and D.R. Cressey. 1970. *Principles of Criminology.* Chicago: J.B. Lippincott.

Sutton, R., and T. D'Aunno. 1989. "Decreasing organizational size: Untangling the effects of money and people." *Academy of Management Review* 14(2): 194–212.

Tajfel, H. 1981. *Human Groups and Social Categories: Studies in Social Psychology.* Cambridge, England: Cambridge University Press.

Tajfel, H., and J.C. Turner. 1985. "The social identity theory of intergroup behaviour" in S. Worchel and W.G. Austin (eds.), *Psychology of Intergroup Relations,* 2d Ed., pp. 7–24. Chicago: Nelson Hall.

Taylor, D.W., and A.A. Warrack. 1998. "Privatization of state enterprise: Policy drivers and lessons learned." *International Journal of Public Sector Management* 11(7): 524–35.

Taylor, D.W., A.A. Warrack, and M.E. Baetz. 1999. *Business and Government in Canada: Partners for the Future.* Scarborough, Toronto: Prentice Hall Canada, Inc.

Taylor, F. 1991. *Principles of Scientific Management.* New York: Harper & Row.

Taylor, F.W. 1947. *Scientific Management.* New York: Harper & Row.

Taylor, F.W. 1913. *Principles of Scientific Management.* New York: Harper & Brothers.

Taylor, M., J. Langan, and P. Hogget. 1995. *Encouraging Diversity: Voluntary and Private Organisations In Community Care.* Hampshire, England: Arena.

Teece, D., G. Pisano, and A. Shuen. 1997. "Dynamic Capabilities and Strategic Management," *Strategic Management Journal,* 18(7): 509–33.

Theil, Rita. 1996. "Learning to apply the lessons of privatization." *International Financial Law Review* (April) 15(4): 51ff.

Thoits, P.A. 1983. "Multiple identities and psychological well-being: A reformulation and test of the social isolation hypothesis." *American Sociological Review* 48: 174–87.

Thompson, J.D. 1967. *Organizations in Action.* New York: McGraw-Hill.

Tolbert, P., and L.G. Zucker. 1983. "Institutional sources of change in the formal structure of organizations: The diffusion of civil service reform, 1880–1935." *Administrative Science Quarterly* 28(1): 22–39.

Tomasko, R. 1990. *Downsizing: Reshaping the Corporation of the Future.* New York: AMACON.

Trevino, L.K. 1986. "Ethical decision making in organizations: A person-situation interactionist model." *Academy of Management Review* 11(3): 601–17.

Trevino, L.K., and S.A Youngblood. 1990. "Bad apples in bad barrels: A causal analysis of ethical decision making behaviour." *Journal of Applied Psychology* 75(4): 378–85.

Tsalikis, J., and D.J. Fritsche. 1989. "Business ethics: A literature review with a focus on marketing ethics." *Journal of Business Ethics* 8: 695–743.

Turner, J. 1982. "Towards a cognitive redefinition of the social group" in H. Tajfel (ed.), *Social Identity and Intergroup Relations,* pp. 15–40. Cambridge, England: Cambridge University Press.

Tversky, A., and D. Kahneman. 1974. "Judgment under uncertainty: Heuristics and biases." *Science* 185: 1124–31.

Tversky, A., and D. Kahneman. 1973. "Availability: A heuristic for judging frequency and probability." *Cognitive Psychology* 5: 207–32.

Tversky, A., and D. Kahneman. 1972. "Subjective probability: A judgment of representativeness." *Cognitive Psychology* 3(3): 430–54.

Tversky, A., and D. Kahneman. 1971. "The belief in the 'law of small numbers'." *Psychological Bulletin* 76: 105–10.

Useem, M. 1987. "Corporate philanthropy" in W.W. Powell (ed.), *The Nonprofit Sector: A Research Handbook.* New Haven: Yale University Press.

Utterback, James M. 1994. *Mastering the Dynamics of Innovation.* Boston: Harvard Business School Press.

Van Til, J. 1988. *Mapping the Third Sector: Voluntarism in a Changing Social Economy.* New York: Foundation Center.

von Finckenstein, K. 1999. Q.C. Commissioner of Competition Bureau, Statement to the "Meet the Competition Bureau," Forum Insight Conference, Toronto, May 3.

Vroom, V.H. 1964. *Work and Motivation.* New York: John Wiley.

Wahba, M.A, and L.G. Bridwell. 1976. "Maslow reconsidered: A review of research on the need hierarchy theory." *Organizational Behaviour and Human Performance* (April): 212–40.

Wanberg, C., L. Bunce, and M. Gavin. 1999. "Perceived fairness of layoffs among individuals who have been laid off: A longitudinal study." *Personnel Psychology* 52 (Spring): 59–84.

Wasney, G. 1997. "A new road for Canadian truckers." *World Trade* 10(2): 48–50.

Weber, J. 1990. "Manager's moral reasoning: Assessing their responses to the three moral dilemmas." *Human Relations* 43: 687–702.

Weber, Joseph. 1998. "Does Canadian culture need this much protection?" *BusinessWeek* (June 18). Online: <http://www.bwarchive.businessweek.com>.

Weber, M. 1979. *Economy and Society,* eds. G. Roth and C. Wittich. Berkeley: University of California Press.

Weber, M. 1947. *The Theory of Social and Economic Organizations.* Edited and Translated by A.M. Henderson and T. Parsons. New York: Free Press.

Weber, M. 1946. *From Max Weber: Essays in Sociology,* eds. H.H. Gerth and C.W. Mills. New York: Oxford University Press.

Weber, M. 1927. *General Economic History.* Transl. F.H. Knight. London: Allen & Unwin.

Weick, K. 1979. *The Social Psychology of Organizing.* Reading, MA: Addison-Wesley.

Weick, K. 1976. "Educational organizations as loosely coupled systems." *Administrative Science Quarterly* 21: 1–19.

White, J.P., and R. Janzen. 2000. "The industrial relations implications of privatization: The case of Canada Post." *Industrial Relations* (Winter) 55(1): 36–55.

Whyte, G. 1993. "Escalating commitment in individual and group decision making: A prospect theory approach." *Organizational Behaviour and Human Decision Process* 54(3): 430–55.

Wild, J.J., K.L. Wild, and J.C.Y. Han. 2000. *International Business: An Integrated Approach.* Upper Saddle River, NJ: Prentice Hall.

Williamson, O.E. 1975. *Markets and Hierarchies: Analysis and Antitrust Implications.* New York: Free Press.

Winston, C. 1993. "Economic deregulation: Days of reckoning for economists." *Journal of Economic Literature* 31: 1263–89.

Woodward, J. 1965. *Industrial Organization: Theory and Practice.* London, NY: Oxford University Press.

World Bank. 1997. "Privatization revenue statistics by regions." Online: <http://worldbank.org/ecsp/finl/html/priv-regions.htm>.

Worrell, D., W. Davidson, and V. Sharma. 1991. "Layoff announcements and shareholder wealth." *Academy of Management Journal* 34 (September): 662–78.

Wren, D. 1979. *Evolution of Management Thought,* 2d Ed. New York: Wiley.

Zahra, S.A., and C.D. Hansen. 2000. "Privatization, entrepreneurship, and global competitiveness in the 21st Century." *Competition Review* 10(1): 83–103.

Zajac, E.J., and M.H. Bazerman. 1991. "Blind spots in industry and competitor analysis: Implications of interfirm (mis) perceptions for strategic decisions." *Academy of Management Review* 16(1): 37–56.

Zucker, L.G. 1977. "Institutionalization as a mechanism of cultural persistence." *American Sociological Review* 42(2): 726–42.